TEILHARD AND THE CREATION OF THE SOUL

Robert North, S.J., S.S.D.

TEILHARD
and the
CREATION *of the* SOUL

Introduction by Karl Rahner, S.J.

THE BRUCE PUBLISHING COMPANY
MILWAUKEE

SAINT LOUIS UNIVERSITY (SAINT MARYS) THEOLOGY STUDIES

Citations from *The Phenomenon of Man* by Pierre Teilhard de Chardin, © 1955 by Éditions du Seuil, Paris; © on the English translation by Wm. Collins Sons & Co., Ltd., London, and Harper & Brothers, New York, are reprinted with the permission of Wm. Collins Sons & Co., Ltd., and Harper & Row, Inc.

Citations from *Letters from a Traveller* by Pierre Teilhard de Chardin, © 1962 in the English translation by Wm. Collins Sons & Co., Ltd., London and Harper & Brothers, New York, are reprinted with the permission of Wm. Collins Sons & Co., Ltd., and Harper & Row, Inc.

Library of Congress Catalog Card Number: 67–15250

© 1967 THE BRUCE PUBLISHING COMPANY
MADE IN THE UNITED STATES OF AMERICA

To

my students, my teachers

Chinese Jesuit Province, 1963

Korea Kwang-Ju Seminary, 1966

ANALYSIS OF CONTENTS

INTRODUCTION
by KARL RAHNER, S.J.

Wenn ich diesem gründlichen und gelehrten Buch eine "Empfehlung" mitgebe, so haben weder ich noch der Verfasser die Absicht, die Verantwortung für die in diesem Buch vorgetragene Auffassung miteinander zu teilen. Der Verfasser trägt sie allein und will sie auch allein tragen. Die Empfehlung ist keine Parteinahme, keine Erklärung der Übereinstimmung, schon weil es in einem so kurzen Vorwort unmöglich ist, in dieser Hinsicht ein Ja oder Nein zu sagen und — was dann notwendig wäre — gar zu begründen. Das Buch empfiehlt sich schon dadurch, dass es eine "Quaestio disputata" mutig und sorgfältig aufgreift, die nicht schon als schlechthin gelöst betrachtet werden kann. Die Auffassungen Teilhards stellen keine Frage, die schon längst beantwortet ist, sie stellen die Frage nicht einmal zuerst und allein; sie sind eher ein Symptom für eine Frage, die vielleicht dann am beunruhigendsten ist, wenn die Frage (schon als solche) unbedacht bleibt und doch "verdrängt" wirksam wird. Schon darum verdient das Buch den Dank der katholischen Theologen.

Die Neuheit der expliziten Frage gründet letztlich darin, dass die traditionelle Weise, wie die bleibende Wahrheit von der Erschaffung der Seele dargestellt wird, nicht genügend erkennen lässt, dass Gott, wenigstens einmal im natürlichen Bereich, nicht als eine kategoriale Ursache

If I offer a "recommendation" along with this thorough and scholarly book, it is neither my intention nor the author's that we should divide the responsibility for the view put forward in it. The author takes this responsibility upon himself alone and willingly. The commendation is no onesided declaration of agreement, were it only for the reason that in such a brief foreword it is impossible to speak out that kind of Yes or No and then justify it as fully as would be required.

The book is its own recommendation from the very fact that it boldly and methodically takes hold of an "open question," a question which cannot be regarded as simply and definitively solved.

Teilhard's views do not pose any question that has long ago been answered. They do not even raise the question foremost and primarily. Rather they are the symptom of a question whose most disquieting feature is perhaps the fact that its very questionableness has failed to emerge in awareness and nevertheless exerts a sort of "repressed" activity. For that reason from the outset this book earns the thanks of Catholic theologians.

The newness of the question in the form here made explicit is due ultimately to this: The traditional mode of presenting the enduring truth of the creation of the soul does not bring out sufficiently the special character of God's causality. God, at least within the domain of nature, may not be viewed as a categorial cause. His causality does not break the flow of natural and finite causes

aufgefasst werden darf, die die Reihe der natürlichen und endlichen Ursachen für endliche Wirkungen und so den Zusammenhang endlicher Phänomene unterbricht. Gott ist — hinsichtlich dieses Satzes ist man heute sehr empfindlich — nicht "eine" Ursache neben anderen für die Phänomene unserer Erfahrung, sondern Ursache für alle Ursachen, der transzendente Urgrund für alle partikulären Begründungszusammenhänge. "Er stopft nicht Lücken", würde D. Bonhoeffer sagen, er trägt, umfasst, und ermächtigt das Lückenlose der Welt, wobei freilich die Lückenlosigkeit nicht ontologische Gleichrangigkeit der Phänomene bedeutet. Tatsache und Weise der Vereinbarkeit dieses Zusammenhangs aller Phänomene mit dem bleibenden Dogma von der unmittelbaren Erschaffung der menschlichen Seele durch Gott ist die Frage, die dieses Buch stellt.

Für das richtige Verständnis der Frage und der Antwort seien mir hier einige Bemerkungen gestattet. Es ist schon betont worden, dass der Zusammenhang der empirischen Phänomene, der es verbietet, im natürlichen Bereich Gott zu einer einzelnen kategorialen Ursache unter anderen zu machen, keine ontologische Gleichrangigkeit der einzelnen Wirklichkeiten impliziert. Mit der ontologischen, "wesentlichen" Verschiedenheit der einzelnen Seienden und Seinsstufen in der einen Welt ist es auch selbstverständlicherweise gegeben, dass die göttliche Ursächlichkeit, die alles einzelne und dessen Zusammenhang trägt, "terminativ" und so auch "prinzipiativ" verschieden ist, je nachdem um welches Seiende

in producing their finite effects, and thus it does not interrupt the interconnection of finite phenomena.

We have here an insight to which the man of today is extremely sensitive: God is not "a" cause alongside others for the phenomena of our experience. He is rather cause for all causes, transcendent ultimate ground of all particular interconnected groundings.

"He does not stop up gaps," Dietrich Bonhoeffer would say. He upholds, encompasses, and makes possible a world without gaps to stop up. This gaplessness does not, of course, mean that all phenomena are set on an equal footing within reality.

The fact and the mode of reconciling this interrelation of all phenomena with the enduring dogma of the immediate creation of the human soul by God form the question posed by this book.

For a right understanding both of this question and of its answer these few observations may be permitted me. It has just been stressed that the interconnection of empirical phenomena precludes making God one single categorial cause among others in the domain of nature. Given, however, this differentiation "in being" among the individual beings and degrees of being within the single universe, it then follows as a matter of course that the divine causality — supporting both the individuals and their interrelation — is in itself differentiated "as to the terminus" and therefore also "as to the principle," depending upon the degree of each respective being constituting the "terminus" of the divine causality.

es sich handelt, das so "Terminus" dieser göttlichen Ursächlichkeit ist. In dem Sinn, in dem die geistig-personale Seele, verglichen mit anderen Seienden, eine unvergleichliche Stelle im Ganzen der Welt hat, ist also natürlich auch ihre Erschaffung eine ganz "besondere". Das hindert jedoch nicht, das Gemeinsame zu bedenken, das allem schöpferischen Verhältnis Gottes zu den endlichen Seienden zukommt, und es auch von dem Verhältnis Gottes zur Seele gelten zu lassen.

Es ist eine Frage, die wohl offen bleiben kann, ob es terminologisch sehr empfehlenswert ist, die schöpferische Verursachung der menschlichen Seele durch Gott "Konkurs" zu nennen, auch nur insofern diese schöpferische Wirksamkeit Gottes in Beziehung gesetzt wird zu der Ursächlichkeit der Eltern auf das Entstehen des einen neuen Menschen. Ich selbst suchte zwar den traditionellen Begriff des "Konkurses" in der scholastischen Philosophie und Theologie und die Verschiedenheit seiner Interpretation in der Scholastik zu verwenden, um eine sachgemässe und doch der Tradition gerecht werdende Vorstellung von der Einheit der schöpferischen Wirksamkeit Gottes und der Ursächlichkeit der Eltern für das Werden des einen neuen Menschen zu gewinnen. Der traditionelle (thomistische) Begriff des Konkurses in seiner thomistischen Interpretation macht nämlich deutlich, dass er immer auch eine (wenn zunächst auch nur "akzidentelle") Selbsttranszendenz des endlichen Wirkenden impliziert. Doch meine ich selbst nicht, dass

In the sense in which the spiritual-personal soul has a unique position in the world's totality as contrasted with other beings, its creation also is an altogether "special" one. But this does not exclude acknowledging also that which it has *in common with all* creative relationship of God to the finite being. What holds for everything, holds also for the relationship of God to the soul.

As a question of simple terminology, it may well be left open whether "Concursus" is the happiest choice of a name for the creative causing of the human soul by God. True, the term does set this creative causality of God in relation to the causality of the parents effecting the emergence of one single new human being. I myself in fact made a point of *adapting* the notion of "concursus," traditional but highly versatile within scholastic philosophy and theology, in order to attain a factually and yet also traditionally correct presentation of the unity between the creative causality of God and the causality of the parents in regard to the emergence of the one single new human being. The value of this approach lies in the fact that the traditional notion of concursus in its Thomistic interpretation always clearly implies also self-transcendence on the part of the finite agent, even if only in some incidental respects. And yet I do not myself mean that simply for this reason the creative activity of God in relation to the soul should be named "concursus."

*man darum schon das schöp-
ferische Wirken Gottes im
Bezug auf die Seele "Kon-
kurs" nennen sollte.*

*Man kann in der katho-
lischen Theologie die Frage
des Polygenismus mit dem
gebührenden Respekt vor
der Erklärung von "Humani
generis" als noch offene
Frage behandeln. Der Mono-
genismus ist gewiss kein
Dogma. Bei sorgfältiger
theologischer Überlegung
lässt sich heute wohl zeigen,
dass das tridentinische
Dogma von der Erbsünde
den Polygenismus nicht aus-
schliesst, dieser mit jenem
zusammen bestehen kann.
Ich selbst habe meine frü-
here Ansicht in diesem Punkt
revidiert und hoffe, das Er-
gebnis dieser neuen Prüfung
der Frage bald in den "Quaestiones disputatae" (Freiburg, Herder) vorlegen zu
können.*

*Das vorliegende Buch ver-
dient nicht nur Lob und
Aufmerksamkeit, weil es
eine wichtige theologische
Quaestio disputata deutlich
reflex macht und zur De-
batte stellt. Das Buch sam-
melt auch ein ausserordent-
lich reiches Material aus
den verschiedensten theo-
logischen Disziplinen zur
Beantwortung der Frage
und erleichtert so dem theologischen Leser ein selb-
ständiges Urteil.*

KARL RAHNER
München, im Dezember
1966

The question of polygenism within Catholic theology may with all due respect for
the interpretation of *Humani Generis* be
treated as still open. There is certainly no
dogma of monogenism. Cautious theological
reflection enables us to show today that
Trent's dogma of original sin does not exclude polygenism. The two can coexist. On
this point I have reappraised my own earlier
view. The results of my new examination
of the question will hopefully soon be available to the public as one in the series of
Quaestiones Disputatae.

The present volume merits praise and interest not only because it brings an important
open question of theology clearly to the forefront of attention and debate. It gathers together also an extraordinary abundance of
materials out of the most varied theological
disciplines relevant to the solution of its
question. This will make it easier for every
theologically-minded reader to form his own
independent judgment.

KARL RAHNER

Munich, December 1966

PREFACE

Pope John XXIII in his encyclical *Peace on Earth* adopted some expressions traceable to Teilhard de Chardin.

So did several archbishops in their proposals for *aggiornamento* at Vatican Council II. The Austrian Cardinal Koenig declared that this French geologist achieved something unique, which Catholic scholarship in its various branches ought to follow up.

And yet from Rome itself have come two distinctly unsympathetic "cautions" against making the thought of Teilhard available to the Catholic public, or especially to seminarians.

One of these could claim the authority of Pius XII, who had shown disfavor in his 1950 encyclical *Humani Generis* for some of the doctrines but without mentioning their author's name.

A sort of climax in the "new look" of Catholic censorship was reached in 1962. American bishops received from the Apostolic Delegate Egidio Vagnozzi a communication of the unofficial but firm will of the Curial head of the Holy Office, Cardinal Ottaviani. Permission for any public lecturing on Teilhard should be refused. Kindred measures should also be taken to discourage the current wave of interest, so that it would die a natural death.

We were left with the view that our leaders in the hierarchy were going in two directions. Meantime from Europe came similarly irreconcilable views from theologians and other specialists of Catholic thought.

Strangely, Teilhard did not fare any better at the hands of the worldwide natural-science community. It is true that his works had been published by a galaxy of top names in science and acclaimed by others especially in his native France.

The adherence of some of these, and of the 800,000 buyers of his books, seems to have been in large measure just a standing vote for freedom of scientific publication as against censorship obscurantism. Of those scientific journals which carried serious appraisals, the consensus was more sharply and wholly negative than among philosophers of religion.

All alike recognized the wizardry of his articulateness.

"What are we to think?" many Catholics not specialized in both theology and science were asking anyone who seemed to be in a position to know. Thus this volume arose, as the answer a Catholic archeologist and exegete would give. Why Teilhard's work should have been linked at all to either archeology or exegesis is part of the enigma. But it was.

This answer ranges far afield: but no farther than is "all in the day's work" for both those professions.

The excavator cannot choose *what* he will find in the ground; *whatever the spade turns up* must be inexorably studied through into a finished volume, invoking or challenging the verdicts of many peripheral experts.

The exegete cannot *make* God's word or the human author's style, but can only sound them by drawing upon a terrifying variety of separate scholarly areas.

Teilhard, because of his personal endowment, offers more of a challenge than is normally met in archeology or exegesis. But that is part of his planned campaign to break through the compartmented self-sufficiency dividing speculative from empirical sciences. It is a breakthrough in which biblical archeology has had an altogether special role to play.

ROBERT NORTH, S.J.

TEILHARD AND THE CREATION
OF THE SOUL

CHAPTER 1

SPIRIT REVEALED BY OBSERVING MATTER

1. Teilhard as Excavator and Observer

Excavation was the act by which Teilhard earned the right to expect scientists to listen to what he had to say.

He was not the discoverer of Peking Man, but his help in unearthing and interpreting its surroundings was immediate. Less immediate was his presence at Piltdown. He was in on one phase of the discovery of what is now known to be a hoax. The one name no less than the other is to scholarship a symbol of the very heart of pioneering into human origins.

Teilhard's earliest adult researches were more concerned with entomology, "insect-lore," as his *Letters from Egypt* bring strikingly alive.[1] A new species was named for its discoverer *plagiociardis teilhardi,* a prickly sea urchin, globular and thus not manifesting the "radial arrangement" of five arms common to the other echinoderms.[2] It was chiefly out of

[1] Teilhard, *Lettres d'Égypte* (Paris: 1963), 283; Eng. tr., *Letters from Egypt* (New York: Herder & Herder, 1965), 237. — On the Piltdown "discoverer," see *Lettres d'Hastings et de Paris 1908–1914,* edited by Auguste Demoment and H. de Lubac (Paris: Aubier, 1965), 70; 303. On Peking Man, see *Teilhard et le Sinanthrope* by George Magloire (Carnets Teilhard, 19; Paris Éditions Universitaires, 1964); Jean Piveteau, "Teilhard de Chardin et la Science," *Livres de France* 17/4 (Apr. 1966), 15.

[2] Charles E. Raven, *Teilhard de Chardin: Scientist and Seer* (London: Collins, 1962), 54, notes also *Lycopoditis teilhardi* named by A. C. Seward in *Quarterly Journal of Geological Society* 69 (1913) 86.

1

rock that Teilhard hammered the secrets of insect life. *"Archeology is not my dish,"* he writes after an admittedly engrossing visit of the Cairo Museum. But his very first publication was "Eight Days in Fayûm Oasis."[3]

As a little boy in the massive mountains of Clermont-Ferrand, Pierre Teilhard de Chardin had acknowledged that a hard lump of matter was for him something to "adore."[4] This verb scandalizes many readers, especially if they have learned that his mother was a relative of Voltaire. But it was from her that he derived an intense piety. His "adoring" the lump of iron is the clue to an essentially God-seeking satisfaction. He was to find in science that appeasement of the quest for God which others find in a litany or a donation.

Not life itself, but the hard brute matter in which it was imbedded, was Teilhard's initial attraction. He really started out as a geologist. But the study of earth's crust quickly tumbles onto fossils, and the geologist is the man best equipped to extract and interpret them. This study of once-living things is a sort of biology, a "biology of the past." It is called paleontology. In adult life, by profession, Teilhard was specifically a paleontologist.

2.   *The Past for the Sake of the Future*

Even as a paleontologist, he saw that the scientist's mission was not just to record the dead facts of the past.

Our way of recording these facts makes a kind of graph. When enough points have been plotted, up to and including the present, they determine a *line*. This line of itself continues even farther into the past, along the direction indicated. But it continues also toward the future. That is the nature of a graph.

Diagnosis is for prognosis. A doctor records the patient's symptoms only in order to foretell how his future condition will combine with available remedies in order to straighten out. To Teilhard it early became apparent that for him at least "there was no future" in a career burrowing ever deeper into what went behind. *"What is past is dead and interests me no more."*[5]

---

[3] *Relations d'Orient* for December, 1907, pp. 274–281. On page 279, next to two Fayûm pyramids, he describes a swarm of bees; and the article ends: "All this is froth. For the serious part, see the Egyptologists, or my collections."

[4] Teilhard, "Le coeur de la matière" (1950), announced as Œuvres 10 (Paris: Seuil, 1966); amply cited in F.-A. Viallet, *L'univers personnel de Teilhard de Chardin* (Paris: Amiot-Dumont, 1955), 27. Pierre was born May 1, 1881, at Orcines (Puy-de-Dôme), Auvergne, and died in New York on Easter Sunday, April 10, 1955. His name is given as Marie-Joseph-Pierre in Michael H. Murray, *The Thought of Teilhard de Chardin* (New York: Seabury, 1966), 1.

[5] Letter of January 18, 1936, cited by Claude Cuénot, *Pierre Teilhard de Chardin* (Paris: Club des Éditeurs, 1958), 257. This most adequate biography is now

"In India with de Terra and in Java with Koenigswald, I fell head-on into two of the most booming sectors of the Prehistory front — and just at the moment of decisive advances in which I was able to take part. This adds considerably to my experience and my platform. But I get only a meagre satisfaction from it all. Less and less my science (to which I owe so much) seems to me an end sufficient for existence."[6]

A popular word for prognosis nowadays is extrapolation. It means taking a graph of your sales for the past ten years and being able to predict from it where you ought to focus your manufacturing and selling staff for the future. Teilhard's *Phenomenon of Man* is often blamed for its extrapolation. But he felt that in thus "predicting" the future, he was no more exceeding the evidence than a mathematician who continues the line of his graph beyond the plotted points.

"The basic plan of this work: Pre-Life; Life; Thought: three events sketching in the past and determining for the future (Survival) a single and continuing trajectory, the curve of the phenomenon of man."[7]

This might have been all right, if he had "predicted" in the non-committal tones of an actuary or statistician. But the function of predicting is instinctively (not altogether rightly) associated with the biblical Prophet. And Teilhard's manner was in every way more akin to that of the prophets.

"Confronting Teilhardian Prophetism" is the title of a recent book full of zeal and rage. It tells us that teilhardism is "a neoplatonic gnostic neurosis . . . an incurable mental disease" and "a mystification like so many others, with its initiates' ritual."[8]

---

available in English: *Teilhard de Chardin: A Biographical Study,* translated by Vincent Colimore (Baltimore: Helicon, 1965). See further Louis Barjon and P. Leroy, *La carrière scientifique de Pierre Teilhard de Chardin* (Monaco: Rocher, 1964); J. Piveteau, *Le père Teilhard de Chardin savant* (Paris: Fayard, 1964); Armin Müller, *Das naturphilosophische Werk Teilhard de Chardins* (Freiburg: Alber, 1964), with comparisons to Eduard Spranger, 119–224.

[6] Teilhard, *Lettres de voyage I. 1923–1939,* January 21, 1936. The volume was edited by his cousin, Marguerite Teillard-Chambon, under the name Claude Aragonnès (Paris: Grasset, 1956), and is now available in English as *Letters from a Traveller* (New York: Harper, 1962), 218. — On the Burma researches along with Harvard's Hallam Movius, see Helmut de Terra, *Memories of Teilhard de Chardin,* translated from the German by J. Maxwell Brownjohn (London: Collins, 1964), 81.

[7] Teilhard, *The Phenomenon of Man* (London: Collins; New York: Harper, 1959), 34. This translation by Bernard Wall (Œuvres 1, Paris: Seuil, 1955) has in general shown up very well to my critical scrutiny, though it contains some few misinterpretations which have been rightly called to public attention. We have substituted a few American spellings (labor, hominization), and other variants indicated by single quotes. — On extrapolation as rather a "converging proof," see Charles Bordet, *Teilhard de Chardin: L'actualité de son message* (Paris: Éditions Ouvrières, 1964), 15.

[8] Arsène Seuil, *Face au prophétisme de Teilhard de Chardin* (Brussels: C. Dessart, 1963), 35; 39, M. de Corte; 43, A. Curvers. Similarly P. B. Medawar, reviewing *The Phenomenon* in *Mind* 70 (1961), 99, calls it "tipsy, euphoric prose-poetry . . .

The phrases in which this hostility is clothed are a useful clue to their subject's uniqueness. He was "charismatic": the kind of personality who is raised up from time to time to shock men out of their bureaucratic routines and slumbering securities. His frankly "mystical" preferences might well embarrass or alienate his fellow scientists.

Mistrust was deepened rather than dissipated on the rare occasions when Teilhard set out to be an interpreter of Scripture — again, in charismatic fashion: "not bound by the rules."

3.   *What Teilhard Felt to Be Lacking*

One claim has been made which is hardly convincing: namely, Teilhard's complaint against theology was that it ought to be vitalized by a more cogent use of the Bible. Certainly he never claimed to be an exegete. In all his voluminous writings, we seldom run across a single express word from Scripture. Conspicuously exceptional is this early Letter recording his reflections as he sailed down the gulf of Suez.

"Between the prodigiously picturesque and desolate lands [SINAI . . .], *lands almost unknown and unvisited, to which perhaps for that very reason are attached the most mysterious phases of our religious history. I would have loved to get off on those rocky coasts, not only to try them with my hammer, but to hear also if I could the voice from the Burning Bush. But is the time not past when God speaks in the desert, and do we not understand that the 'He Who Is' is not heard either there or here, because the summits he inhabits are not an inaccessible mountain, but a more profound sphere of things? The professors of theology would do well to pass, all of them, through a stage like that which I am going through at this moment. I am beginning to think that there is a certain view of the real world just as closed to certain believers as the world of Faith is to those who are not believers."*[9]

His Old Testament reflections do indeed bear upon the dissatisfaction he felt with seminary theology. But what he deplores is its lack of twentieth-century realism rather than of Scriptural basis.

As for the New Testament, we shall see that he often recurs to a thought of St. Paul which influenced him profoundly: "God shall be all in all" (1 Cor 15:28). This doubtless furnished his "Omega Point" as goal of creation.

---

excused of dishonesty only on the grounds that before deceiving others he has taken great pains to deceive himself;" (p. 106) "gullibility makes it possible for people to be taken in by such a bag of tricks as this."

[9] Teilhard (-Aragonnès), *Lettres de Voyage I* (Paris: Grasset, 1956), 25 f (*Letters from a Traveller*), letters of April 25 and 17, 1923. See now his *Genèse d'une pensée* (Paris: Grasset, 1961), translated by René Hague as *The Making of a Mind: Letters from a Soldier-Priest 1914–1919* (New York: Harper, 1965).

He more or less consciously emphasized also the connected Pauline passages: Romans 8:21 about the material creation being redeemed with man, and Colossians 1:15 about Christ the firstborn of the whole creation.[10]

"Despite the spirit (or even the letter) of the writings of Saint Paul and Saint John, there is still something conventional, juridical, accidental about the salvific figure and function of Christ in current dogmatic formulations."[11] Here again: what Christology most lacks is not better use of Scripture, but better incorporation of the *cited* texts into an up-to-date framework of reality.

So it could not truthfully be said that what Teilhard regretted or resented in his seminary course was any lack of scriptural orientation. His defenders, chiefly Tresmontant, have striven to show that Teilhard's earthiness is more akin to the Bible than to scholasticism.[12] But really what Tresmontant proves is that biblical thought itself is "existential." Ironically that is one of the words most spurned by Teilhard throughout his life, doubtless because of the pessimism with which its votaries shrouded it.[13]

The seminary training against which he protested was not merely his own or the Jesuits' or France's. It has been equally true of Catholic seminary training in general up through the past century. There is an emphasis on purely speculative accuracy of formulations and on the history of scholasticism, sharpened into a defensive posture against all-too-legitimate critiques since Descartes. Somewhere along the line, says Seibel, Church authority forgot that its mission was to guide men in their *living* rather than their formulation of abstractions.[14]

Violent and worldwide rebellion of seminarians, which our past decade has seen, was bound to come. Regrettably, like most rebellions, it tends to sweep away much that is irreplaceable in the scholastic heritage.

At any rate, we should not imagine that Teilhard was crusading for a renewal of theology by return to the sources. He was indeed linked in scholarly intimacy with many of the greatest figures in that renewal movement among French Jesuits and Dominicans. But as his sympathizer de Lubac trenchantly remarks, Teilhard never read even the

---

[10] See below, chap. 5, pp. 122–139.

[11] Teilhard, "Un seuil mental sous nos pas: Du cosmos à la cosmogénèse" 1951, in Œuvres 7, *L'activation de l'énergie* (Paris: Seuil, 1963), 271; similarly page 282, in the essay "Réflexions sur la probabilité scientifique," also composed in 1951.

[12] Claude Tresmontant, *Pierre Teilhard de Chardin: His Thought* (Baltimore: Helicon, 1959); *Études de métaphysique biblique* (Paris: Gabalda, 1955), 126. His *Study of Hebrew Thought* (New York: Desclee, 1960) is the translation of an earlier work, *Essai sur la pensée hebraïque* (Lectio divina 12; Paris: Cerf, 1953).

[13] See below, chap. 10, pp. 274–277.

[14] Wolfgang Seibel, "Die pastorale Zielsetzung des Konzils." *Stimmen der Zeit* 173/1 (Oct. 1963), 39.

most elementary essays of his own professors which cast a needed light on those theological problems he himself brushed contentiously.[15]

The author of *The Phenomenon of Man* repeats often with elaborate humility that he is no theologian, no philosopher, but merely an observer of *facts* who defers to the greater competence of such experts in their own domain. Yet this humility is also and at the same time a not-un-warranted defiance.[16]

In an earlier stage he had felt that with a little patience and aid, his eye-catching insights could be translated into orthodox scholastic formulations.[17] We shall cite his dream of forming a bridge between the tortuous involutions of Roman jargon and the simple honesty of a Harvard professor's exposition.[18] But he seems to have given up both these hopes, rather more defiantly than humbly, in later life.[19]

The thorny problem of compartmentalizing in modern scholarship will

---

[15] Henri de Lubac, *La pensée religieuse du père Pierre Teilhard de Chardin* (Paris: Aubier, 1962), 302–308.

[16] Teilhard, "Le sens humain," 1929, cited by N. Wildiers, *Teilhard* (Paris: Presses Universitaires, 1960), 82: "The truth is that if Christianity has today ceased to give satisfaction, this is not at all because (as its defenders claim) it is too difficult and too lofty, but on the contrary because its ideal does not seem either sufficiently pure or sufficiently elevated. Under its actual current presentation, the Christian religion seems narrow to our spirit and chokes our heart." Wildiers on p. 87 records Teilhard's further observation, "Isn't it strange that Christology, in contrast to Mariology, has made no progress for centuries?"

[17] Teilhard, letter of August 16, 1925, to Gaston Fessard, editor of *Études*, published in P. Grenet, *Teilhard* (Paris: Seghers, 1961), 146; see further Cuénot's *Teilhard* (Paris: 1958), 83, 249.

[18] See footnote 52 on p. 25 below, and footnotes 53–69 on metascience. Maxime Gorce, *Le Concile et Teilhard, l'Éternel et l'humain* (Neuchâtel: Messeiller, 1963), 196–198, shows that Teilhard in a letter to the ex-Dominican "G" maintains "The Roman phylum alone bears the future of the world"; see Pierre d'Ouince, "L'épreuve de l'obéissance dans la vie du père Teilhard de Chardin," *Mélanges H. de Lubac, L'homme devant Dieu* (Paris: Aubier, 1963), 3; 332–346. At the Second Vatican Council the four Fathers who spoke in favor of Teilhard were from East Germany, Africa, North and South America.

[19] The General of the Jesuits released for publication a letter addressed to him by Teilhard on October 12, 1951, acknowledging this his *"vision of Christianity was judged at Rome premature or incomplete,"* but *"he can't change it any more than the color of his eyes, and he can't stop seeking* [to be] *himself";* cited by Pierre Leroy in *Pierre Teilhard de Chardin tel que je l'ai connu* (Paris: Plon, 1958), 57.

Teilhard passed his philosophy course with distinction, and after succeeding in the rigorous "long course" examination at the end of theology in Ore Place on the isle of Hastings, made in France the solemn profession of four vows on May 26, 1918. "It was in England where the Jesuits, banished from France, had taken refuge, that his character was shaped by the philosophy and theological teaching of the Company of Jesus. . . . [Teilhard] had an indefinable something that was Anglo-Saxon." Jean Guitton, *Journals 1952–55*, translated by F. Forrest (London: Harvill, 1963), 244 f. On Teilhard's reception in England, see Thomas Corbishley, "The Phenomenon of Teilhard de Chardin," *Wiseman Review*, 502 (Winter 1964–65), 267–277.

occupy us presently. Specialists no longer speak the same language and have no common ground. This barrier separates scientists not only from theologians but also from historians, jurists, and artists. The physical sciences themselves have become so ramified and technical that scarcely anyone can be spokesman for them all. Even to do this would be already "metascience." Indeed, that is roughly what Teilhard claims to be producing.

"I have not tried to discover a system of ontological and causal relations between the elements of the universe, but only an experimental law of recurrence which would express their successive appearance in time. Beyond these first purely SCIENTIFIC *reflections, there is obviously ample room for the most far-reaching speculations of the philosopher and the theologian. Of set purpose, I have at all times carefully avoided venturing into that field of the essence of being. At most I am confident that, on the plane of experience, I have identified with some accuracy the combined movement towards unity, and have marked the places where philosophical and religious thinkers, in pursuing the matter further, would be entitled, for reasons of a higher order, to look for breaches of continuity."*[20]

Scarcely anyone can deny that he was right in seeing the need and brave in setting out to fill it. He has *dramatized* a predicament which after his articulate prodding can never again be ignored. How reliably he has answered his own questions, or rather how faithful he has remained to his own commitment, is another problem. We will take it up toward the end of this chapter, after first concerning ourselves with some of his concrete evidences.

"Like the meridians as they approach the poles, science, philosophy, and religion are bound to converge as they draw nearer to the whole. I say 'converge' advisedly, but without merging, and without ceasing, to the very end, to assail the real from different angles and on different planes. Take any book about the universe written by one of the great modern scientists, such as Poincaré, Einstein, or Jeans, and you will see that it is impossible to attempt a general scientific interpretation of the universe without GIVING THE IMPRESSION *of trying to explain it through and through. But look a little more closely and you will see that this 'hyperphysics' is still not metaphysics."*[21]

4. *New Evidences and the Growing Pattern*

The paleontologist is concerned with fossils. Ideally he should discover new ones, or more importantly ascertain their stratified background. But

---

[20] Teilhard, *Phenomenon of Man*, 29. A footnote is added, to the effect that the "breaches of continuity" for which Teilhard leaves room, are those which in fact form the focus of interest of our present book.

[21] Teilhard, *Phenomenon of Man*, 30.

such a discovery may come once in a lifetime. And even the discoveries simultaneously being made by others during that lifetime are relatively few. The rest of a paleontologist's career is taken up with fitting those few discoveries into a growing pattern.

The pattern into which fossils fit is not a closed system, but is continuous with the biological specimens existing up to our own day. The first effort to record and classify every known "family" or phylum of living things was made by Linnaeus only in 1753. A few dozen fossils were known to him, some only by hearsay, and so he incorporated them into his classifications with a question mark.

Linnaeus was intensely convinced that all the species he recorded were created in that form initially by God. He was an anti-evolutionist. Yet a simple glance at his phyla, merging so gradually with one another, has been historically the most convincing basis of evolution.[22]

Basis rather than proof, we say, because evolution is a framework of our knowledge rather than a specific ascertained fact or event. The framework is a "working hypothesis," and can be proved to the extent to which an ever-widening sampling of the facts *fits* the frame, even if by modifying it constantly.

Fossils date from one billion years ago. They continue as our only evidence of life down to a million years ago: that is to say, "down to our present day minus one-thousandth," a fraction too negligible to be counted. In this negligible fraction may be included the skeletons of early Stone Age man, from a million (more or less, depending on the new Olduvai evidence) down to some two hundred thousand years ago.[23]

All other evidences of evolution date from our own time. It is true that some few biological specimens are known from "history," by descriptions dating back a maximum of five thousand years. But before Linnaeus the features which are today considered important were not recorded with sufficient accuracy, even by Aristotle.

In all these five thousand years, scarcely a single species affords any evidence of change. Hence for measuring the course of evolution we have practically only two sets of observations: the fossil record and the species now current.

This means virtually that we are getting a bearing from two points of time. One point is the present moment, including the negligible changes of the past five thousand years. The other "point" is the fossil record: though it lasts a billion years, its total contribution is small, and in general gives a "point of view" which we might focus at half-a-billion years ago.

---

[22] H. Wendt, *In Search of Adam* (Boston: Houghton Mifflin, 1956), 53; see footnote 3 of chap. 2, p. 36, below.

[23] L. S. Leakey, *Illustrated London News*, 235 (Sept. 12–19, 1959), 217–9; 288.

What a strange clock, that has only two points, "Then" and "Now." We might call these the vertical axis of measurement. But when we take into account the immensity of the durations involved, it turns out that the "Now" has a sort of "spectrum" or horizontal gradation. The finely graduated distinctions between the thousands of species existing today constitute a sort of sundial, on which the light shed by the fossil record enables us to read the course of evolution more accurately.

Unlike the sundial, our horizontal present-day record has also its own x-axis and y-axis.

The living things known today, apart from their purely biological relations to each other, fit into two larger schemes of measurement: the infinitely big, and the infinitely tiny. On the x-axis we can record by billions the atomic elements which go into the structure of a living being. On the y-axis we can record in billions of units how far the individual is surpassed by the universe in which he forms a cog of incessant mutual activation.

"Because of its consequences even up to the genesis of the intellect, we must notice and record the definite connection which, genetically, associates the atom with the star."[24]

This proportion hinted between Complexity and Consciousness is backed up by a diagram with some statistics in *The Human Zoological Group*. The x-axis, giving a rough count of the atomic units in various living things, starts with zero and proceeds to the number of units in the virus, which is 1000 or "ten to the third power." By the time we reach the smallest cell, this number is already increased astronomically, to one trillion, "ten to the twelfth power." Ten more zeroes must be added for the next indicated organism (lemna); and seven more still for man, or possibly for man's brain alone.

The vertical or y-axis of this diagram also starts with zero. Really it starts with "ten to the minus-twentieth power," but a footnote tells us that ten to the minus-thirteenth, the length of the electron in centimeters, has a good chance of being proved to be the absolute minimum unit of length in the universe. On this y-axis the virus measures ten to the minus-fifth power. Man's six feet is in centimeters something more than ten squared. The earth's radius is ten to the plus-seventh. For the diameter of our galaxy add fifteen zeroes more, and for the diameter of the whole universe only five more. This diagram is given in expanded form in a 1942 essay on "Man's Place in the Universe."[25]

What are these charts supposed to show? Mainly they are to familiarize

---

[24] Teilhard, *Phenomenon of Man*, 50.

[25] Teilhard, *Le groupe zoölogique humain* (Paris: A. Michel, 1956), 22 = *Man's Place in Nature*, translated by René Hague (New York: Harper, 1966), also page 22; and "La place de l'homme dans l'univers" (Peking, 1942), in Œuvres 3, *La vision du passé* (Paris: Seuil, 1957), 308 and 317.

us with the infinities both of bigness and of smallness in which man is incorporated. Despite his modest location just above (numerical) zero among the measurements of length, the complexity of his brain structure in number of units (10^{25}) is equal to the diameter of the whole universe in centimeters!

Another approach. Matter looks dead to us. We may quite legitimately express this in quantified terms thus: "Bodies whose molecular composition is in the range of less than a million structural units show no sign of life." But what about some other familiar phenomena like light? The stars are cosmic bodies which we can recognize only because of the light they emit. To have this effect upon our gaze, *"it is required that the complexity of the object has passed beyond a certain critical threshold, short of which we would see nothing. The speed of a body must approach the speed of light before its variation of mass can become apparent to us. Its temperature must pass 500° centigrade in order that its ray may affect our eyes."*[26] Why can it not be that in virtue of just *such* a mechanism, matter *looks* dead until its "life-elements" attain sufficient complexity?

"The cell remains in all cases essentially true to itself. Looking at it, we hesitate to compare it to anything either in the world of the 'animates' or that of the 'inanimates.' Yet cells still seem to resemble one another more as molecules do than as animals do. . . . What we have is really the stuff of the universe appearing once again with all its characteristics only this time it has reached a higher rung of complexity and thus, by the same stroke (if our hypothesis be well founded), advanced still further in INTERIORITY, *i.e. in consciousness."*[27]

5. *Complexity and Consciousness*

The above observations about the cell are flanked in Teilhard with unguarded or at least audacious expressions. He speaks of the *freedom* and *ingenuity* of "non-living matter" in groping toward cell-organization. But let us agree to overlook his metaphors for the moment. Thus we can grasp some more serious and factual statistics of the observable relations between complexity and consciousness.

As a crass and offhand observation, we may say that the more complex structures exhibit more characteristics of conscious life. It is rather a theorizing on this fact to say outright that every increase in complexity of structure means an increase in consciousness:

"The pre-living can be divined, below the horizon, as an object sharing in the CORPUSCULAR *structure and properties of the world. Looked at from* WITHIN, *as well as observed from without, the stuff of the*

---

[26] Teilhard, my rendition of *Man's Place in Nature*, 24.
[27] Teilhard, *Phenomenon of Man*, 87.

universe thus tends likewise to be resolved backwardly into a dust of particles . . . mysteriously connected among themselves by a comprehensive energy. . . . Virtually homogeneous among themselves in the beginning, the constituents of consciousness, exactly as the constituents of matter which they 'underlie,' complicate and differentiate their kind, little by little. . . . Consciousness reveals itself as a cosmic property of variable size subject to global transformation."[28]

"An irregularity in nature is only the 'sharpening,' to the point of perceptible disclosure, of a property of things diffused throughout the universe, in a state which eludes our recognition of its presence. . . . 'Consciousness is only completely recognizable in man,' we are tempted to say, 'therefore it is an isolated instance of no interest to science. There is evidence for the appearance of consciousness in man,' we must continue, correcting ourselves, 'therefore, glimpsed in this one flash of light, it has a cosmic extension.' "[29]

"All cosmic units, somewhat like Man, possess and represent (however dispersedly or fragmentarily) a tiny 'within,' reflecting with more detail or less one particular representation of the world. . . . [This consciousness of things is] *utterly beyond our means of observation short of atomic complexity 10^5 characteristic of the virus. . . . Consciousness is a universal molecular property; and the molecular state of the world expresses the pluralized state of some potency of universal consciousness."*[30]

To avoid misunderstanding, I propose to sift out of these assertions one part which is observed phenomenon, and another part which is legitimate working hypothesis. The only part which we really *observe* is this: The *reactions* exhibited by more complex structures approximate progressively to those prompted by human consciousness. This holds even for inorganic and plant units. On higher levels, concretely, behavior becomes more like human conscious behavior in measurable proportion as the complexity of the nervous system and eventually the size of the brainpan approach closer to those of man.

This is *verifiable* only in a general way, regarding certain key species. Moreover it in no way applies to individual specimens. Not every human with a larger brainpan is more intelligent than other humans.

We are comparing merely the overall size of molecular structure within contrasted groups. There are doubtless samples like the beaver or the bee which do not fit this rule of thumb. Perhaps Bergson, in a rare tenet in which Teilhard disagrees with him, is nearer the truth in claiming that the "manlike" resourcefulness of the insect is not an *approach*

---

[28] Teilhard, *Phenomenon of Man,* 59; see chapter 6, footnote 6, p. 167 below.
[29] Teilhard, *Phenomenon of Man,* 56.
[30] Teilhard, "La centrologie: essai d'une dialectique de l'union," 1944, in Œuvres 7, *L'activation de l'énergie* (Paris: Seuil, 1963), 107.

toward intelligence but a one-way street in the diametric opposite direction.[31]

Otherwise the discrepancy can be in part explained by the fact that we are merely approximating when we assign to the respective animals varying degrees of consciousness varyingly closer to that of humans. We do not possess for their reactions adequately quantified statistics such as the number of neurons involved.

But even suppose there are concrete species in which structure growth is palpably *not* accompanied by an advance toward consciousness. Teilhard might here reply (though he does not seem to have done so explicitly): It is just as in the whole of evolution: an overall forward-moving Progress by no means excludes numerous and titanic regressions. The "failures" have failed only themselves; they have not failed *nature,* since it was their forward *surge* that made possible the maximum attainment in relatively few cases.

As Rabut paraphrases Teilhard, "A Phylum may be compared to a bush whose upward growth is halted by a board containing one small hole. The bush would produce a fan-shaped bundle of sprouts, a probe-fan, of which one sole twig would find the opening and continue its upward growth."[32]

True, there is a "threshold" or gulf which *severs* man from the possessors of various other degrees of approach toward consciousness. It severs also animal from plant, life from inorganic matter. Ormea notes that *every* birth, not only every species change, is a discontinuity as well as continuity.[33] As a maximum defense of the uniqueness of man's soul, post-Cartesian Catholics have loved to dogmatize that every such threshold, and especially the gulf between nonlife and life, requires a uniquely immediate intervention of the Creator. This assertion is simply unproved: whether or not (as seems likely) its contrary is at present in course of being shown experimentally. "The impossibility of life arising from non-life under any conditions whatever cannot be proved. . . . Neither can we prove that the appearance of life required some special intervention of God," says an up-to-date collaborative volume from a seminary in India.[34]

Discontinuity indeed there is. It is an interesting part of the observed phenomenon, and will call for its explanation in due time. But for the

---

[31] Henri Bergson, *Creative Evolution,* translated by A. Mitchell (New York: Holt, 1911), 112; see pages 153 and 166 of *The Phenomenon of Man.*

[32] Olivier Rabut, *Le problème de Dieu inscrit dans l'évolution* (Paris: Cerf, 1963), 16; Teilhard, *Phenomenon of Man,* 132, 118.

[33] Ferdinando Ormea, *Pierre Teilhard de Chardin, il pensiero, l'originalità, il messaggio* (Turin: Contessa, 1963), 117.

[34] J. Misquitta, "How Life Came to Be," in (A. Fonseca), *Origins* (Poona: Pontifical Athenaeum, 1964), 79; see below, footnote 70, p. 31.

moment we are focusing rather the *continuity* of growth toward consciousness proportioned to growth in structural complexity.

"We are inevitably the focus of our own observation. In its early, naïve stage, science, perhaps inevitably, imagined that we could observe things in themselves, as they would behave in our absence. Instinctively physicists and naturalists went to work as though they could look down from a great height upon a world which their consciousness could penetrate without being submitted to it or changing it. They are now beginning to realize that even the most objective of their observations are steeped in the conventions they adopted at the outset and by forms or habits of thought developed in the course of their research; so that, when they reach the end of their analyses they cannot tell with any certainty whether the structure they have made is the essence of the matter they are studying, or the reflection of their own thought. And at the same time they realize that because of the return shock of their discoveries, they are committed body and soul to the network of relationships they thought to cast upon things from outside. . . . Object and subject marry and mutually transform each other in the act of knowledge; and from now on man willy-nilly finds his own image stamped on all he looks at. This is indeed a form of bondage. . . . But what happens when chance directs his steps to a point of vantage . . . from which, not only his vision, but things themselves radiate? In that event the subjective viewpoint coincides with the way things are distributed objectively. . . . That seems to be the privilege of man's knowledge."[35]

The only "consciousness" anyone really knows by experience is his *own*. What man observes in other realities, even other men, is simply a type of *reaction* varyingly similar to the reactions which he sees prompted in himself by his consciousness. If we are careful to keep remembering this, then we may warrantably extend the same observations to plant and mineral structures.

Scarcely anyone will deny that a puppy's reaction to kindness merits the name of both "knowledge" and "love" to a *greater* extent than some other chemical reactions in the universe.

"In the vegetable kingdom we are unable to follow along a nervous system the evolution of a psychism obviously remaining diffuse. That is not to say that the latter does not exist, growing in its own manner. I

---

[35] Teilhard, *Phenomenon of Man*, 32. Teilhard's title seems to be envisaged by Hans Jonas, *The Phenomenon of Life: Toward a Philosophical Biology* (New York: Harper, 1966), not least because p. x says "The reader will find nothing here of the evolutionary optimism of a Teilhard . . . metaphysical success stories"; p. 25, Whitehead's theory of all actuality as "feeling" is on a considerably higher philosophical plane than the panpsychism of a Teilhard; there is a chapter beginning on p. 99 entitled "On the Animal Soul," but the intriguing title is never taken up in the chapter.

would not think of denying it. Indeed, to take one example out of a thousand, is it not enough to see how certain plants trap insects, 'in order to' be convinced that the vegetable branch is, 'at a distance from' the other two, subservient to the rise of consciousness?"[36]

Teilhard does not seem to have made a capital point of Bergson's observation that the "best" consciousness is in the *lowest* forms of plant-life, precisely because they are *nearest* to the stage at which the man-branch turned off into its separate direction! Yet he does enunciate, in subconscious dependence upon Bergson, the law that the development of a base for psychism in the primates was possible because their bodily development remained most primitive (indeterminate) and therefore most *free.*[37]

Any living cell is more complex than the inorganic molecular structure. Among the molecules, scientists detect combining patterns to which they give names like affinity and preference, and other human-sounding terms, while excluding any "purposefulness" implanted within the molecule.

"This law of controlled complication, the mature stage of the process in which we get first the micro-molecule then the mega-molecule and finally the first cells, is known to biologists as orthogenesis. On the pretext of its being used in various questionable or restricted senses, or of its having a metaphysical flavor, some biologists would like to suppress the word 'orthogenesis.' But my considered opinion is that the word is essential and indispensable for singling out and affirming the manifest property of living matter to form a system in which 'terms SUCCEED EACH OTHER *experimentally, following the constantly increasing values of centro-complexity.' "*[38]

As for the atoms, it is doubtless not true to say that silicon exhibits more resemblance to conscious activity than hydrogen, though the heavier

---

[36] Teilhard, *Phenomenon of Man*, 153 n. Page 156 expands: *"Let us leave the insects and return to the mammals. At once we feel at ease; so much at ease that our relief could be accounted for by an impression of 'anthropocentrism.' If we breathe more freely now that we have come away from the hive and the ant-hill, is it not quite simply because, among the higher vertebrates, we feel 'at home' . . . ? We are not making a mistake. . . . If a furry quadruped seems so 'animated' compared with an ant, so genuinely alive, it is not only because of a zoological kinship we have with it. In the behavior of a cat, a dog, a dolphin, there is such suppleness, such unexpectedness, such exuberance of life and curiosity! Instinct is no longer narrowly canalized, as in the spider or the bee, paralyzed to a single function. Individually and socially it remains flexible. It takes interest, it flutters, it plays. We are dealing with an entirely different form of instinct in fact, and one not subject to the* LIMITATIONS IMPOSED UPON THE TOOL BY THE PRECISION IT HAS ATTAINED. *Unlike the insect, the mammal is no longer completely the slave of the phylum it belongs to. Around it an 'aura' of freedom begins to float, a glimmer of personality. And it is in that direction that the possibilities presently crop up, interminate and interminable, before it."*

[37] Bergson, *Creative Evolution*, 114; Teilhard, *Phenomenon of Man*, 159.

[38] Teilhard, *Phenomenon of Man*, 108. On orthogenesis see pp. 76–78 below.

elements are held to be in a certain sense "powers" of hydrogen. Any effort to "reduce" them to hydrogen brings us into the subatomic domain. And there activity is governed by *electric charge.* The resemblance of this phenomenon to the selectivity and jitteriness of consciousness is too well attested in everyday metaphor to be overlooked.

6. *Entropy*

We will not yet draw any conclusion from the simple observed facts of Complexity in its relation to Consciousness. First we will make an effort to pursue more faithfully Teilhard's austere commitment to recording the data in their proper order than he himself has always done in the above excerpts. Let us here make a fresh start from an entirely different datum of experience which he stresses.

In every operation, a certain portion of the available mass or energy is transformed into heat. This heat is simply diffused and is thus no longer available for useful operations of any kind. This unhappy fact is called entropy.

This has now been happening for some billions of years. At that rate, the universe should have "run down" by now. But in fact it has not thus completely decomposed. On the contrary, it is bursting with dynamism more now than ever, or at least not perceptibly less.

"A counterpoise to entropy drives matter into ever more centro-complexified states," wrote Teilhard the year before he died.[39] *"Poking its head up through this rain of ashes is a sort of cosmic whirl, at whose heart twists the World-Stuff, twirling compactly in on itself in ever more complicated and centered combinations by preferential utilization of its chances."*[40]

The dilemma posed by entropy is acknowledged by most scientists. Some few have attempted to solve the problem. A tiny minority even go

---

[39] Teilhard, "Sommaire de ma perspective phénoménologique du monde," 1954, Œuvres 10; M. Barthélemy-Madaule, *Bergson et Teilhard* (Paris: Seuil, 1963), 586.

[40] Teilhard, "La convergence de l'univers," (Cape Town, 1951), in Œuvres 7, *L'activation de l'énergie* (Paris: Seuil, 1963), 303, in reaction to the hypothesis of an exploding universe, itself a sequel to the hypothesis that the redness of the galaxies is due to their movement rather than the fading of their light in the course of time it takes to reach us.

ENTROPY was taken by Clausius in 1850 and Kelvin in 1851 as proof that if the universe were eternal it would by now have run down. But Engels (before Teilhard) declared that there "must" be a natural process whereby entropy is countered. See Wolfgang Büchel, "Entwicklung und Entropie," *Stimmen der Zeit,* 170 (1962), 187, 190. On the equating of consciousness with "triggerable energy," see Oliver L. Reiser, "Energy the Soul of Matter," *Journal of Religion,* 12/1 (Jan. 1932), 74; and "Mathematics and Emergent Evolution," *The Monist,* 40 (1930), 509–525; also the criticism of C. Lloyd Morgan's 1922 Gifford Lectures, by Alphonse M. Schwitalla, "Emergent Evolution," *The New Scholasticism,* 1/1 (Jan. 1927), 33–48.

so far as to postulate "continuing creation." But most of the scholarly fraternity simply and frankly ignore the paradox as a "given" for which they at present see no explanation.

Teilhard's solution must at first sight appear to be no more than a posing of the problem; a mere relocating (in a more remote corner) of the "pocket of ignorance" which science is content to leave out on the table in plain view of all.

Every separate thing whose operation we *can* observe assures us that the universe is running down. And yet we can equally observe that the universe is *not*. We must then conclude that there was in these separate operations a factor which *escaped* our observation. We only saw what was on the *outside*. There must have been an "inner face" of the respective particle of matter accounting for rebuilding of lost energies.

"The evolution of matter reveals itself to us, 'here and now,' as a process during which the constituents of the atom are inter-combined and ultra-condensed. Quantitatively, this transformation now appears to us as a definite, but costly, operation in which an original impetus slowly becomes exhausted. . . . A rocket rising in the wake of time's arrow, that only bursts to be extinguished; an eddy rising on the bosom of a descending current — such then must be our picture of the world. So says science; and I believe in science: but up to now has science ever troubled to look at the world other than from WITHOUT?"[41]

"In the eyes of the physicist, nothing exists legitimately, at least up to now, except the WITHOUT *of things. The same intellectual attitude is still permissible to the bacteriologist, whose cultures (apart from some substantial difficulties) are treated as laboratory reagents. But it is still more difficult in the realm of plants. It tends to become a gamble in the case of a biologist studying the behavior of insects or coelenterates. It seems merely futile with regard to the vertebrates. Finally, it breaks down completely with man, in whom the existence of a* WITHIN *can no longer be evaded, because it is the object of a direct intuition and the substance of all knowledge. . . . The activity of radium had not been neglected, and could not be neglected, because, being measurable, it forced its way into the external web of matter — whereas consciousness, in order to be integrated into a world-system, necessitates consideration of a new aspect or dimension in the stuff of the universe."*[42]

Despite our author's justified vehemence, we must really break in on him to inquire whether this "within of things" is in fact *observed*, or is rather deduced by some kind of speculative reasoning process. This

[41] Teilhard, *Phenomenon of Man*, 52.

[42] Teilhard, *Phenomenon of Man*, 55. See F. Meyer, *Teilhard et les grandes dérives du monde vivant* (Carnets Teilhard, 8; Paris: Éditions Universitaires, 1963). Teilhard in *Études*, 285 (May 1955), 279, had expressed admiration for Meyer's 1954 *Problématique de l'Évolution*.

might seem to be a mere quibble, save for the fact that Teilhard's whole quarrel with the theologians is that it is *they* who too often mistake rarefied theorizings for observed facts.

With due caution, we may say that the "within of things" is in a certain true sense *observed.* It is truly a component of the observed phenomena. It is "observed" as much as the atom, or atom smashing, is observed. These are not merely *postulated;* they are somehow *detected* as underlying the large-scale reactions.

In an equally true sense, the "unperceived force countering entropy" can, with no more paradox than is built into nature itself, be said to be truly a part of the observed phenomenon. And it is a feature of all material reality whatsoever.

Insofar as this "within of things" is simply a factor of thermodynamics, it has no perceptible or a priori relation to consciousness. Nevertheless, as a simple working hypothesis, Teilhard proposes that we *combine* the two observed phenomena into a diagnostic unity. A doctor knows that a festering toe can cause or cure toothache; but when he confronts a patient who has equally inexplicable swellings of the forehead and rheumatism of the ankle, he is at least no worse off in trying to explain them as dual manifestations of a single disorder, especially if a single miracle drug like cortisone is found to affect both beneficially.

In somewhat the same fashion, let us *suppose* that in fact this "inner face" of the tiniest particles is also an infinitesimal approach toward consciousness. The more elaborate and complex are the structures into which these "units of consciousness-stuff" or Pre-Thought are combined in any being, the more perceptible will be that being's overt activities resembling the behavior prompted by consciousness in humans.

This is no observation. It is a hypothesis or framework *invented* to account for the known facts, to be constantly tested and checked against them.

In a 1952 essay, Teilhard offers a new diagram of the curve of man rising midway between the vertical *y*-axis of orthogenesis, and the horizontal *x*-axis of entropy. He there aims to illustrate that the only thing to prevent a falling off definitively toward entropy is a conscious science or Institute of "Human Energetics" — since *"the productivity of a productive enterprise depends functionally on the* ENTRAIN [pep and involvement] *brought by the workers to their task."*[43] By a larger diagram, Meurers endeavors to spell out what Teilhard means, indicating the cases in which radial energy props up an unwinding universe.[44]

---

[43] Teilhard, "La réflexion de l'énergie," from the *Revue des Questions Scientifiques* for October 20, 1952; in Œuvres 7, *L'activation de l'énergie* (Paris: Seuil, 1963), 345, 348.

[44] Joseph Meurers, *Die Sehnsucht nach dem verlorenen Weltbild* (Munich: 1963), 34; reproduced by A. Haas in *Scholastik,* 39 (1964), 336.

7. *The Primacy of the Spirit*

"Primacy of the human spirit" is not an expression antagonistic to scientists. We would be obstinately naïve if we allowed ourselves to imagine that even the most atheistic or materialistic laboratory researchers are not proud of the achievements of man's unfettered soaring spirit. They acknowledge and insist that the mental operations of man far surpass in dignity the other components of the universe.

But they also insist that these operations emerge from a *material being.* And they are dead right!

The thing to explain is *not* how there can be a non-material being capable of thought. This is no part of our experience. The thing to explain is how there can be a *material* being capable of thought.

Too long we have simply taken for granted — duped by siren Plato! — that distinctively human operations of abstract thought and free choice are performed *apart from* any genuine continuity with matter at all. Moreover Christians have further nourished the conviction that from divine revelation itself we are informed: "Only a non-material being is capable of thought; *therefore* we have 'within' us a non-material principle of our thinking."

If this is truly the datum of reason and revelation, then by all means we want to hold on to it. But the recalcitrance of scientists far more intelligent than any particular *I,* ought to make us at least pause for thoughtful reappraisal. When two highly intelligent and courteous individuals find themselves in radical disagreement about an important decision based on identically the same data, what do they do? They go back over the data step by step, and try to *isolate* the precise point from which — *only* perhaps, or at least *first* — they drew diverging conclusions.

This is all very well where their analysis of the situation starts or continues from the same outset point. But the whole problem will often or generally turn out to be that they took radically divergent outset points; and each expert, in step-by-step fidelity to his own base, has flawlessly reasoned himself to the conclusion where he now stands.

In such a dilemma, the only hope of solution is for *one* of the litigants gallantly to agree to rethink the whole problem in *his colleague's* own terms. There is then a chance that he will be able to indicate along the way, with surgical precision, where the flaw in reasoning came in: whether his own flaw or his colleague's. More likely he will *not* be able to do this to the complete satisfaction of his co-searcher, or even of himself.

But they will at least be talking now about the same thing; as Courtney Murray says, they will have climbed up to the plane of rational disagreement.[45] Perhaps the partner will then volunteer to go back over the steps involved in the *alternative* point of departure. Even if he has no greater success, much has been attained. They have both talked about the same things, from two different approaches.

Both sides tend to imagine that our first contact with reality is via matter, and that what we call "man's spirit" is a thing we go on to deduce from our experiences with matter.

This is a delusion. As a delusion it is more pardonable in the so-called materialists than in us who profess to put above all material reality the primacy of the spirit.

What is the true datum of experience? Scientist and speculativist are perfectly agreed on the fact that our contact with the outside world is by means of an act of knowledge.

This is not the same as saying that the thing we know is solely or even firstly our own act of knowledge. Thought truly puts us in contact with outside reality. But in that act, we are aware of the role played by the self as thinking subject.

The reality with which man first comes in contact is not matter *without* (what is popularly called even by scientists) "spirit." Nor is it spirit without matter. It is simultaneously matter and spirit, both of them consciously, but matter *through* spirit. This leaves that "spirit," whatever it is, as in some sense First.

Again: The most immediate datum of adult observation and experience *includes* the mental operation itself, or rather the "me thinking." It is this thought, this thinking ego, with which our book is concerned.

For the Catholic philosopher, that concrete reality is neatly defined "the operation of a spiritual soul." From the fact that such a description is anathema to the laboratory scientist, it would be folly to conclude he denies the operation which is professedly being described.

He recognizes the *existence* of such operations and their *superiority* to anything verifiable in the inorganic or animal world. Why then should we not be friends with him, and agree to cooperate amiably in evaluating that reality? We can describe it in noncommittal terms without renouncing our private convictions as to how it really *ought* to be named and defined.

Experience includes the "thinking Me" immediately, but not any *more* immediately than it includes the outside object. Only a rather sophisticated second look at that act of knowledge reveals the mental activity in isolation, as distinct from its content. Moreover, it is revealed differently to various observers.

To the scientist, what is strictly experienced is only an *act of thought,*

---

[45] John Courtney Murray, *We Hold These Truths* (New York: Sheed and Ward, 1961), 15.

no real thinking subject at all. Whether the "thinking Me" is merely a popular delusion, or whether it is a reality persisting unchanged through all the shifting "thoughts" of varied content — or indeed, whether this is a question solved by immediate experience itself or only by theorizing: on this burning issue there is no longer agreement.

Philosophers do not agree upon it, either among themselves or with the laboratory scientist. The fact that *we* may have ecclesiastical pronouncements guaranteeing our confidence in a dandy explanation advanced by post-Cartesian Thomism does not forbid us to delimit sharply the extent to which our convictions involve a datum of immediate experience agreed upon by all men.

In the adult, matter and spirit are experienced with equal immediacy, yet matter via spirit. It would be interesting to track down whether in the *infant* the priority of spirit over matter in experience is more clearly provable. At the Fordham Teilhard Seminar in 1964, psychiatrist Henry Elkin summarized long-continued observations tending to prove that the infant experiences *before* anything "else" that "Me" which a certain school of philosophy declares to be the principle of mental operations or spiritual soul.

The infant does *not* at first distinguish among the various contents of his observations. It is all one glorious blob, and that blob is "Me." Only after six months, arrested movements of his hands and eyes betray that he has recognized himself as *distinct* from his environment. It would seem then that he now for the first time "knows" anything other than "his knowing self." Up till then he truly and enduringly knew his own thinking spirit, but mistakenly or rather gropingly confused with it all the other things which he would gradually learn to identify as distinct.

These researches into the "dawning of consciousness" have doubtless much more to add to our problem than has so far been made available. As early as 1908 there was a religious-psychology research with the promising title, "Biblical outlook on spirit and soul compared with modern recognition of the unconscious and of self-awareness."[46]

Returning to the adult, let us proceed with our analysis and our effort to leave in abeyance that long and not merely sectarian tradition which claims our thinking can proceed only from an immediately created and immortal spiritual substance which has somehow been encased in the body.

That body of ours possesses "individuality." And by this we really mean something which no other kind of body possesses: neither the diamond, nor the oak, nor the Arabian steed.

We may call those things *individuum,* or we may hesitate to do so.

---

[46] Fr. Sperl, "Die biblische Anschauung von Geist und Seele und die moderne Erkenntnis des 'Unbewussten' und des 'Bewusstseins,'" *Zeitschrift für Religionspsychologie,* 2 (1908), 145–165.

Its root-meaning "indivisible" certainly does not fit; but on this score it is no worse off than "atom" meaning unfissionable.

Rahner claims we cannot know for sure that even the dog is one single individual. I would tend rather to acknowledge that the animal and even the plant exhibit a certain unity of structure and operation more than a crystal or a bonfire, which in their turn also are in our experience not merely "a horde of separate things."

And even that "horde of separate things" itself would be a meaningless expression unless we felt vaguely that the "things" in it were somehow individuals. Such "individuality" pertains to whatever involves a constant operational interchange of dynamic elements for the good of the whole. By this norm, indeed, the whole atom-structured *universe* is a single individual. *"Considered in its physical, concrete reality, the stuff of the universe cannot divide itself, but as a kind of gigantic 'atom' it forms in its totality . . . the only real indivisible. The history of consciousness and its place in the world remain incomprehensible to anyone who has not seen first of all that the cosmos in which man finds himself caught up, constitutes . . . a system, a totum, and a quantum."*[47]

Nevertheless, by the "individuality" of our own body we mean something different. We mean *personality*. The rediscovery of personality has been a great achievement of our age. Or must we call it rather a reaction against some more spectacular achievements of science?

It is OUR BODY which we experience as individual. Immediate experience does not of course answer such conundrums as whether the outgrown hair or fingernails genuinely form part of that individuality. For fringe-cases like that, we have to reason to an answer, and can find none that will convince everybody. How could we even get Khrushchev and the Beatles to agree on when hair is "outgrown"?

Similarly our experience of the body as an individual by no means excludes in advance the possibility that it possesses a "vital principle." Such a principle is, even popularly, assumed as being not mere body in the same way as the animal or inorganic bodies around us, yet more truly substantial and individual than the "tangible body" itself, to which it gives individuality. This assumption, dear to common sense and to Christianity but abhorrent to biology, may yet be true; but its truth is revealed by reasoning and not by experience.

Even the phenomenon of self-awareness is not an immediate experience of something *other than the body,* as such. It is a space-time continuity among our experiencings of various parts of our *body.* Perhaps (and perhaps not) by effort we can remember in isolation a purely abstract thought, of which the remembrance itself is not embodied in an image or formula of words. At the very least, the philosopher should be willing

---

[47] Teilhard, *Phenomenon,* 43. See below, p. 219, n. 41, and on *individuum,* p. 230.

to admit that this "awareness of isolated immateriality" is very difficult to attain, and impossible for many or most men. Its theoretical *possibility* is useful for helping us to grasp what relation exists between men and other material bodies. But we cannot suitably take as point of departure for our whole cognitive structure a "fact" which is relatively unattainable.

Consciousness manifested by bodies, on the other hand, is a genuine and impressive datum of experience.

In me myself, knowledge and self-awareness provoke reactions. Those reactions are betrayed externally, often in spite of my efforts to conceal them, even in playing poker.

The only way I know that other *humans* possess a type of consciousness identical with mine is from the fact that their reactions are *in type* identical. They are by no means identical in numerous individual details which might even seem to be essential. Still, taken as a totality contrasted with the reactions of the dog or horse, human reactions convince everybody that human self-awareness in its totality is of a different order than the type of knowledge which produces animal reactions.

A little boy loves his puppy and his grandpa. He loves his puppy more than his grandpa, really. Yet he sadly realizes that his grandpa is "his own kind," while his puppy is not. How happy he would be if he could confer on his puppy the same type of reality that he himself possesses. What perfect pals they could be then! Pinocchio and Raggedy Ann are masterpieces of storytelling because they capitalize on this instinctive human analysis of the type of underlying consciousness from which behavior proceeds.

It is thought clever to say a rat is more intelligent than Dagwood, or a dog is nobler than Goldfinger. This usage implies that one of the contrasted parties exhibits reactions suggesting a mechanism different from that which its total nature assures us is there.

Consider the differing reactions of Me, other men, dogs, amoebas, mimosas, and electronic brains. They are not all forms of consciousness; they are not necessarily all even reactions to consciousness. But they are all reactions approaching progressively to the reaction of *My* consciousness. Can we reduce these diverging reactions to something measurable and statistical?

The scientist thinks we can. And indeed why should he not? Whatever comes into play in these perceptible reactions is purely material. The Aristotelian does not deny this. He simply is not interested in such statistics. He has discovered in the reality of "self-movement" an altogether adequate principle of unity distinguishing *all* animals (in which he technically includes also humans) from all other beings.

Teilhard claims that if the Aristotelian were only willing to sit still once and look, he would be fascinated by the quantitative statistics relevant to animal consciousness. The most imposing of these is that the more complex structures, and specifically those with largest brainpan, approximate progressively to the special type of consciousness expressed by humans. This *suggests* that there is an uninterrupted continuity of the phenomena of consciousness from the inorganic domain through varying degrees of animals into the highest reaches of the human spirit.

"*Step by step, from the early earth onwards, we have followed* GOING UPWARDS *the successive advances of consciousness in matter undergoing organization. Having reached the peak we can now turn round and,* LOOK-ING DOWNWARDS, *take in the pattern of the whole.* . . . *From top to bottom, from our souls and* INCLUDING *our souls, the lines stretch in both directions, untwisted and unbroken. From top to bottom, a triple unity persists and develops: unity of structure, unity of mechanism, and unity of movement.*"[48]

"*We can see transformed* . . . *not only the individual structure of the organs and the interior ramifications of the species, but even the tendencies and behavior of the 'soul.' In man, considered as a zoological group, everything is extended simultaneously — sexual attraction, with the laws of reproduction; the inclination to struggle for survival, with the competition it involves; the need for nourishment, with the accompanying taste for seizing and devouring; curiosity, to see, with its delight in investigation: the attraction of joining others to live in society. Each of these fibres traverses each one of us, coming up from far below and stretching beyond and above us.* . . . *But each one, just because it is evolutionary, undergoes a metamorphosis as it crosses the threshold of reflection* . . . *discontinuity superimposed upon continuity.*"[49]

8. *Metascience*

There are those of us who within the ample mansions of theology and exegesis have been assigned the more *earthy* chores: investigations which deal more proximately with brute matter. It would seem to be our duty — not our duty to science or to atheism but our duty to the Church — to detect and defend the *relevance* of matter to revelation and to spirit.

Says Rahner: "Natural science is by the theologian's own definition a pursuit that has nothing to do with God. There do in fact exist things distinct from God, possessing their own enduring reality, and immediately accessible to men. . . . Christian theology itself teaches that there is a realm of objects of study in which God and salvation history are not

---

[48] Teilhard, *The Phenomenon of Man,* 220 f; see Hans Mislin, "Zu einer Zukunfts-synthese von Geist und Natur," in Eleonore von Dungern, ed., *Forschung und Lebensordnung mit und ohne Teilhard de Chardin* (Terra Nova 3); (Munich: Reinhardt, 1965), 81–91.   [49] Teilhard, *The Phenomenon of Man,* 179.

included. In that realm, called the world or Nature, God is what he is, namely not present as a reality distinguished from other things alongside it, and forming an object of experience like them. . . . The natural scientist as such does and must value a certain methodological un-theism . . . neither must nor can be pious, since the method and principles of his science bind him to seek the reason of any given phenomenon in another observable phenomenon and not immediately in God as such. . . . And these natural sciences have of their nature a special accessibility, universality, and reliability . . . not *greater than* but *different from* what theology and other researches of the spirit possess."[50]

Even within its own domain, matter is now seen to possess a surpassing unity. *"We have been looking at matter as such, that is to say according to its qualities, and in any given volume — as though it were permissible for us to break off a fragment and study this sample apart from the rest. It is time to point out that this procedure is merely an intellectual dodge. Considered in its physical, concrete reality, the stuff of the universe cannot divide itself, but as a kind of gigantic 'atom' it forms in its totality (apart from thought on which it is centered . . .) the only indivisible,"* as we just saw.[51]

Too often the duty of the theologian is seen to lie in *resisting* the effort and claim of natural science to reduce the phenomena of experience more and more to a recognizable continuity. And yet the whole progress of man out of superstition and magic into religious belief and theology has been a record of progressively eliminating the assumptions of capricious interventions of spirit realities into man's mysterious and uncooperative material environment.

Theology now extols in principle the *economy* of action by which God put into the natural universe secondary causalities whose proper functioning is now seen to be a more marvelous praise of their maker. Yet there remain little pockets of atavism, resisting every new effort to attribute to secondary causality what newly observed facts seem to warrant.

It is really to counter this heritage of hostility toward rational science that our Church steers a notable number of its priests and theologians into fields where matter rather than spirit is the proper object of research. By so doing, she in a certain sense commends to them a duty of *resisting* the yen for discontinuity between matter and spirit which animates the majority of her spokesmen.

This is to create not a schizophrenic dissidence within her own ranks, but a healthy tension of dialogue and dialectic. Even where she gives

[50] Karl Rahner, "Das Selbstverständnis der Theologie vor dem Anspruch der Naturwissenschaft," Sonderheft, *Religionsunterricht an höheren Schulen* (Düsseldorf: Patmos, 1963), 5 f, 21.

[51] Teilhard, *Phenomenon of Man*, 43; see above, p. 21.

an express mandate to refute out of the data of science itself the errors seen to be incompatible with her heritage, it may and must sometimes turn out that her loyal sons show her instead that the incompatibility was only apparent.

Between all the exact sciences and religious philosophy there is a chasm to be spanned. It is not due to any hostility or incompatibility, but simply to the fact that they speak different languages and move in different media. They do not communicate.

Teilhard muses in Peking how *"the day before yesterday, before a Chinese-American audience, a very congenial professor from Harvard explained to us very simply and humbly his manner of understanding the awakening of thought in the animal series. I thought of the abyss which separates the intellectual world in which I find myself and whose knowledge I understand, from the theological and Roman world whose idiom is also known to me. After an initial shock at the idea that this world can be just as real as that one, I told myself that now I would perhaps be capable of speaking that first language so as to express legitimately what the other keeps and repeats in its words which have become incomprehensible for many. Strange as it may at first seem, I ended up realizing that here and now Christ is not indifferent to the concerns of Prof. Parker, and that with certain intermediaries he could have been made to pass from his positivist psychology to something of a mystical perspective. Here is an India that attracts me more than that of Xavier."*[52]

The failure of speculative and empirical research to communicate together adequately is only one aspect of the larger malaise of our academic century. Knowledge about man, or about reality with man as its focus of interest, has become simply too vast and proliferated for any one science to master it.

"Anthropology," if names mean anything, ought to do this. And in fact it approaches that function in the German pattern, as a branch of theology. We do not use the word in English in that sense at all. And throughout the world of science, Anthropology is sharply restricted to what outsiders at least tend to regard as a study of primitive or race-bound behavior.

Anyway it would seem to pertain to the domain of Biology or Biochemistry to evaluate any claim that the meanest sand speck or gas develops in uninterrupted continuity up into the highest flowerings of the human spirit. If the claim is true, the *processes* are biochemical; if

---

[52] Teilhard (-Aragonnès), *Lettres de Voyage I* (Paris: Grasset, 1956), 91, letter of June 19, 1926; alternative translation in *Letters from a Traveller* (London: Collins, 1962), 127. On Georges Gusdorf's complaint about compartmentalized scholarship's resistance to Teilhard, "the biggest name of French anthropology since Broca," see H. de Lubac's essay "Envergure et limites de l'oeuvre teilhardienne" in his *Blondel et Teilhard de Chardin* (Paris: Beauchesne, 1965).

false, biochemistry should be able to refute it. But the *achievements* of man's spirit pertain to fenced-off domains of scholarship far other than biochemistry: history, linguistics, ethics. More recently there have sprung up brand-new sciences trying to bridge the gap between empirically measurable and creatively free behavior: psychology, sociology.

They are not enough. What was once called "Physics" has proliferated into a regular empire of autonomous natural sciences, clamoring imperatively for a unifying and digesting discipline to make their results available even to each other.

But was it not precisely that clamor, heard even in his own day, which Aristotle was satisfying when he invented "After Physics"? This is what he meant by metaphysics, and is in fact what the word itself means: a thing far more pragmatical and empirical than the shuddering abstractions it has come to be associated with.

Maybe that was what Aristotle meant, and maybe it wasn't. But today the name metaphysics has been preempted for something else, and there is *still* room for a cumulative-survey-science "next after Physics." Teilhard himself declares that *The Phenomenon of Man* is this: a "Super-Physics," a "hyperphysics which is still not metaphysic."[53]

"Cosmovision" is a good name, which means the same thing, and has been applied by his evaluators out of a desire to avoid unwanted connotations. "World view," at least as *weltanschauung* is used in English, rather hints at something else. "World vision" can scarcely escape nuances of the visionary or mystic: just as "theory" has come to mean something different from its Greek sense of "a straight look at the facts," which gave to Huyghens already in 1700 the title *Cosmotheoros*.[54] Perhaps the most suitable name of all is Metascience.

Whatever its name, such a super-science is sorely needed by the philosopher too. Some few who bear that title in our day think that there is no need any more for them to know the actual realities of physics, since Aristotle and Aquinas already established a framework of immutable truths which no conceivable alteration in physical science could subsequently affect. For them philosophy's posture vis-à-vis physics is simply to take over the new data to be tucked in wherever they best fit in the *philosophia perennis*.

But many even among the Neo-Thomists realize that the only way we can be faithful to Aquinas in our day is by taking the most reliable existing physics to base upon *it* an architectonic pattern of reality. Was

---

[53] Teilhard, *Phenomenon of Man*, 30; also "La place de l'homme," 1942, in Œuvres 3, *La vision du passé* (Paris Seuil, 1957), 306. See above, p. 7, n. 21.

[54] Christian Huyghens, *Cosmotheoros* (1704), noted by A. Delcourt, "Notions de biosphère et de noösphère," *Revue Teilhard de Chardin*, 8 (Dec. 31, 1961), 13. I. Meilvielle calls it "La cosmovisión de Teilhard de Chardin: una metafísica del unir," *Estudios Teológicos y Filosóficos* 2 (1960), 107–133.

not this what *he* did? Anton Pegis concluded his 1964 Aquinas Lecture at Marquette University with the statement that no *philosopher* can lay claim to being a Thomist unless he rethinks for himself and his own century what Aquinas suggests only parenthetically in his intended *commentary on revelation.*[55] J. B. Metz shows how the Thomist achievement lay in its *re-orienting* of the data of Aristotle rather than in the data thus re-oriented.[56] John Russell from an Oxfordshire Jesuit seminary writes, "when one considers how closely Aristotle integrated his philosophy with the best scientific knowledge of his time, it becomes clear that to remain faithful to his spirit one must [decide] that the old context is obsolete and seek a new one in the world pattern revealed or suggested by modern science. . . . Nor need we be unduly disturbed if, in the process, some of the traditional conclusions of scholastic philosophy are found to be in need of revision."[57]

Yes, the philosophers need a good noncommittal summary of *what science alone* tells us about the entire world of man. Yet they show themselves terribly alarmed that no such summary can be compiled without impinging on their own domain — inevitably, incompetently, and disastrously. And they may well be right. Certainly in the case of Teilhard's own attempt, their protests are not without foundation.

One American Dominican periodical notes that Teilhard has much to say "on actuality and potentiality, on determination and chance, on truth and goodness, unity and diversity, dualism and monism, on the constitutive of personality, on the essential nature of things, on the proper powers and passions of natural bodies, on the nature of men, of the mind, of love, of society. This is philosophy, and the force and moving power of the book lies largely in the way it handles these many topics."[58]

The sketch *Comment je vois* is of special importance, since Teilhard there sets forth expressly a "metaphysic," as *distinct* from his own "phenomenological science." So says Haas, who with Smulders notes as two

[55] Anton Pegis, *Saint Thomas and Philosophy* (Milwaukee: Marquette University Press, 1964), 87. So now with explicit praise for Teilhard's effort, Gerard Smith, "Note sur l'avenir de la philosophie catholique," *Mélanges H. de Lubac, L'homme devant Dieu* (Paris: Aubier, 1963), 3, 283; 277–285.

[56] Johannes Baptist Metz, *Christliche Anthropozentrik: über die Denkformen des Thomas von Aquin* (Munich: Kösel, 1962), 45; see Metz's defense of his contentions in *Theologische Revue,* 61/1 (Jan. 1965), 14–16, against H. Meyer's claim that the Sophists and Plato were already just as man-centered.

[57] John L. Russell, "Teilhard de Chardin: *The Phenomenon of Man,*" *Heythrop Journal,* 1/4 (Jan. 1960), 277. Now E. R. Baltasar, "Teilhard de Chardin: a Philosophy of Procession," *Continuum,* 2/1 (Spring, 1964), 87–97, holds that to solve the central problem of human thought requires in first place a "conversion from the Aristotelian to the Teilhardian or biblical philosophic pattern of thought." In Baltasar's title "procession" seems to mean *process,* but stressing its verbal aspect.

[58] Michael Stock, review of *The Phenomenon: The Thomist,* 23 (1960), 297.

chief philosophical presuppositions the primacy of man and the biological function of society.[59]

Metascience is the term of Guérard des Lauriers.[60] He admits its validity, "constituted by the reflection of science on its own methods and principles: unable to found or criticize these principles, yet capable of disengaging them on the basis of their consequences." He would even admit that there can be a *cosmology* which is only a cosmic view or synthesis of the metasciences. Yet he claims that Teilhard's work is neither of these, nor even a "natural theology," but a theology unlimited. Hinske deplores "casual and questionable philosophical positions."[61] Delfgaauw asks whether hyperphysics has a method, or is just a confusion of science and philosophy.[62]

Congo Jesuit Elliott declares categorically that Teilhard's effort is a philosophy, yet deserves to be called "universal history" and "neither science nor metaphysics but phenomenology."[63] All this is nuanced considerably in the recent giant philosophical disquisition on Teilhard and Bergson: Teilhard says expressly that his work is a phenomenology, but since it is *not* such in the sense that word has in philosophy, a lot remains to be explained before it can be decided in what sense he was a philosopher. His first use of "phenomenology" is coupled with *human*. He appears to be claiming to chart only the "external face" of reality, when it is obvious that his real contribution and concern is "the within of things." His famous letter to Cuénot *denies* that people like Husserl can claim the name "phenomenologist" while they are ignoring "the *big*

[59] Adolf Haas, "Schöpfungslehre als 'Physik' und 'Metaphysik' des Einen und Vielen bei Teilhard de Chardin nach der unveröffentlichten Schrift 'Comment je vois,'" *Scholastik*, 39 (1964), 321–342, 510–527; the citation on page 322 from Smulders is page 31 in the French edition, *Vision de Teilhard* (Paris: Desclée, 1964).

[60] M. Guérard des Lauriers, "Le 'Phénomène humain,'" *Revue Thomiste*, 56 (1956), 518.

[61] Norbert Hinske, "Der Mensch als Achse und Spitze der Entwicklung," *Kommunität*, 5 (1961), 176.

[62] Bernhard Delfgaauw, *Teilhard de Chardin* (Baarn: Wereldvenster, 1961), 84. Now Joseph F. Donceel, "Teilhard de Chardin: Scientist or Philosopher?," *International Philosophical Quarterly*, 5/2 (May 1965), 248–266: Teilhard was right in maintaining that both the without and the within of things must be explained, but wrong in assigning both tasks to the scientist as such; he can hardly be interpreted as having meant the one man, the scientist, *as* philosopher. The scientist in fact cannot help philosophizing any more than he can help breathing. The trouble is, he is philosophizing *most* when making such declarations as "Science needs no philosophy."

[63] F. G. Elliott, "The World-Vision of Teilhard de Chardin," *International Philosophical Quarterly*, 1/4 (Dec. 1961), 620, 643. See further N. A. Luyten, *Teilhard de Chardin: nouvelles perspectives du savoir* (Fribourg: Éditions Universitaires, 1965); N. George, *D'Einstein à Teilhard* (Paris: Éditions Universitaires, 1964); Maurice Gex, *Le problème des rapports du devenir et de l'intelligibilité dans l'évolutionisme de Teilhard de Chardin* (Basle: Recht und Gesellschaft, 1959).

phenomenon" of cosmogenesis. In short, Teilhard has " 'a' philosophy" because he has " 'some' philosophy": after all, *no* philosopher has *la philosophie.*[64]

To James Reilly it is unlikely that this "observation of the phenomenon" is rigorously free from any extra-scientific presuppositions; it is rather a myth like Plato's *Timaeus.*[65] On the other hand, precisely because he tried to dispense with philosophy, Vander Gucht rules him out as the coming master of Christian thought.[66]

Teilhard's enterprise requires more serious philosophy than he possesses, says Dominique Dubarle. If the "outside" of things is precisely everything that scientific observation can reveal, then the "within" of things (though called by Teilhard a part of the total phenomenon) must involve an element of imagined reconstruction or intuition: a Hegel-Husserl style "phenomenology" which means "detachment from metaphysics."[67]

It is difficult to withhold our admiration from the penetrating analysis which Paul-Bernard Grenet penned with a sympathy belying the title "Philosopher in spite of himself" which offends some as a snide allusion to Molière. "A very great mind, wanting to limit himself to science, was forced by the very universality of that science to pose philosophic problems. . . . As his knowledge of philosophic technique was sparse, he seemed a disseminator of poor philosophy to many either whose duty it was to judge of him, or who availed themselves of every reader's right to judge as he reads. But by many others (since his scientific information was immense, his greatness of heart inexhaustible, and the poetry of his expression enchanting), Teilhard was regarded as the *only* philosopher of the future. He complained sometimes of his critics, but not in proportion to what he had to suffer. Against his admirers he defended himself as well as he could, but all his protests never prevented them from taking him for something he professed not to be."[68] In a later

---

[64] Madeleine Barthélemy-Madaule, *Bergson et Teilhard de Chardin* (Paris: Seuil, 1963), 581, 585, 621; see now her *La personne et le drame humain chez Teilhard de Chardin* (Paris: Seuil, 1966); J.-P. Blanchard, *Méthode et principes du père Teilhard de Chardin* (Paris: Colombe, 1961); and L. Barral, *Éléments du bâti teilhardien* (Monaco: Rocher, 1964).

[65] James P. Reilly, jr., "A Student of the 'Phenomena,' " in Robert T. Francoeur's *World of Teilhard* (Baltimore: Helicon, 1961), 60.

[66] Robert Vander Gucht, "L'Église et la crise de l'idée de vérité," *La Revue Nouvelle,* 34/12 (Dec. 15, 1961), 501. But "a cosmic view of the universe asks for a Christianity viewed in proportion to that universe," says Sister Mariella Gable, "The Concept of Fame in Teilhard de Chardin and Dante," *American Benedictine Review,* 16/3 (Sept. 1965), 342 (-358).

[67] Dominique Dubarle, "A propos du 'phénomène humain,' du P. Teilhard de Chardin," *La Vie Intellectuelle,* 27/3 (Mar. 1956) (6–25); 20; 10.

[68] Paul-Bernard Grenet, *Pierre Teilhard de Chardin ou le philosophe malgré lui* (Paris: Beauchesne, 1960), 5. One may regret as rather hasty the review by F. Russo in *Études,* 306/1 (July 1960), 138. Regarding the literary skill and massive

work Grenet adds even more sympathetically, "We showed how despite his ever-clearer intention of presenting only a Super-Physics, he was drawn in spite of himself to present a philosophy . . . [which] did not always ring true. Now it is time to turn the page, and show how even the most expert conventional philosopher must listen to the 'cry' of Teilhard and gaze at the 'vision' which forced the cry from him."[69]

Teilhard's challenge is indeed an unnerving one to the philosopher, who fears that if any such super-science emerges even better than Teilhard's, it will inevitably be an ersatz-philosophy, harmful because popular. Ah yes: popular. If such a super-physics *can* exist, it is inexorably the language of the future. Not the supremacy, and not even the autonomy, of either philosophy or theology is threatened. What is threatened is their *relevance* for a man who cannot know what they are saying until it is translated into his own language.

9. *Continuity Looks Both Ways*

Did Teilhard set a sufficient break between the human principle of operation and those material realities out of which it appears to evolve?

Doubtless most Christian readers will feel that this way of posing the question is all wrong. First we should affirm our unshakable conviction of the soul's spirituality, immortality, and unique origin, as a challenge to this materialistic and unbelieving generation. Only in second place should we listen to what contrary evidence the scientist claims to have discovered in his laboratory. This we may do with the intention of isolating and refuting his errors, but not to find or admit anything that might involve altering our cherished formulas. . . .

Formulas do in fact exist, whose alteration for one reason or another is inadmissible. This is true not only within the domains allied to theology, but in the most empiric sciences as well. But in both areas cases have come to light in which the formula retained its correctness only if recognized as restricted to an assemblage of facts which had meanwhile been broadened. Parallel lines, usury, Galileo, Darwin, and rhythm are key-words recalling such reappraisals which could be repressed only so long.

One frailty our flesh is heir to is that of staking our defense of cherished ideals on one or other slogan of which we feel quite sure,

---

diffusion of Teilhard's writings, see A. Rousseaux, "La stature du Père Teilhard de Chardin," *Littérature du XXᵉ siècle* (Paris: Michel, 1961), 7, 105–114 [6, 155–174]; and J. Hassenforder, *Étude de la diffusion d'un succès de librairie* (Paris: Centre d'études économiques, 1957).

[69] P.-B. Grenet, *Teilhard* (Paris: Seghers, 1961), 146. That this work was intended as an *amende honorable* is denied by Grenet, "D'une très curieuse opinion sur l'être en puissance," *Revue Thomiste*, 65/3 (July 1965), 427.

instead of first reflecting whether we have other equally-operative slogans which might tend to put matters in a slightly different light.

"Matter cannot become spirit, and matter cannot produce spirit." Undeniable. The conclusion seems to impose itself that there is an irreducible discontinuity between matter and spirit.[70]

But . . . "Spirit *can* produce matter." (God created the world.) "Spirit can *become* matter." To omit from our present perspective the mystery of God becoming man, we allude rather to the more accessible fact that "the soul is the form of the body."

Without going into controverted subtleties of Thomism, we take this to mean that the soul in some way gives to the "pure potency" which is called *materia prima* every single one of its perceptible and phenomenological characteristics which we call "matter": that which has weight and/or occupies space.

The soul is not held to "produce" this matter after the fashion of an efficient cause, but nevertheless *this body* which I actually possess is determined by the *form* and not by *materia prima*.

And more properly, when I say my *body,* I mean "individual material *being.*" Form is a principle of a *being,* not of a counter-principle. The soul is the form of the material being which it *is,* insofar as a "form" can be said to have existence at all.

"What we call 'material' is at least in a Thomistic philosophy always regarded [says Rahner] as contained and solidified spirit. It is determinate being, whose being as such [is a thing] apart from the 'real negativity' called generally *materia prima,* which involves no positive reality. . . . The body of man is necessarily a factor of the becoming of man as a spirit, and is thus not the 'un-spirit.' . . . The same holds true of other

---

[70] P. Schoonenberg, "Evolutie," *Bijdragen,* 23/2 (1962), 109–137: "Continuity of evolution" is Teilhard's view, unhesitatingly to be preferred to Aristotle's; but the three planes of matter-life-spirit are called in scholasticism *analogous,* which ought to mean that they are just as fully identical as they are different. Well-meaning believers continue to dogmatize "No pre-life will ever be verified," as now Wolfgang Kuhn, "Teilhard de Chardin y la Biología," *Estudios Centroamericanos,* 18/187 (Nov. 1963), 334–9. But some of the real facts of the case seem hardly intelligible to theologians. "The biosynthesis of deoxyribonucleic acid (DNA) *in vitro,* through polymerization of nucleoside triphosphates in the presence of the appropriate enzymes, was successfully completed by Kornberg, and for this he received the Nobel Prize in 1959" along with Ochoa, who synthesized RNA: Arthur C. Giese, *Cell Physiology* (Philadelphia: Saunders, 1962), 527; see *Science,* 131 (1960), 1503; and Francis Crick and Marshall Nirenberg, "The Genetic Code," *Scientific American,* 20/74 (Oct. 1962), 66–74; 208/3 (Mar. 1963), 80–94: DNA is the giant helical molecule that embodies the genetic code of all living organisms. Further explanation of the DNA genetic code, and of what Berkeley's Calvin calls taming of electrons, in Alfred Herrmann, *Teilhard de Chardin, Melvin Calvin et l'Origine de la Vie sur notre Terre et dans le Cosmos* (Carnets Teilhard, 18; Paris: Éditions Universitaires, 1964), 27. See above, p. 12, footnote 34.

bodies insofar as these are environment and extended embodying of [man's] spirit."[71]

If spirit can produce matter; if spirit can determine the reality of that very matter which is its own being: then in one direction at least there is no discontinuity between matter and spirit.

If *all* the matter which there is was produced by spirit; if *much* of the matter is concretely determined to its individual existing reality by spirit here and now: then it would seem unwarrantable to extend the slogan "matter cannot produce spirit" to imply unwarrantably *"spirit cannot, mediately, produce spirit."*

Is it in fact true that spirit (except God) cannot produce spirit? It may be. But if so, it is not the slogan we started from.

Here is the problem as expressed by a scholar of Teilhard's own tongue recently elevated to the Cardinalate: "Instead of explaining the superior by the inferior, thought by life, life by matter, as materialistic evolution does, [Teilhard] justifies the inferior by the superior, matter and life by the thought to which they are ordered, thought itself by the final collective regrouping of human persons about a super-personal transcendent center . . . whose name Christianity can reveal. . . . [*Materia matrix* is] not Spirit incomprehensibly juxtaposed with matter (Thomism!), but Spirit emerging (by pan-cosmic operation) from matter. . . . Such a view radically excludes the philosophic doctrine which sees irreducible differences of order between matter, life, sensation, thought. . . . If the appearance of thought is the fruit of evolution, how maintain the defined doctrine of creation of the soul?"[72]

Let us take one thing at a time. Is it true that spirit cannot produce spirit?

Obviously if finite spirit exists, it has been produced, therefore it *can* be produced. But it could have been produced by God rather than by another spirit. This cannot just be assumed; it must be proved. We will examine the proof in due time.

But for the moment we wish merely to insist that when theologians say "matter cannot produce spirit," what they really mean is "spirit cannot produce spirit; only God can." And that is quite a different thing. That is the question of whether the primacy of spirit can be salvaged

---

[71] Karl Rahner, "Die Einheit von Geist und Materie im christlichen Glaubensverständnis," Sonderheft, *Religionsunterricht an höheren Schulen* (Düsseldorf: Patmos, 1963), 40 f.

[72] Charles Journet, "La vision teilhardienne du monde," *Divinitas*, 3/2 (Apr. 1961), 331, 334. In "La question des origines: la Bible et les sciences," *Nova et Vetera*, 33/3 (1958), 169, the distinguished critic cites numerous examples of Teilhard's error in locating life itself at the heart of the cosmos, and on pp. 223–230 condemns Teilhard's failure to leave room for the immediate creation of the soul. See below, pp. 206–223 on the "defined doctrine."

without postulating its discontinuity from the material world in which it is imbedded and observed.

In one of his most recently published essays, called "Centrology," Teilhard endeavors to express a limited continuity between matter and spirit in function of the manner in which every particle of reality is *related* to others. He conceives this relatedness as a (metaphorical) *curvature* of each thing, inexorably pointing to a *center* outside itself, serving to relate it first to other "arcs" apparently quite remote from it, then secondly to other centers in a grand super-centering of the whole universe. This centeredness is "genetic," in the sense that it forms part of all productive activity, and in turn plays a large part in productivity, especially the type called reproductivity:

"Regarded as synonyms of multiplicity and unity respectively, matter and spirit are not two heterogeneous or antagonistic things held together by accident or violence. In virtue of the genetic or centrogenetic relation which makes unity and centeredness depend upon the complex multiple, the material and spiritual aspects of the Real evoke each other necessarily and complementarily, like the two faces of a single object, or rather like the terms A QUO *and* AD QUEM *of a single motion. . . . Matter, strictly defined as a 'thing' without trace of consciousness or spontaneity, simply does not exist at all. . . . The determinisms or 'laws' of physics are simply a function of Big Numbers, the* [statistical quantification] *of freedom in matter. . . . But Spirit is not simply the* TOTALITY *of the centers engaged in centrogenesis; . . . from the successive syntheses or segmentations affected by centro-complexity emerge genuinely new centers along the way and only* [these! human souls? SEULS LES NOYAUX RÉ-FLÉCHIS] *reflex-cores represent the irreversible portion of the spiritualized universe. . . . Centreity is interiority (soul), itself function of a proportionate degree of complexity (body). . . . This coefficient of centro-complexity (i.e. of consciousness) is the veritable absolute measure of all the beings surrounding us. It alone can be taken as basis of a truly natural classing of all the elements of the universe."*[73]

---

[73] Teilhard, "La centrologie," Peking, Dec. 13, 1944; in Œuvres 7, *L'activation de l'énergie* (Paris: Seuil, 1963), 131 f, 107.

SUMMARY OF THE FIRST CHAPTER,
ON "MATTER AND SPIRIT"

Teilhard adored matter, and in his own branch of science he was dedicated to finding the traces of life imbedded in it. His interest in the past was only as a clue to the future. He aspired to put theology into contact with the twentieth-century facts of life. This meant incidentally a sympathy for the enrichment of theology by a return to its own sources, insofar as these put a premium on realism and common sense.

As a paleontologist, he did not feel his work was done when he had unearthed new specimens or clarified their prehistoric context. The true goal of the scientist is to fit the separate facts into a growing pattern. His researches showed man's place in the universe to fit into a significant continuity stretching from the atom to the galaxy.

Complexity of molecular structure is at a maximum in man, and so is the manifestation of consciousness. Other structures are progressively less complex in proportion as they recede from behavior resembling that of man's consciousness. All structure is due to incessant interchange and recombining of atomic elements. These operations, though efficient, are always accompanied by entropy, the diffusion and loss of a percentage of the total available mass or energy.

The functioning of entropy through these billions of years should mean that the universe would have run down by now. The fact is that it has not. This can only mean that there was a dynamic "inner face" of matter escaping our direct observation. The two facts which *are* observed, entropy and complexity-consciousness, may lawfully be combined into this "working hypothesis":

"The ultimate source of the rebuilding of the lost energy is identical with the ultimate unit of potential consciousness present in every particle of matter." A *hypothesis;* not an observed fact.

In this hypothesis, the noblest achievements of man's spirit are reduced to ever-more-complex restructuring of material elements. Yet that process involves a *leap* over certain "critical thresholds" in such a way that merely quantified increase produces truly qualitative change.

Human individuality and freedom are not less unique things for being built up out of material units, as long as those units already possessed their "inner face" of dynamic spiritual energy, though in unrecognizably tiny proportions. At any rate, the great enigma posed by the fact of man himself must be realistically formulated, "How is it possible for a *material* being to *think?*"

The progress of man out of superstition and magic into religious belief and theology has been a record of progressively eliminating unwarrantably-assumed capricious interventions of the spirit world where matter is seen capable of doing the job. It is not unworthy of the theologian to magnify the extent to which secondary causality operates in virtue of powers put into it by God. Only when we face dispassionately the "metascience" correlating all we know of what nature itself can do, are we in a position to go beyond and acknowledge how much there yet is for which we have to rely on God.

CHAPTER 2

"BREATH IN CLAY" OR MANY ADAMS?

The aim we have set ourselves in this book is to evaluate whether Teilhard's claims of continuity in the material universe are compatible with revealed truth, or with any possible reformulation of it. Our inquiry will thus hover around the problem of God's "breathing into the mud" of Genesis 2:7. Has this rightly *or at all* been taken by authoritative Christian tradition as a rejection of the measurable continuity of man with the lower creation which is apparent to the scientist?

The question will be whether man's soul required a divine intervention to produce what could not have been produced by the forces imbedded within nature itself.

1. *What God Has Joined, Are We to Sunder?*

This question is in principle entirely distinct from that of bodily evolution. It is also distinct from whether the human race proceeds from one first man or many, since the intervention is required as much for every single man as for the first man.

Yet we must not talk about the latest theology manuals as if they existed in a vacuum, without a history and without a future. The present state of things may quite serenely and accurately be expressed as follows: Less than a lifetime ago, any form of human bodily evolution whatso-

35

ever was rejected as *heretical*. Under pressure of mounting scientific data, the "heresy" of evolution was — not painlessly! — reinterpreted to mean the heresy that man's *total* and not merely "material" reality came from his progenitors.[1] That same continuing scientific pressure is today nudging theology to decide whether original sin or any other dogma indirectly requires that the evolutionary species-transit must have taken place in man without that *plurality* which would normally accompany it in "evolution as such." In this perspective, the creation of the soul is *not* a question so distinct from "polygenism," but is simply one more in a series of reappraisals to which theology and exegesis have been rightly subjecting the creation narrative of Genesis.

Until most recent times it was agreed that man, both as presented in Genesis and as analyzed in his intellectual superiority, could not be the offspring of an animal. Hardening of this conviction in the Protestant Anglo-Saxon nineteenth century has been absorbingly set forth by Gillispie.[2] An even livelier, if less surgically objective, research sets forth the resistance of Catholic northern Europe.[3]

According to religious declarations as recent as the English edition of Ruffini's *Evolution* in 1959, the emergence of thought and will in a material body requires more than the insertion of some purely spiritual reality into that body from outside and without the concurrence of material causes.[4] It requires that the body itself be produced out of nothing,

[1] Maurizio Flick, "L'origine del corpo del primo Uomo alla luce della filosofia cristiana e della teologia," *Gregorianum*, 29/4 (Oct. 1948), 392–416, 413. *Civiltà Cattolica*, 15/8 (1893), 338 had claimed: "Catholic apologists unanimously, restricting themselves within the data of science, have exposed the inanity of evolution: total defeat of the system which is now retained not because it is demonstrated but because it is desired." Quite a different view is expressed in *Civiltà*, 97C (1946), 270, as Flick shows on page 392.

[2] Charles C. Gillispie, *Genesis and Geology* (Harvard: 1951), 223–6: Ignorant clergymen denounced evolution either because of a mechanical literalism in interpreting Scripture, or because they thought man's body had to be a unique, specially created vessel for the soul. But even scientists and the open-minded public were hostile to evolution, because it seemed to sweep away one area of activity of God's Providence. The same kind of public opinion was meanwhile opposing social justice reform: such reform seemed to be against God's intended plan of affording occasion for the practice of charity! See p. 70, below.

[3] Herbert Wendt, *In Search of Adam* (Boston: Houghton Mifflin, 1956). He notes on p. 6 that when Jesuit astronomer Scheiner in 1611 discovered sunspots, he was cautioned by his superior on the ground that Aristotle afforded no basis for supposing their existence. See further Begouën, *Quelques souvenirs sur le mouvement des idées transformistes dans les milieux catholiques* (Paris: Bloud, 1945), cited further on p. 88, n. 11.

[4] Ernesto Ruffini, *The Theory of Evolution Judged by Reason and Faith* (New York: Wagner, 1959), acclaimed with strong anti-Teilhard comments in *Homiletic and Pastoral Review*, 62/5 (Feb. 1962), 468, H. Rope's review of Patrick O'Connell, *Science of Today* (St. Paul: Radio replies, 1961). Similarly, transformism is for Dr. Maurice Vernet, *La grande illusion de Teilhard de Chardin* (Paris: Gedalge, 1964).

or possibly out of mud or some ignoble inorganic substance, but not out of the next-highest form of animal life.

Yet since 1890 numerous Catholic authorities had been maintaining that *bodily* evolution is not incompatible with our faith in Scriptural revelation. One of the most clairvoyant exponents of this view was the American priest John Zahm of Notre Dame University.[5] The facts of his unfortunate silencing are told in the biography by Ralph Weber.[6] A more successful breakthrough was made in the volumes of the British priest Ernest Messenger on evolution and theology.[7]

In fact by 1950 so many Catholic theologians had orally or guardedly adhered to this view that its authorization in *Humani Generis* merely made officially legitimate what was already the consensus of experts. Rahner notes this with the remark, "There is food for thought in the fact that this consensus had been worked out down to the last detail behind a façade of printed theology."[8] The façade was all along saying the exact opposite with varying, thought diminishing degrees of emphasis!

But even the most outspoken Catholic defenders of evolution never called in question two dogmas intimately connected with it.

The single verse of Genesis (2:7) had single-handedly been responsible for resistance to the deriving of man's body from a living animal. But the same verse which says that man's emergence required God's immediate formation of his body, goes on to say with equal objectivity that it required "breathing" into that body "a soul" as it has commonly been translated. We will take up later the exegesis of this passage, but meanwhile no discussion of bodily evolution can leave out of account how closely the terms by which it used to be rejected are interwoven in Scripture with that creation of the soul.

The other dogma intimately connected with evolution is original sin. Really it has nothing to do with the transformist hypothesis as such. But it has very much to do with a more general evolutionist postulate that the mutation of one species into another would seem to happen in numerous individuals simultaneously. We will take up first the relevance of this hypothesis, which is that of "Many Adams" or polygenism. Much

---

[5] John A. Zahm, *Evolution and Dogma* (Chicago: McBride, 1896); attacked in *Civiltà Cattolica* for Dec. 31, 1898.

[6] Ralph Weber, *Notre Dame's John Zahm* (1961); see my "American Scripture Century," *American Ecclesiastical Review*, 150/5 (May 1964), 316 f.

[7] Ernest C. Messenger, *Evolution and Theology* (London: Burns Oates, 1931); *Theology and Evolution* (London: Sands, 1949); "The Origin of Man in the Book of Genesis," in Jacques Bivort de la Saudée, *God, Man, and the Universe* (New York: Kenedy, 1953), 163.

[8] Karl Rahner, *Das Problem der Hominisation* (Quaestiones Disputatae, 12; Freiburg: Herder, 1961), 30; *Hominisation: The Evolutionary Origin of Man as a Theological Problem*, translated by W. T. O'Hara (New York: Herder and Herder, 1966), 29; see below, chap. 8, p. 233.

of what follows here has been documented in our 1963 *Continuum* article.[9]

2. *An Adam for Each Race or Region?*

The disturbing hypothesis that the biblical First Father of the human race might have been many individuals simultaneously is called polygenism. But we are here concerned with only *one* of the three fairly current uses of that term.

By polygenism is elsewhere meant the theory that black and yellow and white races descended from entirely different branches of the primate group. This has been seriously maintained by such experts as Klaatsch, Sergi, Sera, Arldt, and with some nuancing by R. R. Gates of Harvard as recently as 1948.

For this kind of polygenism we may aptly reserve the term "polyphyletism," meaning that the present human race owes its origin to several different phyla. Phylum in turn may be defined "species, as it is constituted at the moment under consideration."[10]

Polyphyletism has almost no scientific defenders today. It cannot truly be excluded on the evidence of paleontology, for the same reasons as will show us that monogenism cannot be excluded on the evidence of paleontology. The distaste we feel today for a "racist" view that Negroes or Chinese do not come from simon-pure Aryan stock is undoubtedly a healthy conclusion from our assurance that polyphyletism is wrong, but it does not "prove" that assurance. Some defenses of the unity of the human race, notably by J. Carles, in claiming to reject polygenism seem really to be rejecting polyphyletism.

A second sense of polygenism, also *not* envisioned here, is the view that human life sprang up simultaneously *all over* the planet as soon as suitable biological conditions existed. This theory was propagated chiefly by Daniele Rosa, who gave to it the name of *ologenesi,* a proper italianizing of the Greek *hólos* "whole (earth)."[11] His admirer Montandon rendered this in French as *ologénèse,* which has been rightly corrected to *hologénèse.*[12] By English norms this would be rather "hologenism," as an alternative to polyphyletism and polygenism.

Hologenism counts even fewer scientific advocates on its side. It is

---

[9] R. North, "Teilhard and the Many Adams," *Continuum,* 1/3 (Autumn, 1963), 329–342.

[10] J. Carles, "Polygénisme et monogénisme: l'unité de l'espèce humaine," *Archives de Philosophie,* 17/2 (1948), 90. See now Carles, *Teilhard de Chardin: sa vie, son Œuvre, avec un exposé de sa philosophie* (Paris: Presses Universitaires, 1964).

[11] Daniele Rosa, *L'ologénèse* (Paris: Alcan, 1931). See note 41, p. 78 below.

[12] G. Montandon, *L'ologénèse humaine* (Paris: Alcan, 1928), 72.

said to be "scientifically or experimentally more probable" by a Canadian
Jesuit, who adds that it has to be evaluated also in the light of "causalities other than material."[13]

Polygenism, as usually understood in theological contexts, has a third
sense. It is the fairly widespread conviction of scientists that human life
emerged in one relatively restricted cradle area, but not from one couple.

It would be unrealistic to deny or overlook an existing presumption
of Catholic theologians that polygenism is wrong and is incompatible
with the dogma of original sin. But an illuminated French Dominican
warns us that it would be equally unrealistic and dangerous to overlook
a counter-presumption of even the most religious scientists and thinkers.

The informed Catholic, says Dominic Dubarle, "will have a strong
psychological tendency to ask whether our attachment to the solitariness
of the original human couple is not ultimately a too-human survival of
the need of basing religious certitudes on naïvely material supports."
Even when the Church takes an explicit position giving rise to scholarly
tensions, the loyal Catholic "is justified in making public this psychological difficulty [though not] in taking it as the basis of a partisan demonstration. . . . The truly religious attitude is to take in stride this polarity
tension between the ingredients of a thinking spirituality and a fruitful
scholarship"; theologians and the Pope himself await clearer light on this
subject.[14]

Hence if we consent to examine this view of scientists without first
laying down our adherence to a theological consensus that they are
wrong, this is not equivalent to saying that the scientists are bound to
prevail and the churchmen will sooner or later have to conform. There
is at least one possible alternative which has been applauded by a fairly
conservative contemporary theologian. We may end up unflinchingly admitting that nature as revealed by science did in fact tend in a certain
direction, while yet we hold from revelation that God simply intervened
to prevent the awaited result.[15]

However, we for our part envision a more satisfactory possibility.
Diligent reappraisal of what both the scientists and the custodians of
revelation are saying may show that there is no unexplainable contradiction between them after all.

"The two chief sources of such apparent contradiction," says the First
Vatican Council, "are that the dogmas of faith were not understood and

---

[13] Guy Picard, "La science expérimentale est-elle favorable au polygénisme?,"
Sciences Ecclésiastiques, 4 (1951), 81; "hologénèse," p. 73.

[14] Dominique Dubarle, "Évolution et évolutionnisme," *Lumière et Vie*, 34 (Oct.
1957), 88 (= 512).

[15] M. M. Labourdette, *Le péché originel et les origines de l'homme* (Paris:
Alsatia, 1953), 165.

set forth according to the mind of the Church, or that merely hypothetical opinions have been taken for scientific facts."[16]

Note that the order in which these two sources of error are presented seems mildly to imply that the *first* effort of the theologian in such cases should be to see whether he has his own facts straight, even before he demands a similarly honest self-criticism on the part of the scientist.

3. *Teilhard Did Favor Many Adams*

The attitude we take toward polygenism will revolve largely around a declaration of Pope Pius XII. Before turning to his 1950 encyclical, we may find it more honest and helpful to admit that the passage in question is directed against Teilhard. He is not named, nor are there any formulations which could truly be called catchwords of his. But a number of such catchwords do in fact enter into the motivation of the Pontiff's remarks on polygenism as analyzed by an eminently qualified co-worker who shortly afterward became a Cardinal.[17]

Other intimates and defenders of the French seer of science did not need these promptings to recognize in the Pope's wording a broad hint that Teilhard's world-view was being impugned, in part on the basis of a belief in polygenism attributed to him. In reaction they formulated the following three claims: (a) he nowhere expressly maintains polygenism; (b) it would be altogether contrary to his explicit principles to do so; (c) the problem is in any case irrelevant to that simple "observation of the phenomenon" by which he repeatedly characterizes his work.[18]

There is a large measure of truth in these three statements. Nevertheless they might seem to be a disservice in the larger perspective of what was aimed at by Teilhard. In any case, the defense is simply not convincing, because it is not faithful to the facts.

Teilhard clearly and vigorously indicates that his own sympathies and those of science lie with polygenism. *"On the one hand, for reasons which are ultimately neither philosophical nor exegetic, but essentially theological (Pauline concept of the Fall and Redemption), the Church holds to the historical reality of Adam and Eve. On the other hand, from internal*

---

[16] H. Denzinger, *Enchiridion Symbolorum* (= DB) 1797; 32d edition revised and renumbered by A. Schönmetzer (Barcelona: Herder, 1963: = DS), 3017.

[17] Augustin Bea, "Die Enzyklika 'Humani Generis': ihre Grundgedanken und ihre Bedeutung," *Scholastik*, 26 (1951), 51.

[18] Édouard Boné, "Polygénisme et polyphylétisme, orientation présente de la pensée scientifique en matière de l'apparition de l'homme," *Archives de Philosophie*, 29 (1960), 99–137; and "Un siècle d'anthropologie préhistorique: compatibilité ou incompatibilité scientifique du Monogénisme?" *Nouvelle Revue Théologique*, 84/7 (July, 1962), 279. He further contests Teilhard's polygenist leaning, on the ground that most modern science does *not* hold man is an animal "like the others"; anyway, science envisions whole populations rather than individual "mutants."

probabilities and comparative anatomy, science left to itself would not even dream (to say the least) of attributing so narrow a base as two individuals to the enormous structure of the human race. . . . The most we can hope . . . is that 'Monogenism' will gradually take on a form satisfying our scientific requirements."[19]

"The scientist can show indirectly that the hypothesis of an individual Adam is rendered scientifically untenable by all that we can now know of biological laws of speciation."[20]

Teilhard here reduces his case for polygenism to the two intersecting axes which he calls Comparative Anatomy and "internal probabilities," by which he seems to mean the analogies of evolution in nature. Before taking up these separate lines of reasoning, it is important to make clear how true it is that he would not consider these or any conceivably attainable scientific facts to be in the philosophic sense a "proof" for polygenism.

In a word: the chances of feeler-specimens to survive are slim.

He proclaimed it to be highly unlikely or virtually *impossible* that science would ever be able to offer fossils or other direct surviving evidence of the very first man. It is of the nature of the evolutionary process that the initial specimens of any new species should be tentative and frail. We should call these specimens the "feelers," the pioneer cosmonauts dangling off into space by a thin cord from their parent capsule.

But Teilhard envisions them rather as the *stalk* or "peduncle" of the tree that is to come. One of his most recurrent motifs is nature's "Law of Suppression of Peduncles." Overlooking of this law has been largely responsible for the rejection not only of polygenism but of bodily evolution as well.

"The favorite argument employed against the transformists has always lain in pointing out their incapacity to prove the BIRTH *of a species in terms of* MATERIAL TRACES. . . . *'However primitive it is, your first mammalian is already a mammal, your first equine already a horse, and so on all along the line. Accordingly, though there may well be evolution within a given type, we see no new type produced by evolution.' So the increasingly rare survivors of the 'fixed-type' school still contend. . . . But their demand that we should show them the 'peduncle' of a phylum is both pointless and unreasonable. To satisfy it we should have to change the very nature of the world and the conditions under which we perceive it. Nothing is so delicate and fugitive by its very nature as*

[19] Teilhard, "Que faut-il penser du transformisme?," from the *Revue des Questions Scientifiques* for January 1930, in Œuvres 3, *La vision du passé* (Paris: Seuil, 1957), 219. Note the quaint implication that what is contained in Genesis is exegetical but what is contained in Paul's epistles is not.

[20] Teilhard, "Monogénisme et monophylétisme," Œuvres 11, subsequent to *Humani generis,* 1950, according to C. Journet, who cites it in *Divinitas* 3 (1959), 338.

[is] a beginning. As long as a zoological group is young, its characters remain indeterminate, its structure precarious, and its dimensions scant. It is composed of relatively few individual units, and these change rapidly. In space as in duration, the peduncle (or, what comes to the same thing, the bud) of a living branch corresponds to a minimum of differentiation, expansion, and resistance. What, then, will be the effect of time on this area of weakness? Inevitably to destroy all vestiges of it. . . . IN EVERY DOMAIN when anything really new begins to germinate around us, we cannot distinguish it — for the very good reason that it could only be recognized in the light of what it is going to be. . . . Where, even after the shortest lapse of time, are the first 'autos, planes, or movies'? . . . Time, like a 'designer' with an eraser, rubs out every weak line in the drawing of life."[21]

A growth midway between two species may technically be called a "monster." Like a baby with two heads, it is a pitiful and fragile thing, without those implications of sensational size and strength which horror fiction has built up about the term monster. The crossover specimen is biologically unhealthy, tottering, and *as an individual* foredoomed.

At any rate, whether weak or strong, the crossover individuals are bound to be negligibly few among the billions of specimens that existed. It is against all the mathematics of chance that out of those billions the fourscore which have been fossilized and so far recognized should ever be augmented as far as to include a probative proportion of the feeler-specimens.

We cannot hope to know the first individuals of the species man any more than we can hope to know who was the first individual Greek or Irishman.[22] Though everyone admits as a proved fact the transformation of Latin into other languages including French, no one would claim to point to any specimen of human speech and say this is the *numerically first* example of a statement made in French and not in Latin.[23]

"The oldest fishes we know are for the most part strongly, even abnormally, scaly. Without this 'bony covering' they would have left nothing behind them and we should never have known of them. Under this first and apparently rather fruitless attempt at external consolidation was an internal skeleton still entirely 'cartilage.' As we go back, the vertebrates appear less and less ossified internally. That is why we lose trace of them,

---

[21] Teilhard, *Phenomenon of Man*, 120.

[22] Teilhard, *Le groupe zoölogique humain* (Paris: A. Michel, 1956), 82; *Man's Place in Nature* (New York: Harper, 1966), 65.

[23] Teilhard, "La vision du passé" *Études*, 263/3 (Dec. 1949), 308–315; "La paléontologie et l'apparition de l'homme," *Revue de Philosophie* (1923) and reprinted in Œuvres 2, *L'apparition de l'homme* (Paris: Seuil, 1956), pages 52, 80. Further, in refutation of Vialleton, "Le paradoxe transformiste," *Revue des Questions Scientifiques* (Jan. 1925), in Œuvres 3, *La vision du passé* (1957), 131.

*no vestige remaining even in sediments that have come down to us intact.
. . . Whatever living group we take, it always ends up by drowning itself
in 'a puddle of softness.' This is an infallible way of causing peduncles
to vanish."*[24]

4. Progress Clocked by Failure

The upward movement of humanity is recorded by paleontology like
the hour hand on a clock. Its reliability does not depend upon even the
sharpest observer's detection of its movement as actually happening.[25]

*"For our mind to adjust itself to lines and horizons enlarged beyond
measure, it must renounce the comfort of familiar narrowness. It must
create a new equilibrium for everything that had formerly been so neatly
arranged in its small inner world. It is dazzled when it emerges from its
dark prison, awed to find itself suddenly at the top of a tower, and it
suffers from giddiness and disorientation. The whole psychology of modern
disquiet is linked with the sudden confrontation with space-time."*[26]

Some talk about "the myth of Progress." Whatever "progress" is, it
proceeds by waves, involving tremendous backwash and underflow, as
well as the ignominious sinking of false starts or failures by the millions.

It would be absurd to claim that every single subsequent form is
automatically superior and preferable to the preceding form. It is not
in spite of, but *through* the efforts even of those failures, that the *whole
of reality itself* constitutes a great forward surge inspiring the radiant
teilhardian optimism.

*"Right up to its reflective zone we have seen the world 'progressing'
by means of groping and chance. . . . How many failures have there
been for one success, how many days of misery for one hour's joy, how
many sins for a 'rare' saint. To begin with we find physical 'disarrange-
ment' on the material level; then suffering, which cuts into the sentient
flesh; then, on a still higher level, wickedness and the torture of the
spirit as it analyzes itself and makes choices. Statistically, at every degree
of evolution, we find evil always and everywhere, forming and reforming
implacably in us and around us. 'It is necessary that scandals should
come.' This is relentlessly imposed by the play of large numbers at the
heart of a multitude undergoing composition. . . . Death 'is' the essential
lever in the mechanism and upsurge of life."*[27]

Chauchard observes that there is nothing more false than to say there

---

[24] Teilhard, *Phenomenon of Man*, 131.
[25] Teilhard, "Réflexions sur le progrès," 1941, in Œuvres 5, *L'avenir de l'homme*
(Paris: Seuil, 1959), 87.
[26] Teilhard, *Phenomenon of Man*, 225.
[27] Teilhard, *Phenomenon of Man*, 310.

is no place for hell in Teilhard's outlook. "There are no crests without troughs."[28]

"Life advances by mass effects, by dint of multitudes flung into action without apparent plan. 'Billions' of germs and millions of adult growths jostling, shoving, and devouring one another, fight for elbow room and for the best and largest living space. Despite all the waste and ferocity, all the mystery and scandal it involves, there is, as we must be fair and admit, a great deal of biological efficiency in the STRUGGLE FOR LIFE. . . . *By reckless self-reproduction life takes its precautions against mishap. It increases its chances of survival and at the same time multiplies its chances of progress. . . . Life passes over a bridge made up of accumulated corpses."*[29]

"What matter the millions of years and 'billions' of beings that have gone before us if those countless drops form a current that carries us along?"[30]

"Love dies in contact with the impersonal and the anonymous. . . . To ward off the threat of disappearance, incompatible with the mechanism of reflective activity, man tries to bring together in an ever vaster and more permanent subject the collective principle of his acquisitions — civilization, humanity, the spirit of the earth. Associated in these enormous entities, with their incredibly slow rhythm of evolution, he has the impression of having escaped from the destructive action of time."[31]

What is fixed in the universe is not the "essences" but the *direction*, and precisely this distinguishes *genesis* in its continuity and regularity from any sort of (sporadic) "evolution." Since science thinks of origins in terms of populations rather than individuals, we should rethink in those terms a constructive explanation of original sin.[32]

As for the common charge that Teilhard too naïvely ignored the presence or the *predominance* of evil and sin in the world: well, he certainly ignored and denied its "predominance" if by that is meant that the perishing drops are of more importance than the current carrying us inexorably forward.

But in large part his alleged "ignoring" of evil is in reality his critics' ignoring of the immense importance he laid upon "critical thresholds." Only by *groping*, that is by "directed chance," can the myriad individuals somehow among them discover the single opening through which only one will pass, and which is the "direction of the future."

28 Paul Chauchard, *Teilhard et l'optimisme de la croix* (Paris: Presses Universitaires, 1964), 44. See below, pp. 63 and 286.

29 Teilhard, *Phenomenon of Man*, 109 ff; William J. Schmitt, "The Vision of Teilhard," *Philippine Studies*, 9/2 (April 1961), 271.

30 Teilhard, *Phenomenon of Man*, 227.

31 Teilhard, *Phenomenon of Man*, 269.

32 Thomas V. Fleming, "Two Unpublished Letters of Teilhard," *Heythrop Journal*, 6/1 (Jan. 1965), 41, 36.

This is not to brutalize the individual, reducing him to a mere cog in the machine, or to a wretched slave vomiting forth his life to add a tiny inch to the height of pharaoh's pyramid. Along with their own failures so numerous even in the very best, individuals also below the level of the human person *joyously cooperate* in carrying forward "the real," which is at every point their own irreducible blessedness: *ens et bonum convertuntur,* good has no other definition than reality.

"Critical threshold" itself is a teilhardian password which has fared cruelly at the hands of evaluators. It may be defined "a point at which continuous injection of energy produces alteration of entirely discontinuous character." Or more concretely, "the stage where purely quantified additions produce of themselves a qualitative alteration."

Example: Every calorie of heat introduced into a pan of water will increase its temperature with mathematical regularity degree by degree up to 100 centigrade. But after that point, as the calorie injection continues, the temperature will not increase by a single degree; instead, the liquid will be transformed into gas.

Teilhard does not seem to have known, or to have cared, that the formulation of this phenomenon by Marx and Engels is rather basic to their dialectical materialism. He would have saved himself and his defenders some embarrassment if he had faced this consciously. After all, "love is good" does not cease to be true and important just because even the worst criminal or demagogue fastens upon it. If in a given case Marx happens to be heading in the direction of history (that metaphor too is his), we cannot "cut off our nose to spite our face" by refusing to be fellow travelers.

"The law of controlled complication, the mature stage of the process in which we get first the micro-molecule, then the mega-molecule and finally the first cells, is known to biologists as orthogenesis . . . the dynamic and only complete form of heredity. Without orthogenesis life would only have spread; with it there is an ascent of life that is invincible. . . . To this grand process of sublimation it is fitting to apply with all its force the word hominization. Because the specific orthogenesis of the primates (urging them toward increased cerebralization) coincides with the axial orthogenesis of living matter (urging all living things toward a higher consciousness), man, appearing at the heart of the primates, flourishes on the leading shoot of zoological evolution." [33] The Critical Threshold marking the transit from animal to man is here declared to mark also a transit of the whole material universe to that higher reality to which it was geared.

---

[33] Teilhard, *Phenomenon of Man,* 180, 108. See footnote 32 on p. 12 above, on the "groping verticil." On Teilhard's not-so-trusting assurance that biologists at large understand "orthogenesis" as he does, see below, chapter 3, page 76.

*"We are disturbed to notice how little 'anthropos' differs anatomically
from the other anthropoids. . . . But is not this extraordinary resemblance
precisely what had to be? When water is heated to boiling point under
normal pressure, and one goes on heating it, the first thing that follows
— without change of temperature — is a tumultuous expansion of freed
and vaporized molecules. Or, taking a series of sections from the base
towards the summit of a cone, their area decreases constantly; then suddenly, with another infinitesimal displacement, the surface vanishes leaving us with a* POINT. *Thus by these remote comparisons we are able to
imagine the mechanism involved in the critical threshold of reflection. By
the end of the Tertiary era, the psychical temperature in the cellular
world had been rising for more than 500 million years. . . . Finally, with
the primates, an instrument was fashioned so remarkably supple and rich
that the step immediately following could not take place without the
whole animal psychism being as it were recast and consolidated on itself.
Now this movement did not stop, for there was nothing in the structure
of the organism to prevent it advancing. When the anthropoid, so to
speak, had been brought 'mentally' to boiling point some further calories
were added. . . . Outwardly, almost nothing in the organs had changed.
But in depth, a great revolution had taken place: consciousness was now
leaping and boiling in a space of super-sensory relationships and repre-
sentations, and simultaneously consciousness was capable of perceiving
itself in the concentrated simplicity of its faculties."*[34]

We have here two analogies: boiling water and the sliced cone. A
third is the piston: energy applied to it will produce no movement at
all until the attainment of a critical point sufficient to effect a movement
both violent and complete. Fourthly, an airplane progressively increasing
its rate on the runway transforms at a given point its wheel-speed into
flight. Fifthly (for those whose higher physics is equal to it): at high
speeds the mass increases so rapidly as to brake completely the increase
of movement.[35]

These analogies are dismissed by Grenet as mere metaphors, and
misleading ones at that.[36] They are in fact not metaphors. They are
parallels or concrete exemplifications, within observable reality, of a
process which is itself not observed but legitimately inferred from the
evidence. But even if the "critical thresholds" as applied to the evolution
of consciousness were a mere metaphor, it is a groping toward the formu-

---

[34] Teilhard, *Phenomenon of Man*, 168 f. The footnote adds that "immediate
creation of the soul" is here not excluded for those who may possess assurance
of it from a source outside science. See pp. 62 and 164 below.

[35] Teilhard, "Transformation et prolongements en l'homme du mécanisme de
l'évolution," 1951, in Œuvres 7, *L'activation de l'énergie* (Paris: Seuil, 1963), 214.

[36] P.-B. Grenet, *Teilhard ou le philosophe malgré lui* (Paris: Beauchesne, 1960),
21, 118; see footnote 68 in chapter 1, p. 29 above.

takes place at about the same time in numerous specimens both male and female.

This leads us into Teilhard's other line of reasoning in favor of polygenism, which he vaguely phrases "internal probabilities." The same factors which postulate evolution at all, and make it a virtual certainty at least up to the emergence of man, tend of themselves to suggest that the transit in man's case as in that of the similarly structured mammals took place simultaneously in numerous individuals.

More briefly: evolution of itself reckons with polygenism.

The anatomical structure of man occupies a demonstrable place in the gradation of animal forms. This is taken to mean bodily evolution. If evolution is a chief motive for holding polygenism, and if the detail of both is interwoven in the interpretations which have been given to the second chapter of Genesis throughout the ages, then we must try to make clear what revelation has to say about evolution itself.

6. *Teilhard and Pius XII on Evolution*

At the very outset and basis of *The Phenomenon of Man,* evolution is declared to be neither a particular theory nor a particular fact, but a "dimension" to which all thinking in whatever area must conform.[43]

"People keep saying, 'Transformism is a hypothesis.'" This was true in the days of Lamarck or Darwin. But *"reduced to its essence, transformism is not a hypothesis."*[44]

Teilhard thus goes farther than his most advanced scientific colleagues in the claims he makes for evolution. Stock warns us that even biology does not warrant the degree of adherence to evolution which Teilhard recommends, and which Bonoure calls "a dream, not science."[45] The tenet, elsewhere even more explicit, that societal behavior is biological and organismic, is a phase which sociology emphatically agrees to have outgrown.[46] On this point Teilhard saw himself forced to take cognizance of a weakness in his formulation: *"It is not rigorously correct (however thought-provoking and useful the analogy may be) to compare the growth*

[43] Teilhard, *Phenomenon of Man,* 218. See now Jean-Paul Dallaire, "Le P. Teilhard et l'évolution, documents inédits," *Revue de l'Université d'Ottawa* (Jan., 1964), 406–416.

[44] Teilhard, "Comment se pose aujourd'hui la question du Transformisme," *Études,* 167/6 (June 5, 1921), 524–544, in Œuvres 3, *La vision du passé* (Paris: Seuil, 1957), 39.

[45] Michael Stock, "Scientific vs. Phenomenological Evolution: A Critique of Teilhard," *The New Scholasticism,* 36/3 (July 1962), 379; Louis Bonoure, "La cosmologie du P. Teilhard de Chardin devant la biologie expérimentale," *Revue des Sciences Religieuses,* 31 (1957), 290 ff.

[46] Don Martindale, *Nature and Types of Sociological Theory* (Boston: Houghton Mifflin, 1960), 122. See now the symposium on Teilhard and Sociology by Pitirim A. Sorokin and others in *American Catholic Sociological Review* 23/4 (1962), 291–335.

of human social consciousness to the formation of a collective brain. Hence appear the elements of both truth and unfairness in the allegedly definitive criticisms of Durkheim, Cournot, Tarde, against any 'assimilation' of sociology to biology. It would be absurd to IDENTIFY *a society with a group of cells, especially if these be wrongly defined as devoid of psychic content.* [But *not,* then, if defined as Teilhard wishes! and at any rate it would be equally wrong and sterile not to recognize in Society a prolongation of the same essential structure.] *The noospheric center, Omega, is not born of the confluence of human egos, but emerges upon their organized totality as a spark bursting forth between the transcendent face of Omega and the vertex of a perfectly unified universe."*[47]

Clearly, Teilhard has come a long way "From the Fact of Evolution to the Philosophy of Evolutionism," as it is put in the title of an essay by Nogar.[48]

And yet these objections leave their target unperturbed. He even feels that at base they are merely a mask for people's true motives in refusing to read the plain facts of science.

"They keep repeating that evolution is an evil doctrine, just the thing to promote materialism and class struggle. To calm or moralize the world, it has to be belittled and discredited. A fatal tactic, we will cry out, and one tending precisely to accelerate the crisis which it claims to overcome. . . . You seek a means to discipline individualism and eliminate laziness. You will find no better than to exalt before men the grandeur of the totality which they ignore and whose success their selfishness tends to counter. As long as they think that only their personal interest is involved in the earth's adventure, the men of our day will never submit their mind and spirit to anything transcendent."[49]

As against all this, Pope Pius XII in his 1950 encyclical *Humani Generis* declared that evolution may be held as a theory but not as a fact. "Regarding the origin of the human body out of already existing and living matter . . . both sides of the question may be set forth . . . but not as if it were already certain and demonstrated" (DS 3896).

Almost the identical words of this encyclical were reaffirmed and imposed by Paul VI in July of 1966, when he summoned a group of Catholic experts of the world to reconsider and set forth the data of their various specialties in relation to the defense of revealed dogmas such as original sin. Hence in analyzing the words of Pius we may hope to be reaching the mind of Paul VI.

Pius XII's dictum can hardly be denied to envisage Teilhard's formu-

---

[47] Teilhard, "La centrologie: essai d'une dialectique de l'union," 1944, in Œuvres 7, *L'activation de l'énergie* (Paris: Seuil, 1963), 120 f.

[48] R. J. Nogar, *The Thomist,* 24 (Apr. 1961), 463–501.

[49] Teilhard, "L'hominisation," 1923, in Œuvres 3, *La vision du passé* (Paris: Seuil, 1957), 108. On Paul VI see p. 206 and its note 4 below.

lations more proximately than any others attested up to that time. We illustrated this from the explanatory article of Cardinal Bea, which he wrote at the time the encyclical appeared.

Some are unhappy at the thought that Pius XII here shows so negative and grudging an attitude toward this defender of a widespread modern consensus. They even point out that Teilhard is *not* the offender, since he calls evolution a "dimension," and altogether spurns those scholastic tags *ratiocinia, certa, deducta, demonstrata,* used by the Pope to delimit what evolution is not.

These efforts seem to me to deprive Teilhard of one of his most deserved and imperishable titles to gratitude. *Because* his teaching on evolution aroused the misgivings of the Pope, it evoked a declaration of supreme ecclesiastical authority which *for the first time in history* expressly legitimated the defense of bodily evolution.

This service is not diminished by recognizing how grudging and negative the Pope's concession is. He *could* not, no matter how grudgingly, leave full liberty of discussing and defending a doctrine incompatible with divine revelation or Christian dogma.

Of course, on the other hand, the pontiff did not *prescribe* evolution. And the fact that he did not is in itself even more liberating, as Rahner has noted.[50] It remains possible that science itself may destroy and reject that form of the evolutionary hypothesis which is now current. This would not diminish papal prestige or alter the theological significance of the pronouncement in the slightest degree. What has been declared is that the truth or falsity of bodily evolution is a matter which must be left to scientific evidence to decide, since neither alternative is incompatible with Christian dogma.

And in fact this papal declaration has been everywhere acclaimed to be far more significant for the *freedom* it allows to evolution, than for the restrictions placed upon it. Should not the instrumentality of Teilhard in effecting this release be gratefully recognized?

But now, what about those restrictions? Even they are in a vocabulary which scientists would not normally resent as constricting. They couldn't care less if a veto is imposed on their right to "act as if bodily evolution were a certain and demonstrated deduction of ratiocinium." This is the jargon of a scholarly world far different from their own. Science is very tenacious of its "laws" and "facts"; but when scrutinized closely these turn out to be *provisional statistical conclusions.*[51]

The "facts" of atomic structure are still being transformed day by day. Whatever atoms are, one thing we know about them is that they

---

[50] Karl Rahner, as in footnote 8 to p. 37 above; also *Kleines Theologisches Wörterbuch* (with Herbert Vorgrimler; Freiburg: Herder, 1961), 98.

[51] George P. Klubertanz, "The Influence of Evolutionary Theory upon American Thought," *Gregorianum,* 32/4 (Oct. 1951), 583.

are *not* what the very name was chosen to describe: unfissionable. Yet no one for an instant doubts the existence of atoms.

May we not feel, then, that Pius XII could agree that evolution is to be called a "fact" or a "law" in the sense in which physical science understands those terms, though only a "theory" in the light of that immutability with which speculative theology regards facts and laws?

In this setting we see no disloyalty in the number of Catholic experts who since 1950 have insisted on pronouncing that transformism is a fact as solid as anything science can call a fact.[52] This is not to overlook that different experts set forth the evolutionary position with varying nuances, with disagreement on minor details, and even with a readiness to adapt this framework considerably in proportion as new discoveries will warrant it.

Vehement denials of evolution continue to appear, even from the highest echelons of the Roman Curia, as we have noted. Yet even those textbooks which for fifty years have been opposing the evolution of man's body in the name of dogma, have had to be reissued in successive editions, which progressively recede from branding transformism as heretical or even as contrary to Catholic doctrine.[53]

We said above that the effect of Pius XII's careful wording is to leave the truth or falsity of bodily evolution to scientific evidence to decide, thus withdrawing it from the domain of theology. In saying this, we were not unaware that the encyclical goes on to say that after setting forth both sides of the question, the experts must be ready to comply with any judgment of the Church in the matter, "not as if there were nothing in the sources of divine revelation which here requires extreme moderation and caution."

These words are thus paraphrased in one of the most lucid defenses of evolution by an American theologian: "Derivation of the human body from a living organism cannot be designated as a freely disputed theological question, if by that is meant a view which no longer interests the teaching authority of the Church."[54] With all respect, we venture to question whether "freely disputed theological question" really does mean exactly that. If it does, then it could not be applied even to such celebrated theses as the ultimate essence of the sacrifice of the Mass or of the Act of Faith. But as long as these remain genuinely probable

---

[52] Henri Breuil, "Teilhard de Chardin et son *Phénomène Humain,*" *La Table Ronde,* 100/4 (Apr. 1956), 109; Msgr. Bruno de Solages, "Christianity and Evolution," *Cross Currents,* 1/4 (Summer 1951), 27; N. Corte (= L. Cristiani), *The Origins of Man* (New York: Hawthorn, 1958), 9; N. M. Wildiers, *Teilhard* (Paris: Éditions Universitaires, 1960), 32, 57.

[53] See footnotes 4 and 1, p. 36.

[54] Cyril Vollert, "Evolution of the Human Body," *Catholic Mind,* 50/3 (Mar. 1952), 142.

and free, it would seem that Pius XII regarded evolution as probable and free.

And in fact there is great difference in his terminology when he turns from this to the question of polygenism. It is crystal clear that he chooses his words carefully in order to accord to transformism a degree of legitimacy which he *denies* to polygenism. "The sons of the Church by no means enjoy the same freedom in regard to another conjectural opinion, polygenism."

Most commentators of all nations in the world quite promptly recognized in this statement a definitive cloture to all debate as to how polygenism might possibly be reconciled with the Catholic and scriptural dogma of original sin. An exhaustive survey by the late Gustave Weigel concludes that the specific *kind* of polygenism banned by the Pope as "incompatible with Catholic doctrine" is "out — now and forever"; but that even Bea finds it "left to the representatives of science to see if perhaps new forms of polygenistic theory can be found which do not contradict dogma."[55]

One wonders why neither Bea nor Weigel proposes as equally legitimate, in the light of the First Vatican norm which we cited above, that the "representatives of theology should see if perhaps new formulations of the revealed content of original sin can be found which do not contradict scientific findings." At any rate, this was the interpretation which a number of theologians, at first small but gradually increasing, put upon the Pope's words.

Especially at Louvain was raised almost at once the question of the *degree of certitude* with which monogenism is imposed by the papal utterance. "Researchers are warned not to continue along that path [of polygenism]. Is there question of a definitive irreformable judgment? Surely not; the Pope's very manner of speaking shows he is not making a dogmatic definition; we may paraphrase 'we really don't see what could lead the Church to alter this rule of conduct.' Let the theologian then examine [what is implied in] original sin."[56]

7. *Genesis, Original Sin, and Polygenism*

Responding to this invitation, the Louvain Jesuit Jean de Fraine in a recent book has shown that no passage in the whole Bible, not even

[55] Gustave Weigel, "Gleanings from the Commentaries on *Humani generis,*" *Theological Studies,* 12/4 (Oct. 1951), 546; citing A. Bea, *Scholastik,* 26 (1951), 54, as in footnote 17.

[56] G. Vandebroek and L. Renwart, "L 'encyclique *Humani Generis* et les sciences naturelles," *Nouvelle Revue Théologique,* 73/4 (Apr. 1951), 351; also 84/6 (June 1962), 632–4, "De nouveau sur Teilhard," by Renwart; and 72/7 (Sept. 1950), 788, by J. Lévie; A. Roets in *Collationes Brugenses,* 71 (1961), 240; and P. Pas in *Collectanea Mechlinensia,* 46 (1961), 606. See also A. Vanneste in *Ephemerides Theologicae Lovanienses,* 38/4 (Dec. 1962), 895.

Romans 5, excludes polygenism directly.[57] In another book he has dealt with the Hebrew word *adam* as meaning "mankind, men," not exactly in contrast to its use as the name of an individual, but as an expression of the characteristic Hebrew thought pattern of solidarity or "corporate personality."[58]

The image of "God breathing soul of life" into the mud which he had molded will concern us in Chapter 6. But for the moment we may notice that Vollert, who takes it to mean "merely the non-living becomes living," goes on to distinguish a *theological* monogenism, which he finds implicit in Genesis 1:26 and 3:20 and especially Romans 5:12, from biological monogenism.[59]

It is increasingly claimed that since Romans 5 rather than Genesis 2–3 teaches original sin, it is there alone that we can look for the virtual revelation of monogenism.[60] Some theologians, basing themselves ultimately on Scripture though proximately on its use in patristic tradition, still assign to monogenism the high note of "proximately or implicitly revealed dogma."[61]

It would seem to be something less than honest for us to say that original sin is taught in Romans 5, without at the same time indicating our answer to the question of where Paul learned about it, if not from Genesis, or from tradition claiming to be rooted in Genesis.[62] Rahner has voiced a protest that the exegete is always putting the theologian off

---

[57] J. de Fraine, *The Bible and the Origin of Man* (New York: Desclée, 1962; = Paris, 1961), 49, 91; following Renié, Chaine, Guitton, and J. Lévie, "Les limites de la preuve d'Écriture Sainte en théologie," *Nouvelle Revue Théologique,* 71/10 (Dec. 1949), 1011.

The statement that polygenism "is a question the ancient author simply did not pose" (de Fraine) is called by G. Fohrer in *Zeitschrift für die alttestamentliche Wissenschaft,* 73/4 (1961), 332 "a too one-sided limiting of the Bible to theological declarations; its authors had doubtless also the intention of describing the origin of the world and of men as appearing to them." See p. 91 below.

[58] J. de Fraine, *Adam and the Family of Man* (New York: Alba, 1965).

[59] Cyril Vollert, "Evolution and the Bible," in B. Boelen, *Symposium on Evolution* (Pittsburgh: Duquesne, 1959), 115.

[60] Herbert Haag, "Das heutige Verständnis der biblischen Schöpfungsgeschichte," *Arzt und Christ,* 7/1 (1961), 1–9.

[61] Heinrich Lennerz, "Quid theologo dicendum de polygenismo?," *Gregorianum,* 29/4 (Oct. 1948), 422; Réginald Garrigou-Lagrange, "Le monogénisme n'est-il nullement révélé, pas même implicitement?," *Doctor Communis,* 2 (1948), 191–202; Ottorino Alberti, "L'unitá del genere umano nell'insegnamento del Magistero della Chiesa," *Divinitas,* 5/3 (Sept. 1961), 735–797.

[62] See André-Maria Dubarle, "Original Sin in Genesis," *Downside Review,* 76/245 (Summer 1958), 241; *Revue Biblique,* 64 (1957), 15; W. B. Neenan, "Doctrine of Original Sin in Scripture," *Irish Theological Quarterly* 28/1 (1961), 54–64.

Bonaventura Mariani, "Il poligenismo e san Paolo," *Euntes Docete,* 4/1 (1951), 142, holds Paul based on Genesis; but he notes on page 121 the paradox that Romans 5:12, though the chief biblical source opposed to polygenism, was precisely the one from which Isaac LaPeyrère in 1657 strove to promote his "Pre-Adamite" brand of polygenism.

by claiming that a Church dogma must be proved from some scripture area *other* than the one under discussion.[63] Rahner's own dogmatic theologian's solution to the problem involves claiming that ever since Trent the rejection of polygenism has been "theologically certain."[64] But he gives to *certain* here the sense of "requiring an internal but not irreformable assent": and this is a use of "certitude" for which I find no basis in experience. Many of our certitudes do end up in fact being proved wrong, that is, proved to have been "purely subjective"; but no assent is ever given as certain if it is accompanied by the proviso that it may eventually cease to be such.

A significant new light on the relation between original sin and the origins of the human race has now been shed by Smulders.[65] He shows that our discussion really ought to begin with the state of mind and of

[63] Karl Rahner, "Exegese und Dogmatik," *Stimmen der Zeit,* 168/10 (July 1961), 245; abridged in *Theology Digest,* 10/2 (Spring 1962), 84.

[64] Karl Rahner, "Theological Reflexions on Monogenism," *Theological Investigations, I* (Baltimore: Helicon, 1961), 250, 233. This essay of Rahner appeared in German in 1954, and is partly summarized in *Theology Digest,* 10/2 (Spring, 1962), 103–105. Rahner evaluates the Catholic theologians who before 1950 expressed a guarded favor for polygenism: Amann, Bouyssonie, Chaine, Guitton; A. Mancini, "Monogenismo e poligenismo: informazioni," *Palestra del Clero,* 28 (1949), 904–908; B. Prete, "A proposito del poligenismo," *Sapienza,* 1 (1948), 420; H. Rondet, "Les origines humaines et la théologie," *Études = Cité nouvelle,* 1 (1943), 973–987. Angelo Zuerich, "Monogenismo teologico," *Divus Thomas Piacenza,* 59 (1956), 230–245, rebuts Rahner.

Joseph Bataini, "Monogénisme et polygénisme," *Divus Thomas Piacenza,* 52 (1949), 187–201, holds it premature to affirm either that polygenism fits the scientific *proofs* as distinct from the scientific *mentality,* or that monogenism belongs to the deposit of revelation; he expresses the need of a Papal intervention! This seems to be reproached by José Sagüés, "La encíclica 'Humani Generis' — Avances teológicos," *Estudios Eclesiásticos,* 25/97 (Apr. 1951), 174; he adds that the encyclical does not determine the theological note of monogenism, which he holds to be "at least theologically certain"; nor does the encyclical exclude a kind of polygenism which would not involve the errors it warns against.

Achille Cardinal Liénart, "Le chrétien devant les progrès de la science," *Études* 255 (1947), 289–300; page 299 holds polygenism scientifically unproved and "no threat": we cannot proclaim a solution without waiting to get the data; page 297 contends that science, in recognizing that species are due not to mechanical interplay but to laws of heredity and the *mystery* of mutations, has *abandoned* Transformism.

Maximiliano García Cordero, "Evolucionismo, poligenismo y exégesis bíblica," *Ciencia Tomista,* 78 (1951), 467–479, denies unnamed statements favoring polygenism attributed to him by T. Ayuso Marazuela, "Poligenismo y evolucionismo a la luz de la Biblia y de la teología," *Arbor,* 19 (1951), 347–372, 354 f.

[65] Pierre Smulders, *La vision de Teilhard de Chardin: essai de réflexion théologique* (Paris: Desclée de Brouwer, 1964), 177; summarized in *Theology Digest,* 13/3 (Autumn, 1965), 172–176. Teilhard's essay entitled "Mon univers" of March 25, 1924, and his "Note sur quelques représentations historiques possibles du péché originel" caused him to be forced to sign an "engagement sur le péché originel" on November 2, 1924, according to Giancarlo Vigorelli, *Il Gesuita proibito: vita e opere di Pierre Teilhard de Chardin* (La cultura 58; Milano: Saggiatore, 1963), 62. See the content of those articles in footnote 70 to page 60 below.

Christian conviction prevailing at the Council of Trent before the formulation of its decrees.

First of all, they were concerned with original sin as a datum of experience in *contemporary adult life.* As was Paul! The Pope's own legate at Trent, Cardinal Pole, expressed it thus: "What original sin is, we feel more in ourselves as a reality than we are able to express in words."

Secondly, the extent to which original sin is present in an *infant* is only a fringe-case, an *extension* of the original problem, even verging on unreality if considered too exclusively apart from the normal unity of this situation with its gradual unfolding in mature life.

Thirdly, the presence of a given quality in *all men today* warrants our concluding to its presence in whatever man was *first,* and even to an organic connection of heredity between that "first" and this present multitude. But the legitimacy of this retracing does not of itself convey any biological information on the precise nature of that "first" man.

Fourthly, Adam's sin is only one of *several* described in Sacred Scripture as transmitted from the father to the sons. Babel and Solomon are other examples. These lines of research which Smulders recapitulates do indeed constitute a response to the *Humani Generis* challenge to theologians to check whether the dogma of original sin is indeed incompatible with polygenism.

An entirely different approach has meanwhile been broached by the Jesuit Blandino of Bologna in a brief printed lecture.[66] He claims that any progenitor introduced into the human race could become within a few thousand years a lineal parent of all living men.

To grasp his viewpoint, we may take as outset the undisputed fact that everyone living today has two parents, four grandparents, eight great-grandparents, and so forth. This amounts to a thousand lineal progenitors since the Mayflower. (Those Americans whose family tree has been traced will note that duplications during those ten generations have been surprisingly few.) Anyone's own lineal ancestors in 1066 amounted theoretically to one billion. In actual fact this number was far

---

[66] G. Blandino, *Deux hypothèses sur l'origine de l'homme* (Florence: 1962; available from the author at Via Irnerio 43, Bologna). A sequel entitled "Il significato del peccato originale" was to be published in *Münchener Theologische Zeitschrift* for 1965. It theorizes that by original sin we mean the fact that God created all men subject to death and pain in punishment of their own foreseen sins, of which the sin of their Head is taken as the symbolic and pedagogical recapitulation.

See now Zolton Alszeghy and Maurizio Flick, "Il peccato originale in prospettiva evoluzionistica," *Gregorianum* 47/2 (Apr. 1966), 201–225; and Flick, "Peccato originale ed evoluzionismo: un problema teologico," *Civiltà Cattolica* 117–IV (1966), 440–447. On Pope Paul VI's reaffirmation of the Pius XII formulation (but with no apparent disclaimer of the interpretations which had meanwhile become common), see below, chapter 7, page 206, footnote 4.

less because many of the progenitors descended from some common ancestor.

Looked at in reverse, however, there is *no* doubling. Any one individual living in 1066, whose line did not die out, has become the lineal progenitor of many million persons.

This mathematical prestidigitation seems to conflict flagrantly with the geographical and racial facts which largely condition reproduction. Still, a single sailor castaway on the North African shore would have sufficed to transmit a tiny proportion of Nordic genes to every baby born 800 years later in south and central Africa. There are undoubtedly enigmas to be ironed out, but it seems salutary to get theologians and demographers thinking along these lines.

A concrete practical conclusion regarding original sin would be this. If "Adam" became the recipient of God's special "elevation" only a few years before Abraham, when the human race was already a million years old, then by the time Saint Paul wrote Romans 5:12 (which is really all we know about original sin), that same Adam *could by natural means have become* the progenitor of every single human living then or later. As is known, there is no theological objection to the "Pre-Adam-ite" hypothesis which Blandino here endeavors to revive.

8. *Science Left to Its Own Domain*

Enough has been said to show that serious divergence prevails among theologians and exegetes as to the dogmatic immutability of monogenism. Is it a truth of revelation? Is it a fact of partially human knowledge, yet genuinely certain and therefore of itself unalterable? Is it a reformable decree of authority? No one can claim a consensus of experts for his answer today.

Nevertheless, it is claimed that *"whether* original sin can be safeguarded without monogenism" is a purely dogmatic issue. And if the answer given by dogma is No, then this further conclusion is drawn: By divine revelation and ecclesiastical decree, no scientific evidence will ever be discovered warranting polygenism.

Not that the Church or revelation is stepping outside its proper domain into that of science; they are simply safeguarding revelation. "Anthropology will never be able to tell whether the human race came from one couple or more. The Magisterium has given the answer: not because it is its function to teach science, but . . . to decide on those matters that pertain to the foundations of the Christian religion."[67]

---

[67] J. O'Neill, "The Bible and Evolution," *Scripture*, 11 (1959), 6–22, 42–51, 50, following A. Gelin, *Ami du Clergé*, 41 (1951), 295. Compare Humphrey Johnson, *The Bible and Early Man* (New York: McMullen, 1948), 73; Raymond W. Murray, *Man's Unknown Ancestors* (Milwaukee: Bruce, 1943), 128.

In this perspective, many recent theologians explicitly declare that no parallel can be drawn between polygenism and the celebrated cases of Galileo or Darwin. There, sad as it is, the mistake has to be acknowledged: "some" defenders of Catholic doctrine unwisely felt that Scripture and dogma had pronounced on facts of astronomy or biology, when in fact these were mere unwarranted *conclusions* drawn by theologians from what the Church really taught.

This posture may seem to some unrealistic. The parallel with Galileo or Darwin founders *if* monogenism is indeed a changeless certitude, especially if it is virtually or implicitly revealed. But on this point we do not possess any infallible decree. The words of Pius XII are surely very weighty and binding, not least of all because they reflect a wide consensus of dogmatic theologians and a theological reasoning which is fairly obvious. But they are now quite generally acknowledged to be not irreformable.

At any rate, can the Catholic historian of theology not ask without disloyalty whether the situation was any different in the epochs when theologians en masse condemned Galileo and Darwin?

The reasoning then too was that no matter *what* evidences the telescope or the fossil-hunter might uncover, no scientific fact ever could be found which would contradict the pronouncements of revelation.

But those alleged scientific facts, which were already perceptible to a few gifted experts, gradually became massive and public. The time came for a pronouncement, not now of theologians, but of supreme ecclesiastical authority. This could only be that no conflict is possible between any alleged revelation and the proved certitudes of science.

Virtually it has been decreed that those theologians, always unofficial however numerous, who claimed heliocentrism and evolution heretical, have been repudiated.

Can we honestly say today that the simple question of *whether or not* fossils or similar evidence *may* come to light at some point in the future, is a question of revealed dogma and not of continuing scientific observation?

Or must we not rather avow that the answer has long ago been given by Saint Thomas Aquinas:

"Whether the Firmament was made on the Second Day: I answer with Augustine that in questions like this we must keep two things before our minds. First, the truth of Scripture must be held inviolably. Second, since the divine Scriptures can be set forth in many ways, no one should cling so insistently to any one explanation, that if this should be proved with certitude to be false, one would be presuming to assert this to be the sense of Scripture. Such declarations would expose Scripture to the derision of unbelievers, and close the path of faith to them."[68]

It is not the function of theology or revelation to pronounce what *facts* the scientist will or will not discover in his laboratory. Even more powerful and relevant are the words of Augustine which Thomas has summarized:

"It happens all the time . . . that even a non-Christian is informed about zoology, botany, geology ['the natures of animals, shrubbery, stones, and such objects'] so accurately that he has utter certitude of reason or experience. It is abominable and pernicious and intolerable that any such well informed unbeliever should hear a Christian claiming to prove from the Christian Bible concerning these matters statements so absurd that he cannot keep from laughing, so diametrically opposed are these babblings to the genuine facts of the case. . . . When well informed experts in a certain field catch a Christian in an obvious mistake, where he claims to prove his unfounded assertion out of our Bible, how can we expect such experts to accept the authority of that Bible at all? [These imprudent Christians] pronounce many words out of Scripture 'without understanding even their own assertion, and much less the facts they are talking about' (1 Timothy 1:7)."[69]

In line with this truly Christian tradition is a paragraph of Teilhard's which for those who admire him is one of the most gripping he ever penned — just as it is one of the most irritating for those who dissent.

"It is a pleasing and dramatic spectacle to see the whole of Humanity divided through history into two camps irremediably hostile. One group stretches out toward the horizon, saying with their new-found conviction, 'Yes, we are moving forward.' The other repeats obstinately, without even getting up, 'No, nothing is changing; we are not moving at all.' These 'immobilists,' in place of the passion they lack (since no one ever became enthusiastic for immobility), have on their side common sense, routine, line of least resistance, and also to a certain extent morality and religion. Nothing seems to have moved, ever since man first handed down the memory of his past: neither the undulations of the soil, nor the forms of life, nor the genius of man, nor even his good . . . suffering, war, vice.

[68] Thomas Aquinas, *Summa Theologica*, First Part. Questions 65–74 deal with "The Work of the Seven Days' Creation." The citation is from the body of Article 1 of Question 68. An unusually perplexing Latin construction of the original has been adapted rather freely in the Dominican version (New York: Benziger, 1947), 1, 338.
[69] Augustine, *De Genesi ad Litteram*, 1, 19, 38; Migne, *Patrologia Latina*, 34, 260; *Corpus Scriptorum Ecclesiasticorum Latinorum*, ed. J. Zycha (Vienna: Tempsky, 1894), 28.

. . . In the name of men's repose, in the name of facts, in the name of the sacred established order, it is forbidden to the earth to move. . . . But the other half of Mankind has simply walked away from where the crew sitting in a circle around the domestic fire keeps on telling the same old stories."[70]

[70] Teilhard, "Note sur le progrès," 1920, in Œuvres 5, *L'avenir de l'homme* (Paris: Seuil, 1959), 13. Alternative translation now by Norman Denny in *The Future of Man* (New York: Harper, 1964), 11. Teilhard's 1924 statements on original sin which on page 55 above are alleged to have cost him his lifelong ostracism are announced for publication in Œuvres 11. Meanwhile a lengthy analysis is offered by Jean Onimus, *Pierre Teilhard de Chardin ou la foi au monde* (Paris: Plon, 1963), 38 ff. In a normal perspective of universal evolution, a large place is vindicated for Evil or Failure as the inevitable by-product of an overall Progress. The emergence of Man, being so evidently a *forward leap,* can on the one hand not so plausibly be seen as a self-perpetuating catastrophe. On the other hand, *not* to recognize such a catastrophe is to ignore the tragic aspect of man's existentiality which calls imperatively for a redemption from beyond his nature. To this dilemma Teilhard replies: First, renounce the biblical image of a couple *born adult,* biological nonsense. Secondly, recognize the "original evil" in the *whole* of the created world: Death is a correlative of Life itself! Thirdly, a wholly special kind of disintegration or failure becomes possible from the moment that complexification brings reflex consciousness and freedom. Within humanity this evil consubstantial with material reality takes on the name of sin. Fourthly, every reality must die to itself to be incorporated in a higher level of being. In man's case, this renouncement involves a reflex decision. Failure on this level becomes *moral* evil — that "original" sin including also *future* sins "on the horizon" — of proportions so terrible that it could jeopardize evolution itself or at least its rate. Teilhard's heroic acceptance of his quite literal banishment from Paris to Peking for these views is expressed in his letters of August 16 and 22, 1925, cited by Onimus on page 42 f. See now Katy Canevaro and Angelo Marchese, *Teilhard de Chardin figlio d'obbedienza* (Rome: AVE, 1965), 10.

SUMMARY OF THE SECOND CHAPTER,
ON POLYGENISM

An interesting and inescapable history of exegesis attaches to the single verse of Genesis 2:7 which is most invoked to prove the spirituality and creation of the soul. The same verse was also most responsible for a century of resistance to bodily evolution by Judeo-Christian theologians of whatever creed. And today the resistance to polygenism cannot be evaluated apart from this verse as a setting of the stage for the Fall narrative of Genesis 3:14, generally assumed to underlie the teaching of Romans 5:12 on original sin.

Most scientists presume polygenism in the sense that the transit to the human species was accomplished in numerous individuals within a relatively restricted cradle area.

Teilhard frankly favors this view, though he insists it can never be proved because of nature's "Law of Suppression of Peduncles." By this he means that the feeler-specimens marking the crossover from one species to another are weak and few and thus doomed to vanish. "Progress" cannot be caught in the act, just as the movement of the hour-hand on the clock cannot be seen with the naked eye. But the presence of "critical thresholds" is our guarantee that at a certain moment, over a fairly large body of individual specimens, "quantitative increase produces qualitative change."

Ultimately the scientist's reasons for inclining toward polygenism are the same that warrant his extending animal evolution to the human species at all. Teilhard's vehemence in finding evolution a dimension of nature everywhere goes beyond what most scientists and especially sociologists would consider factual.

The 1950 encyclical *Humani Generis* of Pius XII envisions views so similar to Teilhard's that it is hard to deny these were being directly disapproved. Yet even more important is the fact that the need of this warning gave occasion for the first explicit authorization of bodily evolution in the history of Catholic dogma. As Rahner puts it, by this decree the façade of Catholic theology was finally made to conform to what had long been solidly built up behind the façade. To have been the evoking or even provoking cause of this decree may well turn out to be Teilhard's most unforgettable service to theology.

In saying that evolution may be defended but not as a proved fact, Pius XII actually calls attention to a general difference in the "certitude" claimed for the statistical laws of physics and the deductive reasonings of speculative theology. In forbidding to polygenism that freedom which he allows to evolution, the Pope has been interpreted as *not* claiming a certitude that would eliminate all further reopening of the question. His State of the Question was reaffirmed by Paul VI.

How polygenism could eventually be reconciled with the revealed truth of original sin is being investigated along three principal lines.

No pronouncements could be more trenchant than those of Augustine and Aquinas to the effect that it is not the function of theology to pronounce what facts the scientist will or will not eventually uncover within his own proper domain.

CHAPTER 3

CREATION, ORTHOGENESIS, AND LAMARCK

1. A Look at the Whole Before the Parts

We have noticed some very bold or even rash statements of Teilhard about the human soul being an uninterrupted continuity with matter. We have also noticed him reproaching his fellow scientists with their neglect of those various "thresholds" which give evidence of *discontinuity*.

At several points in *The Phenomenon of Man* is inserted a footnote acknowledging the creation of the soul, but as a thing not accessible to the scientist without revelation.

"I confine myself here to the phenomena, i.e. to the experimental relations between consciousness and complexity, without prejudging the deeper causes which govern the whole issue. . . . There is nothing to prevent the thinker who adopts a spiritual explanation from positing (for reasons of a higher order and at a later stage of his dialectic), UNDER THE PHENOMENAL VEIL *of a revolutionary transformation, whatever 'creative' operation or 'special intervention' he likes."*[1]

In other words, if one possesses, from sources not available to science, assurance that each human soul is created by God immediately out of nothing, this fits without contradiction into the phenomenon under discussion.

[1] Teilhard, *Phenomenon of Man*, 169. See above, p. 46, and below, p. 164.

62

These insertions have the air of being put in *after* Teilhard's own expression of the facts was complete, in order to satisfy theological censors. Not that there is any doubt of his sincerity in what he there adds. But there may be a doubt whether what he professes here is really necessary, or whether it is coherent with the totality of his system.

The creation of the soul is only one example of creation. We might say it is only one example of creationism. In the long run, the big line of demarcation is between those who admit any creating God at all and those who do not.

Which *particular* movements and mechanisms of creative intervention are to be assigned to God is a relatively domestic dispute. Whatever may have been held by Teilhard on the very specific problem of the soul's origin must first of all be seen as part of his outlook on creationism.

It is of course obvious that he considers himself highly theistic. His whole life-work was to vindicate the claims of God in the scientific world, and reconcile scientists to them. That is why de Lubac and others quite justly insist that it falsifies his thought to focus only upon the scientific half of his writings. This unfairly excludes from view the complementary precisions of religion and faith, contained notably in *The Divine Milieu.*[2]

But *how* does Teilhard try to reconcile scientists with religion? Largely by lopping off growths which religion has inherited or developed out of a pre-scientific framework.

Doubtless most scientists would single out the belief in creation as the one most conspicuous and irritating heritage of superstition. Hence it cannot be blithely taken for granted that Teilhard believes in creation and strives to bring around his fellow scientists to share this belief.

Our misgivings are rendered acute by the extreme diffidence with which he speaks of creation at all, as we shall explain in our next chapter. On the other hand, there is a thing which he does speak of insistently and at great cost to his own scientific standing. That is orthogenesis.

It is important to gain a clear notion of what this key word means in Teilhard's writings. We will try to justify his stand purely on the basis of most recent biology. And we will conclude that he utterly refuses to dispense with orthogenesis, despite its scientific unpopularity. And this is the measure of the intensity of his assurance of creation.

---

[2] Teilhard, *The Divine Milieu,* tr. Bernard Wall (= Œuvres 4, 1957); Henri de Lubac, *La pensée religieuse du Père Pierre Teilhard de Chardin* (Paris: Aubier, 1962), 12; Paul Chauchard, *L'être humain selon Teilhard de Chardin* (Paris: Gabalda, 1959), 19. English translation by George Courtright, *Man and Cosmos: Scientific Phenomenology in Teilhard de Chardin* (New York: Herder and Herder, 1965); *Teilhard témoin de l'amour* (Cahiers Teilhard, 2; Paris: Presses Universitaires, 1962); *Teilhard de Chardin, un guide et un modèle pour notre temps* (Paris: Levain, 1964); *La pensée scientifique de Teilhard* (Paris: Éditions Universitaires, 1965): see footnote 28, page 44 above.

2. *Takeover of Some Biological Terminology*

"I believe in God *and* in evolution" had been convincingly sustained
by various Christians almost since Darwin.[3] Many Catholics were among
these, even before it was officially decreed in 1950 that bodily evolution
is not incompatible with Church teaching. Such believers effected convincing "reconciliations" between faith in an all-creative God, and recognition of natural species developments attested in fossils.

By the time of the Darwin centenary in 1959, Catholics were as loud
as any in generous acknowledgment of his breakthrough. The symposia
of Duquesne and Fordham concretized this Catholic "New Look."[4] Similar volumes of other scientific associations set in sharp focus the various
avenues along which Darwin had surpassed his predecessors.

In such discussions of the achievements of Darwin, one name that never
fails to come up is Lamarck. Almost inevitably it is made to appear
that the real enduring achievement of Darwin was his triumph over
Lamarck. In what precisely this triumph consisted is often regarded as
too obvious to call for comment; "Lamarckism" is a term of abuse which
"every schoolboy knows."

Much rarer in the chorus of praise to Darwin has been any reference
to orthogenesis. Only by the accident that these two words happen to
be important in Teilhard but hard for his votaries to define, are we led
to include them together in one research.

This inquiry will lead the theologian or humanist very far afield from
the areas he knows anything about. Any effort of a non-biologist to
evaluate these terms is foredoomed to end up quite unprofessional. The
case is rather like what an atomic fissionist might produce after six
months of diligently reading up on the Upanishads.

"If these things are done in the green wood, what will be done in
the dry?" Most theologians pronounce with serene assurance on problems
of evolution and Teilhard *without* having endeavored to penetrate into
the technical literature. One thing we can really hope from making that
effort is a salutary awareness of our own ignorance and our own dependence upon experts.

Incidentally, though, apart from the validity or even rationality of
our conclusions, we can hardly fail to end up with *some* more coherent
ideas about the terms "orthogenesis" and "Lamarckism" than before

[3] William W. Keen, *I Believe in God and in Evolution* (Philadelphia: Lippincott,
1922); cf. Russell L. Mixter, *Evolution and Christian Thought Today* (Grand
Rapids: Eerdmans, 1959).

[4] B. Boelen, ed., *Symposium on Evolution* (Pittsburgh: Duquesne, 1959); Walter
J. Ong., ed., *Darwin's Vision and Christian Perspectives* (New York: Macmillan,
1960) = *Thought*, 34/133 (June, 1959).

starting. And since these two words, indexed eleven and four times respectively in *The Phenomenon of Man,* are of considerable nuisance value in the contexts where they occur, it can hardly be time wasted to try to set them straight.

Our own conclusions here were reached most reluctantly. They seem aimed at downgrading the achievement of a very great man. It is almost useless to protest that we are not diminishing Darwin's stature by cutting away claims of his admirers to which he himself did not and would not subscribe. Teilhard too has had to suffer from that kind of veneration.

Here is what these pages will tend to show. Biologists, whether Catholic or uncommitted, but desiring simply to be objective, have taken over from the early Darwinists as a matter of mere *terminology* something which in fact was a *thesis* going considerably beyond what anyone today would consider essential to Darwin.

In a word, they took over that there is no finality. This ultimately is what we will show to be really meant by the oft repeated statement, "Lamarck was wrong, and Darwin was right."

Obviously our intention here is not to tell biologists that we know more about their terminology and its implications than they do. Still less is it to induce theologians and other talented minds without empirical formation to rally around an "anti-biology" standard.

We *depend* on experts on biology. We *cannot* tell them what they should or must find in their laboratory. But we can try to formulate our bewilderments with such pinpointed exactness that a basis for clarification may be laid.

Our firm stand is simply this. "If there is no finality, there is no creation." If by rejecting Lamarckism, the scientist means there is no finality: then even if he is a daily communicant, he is simply rejecting creation.

Teilhard, on the contrary, makes of the words "Lamarckian orthogenesis" a sort of Maginot Line from which there is no retreating: because bad as the phrase is, it is less odious to scientists than outright "creation."

3. *Lamarck's Evolutionism*

The life of Jean-Baptiste de Monet de Lamarck, of Picardy, 1744–1829, was written in English by Packard, and more bibliographically in French by Landrieu.[5] Let it not be thought that some Catholic piety makes him an appropriate vehicle for creationism. He rejected efforts to make a priest of him. He fell deeply under the influence of Rousseau

---

[5] A. S. Packard, *Lamarck, the Founder of Evolution* (London: Longmans, 1901); Marcel Landrieu, *Lamarck* (Paris: Société Zoologique, 1909).

and Diderot. He frankly scorned the creation narrative of Genesis, along with all the conclusions drawn from it by Church authority.[6]

He was a botanist until the age of forty-nine. Then by political appointment he became a zoologist. This will perhaps not seem such an about-face to outsiders as it does to the key men of those specialties. It was Lamarck who invented the little word "biology."[7]

Those were the days in which, by a deplorable regression from the principles we quoted from Augustine and Aquinas, it was commonly held as somehow connected with faith and Scripture that God created all the species separately, or even that reason itself postulates this "Great Chain of Being."[8] Lamarck's was not the first voice raised in protest.

The first steps were taken by William Harvey in 1651. In his wake, more plainly, Pierre Maupertuis in 1745 included under the name of *epigenesis* "virtually every idea of Mendelian heredity and classical Darwinism": heredity due to particles deriving from both father and mother; affinity of particles making them pair off; dominant and recessive traits; notions of phenotype and mutation; "and these fortuitous changes might be the beginning of new species, if acted upon by a survival of the fittest and if geographically isolated."[9]

In fairness to Teilhard and to France, it seems advisable to bring out into the open the strong trend which any reasonably loyal Frenchman would have, to make Lamarck rather than Darwin the real father of evolution. To succumb to that temptation would be rather poignant and frustrating for the Frenchman himself, as André Senet tells it.[10]

Lamarck had indeed maintained, or rather borrowed from Buffon: "All species derive from one another, simple to complex." This principle was completely scorned in scholarly France. An Englishman named Lyell recognized that in holding this, Lamarck had truly anticipated what would seem to be Darwin's main achievement. To counter this impression, Lyell set himself industriously to keep before the public eye details by which "Darwin was right, and Lamarck was wrong." Only this diligent publicizing by Lyell preserved Lamarck's insight from the oblivion

---

[6] Lester G. Crocker, "Diderot and Eighteenth Century French Transformism," in [H.] B. Glass, *Forerunners of Darwin: 1745–1859* (Baltimore: Hopkins, 1959), 128, 143; see also pp. 238–248 by F. Haber.

[7] Erik Nordenskiold, *The History of Biology* (New York: Knopf, 1928), 320.

[8] Arthur O. Lovejoy, *The Great Chain of Being* (Harvard: 1953), 329. Page 145 shows Aristotle culminating in Leibniz; see further H. F. Osborn, *From the Greeks to Darwin* (New York: Scribners, 1924). On Augustine and Aquinas see footnotes 68 and 69 in Chapter 2, pp. 58–59 above.

[9] H. Bentley Glass, *Forerunners of Darwin* (Baltimore: Hopkins, 1959), 60. Maupertuis is made out to be considerably less important in L. Eiseley, *Darwin's Century: Evolution and the Men who Discovered It* (New York: Doubleday, 1958). See further H. F. Blum, *Time's Arrow and Evolution* (Princeton, 1955).

[10] André Senet, *Man in Search of his Ancestors* (New York: McGraw-Hill, 1956), 192, 223.

to which it seemed destined on French soil. As they say it in French, "It was through Lyell that Darwin absorbed Lamarck's ideas and thereby brought Darwinism to success."[11] It is amusing to read Schopenhauer's deadly serious explanation of why Lamarck's evolutionism had to be wrong because the French lack metaphysical insight.[12]

Lamarck's views on evolution were formulated in 1809 as two laws, which we may summarize:

I. Use strengthens, disuse atrophies, any organ.
II. Every such adaptation of an organ is transmitted by heredity.[13]

Six years later, in 1815, he reformulated these laws as four:

I.   Life, by its own force, tends continually to increase the volume of every living body and to extend the dimensions of its parts, up to a limit which it imposes.
II. The production of a new organ in an animal body results from a new need (*besoin*), which continues to make itself felt, and from a new movement that this need brings about and maintains.
III. The development and effectiveness of organs are proportional to the use of those organs.
IV. Everything acquired or changed during an individual's lifetime is preserved by heredity and transmitted to that individual's progeny.[14]

It is indubitable that this Fourth Law includes the "Transmission of Acquired Characteristics," in a sense incompatible with current mendelianism.

Three other facts are less commonly mentioned: (1) Darwin himself accepted and maintained this "Transmission of Acquired Characteristics" to the full extent in which it was understood by Lamarck. (2) Even in modern mendelianism, the origin of species is ultimately explainable only by *some* effect of environment upon the organism, transmitted by heredity. (3) Darwin had no more inkling than Lamarck of the actual microscopic mechanism by which both heredity and species-alteration were effected.

How is it then that Darwin is by universal agreement called (with Wallace, purists will add) the *inventor* of an evolution theory which shares with Lamarck not only its basic *positive* content, but also its most notorious deficiencies: phenotype transmission and unawareness of gene mutation?

[11] Alfred Giard, first to apply the Lamarck principle to environment modifying germ cells; cited by Senet.

[12] Arthur Schopenhauer, *Der Wille in der Natur* (1854), with comments collected by Lovejoy in his contribution to H. Glass, *Forerunners of Darwin*, p. 421.

[13] J. B. Lamarck, *Philosophie zoologique*. My citations are from pp. 204 and 211 of the 1907 Paris Schleicher edition.

[14] Lamarck, *Histoire naturelle des animaux sans vertèbres* (Paris: Verdière, 1815), 1, 181. The translation is from page 51 of Cannon [footnote 18 below], which is referred to a different French edition.

Our chief answer is to be found in the ridicule heaped upon Lamarck's alternative to the famed Darwinian "Natural Selection." This ridicule was not due to Darwin himself in his published works, though somewhat in his letters.[15] Thomas Huxley and other popularizers of Darwin turned the trick.[16]

Ultimately their ridicule must be traced back to the notorious "Eulogy" over Lamarck pronounced by Georges Cuvier, misinterpreting the word *besoin* to mean "conscious desire."

The truth is, and Lamarck really said, environment acts upon the organism mechanically. What is transmitted to progeny? Not the product of conscious striving, but blind adaptation to environment. This adaptation consists chiefly in the perishing of what is not suited to survive.

Whether the giraffe's *besoin* of the upper foliage lengthened his *legs,* as Lamarck actually said, or his *neck,* as his critics found made a better joke of it, is irrelevant. Lamarck was sincerely convinced, *and so was Darwin,* that the transmission of visible external characteristics accounts for the diversification of species. Ultimately the changes introduced in course of transmission do not take place at the instant of separation of sperm from the parent body, but consist in *unaltered* transmission of something which has been altered *within* the parent body.[17]

---

[15] *Darwin's Life and Letters,* 2, 207, reports, "He was annoyed when Lyell used the expression, 'Lamarck's views improved by yours.'" See John C. Greene, *The Death of Adam: Evolution and Its Impact on Western Thought* (Ames: Iowa State, 1959), 285, and his "Darwin and Religion," *Proceedings of the American Philosophical Society,* 103 (1959), 716–725; also P. Schmidt, "Darwins Stellung zur Religion in neuester Schau," *Orientierung,* 24 (1960), 83.

[16] Lovejoy's paper in Glass, *Forerunners of Darwin,* is entitled "The Argument for Organic Evolution [was already complete] Before the *Origin of Species,* 1830–1858." On page 357 he shows that T. H. Huxley's paper on the reception of the *Origin of Species,* published as Chapter 14 of F. Darwin's *Life and Letters of Charles Darwin* (London: Murray, 1887; Vol. 1), is an unfair and distorted account which is at the base of most current information on the subject. Page 370 demonstrates how most of Lyell's criticisms of Lamarck were "devastating but beside the point." And page 379 cites Joseph Leconte's *Evolution and its Relation to Religious Thought* (1905); 65: "We are confident that evolution is *absolutely certain.* Not, indeed, evolution as a special theory — Lamarckian, Darwinian, Spencerian — for these are all more or less successful modes of explaining evolution."

[17] D. Dwight Davis, "Comparative Anatomy and the Evolution of Vertebrates," in Glenn L. Jepsen, *Genetics, Paleontology, and Evolution* (Princeton: 1949), 78: "Among the higher vertebrate categories adaptation is an empirical fact, and here the problem is not whether adaptation exists, but how and why adaptations arose, and what part they have played in evolution. . . . The basic morphology of most and probably all vertebrate orders [is] a major adaptation to a particular way of life. . . . Both Lamarck and Darwin regarded adaptation as indicated in any change in the structure of an animal that better fitted it to its organic or inorganic environment." So in the Darwin *Centennial Proceedings of the American Philosophical Society,* 103/2 (1959), 190–220, Arne Muntzing, "Darwin's Views on Variation under Domestication in the Light of Present-Day Knowledge," p. 191: "Being influenced by Lamarck, Darwin is convinced that biological variation is chiefly

In explaining the adaptiveness of species, the only serious difference between the two men was this. Darwin stressed and explained "survival of the fittest" as a blind natural selection. Lamarck used for this adaptiveness a French word which really means "a need of nature," but in certain idiomatic contexts or by punning could be taken to mean "conscious desire."

The sole word "blind," therefore, puts us on the track of what is acclaimed as the ultimate superiority of Darwin.

4. *Some Recent Critiques of Lamarck*

An explosive little book by Cannon maintains that the denigration of Lamarck is a mechanism for covering up the inadequacies of mendelianism.[18] It is emphatically not our purpose to follow him here in this. Teilhard would not wish to see his own work defended by calling into question the theory of species mutation universally accepted today, which involves the rectification of darwinianism by mendelian elements.[19] At most

---

conditioned by direct influence of the environment on the organisms, believing that the changes thus induced become inherited"; and pp. 183–9, Curt Stern, "Variation and Hereditary Transmission," p. 186: "The causes of hereditary variation, of mutations, according to Darwin lie in the environment."

[18] H. Graham Cannon, *Lamarck and Modern Genetics* (Manchester: University, 1959). On page 67, he quotes Julian S. Huxley, *Evolution, the Modern Synthesis* (London: Allen Unwin, 1942), 54: "It may be legitimately argued that the majority of all inherited characters must rest on a Mendelian basis." To this Cannon adds, "Unfortunately he does not tell us how the minority of characters are inherited, neither does he give us any indication as to what type of character is included in the minority." He then quotes E. B. Ford, *Mendelism and Evolution* (London: Methuen, 1957, [1]1931), 43: "The characters studied by geneticists do in fact differ fundamentally from those which appear to be responsible for evolutionary progress in nature." On page 68 Cannon notes that Sir Gavin de Beer holds hereditary resemblances are determined by genes, "then with amazing ignorance of what Lamarck really said, he condemns him outright, while he lauds Darwin to the skies. His laudation, however, consists almost entirely of pointing out that the real merit of Darwinism is that it establishes the fact that the modern orthodox theory of the gene complex is correct." On page 83 Cannon denies that darwinian and neo-mendelian hypotheses reciprocally support each other; and on pages 86–106 he formulates seven pungent questions to show that biology answers more in favor of Lamarck than of neo-mendelianism.

[19] Cannon on page 46 admits that Kammerer's claim to have produced a permanent new adaptive character was a forgery, though it was espoused by E. W. MacBride's *Introduction to the Study of Heredity* (London: Williams and Norgate, 1942), 68. Perhaps to keep this chapter up to date it ought to be noted that Frank L. Horsfall, "Inheritance of Acquired Characters," *Science*, 136/3515 (May 11, 1962), 472–6, holds that *cancers* in general represent such inheritance at the cell level. Moreover, C. P. Martin, *Psychology, Evolution, and Sex* (Springfield, Ill.: Thomas, 1956), 84, and G. Vandebroek in J. de Bivort de la Saudée, *God, Man, and the Universe* (New York: Kenedy, 1953), 95, show that modern mendelians admit that the inheriting of acquired characters has never been *dis*proved.

we may admit that a small portion of the credit for this present consensus is due to Lamarck, as claimed by Cannon.

We must take up at greater length the critique of Lamarck by an
author who merits our considerable admiration. Gillispie in a brilliantly
readable book called *Genesis and Geology* had already established his
competence to deal with any of the ramified problems accounting for
the strong initial hostility of English Protestantism to evolution.[20]

With an incisiveness and an awareness of the history of ideas which
his earlier work would have led us to expect, Gillispie declares: "Lamarck's
theory of evolution belongs to the contracting and self-defeating history
of subjective science." It was biological pre-newtonianism, and "could no
more have distinguished the study of variations from the study of the
organism as a whole than the impetus school could separate motion from
the missile."[21]

Gillispie reduces to the single phrase "by chance" the ultimate difference
and glory of Darwin vis-à-vis Lamarck.

"Darwin was the first to make [the distinction] between the origin of
variations and their preservation. Variations arise by chance. But they
are preserved according as they work more or less effectively in objective circumstance. In Lamarck, on the other hand, the two problems are
handled as a single question, which in effect is begged by its solution
in the inheritance of acquired characteristics."[22]

Surely the lucid commentator is not unaware that Darwin himself
firmly held the *transmission of acquired characteristics,* and firmly denied
the legitimacy of the term *chance,* as we shall see.

Because of its unique emphasis on *fire* as accounting for all chemistry,
even the continuity of mind with nature, Gillispie continues, "Lamarck's
philosophy is no anticipation of Darwin, but a medley of dying echoes
. . . a life process as the organism digesting its environment."

He quotes Sainte-Beuve, making Lamarck "last representative of that
great school of naturalists and general observers who held sway from
Thales and Democritus right down to Buffon . . . the mortal enemy
of the chemists, of experimentalists and petty analysts, as he called them.
No less severe was his philosophical hostility amounting to hatred for the
tradition of the Deluge and the Biblical creation story, indeed for anything which recalled the Christian theory of nature. His own conception
of things was simple, austere, and full of pathos. He constructed the
world out of the smallest possible number of elements, and with the
fewest crises and the longest duration imaginable. . . . Similarly in the

---

[20] See above, footnote 2 in chap. 2, p. 36.
[21] Charles C. Gillispie, "Lamarck and Darwin in the History of Science," in [H.]
B. Glass, *Forerunners of Darwin 1745–1859* (Baltimore: Hopkins, 1959) [265–291],
287.
[22] Gillispie, in Glass, *Forerunners,* 287.

organic realm, once he had admitted the mysterious power of life, in as minimal and elementary a form as possible, he supposes it developing on its own, building itself up, complicating itself little by little. Various organs were born of unconscious needs, of simple habit working in the different environments against the constant destroying power of nature. For M. de Lamarck separated life from nature."[23]

We do not think that any admirer of Teilhard should ignore these sweeping and thought-provoking observations about Lamarck. Sainte-Beuve and Gillispie like Teilhard himself do not disdain helping themselves over difficult passages in the argument by spellbinding poetic prose. But let us direct attention to two admissions let in by the back door.

First, even Darwin's heirs were as guilty as Lamarck of a Cartesian identifying of cause and operation. "Both Nägeli's ideoplasm and Weissmann's germ plasm were analogous to that Lamarckian inheritance of acquired characteristics which they repudiated. For both concepts gave at once a theory of heredity and development. . . . Darwin and Lamarck, therefore, speak their parts in that endless debate between atoms and the continuum, the multiplicity of events and the unity of nature . . . not simply the wrong side [Goethe espoused the continuum of personality, and Einstein the continuum of geometry!]. For Lamarck the rational continuum resided in life."[24]

Secondly, many who rejected Darwin's evolutionary principles "thought it worthwhile to impugn his originality [by inconsistently making it a defect in him that] Lamarck had had everything essential to an evolutionary biology. And in the face of the enterprise on which the contributors to the present volume are engaged, it would be difficult indeed to claim the fact of the evolutionary variation of species as a Darwinian discovery. It is true that Darwin disposed of a greater fund of species than had Lamarck. . . . It is to be doubted, however, whether the uniformitarian philosophy of Charles Lyell was as essential to Darwin's success as is usually said, or as I once said myself. For Lamarck had been his own Lyell . . . more interesting and elegant. [Yet] his theory failed to compel assent. It scarcely even won attention. [Darwin's success was not due to the 'mechanistic equals scientific' character of his age.] The one thing Darwin did not, and could not, specify was the mechanism of variation or heredity. All he could do was postulate its naturalistic mode. . . . It is no compliment to Lamarck's own conception of his lifework to make him out an unappreciated forerunner of Darwin. I recently asked a friend who is a biologist specializing in evolution what he and his colleagues understood by Lamarckism, and the first thing he said

---

[23] Gillispie in *Forerunners,* 276; the citation is from Sainte-Beuve's *Volupté* (Paris: 1927 edition), 192–194.

[24] Gillispie, *Forerunners of Darwin,* 289 f.

was the inheritance of acquired characteristics, and after that a lingering temptation in biology generally to indulge in an 'Aristotelian vitalism.' "[25]

This is so very important that it will perhaps justify the length of the citation. The sum of Gillispie's evaluation of Lamarck amounts to two assertions. He held inheritance of acquired characteristics: which leaves him identical with Darwin. And he held "vitalism": which distinguishes him from Darwin.

5. Not "Acquired Characters" but "Vitalism"

Let us now pass to Carter's recent reappraisal of Lamarck. This may or may not win approval of biologists. It will doubtless evoke a more instinctive assent of theologians, for the pardonable reason that it speaks a language more intelligible to them. This work states bluntly: Darwin and Wallace founded evolution, *because* Lamarck's "Laws" are clearly vitalistic and not mechanistic. "Since scientific biology is necessarily mechanistic, they have been almost entirely disregarded by later biologists."[26]

There was a strange "blind spot" in Darwin's outlook, Carter continues. "What he did not consider was that any large change in any part of the body is impossible, if the animal is to remain viable, without correlated change in many other parts. . . . It was inherent in [Aristotle, Cuvier, and] Lamarck's third law. But Darwin could see little good in Lamarck." Macroevolutionary changes "must have always taken place in many steps. Birds at first developed their wings as organs for gliding from tree to tree, and only later learnt to use them for active flight."

This 1957 formulation of the phenomenon may or may not be acceptable. But it can hardly be considered notably different from Lamarck's much abused giraffe.

Carter maintains further, "Since small changes are not difficult, it may be that a series of them might without difficulty give rise to one of these large changes. But a series of small changes, if it were to lead to a large change, would have to be accurately correlated with evolution in new characters of the body as it progressed. . . . It is possible that another direction in which our present [Neo-Darwinian] theory may be modified is by return toward [!] Darwin's belief that Lamarckian heredity plays some part in evolution. The present discredit of the Lamarckian assumption that acquired characters are inherited arises from our inability to see how changes produced in the body during the life history could induce changes in the genotype which will give rise in the bodies of the new generation to characters similar to those acquired

---

[25] *Ibid.*, 266 ff. The biologist friend is Colin Pittendrigh of footnote 40 below.
[26] George S. Carter, *A Hundred Years of Evolution* (New York: Macmillan, 1957), 34.

by their parents. But it is always unsound in science, and especially in biology, to say that an effect is impossible because we cannot see how it could be brought about."[27]

This citation is not invoked as a rejection of mendelianism, which as explained above forms no part of our purpose here. We wish to establish only that neither "acquired characters" nor any other essential of species mutation is differently explained by Darwin than by Lamarck except that which concerns the alleged flaw of vitalism.

6. *The Mendelian Contribution*

The experiments of the Augustinian abbot Gregor Mendel in 1866, duly recognized only in 1900, proved conclusively that neither Lamarck nor Darwin had suspected the ultimate microscopic mechanism accounting for the "phenomena" which their respective evolutionisms were describing.[28]

The factor ultimately responsible for species differentiation is not Mendel's genes themselves, which are constant, but their "mutations" caused by chance or accident or some factor which so far escapes us.[29]

In *The Origin of Species,* Darwin wrote, "I have sometimes spoken as if variations . . . were due to chance. This, of course, is a wholly incorrect expression, but it serves to acknowledge plainly our ignorance of the cause of each particular variation."[30] The addition of Mendel's gene mechanism to Darwinian "survival of the fittest" does not in the

---

[27] Carter, *A Hundred Years of Evolution,* 51, 176, 191 f.

[28] Gregor Mendel, "Versuche über Pflanzen-Hybriden," *Verhandlungen des Naturforschung-Vereins Brunn* 4 (1866), 3–47. See the Mendel Jubilee volume edited by L. C. Dunn, *Genetics in the Twentieth Century* (New York: Macmillan, 1951).

[29] In order to adapt to Mendelianism, "the Lamarckian 'impurities' had to be eliminated from the Darwinian concept," says Alexander Wolsky, "A Hundred Years of Darwinism in Biology," *Thought,* 34/133 (June 1959), 171 = [W. Ong, ed.] *Darwin's Vision and Christian Perspectives* (New York: Macmillan, 1960), 12. If our present chapter is well founded, what Wolsky really means is "The *Lamarckian-Darwinian* impurities had to be eliminated from the *Lamarckian* concept and replaced by valid Darwinian-Mendelian factors."

[30] Charles Darwin, *Origin of Species,* at beginning and end of Chapter 5 (Harvard Classics edition: New York, Collier, 1909), 145, 175. — Roger Baja, "Aspects actuels du problème d'évolution," *Revue Thomiste,* 52 (1952), 196–[208] professes that ultimately mutation does not explain the facts any more definitively than either Darwin or Lamarck; along the same lines A.-M. Perreault, "Mutations et évolution," *Revue Thomiste,* 55 (1955), 223, supports the "heated" call for a better explanation of mutations, in Adolf Portmann, "Die werdende Menschheit," in F. Kern's *Historia Mundi* (Bern: Franke, 1952), 1, 21. It is hardly fair to Darwin's express assertions to entitle one's work a "refutation of Darwin's theory of chance," as does Oscar Hertwig, *Das Werden der Organismen: zur Widerlegung von Darwins Zufallstheorie durch das Gesetz in der Entwicklung* (Jena: Fischer, 1922).

least dispel, but only increases, the enigma of how it is that *changes* in species *do* occur.

Not *mere* mutation, but survivals and combinations of mutant and recessive genes, differentiate species.[31]

In this process, great importance attaches to "isolating mechanisms," in which survival of the fittest is conspicuously operative. Even the mutation of the gene itself, but more especially its survival and recombination, must truly be called the effect of environment.[32]

Couple this with the fact that the recognizable existing species (attested by survival or fossildom) show undeniable changes of structure *suited* to the altering environment. We are thus forced to conclude that in species differentiation the gene is truly, in a sense not only more microscopic but also less immediately *purposeful* than Lamarck suspected, an "acquired characteristic which is inherited."

Not for easy reading, surely, but for convenience of reference, it may be desirable to provide here for the theologian a fairly extended updating on the biological facts as set forth by Dobzhansky.

"The adaptation to the environment is achieved in animals and plants by changing their genotypes. . . . Genetics does assert that the organism is not endowed with providential ability to respond to the requirements of the environment by producing mutations adapted to those requirements. The mutations produced are, however, determined by the structure of the organism itself, which is of course the result of an historical evolutionary process in which the environment has played a part. The historical process itself . . . is conditioned by the environment through natural selection. . . .

"Mutations are haphazard in that they arise regardless of the needs of the organism at a given time, and hence are far more likely to be deleterious than useful" then and there, Dobzhansky continues. But they establish an adaptiveness *more* useful for long-term survival, and "they are controlled by the structure of the gene itself as well as by the genetic constitution of the organism."

It was held by such biologists as Jordan and Rensch that a normal antecedent of species formation is *allopatry,* meaning isolation from the parent stem. "These views were more or less strongly tinged with

---

[31] Richard Goldschmidt, *The Material Basis of Evolution* (Yale: 1949; ²1960), 249, holds gene-*pattern,* admittedly hostile to neo-darwinism; but pages 70, 89, 104 are even more frankly against Lamarck. And page 384 praises O. Schindewolf, *Paläontologie, Entwicklungslehre und Genetik* (Berlin: Borntrager, 1936), as the only paleontologist whose data permit him *not* to be Lamarckian!

[32] See now Eric C. Rust, "Creation and Evolution," *Review and Expositor* 59/2 (April 1962), 189, citing L. von Bertalanffy, *Problems of Life* (New York: Harper, 1960), 103: "orthogenetic trends may eventually create prerequisites for other and higher achievements. . . . Evolution is not determined merely by accidental factors and the resulting struggle for existence, but also by internal factors."

Lamarckism. Allopatric populations become genetically different, and diverge more and more in the course of time, because they are changed by the different environments which prevail. . . .

"Unsatisfactory as this formulation sounds today, it is only fair to note that while genetics was only groping for its fundamental concepts, the view that organisms are changed by the environment represented no more than a restatement of the observed facts in ambiguous terms."

The twofold ultimate explanation is, for Dobzhansky: (a) differentiation due to modification of gene-frequencies; and in this, environment is in final analysis the directing agent! (b) reproductive isolation effecting species status.

"Organic diversity may be considered an outcome of the adaptation of life to the diversity of environments on our planet. . . . The number of homozygous gene combinations which [one] organism is potentially capable of producing is . . . vastly greater than the estimated number of electrons and protons in the visible universe."

Out of this stupefying number of possible combinations, relatively few "are suitable for the occupation of the existing ecological niches. The observed discontinuity in the body structures and in the ways of life is a result of adaptation to the discontinuity of the secular environments on our planet."

The mechanism of mutation and reproduction is by trial and error.

"This does not mean that the modern theory of evolution is based on a belief in 'chance,' as is often but groundlessly alleged. . . . Evolutionary changes are far from automatic results of lucky throws of the genetical dice, or even of the demands of the environments. The relations between the genetic system and the external milieu are so complex that the evolutionary process can be described as a creative one." By this creative evolution, Dobzhansky seems to mean no more than that the *compounding* of mutational steps involving numerous chromosomal structures is required.

"The opinion of some early geneticists that new species arise by mutation is false as a general proposition."[33]

Here is how we might endeavor to formulate in layman's language our conclusion from this eminent biologist's studied phrases:

Neither lamarckism, nor darwinism, nor mutation, can stand as a global and ultimate explanation of known facts of evolution. Each contributed its element which is still valid today. Each contained errors which had to give way to a more recent formula. Indeed, *all* "laws" of science are provisional formulations in constant growth.

---

[33] Theodosius Dobzhansky, *Genetics and the Origin of Species* (New York: Columbia, 1959 = 1951; 1937), 308, 51, 60, 74, 204 f, 254 f, 278 f. An exception to the last statement is admitted in the relatively rare cases of hastening by polyploidy.

If this be true, then how are we to account for the fact that to scientists "lamarckism" without qualification is pejorative, while darwinism is respectable?

This would seem to be due to the fact that even the *legitimate* aspects of Lamarck lend themselves more readily to a *teleological* and therefore theistic view of the universe. Natural selection, on the other hand, is more congenial to a mentality which prefers to leave "creation by God" out of account without denying it. "Darwinism became the symbol of materialistic thought."[34]

7. Neo-Lamarckism and Orthogenesis

In Nordenskiold's history of biology the movement called neo-lamarckism is grouped along with or in direct succession to Eimer's "orthogenesis." Eimer was in fact hostile to Darwin, and like Hertwig stressed the inner forces of organisms as distinct from mere external selection.

August Pauly, 1850–1914, explicitly advocated what Lamarck is unfairly taxed with: organs changed by "conscious striving towards a goal," then transmitted by heredity. R. Semon, 1859–1919, thought the problem solved by substituting for the one Greek word *character,* another which meant the same thing, *engramm,* in the sense of a genic "recording" of the change. Ludwig Plate at the same period strongly stressed finality, though claiming to be pro-Darwin and anti-Lamarck. Actively antireligious Ernst Haeckel saw his evolutionism as a synthesis of Lamarck, Darwin, and Goethe.

The United States paleontologist Edward Cope reiterated, "Darwin failed to explain 'the *origin* of the fittest.' " Samuel Butler too protested against Darwin's neglect of the active and reactive nature of the organism. "Since the effects of activity can only influence the evolution of the race if they are inherited and passed on to the next generation, all such theories are necessarily Lamarckian."[35]

Currently the most acknowledged "neo-lamarckists" are Lysenko and

---

[34] Oswei Temkin, "The Idea of Descent in Post-Romantic German Biology," in [H.] B. Glass, *Forerunners of Darwin,* p. 325. — "Both classical and modern Darwinism rest the development of their theory upon a denial of intrinsic finality in nature," states Raymond J. Nogar, "The Darwin Centennial: A Philosophical Intrusion," *The New Scholasticism,* 33/4 (Oct. 1959), 411–445. See now S. Cevallos, "Después del centenario de Darwin," *Ciencia y Fe,* 17/3 (July 1961), 289–311. James Collins in the Ong edition of *Darwin's Vision* (footnote 29 above), page 43, modifies his earlier Fordham paper to add: "But Darwin's theory is sufficiently complex to bar the flat alternative that he must either accept or reject this finality."

[35] G. Carter, *A Hundred Years of Evolution,* p. 88. A detailed and quite Teilhardian exposé of neo-lamarckism is given by R. de Sinéty, "Transformisme," *Dictionnaire Apologétique de la Foi Catholique* (Paris: Beauchesne, 1928), 4, 1824–1830.

the Russian biologists as a solid block. It is hardly to be suspected that their motivation is creationistic or theistic. But there is a congeniality to other aspects of marxist ideology in the notion of man *making* his future rather than being tossed about in streams of chance.

The term *orthogenesis* was proposed in 1893 by W. Haacke.[36] It became popularized only in 1897 in the title of a book on butterflies.[37]

Here is one expert's summary of the facts which seemed to warrant the recourse to a term like orthogenesis:

"We often find change continuing in the same direction in a group of animals through very long periods. [In the horse it amounts to sixty million years.] Size should gradually increase — until a point was reached at which further increase of size was no longer beneficial. . . . There is then no difficulty in understanding change in the same direction going on for some time under the influence of selection acting continually in the same direction. . . . Still, the very long periods of these trends of change [as compared with how much has been achieved by domestication in the course of even a few thousand years] has seemed surprising to many biologists. [These postulate orthogenesis:] some inherent character in the animals causing them to evolve in this direction and not in others." The opinion of biologists is almost universally against the necessity for demanding any inherent orthogenetic tendencies to explain these long-continued trends; the evidence is clearly against the need for postulating them.[38]

Now we come to Simpson, one of the greatest biologists of our time. He has made himself resolute spokesman of hostility to orthogenesis, largely in relation to the key use of that term made by Teilhard de Chardin.

He finds orthogenesis variously defined by Teilhard as the "law of controlled complication," which acts "in a predetermined direction," as "the manifest property of living matter to form a system in which 'terms *succeed each other* experimentally, following the constantly-increasing values of centro-complexity,' " or as *"directed* transformation (to whatever degree and under whatever influence 'the direction' may be manifested)."[39]

---

[36] W. Haacke, *Gestaltung und Vererbung* (Leipzig: Weigel, 1893).

[37] G. Eimer, *Die Entstehung der Arten II. Orthogenesis der Schmetterlinge* (Leipzig: Engelmann, 1897).

[38] G. Carter, *A Hundred Years of Evolution,* 173 f. See Wilfrid Le Gros Clark, *The Fossil Evidence for Human Evolution* (Chicago: University, 1955); E. Ford in G. R. de Beer, *Evolution* (London: Oxford, 1938), 43; T. Dobzhansky, *Evolution, Genetics, and Man* (New York: Wiley, 1955), 363, preferring the term "orthoselection."

[39] George Gaylord Simpson, "On the Remarkable Testament of the Jesuit Paleontologist Pierre Teilhard de Chardin," *Scientific American,* 202/4 (April 1960), 204.

Simpson concludes that what Teilhard calls orthogenesis is mere tautology. Evolution is "erratic and opportunistic." The main thesis of *The Phenomenon of Man, "faith* in progress," is to be rejected: not because it is religious, but because it wrongly claims to be scientifically demonstrable.

On the face of it, Simpson seems to be here chiming in with the many theologians who chide Teilhard for destroying the supernatural by claiming to prove it from biology. Looked at more deeply, it must be admitted that for Simpson the ultimate vice of orthogenesis is that it is correlative to theistic creation. Or rather it is the only kind of theistic creation suitable to a specifically evolutionist system.[40]

As against this, we have Dobzhansky situating macroevolutionary changes inside the organism, or inscrutably outside it ("this escapes rigid proof"), a thing which can be called *finalism* as well as orthogenesis.[41]

8. *Theistic Creation and Evolution*

We turn now from a loyal tracing of what biologists have to say in their own terms and categories to append a couple of remarks from scientifically trained theologians.

Overhage adds several names to the minority maintaining orthogenesis as against chance to account for man's biped and cerebral uniqueness.[42]

---

[40] In his *Tempo and Mode in Evolution* (New York: Columbia, 1944), 150 ff, Simpson notes that the name orthogenesis is now often confused with what in 1934 Osborn named aristogenesis; and he includes Teilhard among those who smuggle in a theological or kindred principle in orthogenesis. In *The Meaning of Evolution* (Yale: 1960 = 1949), 292; 186, Simpson calls the teilhardian analogies pernicious. Lamarck is rejected chiefly for his "inner perfecting principle" drawn from Aristotelianism, in the college textbook *Life* (New York: Harcourt, Brace, 1957), 442, which Simpson coauthored with Colin S. Pittendrigh of footnote 25 above; p. 72.

[41] T. Dobzhansky, *Genetics and the Origin of Species,* p. 17. He equates with the term orthogenesis also *hologenesis,* apparently in a sense quite different from that popularized by Daniele Rosa, *L'ologenèse* (Paris: Alcan, 1931), "ubiquitous polygenism," as in footnote 11 to chapter 2 above, p. 38.

[42] (K. Rahner-) Paul Overhage, *Das Problem der Hominisation* (*Quaestiones Disputatae* 12; Freiburg: Herder, 1961), 213: "Denial of orthogenetic or structure-producing procedures in the course of evolution is a necessary outcome of the basic concept of Neo-Darwinism, thus expressed by M. Greene in the *British Journal of Philosophy of Science,* 34 (1958), 125: 'A gene-complex is a sum of independent units . . . of a mosaic rather than a comprehensive kind' "; see further Overhage's pages 100 and 157 on acquired characteristics. Support of Simpson against orthogenesis is noted in G. Heberer's contribution to H. Hofer, *Primatologie* (Basle: 1956), 1, 379–560. But Overhage on page 208 cites these authors as now favorable to orthogenesis: H. Böker, *Einführung in die vergleichende biologische Anatomie der Wirbeltiere* (Jena: 1937); F. Weidenreich, "The Trend of Human Evolution," *Evolution* 1 (1947), 221–236; F. Grünthal, "Zur Frage der Entstehung des Menschenhirns," *Monatsschrift für Psychiatrie und Neurologie,* 115 (1948), 129–160; K. Saller, "Das Menschenbild im Spiegel naturwissenschaftlicher Anthro-

Haldane's (*Paleontology and Transformism*) "There is such a thing as extranuclear heredity," and Cuénot-Tétry's (*Biological Evolution*) "In a general way, nature tends to replace accommodations by a corresponding germinal mutation," both lead Rabut (*Problem of God Engraved on Evolution*) to pose the question, "Does not all this amount to a lamarckian outcome, whatever be the mechanism?"[43]

The doctrine of Creation is shared by Catholics with practically all believers in Christianity or even in monotheism. How precisely this doctrine is to be reconciled with prevailing norms of contemporary science has always been a thorny problem. Diverging solutions have been progressively given.

It was thought until quite recently that evolutionism in any form was incompatible with the divine revelation in the book of Genesis. Even today, not all "believers" admit evolution. We may acknowledge a certain sympathy and respect for fundamentalist Protestants who pursue their convictions in this regard. But it is hard to see how after the pronouncements of Pius XII anyone could still hold evolution to be irreconcilable with Catholic doctrine.

Since no one who accepts scriptural revelation denies the fact of creation by God, it lies outside the purpose of this book to set forth the passages by which this dogma is proved in Scripture. The first verse of Genesis does not perhaps make out as strong a case as is often imagined. What we mean by "immediately out of nothing" is a rather sophisticated concept which is hard to track down in the Semitic mentality. Yet surely the whole burden of all parts of the Bible is that whatever we see around us owes its whole being to God.

Monotheists generally maintain that creation is a tenet not merely of revelation but of purely natural philosophy.

In fact, though few people seem to have noticed this and many perhaps would incline to deny it, reason cannot prove even the existence of God except in and through the proof of creation. Paradoxically, "God as creator" is grasped by our minds *prior* to "God in himself."

Within the domain of purely natural philosophy, a rather limited and post-cartesian group tends to hold that God's creative intervention was necessary at *three* stages: at the first production of anything whatever outside himself, at the emergence of life out of non-living matter, and in the production of every rational soul.

---

pologie," *Umschau,* 52, (1952), 10–13, cf. *Naturwissenschaftliche Rundschau,* 5 (1952), 446–450; H. J. Stammer, "'Trends' in der Phylogenie der Tiere," *Zoologischer Anzeiger,* 162 (1959), 187–208; K. Beurlen, "Die Menschwerdung als paläontologisches Forschungsproblem," *Saeculum,* 1 (1950), 417–428.

[43] Olivier A. Rabut, *Le problème de Dieu inscrit dans l'Évolution* (Paris: Cerf, 1963), 38. Rabut's p. 61 seems to confuse Pre-Thought with orthogenesis in Teilhard. On planetization = hominization see below, pp. 99; 262.

The third stage forms the object of this book. As for the second stage, we will simply dismiss it. Though it has become intrenched in seminary textbooks, it is directly contradictory to the express teaching of Thomas Aquinas and the other leaders of scholastic thought. It is founded on apologetic and theorizing reactions to Descartes, and is extremely liable to disproof experimentally in the laboratory within our own lifetime, as shown on page 31 above.

Reduced to its minimal terms, *creationism* means that whatever *is* owes its ultimate being to at least one initial intervention of God. And what this chapter has wished to insist upon is that there is no conceivable possibility of salvaging Genesis or creation or *theism* on the assumption that God created matter *without knowing what would eventually become of it.*

Vitalism in the hoary sense of "an essential distinction between life and non-life" no longer fits the purviews of either science or theology; but in the sense of "an inner purposeful direction of organisms toward a chosen goal," it is an inescapable correlative of creation by a personal God.

Orthogenesis may be distasteful to scientists as a kind of double talk. But one must ask whether they are really complaining of "ambiguity," or of an all-too-unambiguous influence and plan of a spiritual being whose reality is not measurable or verifiable by experiment.

Does *darwinism* mean "blind chance governing the universe"? Then Darwin is no theist, however much he may have claimed personally to reverence Scripture and the Church of which Queen Victoria was the head.

Does *lamarckism* mean "nature evolving in accord with purposeful intention"? Then however much Lamarck may have claimed personally to despise Scripture and the form of Catholicism which reached him in France, theists are lamarckists, and have no choice except to stand up and be counted.

Preferably, however, it would seem that the tags "darwinian, all good" and "lamarckian, all bad" should be abandoned by biologists in favor of descriptive titles that show accurately where each expert stands on the issue "Is purposeful directedness *compatible with* (even if not *proved by*) the facts firmly ascertained by controlled experiment?"[44]

---

[44] The truth seems to be, however, that Darwin disbelieved in Providence and gradually lost all faith [J. Collins, *Thought* 34 (1959), 193], whereas Lamarck in his *Histoire naturelle des animaux sans vertèbres*, 1, 325, eloquently confesses "The will of God is everywhere expressed by the laws of nature." Lamarck's real insight was that *evolution has a direction*, according to Ruth Moore's survey, *Man, Time, and Fossils* (New York: Knopf, 1953), 88: he was thus the real founder of evolution; in a subtle sense as unsuspected by him as by Darwin, "environment does affect the individual's inheritable make-up." — The zoologist Paul Moody concludes his *Introduction to Evolution* (New York: Harper, 1953), 432, with personal acceptance

For the moment, scientists' hostility to Teilhard's "lamarckian" orthogenesis may be taken as the surest sign he had *not* fallen short of requirements which the dogma of creation irreducibly imposes upon a Catholic.

"Teilhard's thought is unmistakably evolutionary; it is also unmistakably revolutionary; for his is evolution with a difference. It is teleological as opposed to the purely mechanistic form which has long dominated scientific thought. . . . It is goal-directed; indeed evolution is nothing but the continued striving of the cosmos to reach its goal."[45]

---

of God as the source of natural laws of life and the goal of evolutionary process. See also Jaroslav Pelikan, "Creation and Causality in the History of Christian Thought" along with J. F. Ewing on Catholic teaching, in Sol Tax, *Evolution after Darwin* (Chicago University Symposium, 1960), 3, 29–40.

[45] James Quin, "God and Science 6: Teilhard's Visionary Synthesis," *Christian Order* 5/8 (Aug. 1964), 460. Teilhard's *"directed* evolution" supposes someone *directing,* says Paulo Lopes, "Poligenismo e antropologia teológica," *Revista Eclesiástica Brasileira* 21/1 (Mar. 1961), 28–38; 27. Rather than finality, simple direction or trend is often uppermost in Teilhard's mind when he speaks of orthogenesis. But he himself seems to acknowledge that among inner-directed movements of such multiple complexity, genuine direction cannot long be acknowledged without finality: *"I take 'orthogenesis'* in its etymological sense of oriented *development, a purely 'vectorial' quality (without which one could not speak of* TRENDS *or* PHYLA) *which does not in itself convey any idea either of monophyletism* [but see the citation on pages 21 and 24 above] *or (at least in the beginning) of finality":* "Singularities of the Human Species," *Œuvres* 2 = *Appearance of Man* (New York: Harper, 1965), 215 *n.* On page 221 of that essay Teilhard shows by diagram that there is a *twofold* orthogenesis: the outward-going *ramifying* of species which we discuss on page 100 below is a trend *in principle* diverse from nature's other trend toward maximal corpusculization and complexity; only by a singular privilege (called "coincidence" but in its etymological sense of "occurring simultaneously") does the *one* phylum of man express both these trends, because *"the phyletic drift, instead of principally affecting the structure of the limbs, is merged with cephalization."* See also John L. Russell, "The Principle of Finality in the Philosophy of Aristotle and Teilhard de Chardin," *Heythrop Journal,* 3/4 (Oct. 1962), 347–357; 4/1 (Jan. 1963), 32–41, holding on page 40 that by restoring finality on the best empirical basis it has yet had, Teilhard made a clean break with Descartes and William Paley. So too J. Langlois, "Teilhard et la cosmologie," *Sciences Ecclésiastiques,* 16/2 (May 1964), 338. Yet according to W. A. Wallace in *The New Scholasticism* 36/3 (July 1962), 353–367, "The Cosmogony of Teilhard de Chardin" sounds somehow Cartesian, as Louis de Broglie admitted he himself just couldn't help being (p. 362). See Martin Brennan's review of *The Phenomenon* in *Studies,* 49/194 (Summer 1960), 117–130; 119, claiming that sometimes without warning Teilhard attaches new meanings to old words like orthogenesis.

SUMMARY OF THE THIRD CHAPTER,
ON ORTHOGENESIS

Teilhard's view of the creation of the soul should not be evaluated apart from his convictions on creation in general. The great divide in the world of thought is between those who admit any creating God at all and those who do not. Scientists tend to look askance at creation as a thing which cannot be proved. Teilhard preferred not to come to grips with this attitude directly.

Instead he laid great emphasis on the term "orthogenesis," though he knew most scientists spurned it, largely because it was associated with "lamarckism."

Lamarck was a forerunner of Darwin. The difference between them is commonly imagined to consist in the fact that Lamarck considered one species to transform itself into another by the individual specimen's conscious purposeful effort, while for Darwin it was simply a matter of "survival of the fittest" among various births produced altogether by chance. Yet Darwin acknowledges "chance" is the wrong word here, and in fact he subscribes one hundred percent to the transmission of acquired characteristics.

The real difference between the two must then be sought elsewhere. It will be found to consist in the greater emphasis laid by Darwin on the blind or random directions which evolution takes, but by Lamarck on the coherent and continuous trend toward recognizable goals. The hypothesis of a creating God also emphasizes purposefulness in the existing universe. Hence in a general way it must be expected that around Darwin, as against Lamarck, will be polarized the disinclination to admit creation.

Orthogenesis is simply a neutral term to describe the purposefulness or finality observable in the world. But scientists now universally admit, as an indispensable corrective to Darwin's own view, the mechanisms of mendelian heredity. Insofar as these mechanisms are now understood, they unmistakably favor the view that blind random chance or "sport" alone accounts for the transit from one species to another.

Yet experts will agree that Mendel's "genes" precisely do *not* provide the explanation of *why* occasionally there is transmitted from parent to offspring a *species-change*. In the last analysis, this alteration of species is an "acquired character which is transmitted," though not in the sense in which the phrase is commonly taken. Dobzhansky sets forth the facts in technical but understandable terminology.

Yet Teilhard's biologist friend Simpson attacked him strongly for his insistence on orthogenesis. He calls this simply a tautology to cover our failure to discern anything other than the "erratic and opportunistic" in the evolutionary process.

But to maintain that evolution proceeds *altogether* without a plan is ultimately to deny a creating God. Conversely, to cling relentlessly to "Lamarckian orthogenesis" in face of his colleagues' opposition was Teilhard's scientific-jargon way of affirming a creating God as known even to science.

CHAPTER 4

CREATION AS ALPHA POINT

The word *creation* does not occur in the Index of *The Phenomenon of Man*. The fact or mode of the primal origin of matter from God is nowhere made explicit: not even as much as the creation of the human soul in several footnotes. In Teilhard's other writings there is an almost equal reserve.

This silence is understandable and has not in fact scandalized even the most uneasy critics. They could not deny that the whole aim of *The Phenomenon* and of its author's life was to show God's relation to the world of facts known by science. And this relation could be none other than creative.

1. *The Razor-Edge of Conceptual Accuracy*

When the author is not a theologian, it is understandable that he does not subtly refine on the two dangers into which our notion of creation is apt to fall. It can be distorted by excess and by defect. This is not a snare special to the case of creation. Truth itself, the truth of any concept involving judgment, is a thin line; and error lies in deviating a hair's breadth on the side of the angels just as surely as on the side of the rebels.

By defect, creation risks being seen as mere carpentry. If chaos or formless matter was already there before the creative activity of God, then his contribution must consist simply in a clever reassembling of the elements to make them go. This is precisely what "creative" means nowadays: one of the key words in the valuation of personality and self-realization.

On the other hand, "out of nothing" is a rather hoary embalmed concept. But it is also a highly sophisticated concept, which not everybody is capable of understanding. And no passage of divine revelation, not even the opening word of Genesis, excludes preexisting material with that explicitness which is often too casually assumed.

By excess, creation risks being seen as a snipping off of some of the substance of God. Only by setting ourselves in the direction of this error, can we rectify our imagination's grasp of nothingness as building blocks.

Creation *is* in simple fact a communication of something from within God himself, not once for all many centuries ago, but continuing at moments ever equally present to the point-size eternity of God.

That something communicated by God is Being or Reality. Whatever we mean by Being, it is within God in its totality, and there is nothing else whatever within God. So here again, it is not child's play to form a notion of creation which will be completely free from pantheistic notions.

Let us admit it: *these two snares* were not fully escaped by Teilhard. He speaks expressly of "his own pantheism," which he tries to hedge by suitable qualifications.[1] But he is also accused of ascribing to matter some reality independent or prior to the creative activity of God.

Our concern here is not to defend him from these charges. Much less is it to make him out guilty of them, as some have felt to be the aim of an article which we published on this subject.[2]

What is needed here is simply an appraisal of the elements which Teilhard's view on creation in general contributes to a sound Christian doctrine on the creation of the soul.

2.   *Eternal Matter and Creative Union*

The fear that for Teilhard the visible universe depends *insufficiently* upon God revolves chiefly about three points. Matter seems to be eternal. Its presence and evolution seem to be somehow necessary even to God himself. And the very nature of the creative process is presented as a bringing together of preexisting realities.

Matter eternal? One verdict is that in Teilhard's writings, "creation

---

[1] See footnote 77, p. 112, below.

[2] Robert North, "Teilhard and the Problem of Creation," *Theological Studies,* 24/4 (Dec. 1963), 577–601.

is so little brought out that the reader is left with the impression that matter is eternal in itself."[3]

This judgment hits more directly at uncautious readers than at the man himself. Moreover, the critic wrongly implies that the eternity of the visible universe is automatically incompatible with creation. Efforts to prove this are well known to the history of scholastic thought. They involve highly controverted speculations and end up without agreed probative force. "Of its nature, time does not suppose a real beginning or a real end. Creation *ab aeterno* is considered possible by many."[4]

To say that for Teilhard matter is "eternal" can mean no more than that it possesses a *duration* without beginning or end. But this is not the real definition of eternity, "simultaneous and interminable possession of one's total reality." In neither of these senses does Teilhard regard matter as eternal. For him the very nature of the evolutionary process is tightly bound up with space and time.

His calculations, which carry us back millions and billions of years behind the state of things perceptible today, would have no force except in relation to some "absolute zero." Such a zero can itself doubtless never be attained by our measurements. It may even be considered devoid of interest for the scientist, just as he would think the effort wasted to get out to the "absolute farthest" point of the cosmos in any direction. Such an enterprise would be foredoomed to vague and hypothetical conclusions reached by brushing past many concrete and measurable data along the way.

Finally, Teilhard's pattern of evolution, closing in upon itself since the arrival of man and converging toward the unity of a single point, implies that its origin was equally from a single point, as we shall see.

Creation necessary? One of the earliest and most slashing attacks upon Teilhard declares that for him creation is necessary and not gratuitous.[5]

In a way this charge already involves a kind of admission that Teilhard truly believed in creation. But the situation is not the same here as with "creation from all eternity." In principle, or rather as a quibble

---

[3] Michelangelo Alessandri, "Il pensiero di Pierre Teilhard de Chardin," *Divinitas*, 3/2 (1959), 342.

[4] A. Michel, "Éternité," *Dictionnaire de Théologie Catholique* (Paris: Letouzey, 1913), 5, 921. According to A.-D. Sertillanges, *L'idée de la création* (Paris: 1945), 5–24, the last word of Saint Thomas (*Gentes* 2,31–37; *Potency* 3,17; *Summa* 1,46, 1) is that *faith* compels us to reject the eternity of the world, but from reason alone no proof can be given. See now Sertillanges "L'évolution selon saint Thomas et Teilhard de Chardin," *L'univers et l'âme* (Paris: Éditions Ouvrières, 1965), 19–50.

[5] Louis Cognet, *Le père Teilhard de Chardin et la pensée contemporaine* (Paris: Flammarion, 1952), 146.

of metaphysical terminology, it is possible for the whole universe to *depend* upon God for its being, but from eternity. But if God did not *freely* create, then the universe does not *depend* upon his will, in the sense which creationism has in Catholic theology.

Of course there are many ways in which reality depends upon God other than by a free act of his will. Notably a man's act of wickedness or sin could not be performed without many kinds of God's present co-operation, but this does not mean that God freely chooses to cooperate with the sinful act. God's freedom is considered to be limited by the internal possibilities of things; he cannot make a triangle other than with three sides, or a free agent other than with power to make an effective free choice.

Outside God too, one thing can "depend" upon another which has no choice in the matter. A child's red hair or male sex "depends" entirely upon the two parents who proximately furnished the gene determinants, even though they with all their hearts wanted a black-haired girl. But the parents are at least free (individually if not sociologically) to have a child or not to have one. Suspension of iron filings from a magnet "depends" upon the magnet, even though there is no free choice at all in that case.

Does the universe depend upon God only like the iron filings, in the sense that God furnishes its being because it is his nature to do so and he has no choice in the matter? In this case the universe must be regarded as a mere working out of the being of God; or, what amounts to the same thing, this alleged God is merely one of the component forces of the universe.

The situation is essentially the same if God is like the parents, free only to produce or not to produce, yet unable to determine the detailed nature of the product. In either case, what is called "creation" is in reality a mechanical working out of forces planted within the agent and beyond his control.

This is not creation at all. It is not even a claim that matter is preexisting in expectation of God's creative activity. It is rather a form of pantheism.

In this sense, as we shall see, Teilhard does indeed leave himself open to the charge leveled by Cognet. He holds that not only creation but even incarnation and redemption are in some sense necessary.[6]

---

[6] "The primacy of the Incarnation implies a certain necessity of creation": Adolf Haas, "Schöpfungslehre . . . bei Teilhard," *Scholastik*, 39 (1964), 512. — "No one can explain how and why matter was in a position to become self-conscious and loving. We are confronted with the fact, but it is too much for us. It is a supreme creation; we call it God's image [God brought man to be from the seeds he planted at the start.] God's whole creation, including the Incarnation, is evolutionary cosmogenesis": Joan Vandenberg, "Drie typen in evoluerend Kristendom," *Bijdragen*, 22/1 (1965), 26 f. See further p. 147 below.

But words must not be pressed without regard for their setting. The Church calls Adam's sin "truly necessary," and precisely *because* it brought about the Redemption: which therefore must be in turn even more necessary. But the "necessity" here is unquestioningly taken as "involving certain suppositions." When these are enumerated, the "truth" of the assertion turns out to be not noticeably different from that of a "poetic exaggeration." At least it will look that way to the person inexperienced with such juggling.

Teilhard deplored the manner in which classic philosophy and theology regards creation as "an arbitrary gesture of a first cause." He hints that there would be no God without creation; that there is a blank which somehow has to be filled. Creation is thus not absolutely gratuitous but instead represents a work of almost absolute self-interest on God's part. This has caused considerable dissatisfaction to a competent theologian whose views were given a spurious air of official ecclesiastical promulgation.[7]

We will try to see how the "necessity" of redemption and of creation itself is seen by Teilhard as a corollary of a greater and divinely revealed "necessity" that Christ should be "all in all." It may be serenely debated whether *within that framework* it is desirable to speak of any "necessity" for creation at all, or whether Teilhard would have been better advised to steer clear altogether of such implications.

Creative Union? Very early in his priesthood, Teilhard formed a notion of "creative transformation," in reacting to an article of de la Taille on Contemplative Prayer.[8] This was doubtless linked with similar-sounding insights of Bergson, especially his *élan vital*. Indeed, it has been claimed that the whole first period of Teilhard's writings, from 1909 to 1926, is characterized by an effort to break away from Bergson's influence.[9]

[7] [Jean Rambaud] Philippe de la Trinité, "Teilhard de Chardin: Synthèse ou confusion?," *Divinitas*, 3/2 (1959), 320, 285–329. This essay seems to be at the base of an article, unsigned and not of Père Philippe's authorship, in *Osservatore Romano* for July 1, 1962, a copy of which was sent around along with the *Monitum* of June 30 under the letterhead of Holy Office secretary Sebastian Masala; see Anastasio Gomes, "A New Monitum," *Eucharist and Priest*, 68 (1962), 246–9. The *Osservatore* article and the legitimacy of its vaguely official character are defended by Philippe in *Seminarium*, 16 (1964), 79(–121), mostly against R. Leys, "Teilhard dangereux?," *Bijdragen*, 24/1 (Jan. 1963), 9. On page 81 Père Philippe has this remarkable judgment: "Teilhard does harm. That is a fact. He was a great mind but in dogma a false mind; therefore a great false mind."

[8] Maurice de la Taille, "L'oraison contemplative," *Recherches de Science Religieuse*, 9/5 (Sept. 1919), 273–292; on page 287 is expressed the law of progress and development, even by means of frustration.

[9] Herbert Musurillo, review of *The Phenomenon of Man*, in *Thought*, 35/138 (Oct. 1960), 450; see also August Brunner, "Pierre Teilhard de Chardin," *Stimmen der Zeit*, 165 (1959), 210–222 [= *Theology Digest*, 8/3 (Autumn 1960), 143–7], and Adolf Portmann, *Der Pfeil des Humanen: Über P. Teilhard de Chardin* (Freiburg: Alber, 1960), 9.

"Creation is an act of uniting" is a favorite Teilhard expression, which even his warm friend de Lubac deplores as a kind of admission of preexisting matter. However, in his 1917 article entitled *L'union créatrice,* Teilhard had clarified, "There where is found complete disunion of the cosmic stuff (at an infinite distance from Omega), there is *nothing.*"[10]

As he grew older, he owned up to a great sympathy for the writings of Lecomte du Noüy and Édouard Le Roy in defense of "creative evolution."[11] Le Roy was in fact made the target of an ecclesiastical condemnation for ideas which Teilhard continued admitting to be very close to his own.[12] The work of Lecomte du Noüy is often cited as relevant to Teilhard, but I have found in it nothing to compel comparison.[13]

The objections against *l'union créatrice* are summed up somewhat as follows. The "subject" on which the creative act is worked out seems to be a nothingness which is too "positive." Actually this is good scholastic terminology: "absolute" nothing is that which cannot be created at all, because it is a contradiction in terms; "positive" nothing is that "out of which" God creates, and which is defined as "the *possibility* of being created or of becoming *something.*"[14] In the light of these textbook commonplaces, there should be nothing at all shocking when Teilhard

---

[10] Teilhard, "L'union créatrice" (1917), *Écrits du temps de la guerre (1916–1919)* (Paris: Grasset, 1965). See p. 208, footnote 6, below.

[11] Max Begouën, *Quelques souvenirs sur le mouvement des idées transformistes dans les milieux catholiques* (Paris: Bloud, 1945), 27, notes pioneering of Jesuit Carbonelle in the 1887 Brussels *Revue des Questions Scientifiques;* also J. Guibert, *Les origines* (Paris: Letouzey, 1896); but page 34 declares that Teilhard by his articles in *Études* and *Scientia* "affirmed himself as uncontested leader of Catholic transformist teaching," in relation to Le Roy and Lecomte du Noüy.

[12] Édouard Le Roy, *Les origines humaines et l'évolution de l'intelligence* (Paris: Boivin, 1931), the work which was put on the Index, entitles its first chapter *Le phénomène humain,* and says on page 8 that the book is altogether dependent upon discussions with Teilhard de Chardin and implicit citing of even his unpublished works, especially "L'hominisation" [Œuvres 3, *La vision du passé* (Paris: Seuil, 1957), 75–111]; Chapter 3 is entitled "La noösphère et l'hominisation"; Chapter 9, "L'apparition de l'homme." Le Roy earlier wrote *L'exigence idéaliste et le fait de l'Évolution* (Paris: Boivin, 1927); and now *Essai d'une philosophie première* (Paris: Presses Universitaires, 1956), of which Émile Rideau says in *La pensée de Teilhard* (Paris: Seuil, 1965), 92, that Teilhard's realism sundered him from Le Roy, an idealist admitting only thought.

[13] Pierre Lecomte du Noüy, *Human Destiny* (New York: Longmans, 1947); *Le temps et la vie*[25] (Paris: Gallimard, 1936); *La dignité humaine* (New York: Brentano, 1944). This last work, on page 169, in noting the resistance of the churches to evolution, praises the Catholic Church for having "given in"; and points out the real enemy of the churches is superstition.

[14] P.-B. Grenet, "D'une très curieuse opinion sur l'être en puissance," *Revue Thomiste,* 65/3 (July 1965), 427–436, defends his view that potency is simply the negation of realization, against the equating of potency with Teilhard's pre-life in P. Smulders, *Vision de Teilhard* (Paris: Desclée, 1964), 78. On page 434 Grenet claims that both Bergson and Teilhard err in too strongly rejecting all negativity. See above, Chapter 1, footnotes 68 and 69, pp. 29–30.

speaks of a creatable nothingness which has already sufficient reality to
enable it to be called "a plea for being."

Nevertheless, the sentence "To create, following our appearances, is
to unify" is criticized as implying that there exists a Thing, dissociated
by nature, and prerequisite to the act of creative union. This is said to
mean that the Creator has found outside himself a beachhead or at
least a reaction.

These objections, as we just showed, can be handled within the traditional scholastic terminology, or rectified with its help. But a different
path is taken by Tresmontant, a layman who has been justly praised for
restoring Old Testament categories to a milieu dominated by Greek
speculative patterns.[15] He asserts that Teilhard has performed a valued
service in clarifying the notions of creation and omnipotence.[16]

Our common or at least implicit Christian view is that God had the
freedom and the capability to make participated being arise in any state
of perfection and association at all. This seemed to Teilhard a fantasy
incompatible with the deepest conditions of being as manifested by our
experience. Beirnaert defends Teilhard by an appeal to Irenaeus, paraphrased as saying "God of himself could have created man 'done'
(*téleion*), but man's own nature is incapable of such an operation."[17]
To create must not be taken by us after the fashion of an instantaneous
act, even on the part of omnipotence. If God leaves us to suffer, to sin,
to doubt, it is because he could not, now and at one stroke, heal us
and show himself. Our doubts, as our evils, are the price and condition
of a universal perfecting.[18]

---

[15] Claude Tresmontant, *Study of Hebrew Thought* [= *Essai sur la pensée hebraïque*, Lectio Divina 12 (Paris: Cerf, 1953)] (New York: Desclee, 1960).

[16] Tresmontant, *Études de métaphysique biblique* (Paris: Gabalda, 1955), 126.

[17] Irenaeus, *Heresies* 4,38,4; *MG* 7,1109: "Altogether unreasonable are those
who do not await the time of growth, but blame the weakness of their nature on
God. . . . We blame on him that we were not made gods at once from the
beginning, but first men and then gods: though God did this according to the
simplicity of his goodness, in such a way that none should think him jealous or
ungenerous. He indeed said [Ps 82H,6] 'You are gods, and all sons of the Most
High'; but when we were unable to bear the power of divinity, he said, 'You will
die as men.' " — Louis Beirnaert, "Temps et croissance spirituelle," *Construire*
[= wartime *Études*, after Volume 143], 13 (1943), 81; 75–91.

[18] Claude Tresmontant, *Teilhard de Chardin* [= *Introduction à la pensée de
Teilhard* (Paris: Seuil, 1956)] (Baltimore: Helicon, 1959), 23. The summary of
Eva Kushner, "Tresmontant on Teilhard de Chardin," *Revue de l'Université
d'Ottawa*, 35/1 (Jan. 1965), 103, holds that Teilhard's "scientific" synthesis, distinct from the "theological" and followed by Tresmontant, is "the description
of a unifying and ultimately convergent Evolution without the slightest appeal
or even reference to the existence or nature of its final cause"; but as the last
term of this *scientific* part "we are told that this final goal of evolution must be
of a personal nature, that it must have immense powers of attraction and must,
furthermore, transcend the cosmic process of evolution in order to be able to pull
that process towards itself." See pp. 5 and 81 above.

Perhaps Tresmontant is on the right track in vindicating a certain literalness for some biblical expressions that have been too readily dismissed as anthropomorphisms. But I do not think that either the defense of Tresmontant, or the disapproval of de Lubac, really does justice to the meaning Teilhard himself attached to the bold expressions he used.

In a mature refocusing of his youthful views, Teilhard declares it is wrong to imagine that the act of unifying can be exercised *only* on a preexisting substrate.[19] This claim is rather hard for our imagination to grasp, and may even end up being rejected as double-talk and metaphysical contradiction. Nevertheless, it shows that its author did *not* have the intention of seriously defending a creation in which God would be either not free or not the genuine cause of all reality whatsoever. Teilhard was fumbling or groping for suitable expressions to reconcile these convictions with observed phenomena which had been too little taken into account.

3. *Chaos and Nothingness in Creation Narratives*

We have seen Teilhard's express statement that he did not mean to affirm or suppose a chaos or preexisting matter prior to God's creative act. But neither does he presume to clarify, as part of the observed phenomenon, what exactly is the "nothing" which "pleads for being" and "out of which" God drew the universe.

In this reserve, Teilhard is faithful to the hard-won insights of the best present-day exegesis.[20] There is simply no correlation between the imagery of Genesis and the ultimates of geology, or the concrete traits of paleontological man.

Some Catholics go rather far in denying to the author of Genesis *all* intention of describing the physical and cosmological facts of the origin of the universe. "Genesis has nothing to tell us about the structure of the universe or the processes of its development. The author had no thought of inquiring whether the setting he designed for his religious teaching corresponded or not with objective reality; this aspect of the question did not figure in the religious plan he had conceived. . . . There is no error when nothing is asserted, or when an assertion is true except from a standpoint wholly foreign to the meaning a writer intends to convey and to the expectation of the readers to whom he addresses his words. [If God *had* intended to reveal geogony,] what words could he have found? Would he have employed a scientific terminology such as is

---

[19] Teilhard, "Comment je vois," not in Œuvres 1–7; cited by de Lubac, *Pensée*, 288; "Comment je crois" (1934) as well as "Comment je vois" (1948) is announced for Œuvres 10. See M.-Michel Labourdette, "L'œuvre de Teilhard," *Revue Thomiste* 64/3 (July 1964), 432.

[20] On Teilhard and Genesis, see footnote 9, Chapter 1; and footnote 2, Chapter 6, pp. 4 and 164.

current among astronomers, chemists, and physicists of today? What could his readers have made of all this?"[21]

Well-founded and impressive are the words with which Vollert here concludes, and those of Hauret which they echo.[22] But not all will agree that his preceding assertion is the necessary or only corollary. It is hard to withhold our approval from recent Protestant insistence that the author of Genesis 1 surely *did* intend to give a description of the *physical* origins of the world, not *merely* its theological significance.[23] This is a corollary of Fohrer's earlier-noticed claim that de Fraine unduly whittles down what Genesis intended to tell us about the physical state of our first parents.[24]

At any rate, where Vollert says the author had no thought of whether his setting corresponded to objective reality, we should greatly prefer to say this: "The objective reality *which* the author indubitably felt to correspond with the setting he designed, was not necessarily 'scientific' or 'historical' in our atomic-age understanding of the elements involved;

---

[21] Cyril Vollert, "The Bible and Evolution," in B. Boelen, *Symposium on Evolution* (Pittsburgh: Duquesne, 1959), 92; cf. 107; and his "Evolution of the Human Body: Scientific *Status Quo* and Theological Implications," *Proceedings of the Catholic Theological Society of America*, 6 (1951), 122–145 [= *Catholic Mind*, 50/3 (March 1952), 135–154]. Further Nicolas Corte (pen-name of Léon Cristiani), *Origins of Man*, and Rémy Collin, *Evolution*, both in H. Daniel-Rops, *Twentieth Century Encyclopedia of Catholicism* (New York: Hawthorn, 1958–9); P. Hermand, "Les origines de l'homme," *Revue Thomiste*, 57/1 (Jan. 1957), 129–188; H. Renckens, *Israel's Concept of the Beginnings* (New York: Herder and Herder, 1963); M. Grison, *Problèmes d'Origines* (Paris: Letouzey, 1954), 25. For technical details see Wilfrid F. LeGros Clark, *The Fossil Evidence for Human Evolution* (Chicago: University, 1955), and Loren C. Eiseley, "Fossil Man and Evolution," in W. Thomas, *Current Anthropology* (Chicago: University, 1956: an updating of A. Krober's 1953 *Anthropology Today*, to which Teilhard contributed pages 93–101, "The Idea of Fossil Man").

[22] Charles Hauret, *Beginnings: Genesis and Modern Science* (Dubuque: Priory, 1955), 56: If God had had Genesis written to embody a maximum of scientific truth, he would have said, "In the beginning, two billion years ago, the earth, a tiny bit of an immense gaseous mass, was hurled some 100,000,000 miles into space, away from the sun of which it was a millionth. God then caused life to appear, over 800,000,000 years, culminating in man." Hauret notes that the listeners would have been crushed at the implication that God was so weak he needed millions of years. More relevant, though, is the likelihood that if human science continues its growth for another 3000 years, its formulations will then make ours seem as naïve as Genesis by comparison.

[23] Siegfried Herrmann, "Die Naturlehre des Schöpfungsberichtes: Erwägungen zur Vorgeschichte von Gen 1," *Theologische Literaturzeitung*, 86/6 (June 1961), 413 (–424); Gerhard von Rad, *Old Testament Theology* (New York: Harper and Row, 1962), I, 148, and "Aspekte alttestamentlichen Weltverständnisses," *Evangelische Theologie*, 24/2 (Feb. 1964), 58.

[24] See above, footnote 57 to p. 54; further Ivan Engnell, "Die Urmenschvorstellung und das Alte Testament," *Svensk Exegetisk Årsbok*, 22/3 (1958), 265–289, regarding Sigmund Mowinckel's "Urmensch und 'Königsideologie,'" *Studia Theologica*, 2/1 (1948), 71–89. Engnell denies that Adam as "corporate mankind" fits the intention of Genesis 1–3.

but it nevertheless was felt to be and *was* a truly suitable description of the phenomena *as* grasped by unsophisticated observers." In the same way the Genesis author puts "relationships" of blood between Semite and Hamite tribes in a way which corresponded to his proximate experience of unities among his neighbors rather than to ethnic biology. In the same way it is still "true" today to say "the sun has *set*" to express the fact that we can actually *see* it "setting": irrespective of whether or not we happen to know that the phenomenon would be described differently by an astronomer or even by a plain uneducated observer situated elsewhere in the solar system.

Another Jesuit scholar proposes a formulation which is perhaps more guarded and accurate. The Genesis redactor, in merely juxtaposing two separate creation narratives without any concern for harmonizing them, "thereby informs us, after his fashion, that neither of these popular narratives can lay claim to a rigorous objectivity and that consequently he himself was not making each of the details of these accounts the object of an affirmation."[25]

Yet he *was* making *some* affirmation, not only about the divine nature and activity and men's consequent orientation, but also about how the material universe in fact came into being.[26] This affirmation, however, is limited to what the author could and did know about the matter, largely from Babylonian and Egyptian sources couched in mythological though not thereby automatically "erroneous" terms.[27] At any rate he was certainly not making affirmations in the terms of a science and a world outlook utterly alien to his perspective.

Three incalculably valuable truths about the fact and manner of creation are conveyed in the carefully chosen and expurgated Babylonian imagery of Genesis 1–2. The activity of Israel's sole God, unlike that

---

[25] Gustav Lambert, "L'Encyclique 'Humani Generis' et l'Écriture Sainte," *Nouvelle Revue Théologique,* 73 (1951), 242; further "Le drame du jardin d'Éden," 76 (1954), 917–948, 1044–1072; and "La création dans la Bible," 75 (1953), 256: "Israel did not succeed without difficulty in liberating itself from ancient oriental conceptions of a primordial state of things before the orderly operative creation."

[26] See now G. Gloege, "Schöpfungsglaube und Weltbild," in Festschrift H. Vogel, *Vom Herrengeheimnis der Wahrheit* (Berlin: 1962), 158–178.

[27] On the problem of Babylonian materials, see John L. McKenzie, "The Literary Form of Genesis 1–3," *Myths and Realities* (Milwaukee: The Bruce Publishing Company, 1963), 154; Luis Arnaldich, *El origen del mundo y del hombre según la Biblia* ² (Madrid: Rialp, 1958), 43. On the Egyptian Hermopolis belief in primeval powers raising out of the great deep a hill topped by light, see K. Sethe, *Amun und die acht Urgötter von Hermopolis* (Berlin: Preussische Abhandlungen, 1929); A. H. Sayce, "The Egyptian Background of Genesis 1," *Studies Presented to F. L. Griffith* (London: Egypt Exploration Society, 1932), 419–423; H. Bonnet, "Achtheit," *Reallexikon der ägyptischen Religionsgeschichte* (1952), 293 and 8.

of the multiple and quarreling pagan titans, is shown to be utterly un-hampered by: (a) resistance of any material; (b) intrigues of rival divinities; (c) false starts of his own.

This amounts to an impressive affirmation that the whole of the visible universe as we see it around us owes its total reality to the irresistible will of one sole God. This, as far as it goes, is a great deal: even though upon closer look it leaves certain questions unanswered, or rather simply unasked.

The two chapters when compared together do not in fact categorically clarify what part of their expression is anthropomorphism and what is not. Specifically, they do not put beyond doubt that God's creative act was solely one of will, not even a "word" in the human sense of that term, especially in the *sequence* of separate words so vividly distinguished in the first chapter. God's "molding mud and blowing breath" are doubtless meant to imply in men's regard some activity more "attentive" than the general decrees by which subhuman reality came into being. But there is really no hint that these various dramatizations are to be all reduced to one single act of will involving no change in God!

Granted these irreproachable *omissions* of the narrative, there need be no hesitation in admitting that the text simply does not pronounce upon the nature of that prior condition *"out of* which" God created the universe.

The word nothingness or nothing does not occur in Genesis. And this would not surprise us if we realized how relatively late and sophisticated this notion is in human experience. The invention of the zero was a surprisingly tardy forward step in the history of mathematics; and even our "zero" represents a midpoint among positive quantities (as on a thermometer); we have come to regard it as an amount from which a good deal can still be subtracted.

The notion of "nothing" is in Hebrew expressed rarely and awkwardly by terms like *epes,* "absence or negation of."

The embarrassment at dealing with nothingness finds an echo in the very latest development of modern philosophy. The importance and positive content adjudged to "nothingness" by Sartre is well known to be one of the admired and not easily refuted currents of existentialism. Trained philosophers disgusted by this trend would perhaps be open-eyed if they could gather some data about the manner in which various devout Christians represent to themselves the "nothing *out of* which" God created the universe.

When once we accustom ourselves to the historically documented difficulty which blocked the human mind in arriving at a notion of genuine zero or nothingness, we will be in a position to evaluate what the author of Genesis 1 was aiming to say.[28] The "primeval ocean" familiar from Babylonian myths may well have been the nearest expression a Hebrew writer could find for his conviction that before God's activity there was nothing there at all.[29]

In taking up this view against Barth's claim that the chaos is a diabolical and caricatured reality "which cannot make anything better of itself," Galling has shown that there is no *dissent* between the priestly writer of Genesis and the author of Second Maccabees 7:28 describing creation "out of nothing."[30] The nature of the "abyss," too, is better understood when we reflect that the "Spirit of God" hovering over it *may* perhaps according to normal Hebrew parlance be translated simply "a strong wind."[31]

---

[28] P. de Haes, "Het scheppingsgeloof in het Oude Testament," *Collectanea Mechlinensia*, 46/5 (Aug. 1961), 449–461; 463: *"Everything is created by God: that is the reality and the fact. . . . All the rest is illustration of this basic affirmation";* further his *De schepping als heilsmysterie; onderzoek der bronnen* (The Hague: 1962).

[29] Walther Zimmerli, *1. Mose 1–11: Die Urgeschichte* (Zürich: Zwingli, 1943), 36: "Can even we do any better? can that Nothingness really be 'rightly' described?" So also John L. McKenzie, *The Two-Edged Sword* (Milwaukee: Bruce, 1956), 84. According to Erik Hornung, "Chaotische Bereiche in der geordneten Welt," *Zeitschrift für ägyptische Sprache*, 81 (1956), 28 f, "Un-World" rather than chaos would be the better term; the creation is not strictly delimited as against that which was before it; in *ZäS*, 67 (1931), 34–38, Hermann Grapow, "Die Welt vor der Schöpfung," contends that the portrayals of "nothingness" in the Egyptian Pyramid texts and elsewhere are not borrowed from Babylon, nor vice versa, but reflect a common experience of humanity everywhere. But E. F. Sutcliffe, "Primeval Chaos not Scriptural," *Miscellanea Biblica* (Rome: Pontifical Biblical Institute, 1934), 2, 203–215, holds that the now all-but-universal view of the "chaotic" first state is without foundation; the terms "empty" and "void" mean simply there was no vegetation or people yet.

[30] Kurt Galling, "Der Charakter der Chaosschilderung in Genesis 1, 2," *Zeitschrift für Theologie und Kirche*, 47/2 (1950), 145–157; Karl Barth, *Kirchliche Dogmatik*, 3/1 (1945), 119. — Otto Kaiser, *Die mythische Bedeutung des Meeres in Ägypten, Ugarit und Israel* (Beiheft 78 to *ZAW;* Berlin: Töpelmann, 1959), 120: Genesis 1 leads inevitably *behind* the tensions in its expression, to a transcendental God creating out of nothing; the "divine-fiat strand" is *later* than the "seven-day-toil-strand," as held by G. von Rad, *Priesterschrift im Hexateuch* (BWANT 65; Stuttgart: 1934), against J. Morgenstern, *American Journal of Semitic Languages*, 36 (1920), 169–212. — Against H. A. Brongers, *De scheppingstradities bij de profeten* (1945), J. van der Ploeg, "Sens du verbe *bara*" *Le Muséon*, 59 (1946), 143–157, holds *bara* is not a simple synonym of *yaṣar/'aśa* ("fashion; make"): "God could make whatever he wanted, immediately and without effort; that *implies* the idea of creation out of nothing . . . always with a margin of uncertainty from the purely exegetic standpoint."

[31] W. H. McClellan, "The Meaning of *rûaḥ elōhîm* in Genesis 1, 2," *Biblica* 15 (1934), 517–527, aims to show that the rendition "strong wind" adopted by the Chicago Bible was not in fact favored by the Church Fathers: thus correcting Kazimierz Smoroński, "Et spiritus Dei ferebatur super aquas," *Biblica*, 6 (1925), 293; though the rest of Smoroński's article (pp. 140–156, 275–293, 361–395) favors a rendition guardedly approaching "God's (Holy) Spirit." See below, footnote 83 to chap. 6, p. 195.

The extent to which "creation out of nothing" may be found in Genesis 1 will depend largely on whether the second verse (chaos) is taken as parenthetical to describe a state of affairs which really preceded the first (God's total creativity). The controversy over this point continues unabated, thanks largely to one of Humbert's statistically documented researches. He translates, "When God began to create (the world being then chaos), he said, 'Let there be light.' "[32]

Refutation of this position by other experts more recently is impressive but can hardly be called definitive.[33] Among these refutations, there is a Catholic one which goes on to add, "The message of Genesis 1 against all ancient cosmogonies, in which a theogony always forms part, is that the Creation God did not become such at some point in the past, but showed himself ever present as such."[34] This formula will be seen to fit our own approach to justifying theologically the oft-repeated teilhardian claim that "creation is cosmogenesis" continuing constantly around us.

In this connection we may anticipate here also another thing which we will have to say later about Teilhard's *alpha* discernible only in his *omega*. The chaos with which Genesis opens has been evaluated as a reflection of the cataclysm expected to occur at the end of time. This "eschatalogical" insight already in 1895 gave the title to Gunkel's "Creation and Chaos at the Beginning and End of Time."[35] Others too have noticed

---

[32] Paul Humbert, "Encore le premier mot de la Bible," *Zeitschrift für die Alttestamentliche Wissenschaft,* 76/1 (1964), 121–131, and *Interpretationes S. Mowinckel* (1955), 85; similarly W. Lane, "The Initiation of Creation," *Vetus Testamentum,* 13/1 (1963), 63–73. Humbert's "Emploi et portée du verbe *bârâ* (créer) dans l'Ancien Testament," *Theologische Zeitschrift,* 3/6 (Nov. 1947), 401–422, holds the portrayal to be practically of exilic origin (p. 415): not a monolithic fixed concept but a moving theologumenon (p. 421).

[33] Walther Eichrodt, "In the Beginning," in Festschrift James Muilenburg, *Israel's Prophetic Heritage,* edited by B. Anderson (New York: Harper, 1962), 1–10, holding an *absolute* beginning, not merely relative as Humbert.

[34] Hubert Junker, "In Principio Creavit Deus Coelum et Terram: eine Untersuchung zum Thema Mythos und Theologie," *Biblica,* 45/4 (Oct. 1964), 488, 477–490. In his "Die theologische Behandlung der Chaosvorstellung in der biblischen Schöpfungsgeschichte," *Mélanges A. Robert* (Paris: Bloud, 1958), 27–37, Junker interprets the biblical chaos as "the building-stones of world-order corresponding to the incomprehensible power and greatness of the creator" (p. 37), neither excluding nor clearly implying "out of nothing."

[35] Hermann Gunkel, *Schöpfung und Chaos in Urzeit und Endzeit* (Göttingen: Vandenhoeck, 1895 ²1921), 67, sees the sea, reeds, Rahab, and Leviathan as alternative "Chaos-beings." But page 112 says that in Israel as in Babylon the original All was ocean. — For Sverre Aalen, *Die Begriffe 'Licht' und 'Finsternis' im Alten Testament, im Spätjudentum und im Rabbinismus* (Oslo: 1951), 9, "Darkness and especially the primitive ocean are indeed 'chaos' powers, but the victory over them lies not in their annihilation but in a demarcation which effects an equilibrium."

that the Bible makes creation an echo or aspect of the awaited eschatological consummation. This is true most strongly in Second Isaiah.[36] But it is variously illustrated in the Priestly Creation account, notably in the fact that for God to call his work "very good" and to "rest" means to regard it as having in some sense reached its *term,* just as for New Testament eschatology the (first) coming of Jesus is itself already in a certain true sense the End of the World.[37] We may hold with some assurance that what the biblical writers have to tell us about the *beginning* of the world is at least in part an extrapolation from what they know by revelation about its *end.*

Whatever the relevance of this rather fresh approach to the chaos-nothingness equation, we can no longer deny that the opening chapters of Genesis are in a true sense extrapolation. Though inspired, they are not a transcription of events either historically recorded or explicitly revealed. They are a *reasoning backward,* from the facts known in the time of the author, to the initial state which must be presumed in order to account for them. Thus they are a form of "Biblical Wisdom Literature."[38] As such, they utilize Egyptian inventories and other acknowledged source materials of the Biblical wisdom.[39] They may well be called etiology, in the sense that they produce by speculative reflection an account of the state of things which must have preceded in order to account for phenomena known to the author in his own day.[40]

See further Herbert G. May, "Some Cosmic Connotations of *mayim rabbim,*" *Journal of Biblical Literature,* 74 (1955), 9–21; J. Hempel, "Gott, Mensch und Tier im Alten Testament [Gn 1–3]," *Zeitschrift für systematische Theologie,* 9 (1931), 232 = *Apoxysmata* (Beiheft 81 to *ZAW;* Berlin: 1961), 215.

[36] Rolf Rendtorff, "Die theologische Stellung des Schöpfungsglaubens bei Deuterojesaja," *Zeitschrift für Theologie und Kirche,* 51 (1954), (1–) 13: Mostly in his *hymns,* like 51,9–15 and 44,24–27, Second-Isaiah *changed* the prevailing "P" view of Genesis 1, by making YHWH's creation-act no longer a datum of the past, but a part of current salvation-dealings.

[37] Hans-Joachim Kraus, "Schöpfung und Weltvollendung," *Evangelische Theologie,* 24/9 (Sept. 1964), 462–485.

[38] Luis Alonso-Schökel, "Motivos sapienciales y de alianza en Gn 1–3," *Biblica,* 43/3 (Bea-Vaccari Festschrift, July 1962), 309 f [= *Theology Digest* 13 (1965), 3]; Karl Rahner, "Ätiologie," *Lexikon für Theologie und Kirche*[2] (Freiburg: Herder, 1957), 1, 1011: In making a "myth" to *express* the *present* reality, a human author is not always conscious of the extent to which he is thereby expressing also its (historical) *cause;* queried by Norbert Lohfink, "Gn 2 f als 'geschichtliche Ätiologie,'" *Scholastik,* 38 (1963), 321–334 [= *Theology Digest,* 13 (1965), 11–17].

[39] Hans Lubsczyk, "Zur Theologie des priesterlichen Schöpfungsberichtes," *Roczniki Teologiczno-Kanoniczne,* 11 (1964), 27–37.

[40] André-Maria Dubarle, *Sages d'Israël* (Lectio Divina 1; Paris: Cerf, 1946), 21; *The Biblical Doctrine of Original Sin* [= *Le péché originel dans l'Écriture* (Lectio Divina 20; Paris: Cerf, 1958), New York: Herder and Herder, 1964], 222: original sin did not become known through historical tradition or immediate revelation, but as the result of a mental reconstruction [as shown by H. Renckens, *Israel's Concept of the Beginnings*]; 58: "the facts were reconstructed by reason and imagination directed by the Yahwist belief . . . this reasoning, which we can con-

Whether as wisdom or as etiology, the opening pages of Genesis belong to the genre of philosophy rather than of what is today called history, "man's remembered and chronicled record of his own past." In this sense must be taken the words of Church authority that Genesis 1–11, "while not strictly conformed to the method of Greco-Roman historians, yet pertain to the genus of history in a true sense, which exegetes have still to study and define."[41] The creation narrative is "historical" in the sense that it is *true*. It relates "past events that really happened. The creation of the universe, the formation of the first human beings, and the original state of innocence are facts."[42] Nevertheless, "in our sense of the word, these chapters will not be called history. They relate events that took place before the dawn of history. . . . To distinguish fact from fancy, the true from the imaginary . . . can be called historical."[43] But in our current usages of terms, an account of the origins of the universe is *not* history but philosophy.

We may take it as admitted among Catholics that the Genesis narrative at least uses the *terms* for some chaotic or unformed material upon which God's creative activity was exercised. According to Père de Vaux the three separate terms, Chaos-Darkness-Water, represent symbolically three successive stages of nothingness.[44] Whether we accept this, or prefer the simpler Zimmerli-McKenzie formula that "chaos" itself is as close as the biblical writer could come to a concept of nothingness, we must not exaggerate the extent to which his *concept* was superior to his term. We must not imagine him having in his own mind a crystal-clear scholastic precision as to what this "nothingness" was which alone preceded God's creative act, then setting about to pick among the crude terms existing in his Hebrew vocabulary the one which would best fit his view.

Rather his knowledge itself was only vague and approximative. Since he had no familiarity with the negation of all contingent reality what-

---

struct and express logically, was never present as an abstraction to the mind of Israel"; (p. 45) Genesis "traces the origins of everything that might raise a problem in the Israelite mind . . . by fairly arbitrary juxtaposition of pre-existing sources."

[41] Biblical Commission Reply to Cardinal Suhard, January 16, 1948; *Acta Apostolicae Sedis,* 40 (1948), 46; DS 3864 = 2302.

[42] Cyril Vollert, "Evolution and the Bible," in B. Boelen, *Symposium on Evolution* (Pittsburgh: Duquesne, 1959), 85. Vollert continues, "and the reporting of these facts is history," and he interprets *this* history to differ from our normal understanding of the term primarily in that it does not use Greco-Roman research techniques.

[43] Bruce Vawter, *A Path Through Genesis* (New York: Sheed, 1955), 31. It is not clear whether he intentionally recedes from this position in *Proceedings of the Society of Catholic College Teachers of Sacred Doctrine,* 6 (1960), 25.

[44] Roland de Vaux, *La Genèse* (Paris: Cerf, 1951), 39. — Nic. H. Ridderbos, "Genesis 1, 1 and 2," *Oudtestamentische Studiën,* 12 (1958), 214–260; 224 notes that "chaos" is made a combination of "abyss" and "vastness" [*tohû* = *tᵉhôm* + *bohû*] by W. Albright in *Journal of Biblical Literature,* 43 (1924), 366.

soever, he simply never posed the question of whether that was the state of affairs preceding creation. He is only concerned to account for the origins of the visible universe as we see it around us, and he declares that everything we see owes its actual reality to God's formative act.

Therefore it is not *stated* that before creation there was nothing. It even *is* stated that there was "something" besides God. However, that something is a term whose implication remains open to ulterior determination, like all the other approximations and anthropomorphisms needed to express the divine activity.

Can we go on to infer from what the sacred writer *does* say, that *if* he had been confronted with the notion of "nothingness," he would have been forced to conclude from his own data and convictions that *that* was in fact the state of affairs preceding creation and loosely called by him chaos or primeval flood? I think the inference warranted, even inescapable. If so, it is not explicit in revelation (at least not in Genesis 1, the likeliest place), but is a legitimate theological conclusion.

Others may judge differently, and may claim that the sacred writer really thought there was a reality, distinct from nothingness and from God, preexisting before creation. But even if he thought this, the terms which he chose to express it do not of themselves say to the Hebrew listeners more than "the remotest retreat from reality that the mind can possibly conceive." It is only this much which is asserted to be present before God's creative act.

4. *Omega as Vertex of the Lozenge of Evolution*

We will conclude that if Teilhard errs "by defect" in his concept of creation, that is to say by not making sufficiently explicit the *nothingness* which preceded, in this he must not be judged by a standard more severe than is applicable to revealed sources or to the complexity of the existential situation.

We must now turn to the other half of the problem, and see whether he does not err rather "by excess," in making the created universe a part of the divine substance. He speaks of himself as, in some special sense, both a monist and a pantheist. Before we attempt to evaluate what his pantheism really means, we must devote some rather lengthy attention to setting forth the diagram or graph which is implicit in his term "omega point."

The whole course of evolution, expressed as a graph, will take the form not of a straight line nor of a curve, but of a lozenge or rhombus, the "diamond" of our playing-cards or baseball field.

More properly, the actually charted facts do not have any unity of direction at all. They tumble every which way, and go off in completely

HOMINIZATION
CRITICAL THRESHOLD

opposite directions. But they are like the leaves on a tree. Though hardly a single leaf points in the direction of the branch itself, still in and through the jumble of leaves can be easily discerned an arrow or direction toward which their ensemble tends. It is *this* arrow which according to Teilhard can be plotted, and recognized to form not one line but four. Two proceed upward and outward. But at a certain stage they are cut at a brusque angle by other lines heading still upward but now inward. The purpose of the diagram is to show that man is leading the whole creation toward convergence at a single future omega point. By equal right, the lines can be completed toward the past, toward a single point.

With majestic convincingness, Teilhard shows how fossil data are already sufficient to indicate that with the emergence of man an essentially different direction of evolution had set in. This event is called hominization. But it can also be called "planetization," in referring to its effects later in time than man's first appearance. And it can justly be equated with "orthogenesis," in referring to its processes needed as preliminary to man's appearance.

Before man emerged, all minerals, plants, and animals had evolved centrifugally. There was an ever greater diversification and diffusion away from their area of origin. Nevertheless, in this proliferation of species, nature was somehow coming ever closer to the ideal complexification. This "progress" was inexorable, but it was also in the highest degree *implausible,* as has been brought out by another recent Jesuit scholar quite different from Teilhard.[45]

---

[45] Bernard J. F. Lonergan, *Insight: a Study in Human Understanding* (London: Longmans, 1957), 113–123.

Nature's resistless tendency involves at one and the same time blind unlikely chance and inescapable destiny toward a goal. These contradictory qualities constitute what Teilhard means by orthogenesis, as we showed in our preceding chapter. It is no wonder that he always exhibits embarrassment when forced to define or defend this concept. Let us say that for him it is a sort of natural mystery.

Tenaciously defying the scorn of fellow scientists, he holds to the *purposiveness* of evolution. Purposiveness implies plan and mind in the agent that set the procedure going. Here we have the root of Teilhard's ineradicable conviction of creation.

Orthogenesis, from another point of view, is the "boiling-point." As we have seen, there are in nature some *thresholds* at which the continuing inflow of identical energies produces an alteration now no longer quantitative, but qualitative.[46] Because of some innate directive force, the same external causes which had previously made some unvarying qualities increase in *degree,* now alter the qualities themselves. This alteration may even be called substantial, since it results in a new reality of a higher order.

The maximum expression of this phenomenon is hominization. In the emergence of man, two essential characteristics of evolution are radically altered. Speciation ceases, and the direction becomes centripetal.

(a) *Speciation ceases.* The uninterrupted proliferation of animal species had been due to the need of adapting to the environmental milieu. Various diversifications of bodily organs arose "by chance," or rather by causes unknown to us, apparently not called forth directly by environmental needs.[47] But environment thereupon directed "the survival of the fittest," so the fact that some new species survived and replaced the old ones is ultimately an organismic reaction to environment.

Depending on where they found themselves, various animals throve by the hyperdevelopment of beak, tusk, tail, or arm web. As the unfit died off, older species became extinct; and their place was taken by what had been freaks or monsters in the former species.

But from the moment humanity appeared, no human group has altered its "specific" physical characteristics in order to profit better by its environment. Instead, by the mind's liberating inventiveness, it produces for this purpose *tools* identical in function: shovel, saw, boat, airplane.[48]

Tools are truly the prolongations of man's physical organs. This is just as true as in the case of the altering animal species. But man's

---

[46] See above, pp. 45–47.
[47] See above, pp. 70 and 75.
[48] Teilhard, "L'hominisation" (1924), in Œuvres 3, *La vision du passé* (Paris: Seuil, 1957), 84.

tools are due to intelligence and leave the corporal structure intact.[49] This is a unique new direction in evolution.

(b) *Dissipation ceases.* Before man, each separate species had a relatively limited geographical extension. As it moved farther from its origin, it also moved farther from its nature.

The world was covered by living things, but not united by them, because as they went farther apart they also became different in species.

Then man appeared. In the perspective of geological billions of years, he attained with relative instantaneity his diffusion over the whole habitable globe. This remains true even if we are impressed by the fact that only in the last few hundred years, the last *two-thousandth* of his "instant" on the planet, man has effectively occupied the last *half* of the available space.

But when the planet has been once thus occupied, there is nowhere else to go.[50] The human race has been thus turned back and in, inexorably, upon itself.

Man impinges upon man aggressively. This does not mean always or only with hostility. Little boys at school normally become friends by getting into fights. Man's encounter with man is unifying even where it is hostile.

"The weapons which each people forges desperately to defend and separate itself become immediately the property of all the others, and are transformed into bonds augmenting human solidarity."[51]

The arrow of evolution has thus become centripetal instead of centrifugal. Its graph, perceptible under the foliage of outbranching curlicues, had been a V with top-points ever more separated. With man's coming, the top-points while continuing upward turn inward once again. The graph takes the form of a diamond.[52]

---

[49] On Teilhard's objection to considering the artificial as "unnatural" when in reality it is the "human way of being natural," see below, p. 262.

[50] Teilhard is not unimpressed by the possibility of life on other planets, or occupation of them by earth's inhabitants; but he does not feel that it invalidates the basic lines of the present analysis. See below, p. 262.

[51] Teilhard, "Les unités humaines naturelles," *Études,* 240 (1939), 25 [= Œuvres 3, *La vision du passé* (Paris: Seuil, 1957), 245]; see p. 264; compared with Louis-René Nougier, *L'humanité en expansion,* by Paul-Émile Duroux, *Histoire naturelle de l'humanité selon Teilhard* (Carnets Teilhard 13; Paris, Éditions Universitaires, 1964), 37.

[52] The diagram on p. 99 is suggested by Teilhard, Œuvres 2, *L'apparition de l'homme* (Paris: Seuil, 1956), 323; pp. 293–374 and 185–234 there reproduce articles from *Annales de Paléontologie,* 41 (1955), "Les singularités de l'espèce humaine" and "La structure phylétique du groupe humain"; in the English translation by J. M. Cohen, *The Appearance of Man,* with preface by Robert T. Francoeur (New York: Harper, 1965), pp. 232; 208–270; 132–171. Actually Teilhard's diagram is more schematic, and the inward-turning is in fact shown as a curve; but the point at issue *there* is how *today* man gradually "turns in on himself."

Teilhard does not seem to hint that the trajectory ought to be smoothed off in the form of an appropriate curve or parabola. At any rate, he would demand that the four points of the diamond mark resolute breaks in continuity.

The new direction of evolution guides not only man himself but the whole of material and animal reality. True, the subhuman species continue to proliferate and apparently to disperse. But such further spasmic gestures, after once an ultimate goal has been attained, are merely those decadences and failures which, like male tits or human tailbones, are a normal residue of the general forward-moving success of evolution.

The new direction of orthogenesis furnishes some implications for man's social and political life with which we will conclude in Chapter 10. The name "planetization" may be reserved for the portions of the two *upper* and inward-converging lines which stand between the present state of humanity and its final goal.[53]

At present we are concerned solely with the single point which is the goal itself. It is Omega Point at which those lines converge in the future. From this we will draw the needed implications about the single point Alpha from which the lower lines set out upward.

It is in the nature of a graph that the plotted points themselves, taken from the observed data, give us only the *middle* of a line. But once the shape and direction of the line are firmly established, it can warrantably be prolonged in both directions, forward and back.

The biblical writers, sapiential and priestly, formed their declaration of what happened at the beginning by reasoning back from what was observed in their day. They were helped in this reasoning process by what they saw more clearly was destined to happen at the end.[54]

With Teilhard too we will see that the point of man's origins, though it is past and done, can be better grasped from our understanding of a future point which does not yet have any existence at all!

5. *Is Omega Christ, or God?*

The point of the inverted V toward which all reality under the leadership of man is now tending is called Omega Point. It is something *more* than merely the convergence or unification of all humanity. It is even more than the gathering up of all material creation into the awaited higher unity of man.

How strange! Teilhard, who in speaking for scientists is so uneasy

---

[53] Teilhard's planetization, with hesitancies and correctives, is taken as the goal of history in M. C. D'Arcy, *Meaning and Matter of History* (New York: Farrar, 1959), 255–280; see too chapter 4 of Th. G. Chifflot, *Approches d'une théologie de l'histoire* (Paris: Cerf, 1960).

[54] See above, p. 95, footnotes 35–38.

about mentioning the fact of God at all in connection with creation or the soul, now becomes defiantly and triumphantly open in his claim that the goal toward which man's universe is tending is a Personal Being.

Does this mean that Omega Point is identical with God himself? This seems often enough to be the implication or even the direct assertion. But this involves pantheistic overtones, and Teilhard shows himself aware of it.

An escape seems, at first sight, to be provided by making Omega Point identical with Christ, a material being who is yet God and can thus serve as link between the two orders of reality. Yet here we are dismayed at making the Incarnation a necessity and a part of biological evolution, to say nothing of the absurdity of finding it to be a part of the observed scientific phenomenon at all.

Hence concretely Teilhard finds himself ever forced backward into qualifying Omega expressly as a point of convergence and unification *within* the natural order, but *open* toward, and in some sense *demanding,* a God both transcendent and incarnate.

These avowals, though explicit, scarcely satisfy anyone that they correspond fully to what Teilhard really meant. Or rather, let us say, even as the words stand they leave the difficulty essentially as great as it was before. God or Christ can be part of the material universe not only as a goal to be realized within that universe itself, but also as a further goal outside it toward which the universe has an innate tendency, and without which its fulfillment will never be complete.

In this sense Teilhard never really took back what he said: *"If for Saint Paul 'God will be all in all things,' surely it can't be so bad for us to say the same thing."*[55]

Here he would seem to be rashly flinging aside his claim to report only the observed phenomena, leaving not only revelation but even natural metaphysics completely out of the picture. But it must be remembered that on this level he is defending himself against accusations of heresy or unorthodoxy.

What he *had* reported was, to his mind, noncommittal and scientific, though *coherent* with what he knew by faith. But insofar as his report seemed to involve a final merging of material reality with a transcendent personal being beyond the universe or incarnate in it, his *Phenomenon* was taxed with being "incompatible with Scripture, therefore wrong." In answer, what else could he say except, "It is *not* incompatible with Scripture, *therefore* its truth stands or falls on the same phenomenological premises on which it was proposed."

He is so right, in protesting that he is being crucified by a standard

---

[55] 1 Cor 15:28; Teilhard, letter of Dec. 17, 1922, to Père A. Valensin, cited by Henri de Lubac, *La pensée religieuse de Teilhard* (Paris: Aubier, 1962), 227.

of orthodoxy more severe than is applied to the countless sermons, meditations, or poems which make God the goal of nature's striving. And yet it is not altogether unfair to judge him by a more severe norm. The language of mysticism is mystery, the language of oratory is hyperbole, the language of poetry is polysemy. But the language of science is hard cold fact. If that is the language he claims to be speaking, then he lays himself open to criticism on that basis.

Before taking up the possibility of defending him on his own ground, it may be of interest to notice that he was not the first or only believing scientist to express in a general way the edifying and Pauline notion that the Incarnate God is the crown of his creation. The following lines were penned by a Protestant geologist a hundred years before him:

> The truths of geology appear destined to exercise in the future no inconsiderable influence on natural theology. . . . Of that long and stately march of creation with which the records of the stony science bring us acquainted, the distinguishing characteristic is progress. . . . The existing scene of things is not destined to be the last. . . . Revelation and the implanted instincts of our nature alike teach us to anticipate a glorious *terminal* dynasty . . . the "kingdom" — not of glorified man made in the image of God, but of God Himself in the form of man. [In the] dynasty of Him, in whom the natures are united, we find that required progression beyond which progress cannot go. Creation and the Creator meet at one point, and in one person. The long ascending line from dead matter to man has been a progress Godward . . . destined from the beginning to furnish a point of union. . . . It is, as urged by the Apostle, the especial glory of our race, that it should have furnished that point of contact at which Godhead has united himself, not to man only, but also, through man, to His own Universe — to the Universe of Matter and of Mind.[56]

These clairvoyant anticipations of the most cherished teilhardisms would seem uncanny, unless they were more immediately recognized as a simple optimistic formulation of the basic gospel belief in God Incarnate.

And yet there is a sense in which such "pan-Christism" is even more alien to our supernatural revealed religion than pantheism.[57] God

---

[56] Hugh Miller, *My Schools and Schoolmasters* (Edinburgh: Constable, 1859), 381 ff. — Ernst Benz, "Teilhard de Chardin und die Zukunft des Menschen," *Zeitschrift für Religion - und Geistesgeschichte*, 14 (1962) [229–246], 316–333, notes on p. 328 pertinence of Henry Drummond, Minot Savage, *Religion of Evolution* (1876), F. Œtinger and James McCosh, *Religious Aspect of Evolution* (New York: Scribners, 1890); but this latter work on p. 94 is lamentably concordist.

[57] Teilhard himself said that he was strongly influenced by the "Panchristism" of Maurice Blondel, *Une énigme historique: Le "Vinculum substantiale" d'après Leibnitz* (Paris: 1930; adapted from the Latin of 1893); see Yves de Montcheuil, "Les problèmes du 'Vinculum' leibnitzien d'après M. Blondel," *Mélanges Théologiques* (Paris: 1946), 294; now H. de Lubac, *Blondel et Teilhard de Chardin: correspondance commentée* (Paris: Beauchesne, 1965); Jean Rimaud, "Vie spirituelle et philosophie," *Christus* 9 (1962), 272–288; documentation by Christopher F. Mooney in *Theological Studies*, 25 (1964), 609 *n* 72. Now Mooney's *Teilhard de*

as an indispensable part of creation is not a *mystery* and is not *supernatural.* He is a part of nature, and is knowable by reason alone. No matter how badly we may clarify the exact role which he plays as origin and goal of nature, reason itself *forces* us to take a stand on this.

This is not to deny that it is *difficult,* and even "morally impossible," for human nature *generally* to attain *suitable* knowledge of God. Even some areas of our scientific knowledge are enshrouded in a similar sort of "natural mystery." God is not *more* knowable or *less* mysterious than other specific objects of human knowledge.

Nor are we claiming that God is "within" nature in the sense that his activity is just one beside all the others in a series of natural causalities. Rather he is part of nature as the Thing *outside* all *contingent* reality, *required* by it for bringing it into being.

But God is "natural" to the extent to which supernatural is defined as "not due to our nature in any way, either for constituting it or for completing it or for fulfilling its genuine needs." The very existence of such a "supernatural" as distinct from "man in the only order in which he has ever in fact existed," is the object of an intense controversy in recent Catholic theology. But the attackers of Teilhard's position base themselves on such a "supernatural."

In that very sense, Christ *is* supernatural. The Incarnation is *gratuitous,* meaning that nothing in our nature required it. The Incarnation is a *mystery,* meaning that it could not be known or even understood by reason. Hence we say it is more perilous to claim fulfilment in the Incarnate Christ as the inevitable goal pointed out by the observed facts of science, than to say that science itself shows the material universe becoming eventually somehow reabsorbed in God.

One of the most profound and sympathetic studies of Teilhard's thought is by his lifelong friend Père Henri de Lubac. And it is precisely he who out of the whole world of Catholic theology is most linked with the trend to deny the validity of current distinctions between natural and supernatural.[58] And yet the one point on which he emphatically and repeatedly deplores his confrère's theological inaccuracy is this one.

In at least four connections de Lubac pronounces that Teilhard's terminology about "Christ the term of growth" is imprecise and inadmissible.[59] Unfortunately de Lubac does not do here what the book often com-

---

Chardin and the Mystery of Christ (New York: Harper, 1966), 72, explains from *The Divine Milieu,* 104, why the Christ of the Gospel comes up so rarely. "Limiting oneself intellectually and spiritually to the daily life of Christ on earth, Teilhard felt, was not the way to understand the Incarnation or grasp its ultimate meaning." See his page 85 on the Eucharist as a "biological center."

[58] See Chapter 8, footnote 21, p. 234, below.

[59] H. de Lubac, *La pensée religieuse de Teilhard* (Paris: Aubier, 1963), 174, 181, 196, 202.

mendably does for other aspects of Teilhard's thought: cite examples of the offending formulas. The relevant phrases which are cited do not seem to be the worst that one could find; there is even an astute cautiousness and depth in this one: "Science alone cannot reveal Christ — but Christ fulfils the yearning that the school of science rouses in our heart."[60] Really de Lubac does not state whether he finds this formula sufficiently guarded to redeem those other "imprecisions" which are *not* cited.

And de Lubac nowhere indicates exactly what relation *he* thinks the Omega Point bore to Christ in the mind of Teilhard. Is it asking too much of so great and good a scholar to say that he really owed it to his readers to *reformulate* the relatively delimited content which Teilhard had formulated badly? Perhaps in endeavoring to do this he would have had simply to *excise* what was inadmissible, while showing exactly how much of Teilhard's synthesis remained worthy of consideration after the excision. As things stand now, if the *whole* Omega-Christ concept is simply "wrong," then *nothing* in the whole synthesis would seem to Teilhard worth retaining.

It must be confessed that a more loyal service has been rendered in this area by a Protestant pastor who has devoted himself enthusiastically to the Teilhard spirituality. Crespy concludes that as far as *The Phenomenon of Man* is concerned, it presents the Omega Point merely as "related" to Christ. But in Teilhard's unpublished brochure called *Super-humanity,* Christ is *identified* with Omega. The body of Christ is humanity united biologically here on earth, in a fashion which must be called Gnostic.[61]

"At the very moment when he stresses the distinction of the biological

---

[60] Teilhard, "La science et le Christ" (1921); de Lubac, *Pensée religieuse de Teilhard,* p. 101. Œuvres 9, *Science et Christ* (Paris: Seuil, 1965).

[61] Georges Crespy, "Le Christ du Père Teilhard de Chardin," *Revue de Théologie et de Philosophie* 9, (1959), 305, 310. In *La pensée théologique de Teilhard de Chardin* (Paris: Éditions Universitaires, 1961), 61, Crespy notes the ambiguity of Teilhard's equating the Omega Point of Evolution with either God or Christ; in the *Phenomenon* the summit of the world is something in line with, but more elevated than, Omega (p. 53); "Christianity is far from countering my deep pantheistic tendencies" (p. 58, from Teilhard). — Émile Rideau, *Pensée de Teilhard* (Paris: Seuil, 1964), 327, "Omega is at once God and not God"; p. 154 by a diagram shows an "Omega of humanity" as a *block,* between the arrows of history tending both toward and away from it, and the Omega of both God and Christ tending toward it from the opposite side. This is *not* a teilhardian diagram, and is denied by Abel Jeannière, "Approches christologiques," *Recherches et Débats CCIF 40, "Essais sur Teilhard"* (1962), 95: "Must we make *two* Omega-points? Must we finally refer Omega to *two* modes of historical synthesis? an *impossible* hypothesis; there can be only one single absolute as term of history. What refers to Christ must somehow *complete* what reason reveals."

Now Crespy's Chicago lectures, *De la Science à la théologie: essai sur Teilhard de Chardin* (Cahiers théologiques, 54; Neuchâtel: Delachaux, 1965), 68, show the Christ of Teilhard as fundamentally the Christ of the *parousia.*

and the moral, Teilhard causes a fatal deviation of their conceptualization by insisting on their fusion, by prolonging the biological and its laws even into the heart of human history and the formation of the Mystical Body of Christ."[62] That was the judgment of the continuer of a movement called "Personalism," whose founder Mounier was profoundly congenial to Teilhard, as we shall see in Chapter 10.

6. *"Redemptive Evolution" Under Attack*

It is natural therefore that trained Catholic theologians find great scandal in Teilhard's apparent claim that Christ is part of evolution.

His "redemptive evolution" was the target of a violent attack, which by its cloak of anonymity renounced hope of being taken seriously.[63] It was emphatically denounced by Teilhard as a distortion of his true meaning:

"Even the title insinuates that I ascribe a properly salvific virtue to the cosmic process. On the contrary, my constant preoccupation has been to have radiate from a transcendent Christ the 'redemptive' qualities of the pain engendered by evolution."[64]

It remains true that Teilhard has declared the Incarnation to be "necessary": not in the hypothetic framework *"if* man is to be redeemed," as has always been a commonplace in Christian theology; but as somehow a needed complement of the evolutionary process.[65] Even more

---

[62] Jean-Marie Domenach, "Le personnalisme de Teilhard de Chardin," *Esprit,* 31 (1963), 359; see p. 277, note 48. He refers to Charles (now Cardinal) Journet, "Pierre Teilhard de Chardin penseur religieux," *Nova et Vetera,* 37/4 (Oct. 1962), 284–313. This is an evaluation of several recent critics, and is not basically hostile to Teilhard; it emphasizes the dangers, but unfailingly balances them with the legitimate Christian perspectives which accompany them.

See now H. Huybens, "Ébauche d'une Christologie Teilhardienne," *Revue du Clergé Africain* 21/2 (March 1966), 129–146; Cornelius Van Til, "Pierre Teilhard de Chardin," *Westminster Theological Journal* 28/2 (May 1966), 109–144; and Eusebio Martinazzo, *Teilhard de Chardin: conamen lecturae criticae* (Rome: Herder, 1965), 144–150.

Note the severe judgment of [Jean Rambaud] Philippe de la Trinité, *Seminarium,* 16 (1964), 84, on Claude Cuénot's *Lexique Teilhard* (Paris: Seuil, 1963), p. 29 and especially 63: Omega: (1) Center of concentration of the noosphere; (2) God, end, and consummation of the universe, and especially the risen Christ. This *Lexique* starts out with a facsimile of Teilhard's handwritten effort "to make a lexicon of my terms." In the *Phenomenon,* p. 270, Teilhard enumerates as the four qualities of the Omega: autonomy, actuality, irreversibility, and transcendence.

[63] *L'évolution rédemptrice du P. Teilhard de Chardin* (Paris: Cèdre, 1950).

[64] Teilhard, review of *L'évolution rédemptrice* in *Études,* 266/6 (Sept. 1950), 284.

[65] Hans-Eduard Hengstenberg, "Untersuchungen zur Christologie Teilhards de Chardin," *Wissenschaft und Weisheit,* 26/3 (1963), 165–179; page 169 rejects as untenable Teilhard's "unfinished Incarnation"; see further Hengstenberg's *Evolution und Schöpfung: eine Antwort auf dem Evolutionismus Teilhard de Chardins* (Salzburger Studien zur Philosophie 3; Munich: A. Pustet, 1963); and Alois Guggenberger, "Wissenschaftliches Weltverständnis und christlicher Glaube nach Pierre

audaciously a recent work, original but penetrated with the Teilhard approach, asserts, "God's whole creation, including the Incarnation, is evolutionary cosmogenesis."[66]

Responsible and sympathetic theologians see themselves forced to point out, as the gravest of all dangers in Teilhard's system, the apparent destruction of the abyss between what is owing to man's nature and what is God's gratuitous gift.[67]

When Teilhard writes, "The Christ of revelation is nothing other than the Omega of evolution," and "Let us in fact identify (at least by its 'natural' face) the cosmic Christ of faith with the Omega Point of science — all becomes clear, simple, harmonized in our perceptions," he understandably provokes the expostulation: "On the most important points, on which the whole structure depends, as for example 'the two faces of Omega' . . . the reader is invited to rest content with images. A loyal effort of intense metaphysical concentration would be needed even to pose these questions, to say nothing of solving them. To replace this by play of imagination is movie trickery."[68]

Other theologians, no less capable, have on these very points risen

---

Teilhard de Chardin," in *Gott, Mensch, Universum* (Graz: Styria-Verlag, 1963), 452–499; Eusebio Colomer, "La evolución cristocéntrica en Teilhard de Chardin," *Espíritu*, 12 (1963), 112–126.

[66] Joan Vandenberg, "Drie typen in evoluerend Kristendom," *Bijdragen*, 22/1 (Jan. 1965), 27, 1–128. — George Magloire and Hubert Cuypers, *Présence de Teilhard de Chardin* (Paris: Nouvel Office, 1964), 220, notes these parallels in Berdyaev: "We must insist upon the elements of enrichment which man's creation brought to the divine life itself; man's response to God's appeal." [In *Sens de la création:*] "If the Redemption consecrates only one aspect of Christ, that of suffering and dying Son of God, creation must turn to another aspect, glorious and omnipotent. . . . Via redemption, man returns to his creative freedom; . . . the Christianity of today must stand under the sign of evolution, of spiritual tension." The authors add, "We know that Père Pouget bases similar views on St. Paul." See also Valeria Lupo, "La mística dell' Incarnazione in Pierre Teilhard de Chardin," *Humanitas*, 19 (1964), 293–314; L. Lochet, *Fils de Dieu* (Paris: Cerf, 1963), Chapter 11.

[67] Aldo Locatelli, "Il punto Omega di Teilhard de Chardin," *La Scuola Cattolica*, 90 (1962), 112.

[68] M. L. Guérard des Lauriers, "La démarche du P. Teilhard de Chardin: Réflexions d'ordre épistémologique," *Divinitas*, 3 (1959), 232, citing Teilhard's "Christianisme et évolution" (1945, p. 8), and "Le Christique" (1955, p. 8).

In comparison with these seriously formulated criticisms, we find genuinely preoccupying the language of Giacinto Scaltriti, *Teilhard de Chardin tra il mito e l'eresia* (Studio Generale Domenicano, Teologia y Vita, 2; Rome: Idea, 1964), 30: "Teilhard would certainly have been affronted if his sanctum of paleontological studies were invaded by sports reporters. What is to be said of a paleontologist who without asking permission enters the hall of dogmatic theology and of Aristotelico-Thomistic philosophy, noisily flinging on the cathedra his 'skeletons' and his 'rocks'?"; page 59: with his theological eclecticism and his moral empiricism, he was a real though not a perfect Jesuit; page 53, he suffered a trauma during military service in 1914; he was mad, as are many geniuses; page 166, he was not really Marxist, just used by them.

to Teilhard's defense. His expectations are declared to relate merely to what data observation itself would suggest: "the unity prophesied by Teilhard is still on the phenomenological plane and does not compromise the gratuity of grace."[69]

Similarly: "Just because God has gratuitously engaged himself in the universe, a true phenomenology is bound to be up to a point a theophany."[70] By theophany is normally meant a preternatural intervention of God revealing himself within his creation, rather than that "knowableness of God from the material universe by reason alone" which is found in Romans 1:20 and which is sometimes justifiably called a *natural* revelation. But whether we call it a theophany or not, God's revealing of himself by the processes imbedded in his creation is something quite distinct from the claim that the incarnate Christ is the term of biological evolution.

Hence others attempt the defense on a different basis. One inquirer admits that in the Teilhard system the counterpoise to entropy is ultimately Christogenesis.[71] Here are some of the passages which give this impression:

"The universal Christic energy simultaneously supernaturalizes and ultra-humanizes. . . . Christ is not content to sanctify a crop of souls." "Despite the spirit (or even the letter) of the writings of St. Paul and St. John, there is still something conventional, juridical, accidental about the salvific figure and function of Christ in current dogmatic formulation."[72]

Dolch finds Teilhard's equating of the Christic energy with a remedy for entropy to be tolerable on the ground that his literary genre is "witness" rather than instruction. This seems to be a cloudy way of saying that Teilhard has here abandoned his claim of recording the scientifically observable facts, and is resorting to a poetic or mystical insight which he holds with confidence but cannot prove. This may well be a valid assessment; but one must wonder whether Teilhard would agree.

Even more assertive is a Spanish Franciscan in two articles defending the Teilhard asceticism. Christocentric ordering of all reality is declared to be fully along the lines recommended by Ignatius Loyola in the *Spiritual Exercises,* but even superior to him. It is moreover in the spirit

---

[69] Cyril Vollert, "Toward Omega: Man in the Vision of Teilhard de Chardin," *The Month,* 23 (1960), 265 [= *Catholic Mind,* 58 (1960), 402–409; *Theology Digest,* 8 (1960), 133–136].

[70] William Donnelly, "The Thought of Teilhard de Chardin," *Clergy Review,* 45 (1960), 335, with the further observation that the Pauline vision commands Teilhard's outlook but does not determine the movement of his dialectic.

[71] Heimo Dolch, "Erwägungen über die Aussage Teilhards de Chardin," *Catholica,* 16 (1962), 96, 100.

[72] Teilhard, "Un seuil mental sous nos pas," in Œuvres 7, *L'activation de l'energie* (Paris: Seuil, 1963), 271 f. The date of this opusculum is given as 1961; presumably 1951 is meant.

of John XXIII's *Mater et Magistra,* and affords "a more concrete or comprehensible sense of the glory which man is to give to God."[73] Here again, one must recall that the state of the question is not whether Teilhard does well in praising the position held by Christ in the universe *after* the Incarnation had become a gratuitously realized fact or decree; but whether this fact known only to faith can be found within the data of physics as "a counterpoise to Entropy"!

And yet we do not wish to imply that these efforts to defend Teilhard's position are without their relevance. What Teilhard says, *sounds like what Saint Paul says.* If he invokes Paul, or any other part of revelation, it is *in principle* only to defend himself against the *theologians'* charge that his "observation of the phenomenon" is *contrary* to revelation. This is true proximately only of *The Phenomenon of Man* and those other essays in which Teilhard professes *not* to be basing himself on truths of faith or theology. Such works as *The Divine Milieu* do not in principle need such a defense, since in them he professes to *combine* the observations of reason with what is known by faith. However, even there he is rather careful to say only what he feels he can prove; and so ultimately the relevance of revealed doctrines is somewhat *ad hominem,* as in *The Phenomenon.*

"The purpose of this [Divine Milieu] is to prove . . . that the most traditional Christianity, expressed in Baptism, the Cross, and the Eucharist, can be interpreted so as to embrace all that is best in the aspirations peculiar to our time. My hope is that it may help to show that Christ, who is ever the same and ever new, has not ceased to be the 'first' within mankind. . . . Is the Christ of the Gospels, imagined and loved within the dimensions of a Mediterranean world, capable of still embracing and still forming the centre of our prodigiously expanding universe? . . . We shall listen to St. Paul telling the Areopagites of 'God, who made man that he might seek him.' "[74]

Teilhard's own grasp of the Omega Point toward which evolution was tending was admittedly obscure. He sees only that it bears a relation of intimacy amounting almost to identity with *God,* God a part of the natural order as origin and goal of the evolutionary process. But insofar as there are difficulties in the way of simply identifying this "point of convergence *within* creation itself" with a God who must necessarily be transcendent, there hovers before Teilhard's gaze the purely natural pos-

---

[73] Celestino Solaguren, "La cristología del P. Teilhard de Chardin y el Principio y Fundamento de san Ignacio," *Manresa,* 35 (1963), 14–22; "El cristocentrismo cósmico de Teilhard de Chardin," *Verdad y Vida,* 19 (1961), 131–143. On Teilhard's "Ignatian tradition," see H. de Lubac, *Prière du P. Teilhard* (Paris: Fayard, 1964), 126.

[74] Teilhard, *The Divine Milieu* (London: Collins Fontana edition, 1964), 43, 46.

sibility of some reality which may bridge this gap between God's transcendence and the need for him as goal within his creation.

Only when he allows a hearing to the claim of faith that this "God embodied in matter" *does* in fact exist, and is Christ incarnate, but that it is heretical to claim that one could have seen the need for this from an observation of biological evolution alone, Teilhard lawfully counters, "Well then, what *does* St. Paul mean when he says that Christ is 'the firstborn of the whole creation' by whom 'the whole creation is redeemed'?" He gives no exegetical answer; he never even tied down his vague "St. Paul" to the two passages here hinted. But essentially he is on secure ground in protesting that his terminology is of itself no more paradoxical and disquieting than St. Paul's.

We will see in the next chapter how these fleeting New Testament allusions — really no more focused than by Teilhard — gave rise to a whole school of Catholic theology, whose "orthodoxy" was never impugned and in fact was *enhanced* by the fact that for over six hundred years it could not be dislodged by the ever more monopolistic majority opinion.

We will there endeavor to pursue every slightest trace in the history both of exegesis and of dogmatic theology which may help us to shed light on the Teilhard position. But we wish to acknowledge frankly here that we foresee no benefit for readers who will choose to retrace these steps with us. By flitting rapidly through those pages they can assure themselves that nothing has been omitted which might have been *hoped* to prove instructive. They will agree that the job had to be done, sooner or later. But in the end we will find ourselves exactly where we are now.

As Teilhard puts it, "TOUT DE MÊME, *we have the right to talk like Saint Paul.*"

As John McKenzie puts it, "He resolutely reaffirms the biblical truth that the redemption of man is also the redemption of the cosmos."[75]

7. *"My Pantheism"*

God is in many ways a "part," a "necessary part," of creation and the natural material universe, in an antecedent absolute sense which is not true of Christ. Hence no ultimate grappling with reality can fail to exhibit *some* presupposition concerning the intimate relation of nature to its creator.

The concise surgical formulas by which this relation is expressed in Christian theology do not really eliminate as much of the apparent contradiction as is commonly imagined. The whole of Thomism rests upon "the

---

[75] John L. McKenzie, review of *The Divine Milieu* in *The Critic* (Jan. 1961), 29 f.

Analogy of Being" and the threefold way of reaching knowledge of God, Affirmation followed by Negation then Heightening. Taken together, these amount to the fact that we do not *quite* know *what* we mean by the formulas we adopt to describe God's complex activities, those which involve what for our mode of conceiving is something other than a pure perfection.

Ultimately knowledge of God is possible only on the assumption that there is *something* in common, or conceived as common, between God and creatures. This something is Being. It is not *precisely* the same as found in God and in creatures, but it is not wholly different. And moreover it is ultimately the *only* thing which is found in God at all. In a certain less obvious sense, it is the only thing which is found in creatures at all, since the factors which *distinguish* from "being" any other perceptible characteristics are themselves already "something, reality, being."[76]

All this makes dull reading. To our age it is a distasteful sort of mental gymnastics. Nothing sounds to us more "unreal" than what the medieval scholastics have to say about "Reality." The whole twentieth-century vogue of Existentialism is a revolt against that unreal tone of a philosophy concerned with the *essences* of things or their "ultimate realities."

Even if the formulas of scholasticism commanded more general respect than they do, it is important to recognize again what a thin line they are walking between the errors that would engulf them by the slightest deviation to either side. The alternative to seeing God too little in the material universe is almost inescapably to see him there too much.

"All real religions are of the monist-pantheist type," wrote Teilhard in one of his latest works. The editor's footnote adds that Teilhard uses the word "pantheism" in various senses: sometimes approvingly, but then only in the spirit of First Corinthians 15:28, "that God shall be all in all."[77]

---

[76] Teilhard, *The Divine Milieu* (Fontana edition), 122: *"The divine omnipresence in which we find ourselves plunged* [is] AN OMNIPRESENCE OF ACTION. *God enfolds and penetrates us by creating and preserving us. . . . Under what form, and with what end in view, has the Creator given us, and still preserves in us, the gift of participated being? Under the form of an essential aspiration towards him* [by a] UNITIVE TRANSFORMATION."

[77] Teilhard, "Pour y voir clair" (1950), in Œuvres, 7, *L'activation de l'énergie* (Paris: Seuil, 1963), 227. — *Phenomenon of Man* (New York: Harper, 1959), 294: "GOD SHALL BE ALL IN ALL. *This is indeed a superior form of 'pantheism,' without trace of the poison of adulteration or annihilation: the expectation of perfect unity."* In a letter of December 17, 1922, to Père A. Valensin, author of the article "Panthéisme," in the *Dictionnaire Apologétique de la Foi Catholique*, cited in E. Rideau's *Pensée de Teilhard*, 396, Teilhard protests, *"How is it that you did not make clear that between Spinoza's 'incarnation,' where Everything is hypostatically divine, and the 'Incarnation' of timid extrinsicist theologians in which the Pleroma is only a social aggregate, there is place for an Incarnation terminating in the construction of an organic whole, where physical union with God has DEGREES?"*

It is *not* true that Teilhard found his inspiration in the pantheist religions of India and China. On the contrary, he was repelled by them. He speaks of them with a cold lack of sympathy which accords badly both with our ecumenical era and with his own normally radiant human openness. Consequently we can only dismiss as an unrealist distortion the fantasy that "after having experienced the attraction of humanitarian pantheism and of the oriental mysticisms, it was in the Catholic faith of his childhood that Teilhard de Chardin could finally find the entire satisfaction of this need of the Absolute." This claim is advanced in a book of "meditations evidently not Teilhard's own and not likely to be acknowledged as his thought" by his admirers, though prompted by admiration for Teilhard and by the author's own conversion due to "non-intellectual reading, repelled rather than helped by theology."[78] The truth is that whatever pantheism may ever have received Teilhard's sympathy, came as the culmination and completion of the ever operative faith of his childhood, not as a temporary aberration from which he turned away.[79]

"While using the formula 'Christian pantheist,' he keeps himself from being a pantheist."[80] Statements like this merely pose a problem without solving it. They assume precisely what cannot be so readily assumed: namely that a man deeply sensitive to the nuances of words would deliberately choose and insist upon so shocking a term when what he meant could just as well have been conveyed by a less offensive expression.

Not that he is defiant or challenging about the term, or even insistent. He remarks that he has been *"accused* of pantheism,"* by readers who fail to note that for him understanding is not a continuous forward surge but a *spark* oscillating between two poles, the best known and the least

---

[78] Ignace Lepp, *Teilhard et la foi des hommes* (Paris: Éditions Universitaires, 1963), 115, 9 f. — "The oriental religions seduced Teilhard for a while by their pantheism," is a statement given without documentation in É. Rideau, *Pensée de Teilhard* (Paris: Seuil, 1965), 19. Unless he is subconsciously quoting Lepp, it would seem that both are recalling an authentic phrase. But Rideau on page 528 f more understandably *negates* that Teilhard's thinking ever involved any serious temptation to oriental pantheism.

[79] Note the overgeneralizing and vague use of "suggestion" and "consist" in Pier Carlo Landucci, "Pierre Teilhard de Chardin: aberrazioni ideologiche," *Palestra del Clero,* 43 (1964), 1194: "The pantheistic suggestion of matter: . . . The aberration consists essentially in the notion of absolute, of consistence, of richness of being . . . seen in the solidity of matter and of the world." An "aberration" can scarcely "consist in the notion of absolute": even if this absolute be *learned from* sensibly perceived objects, as in fact our idea of God *is* learned.

[80] Bernard Charbonneau, *Teilhard de Chardin, prophète d'un âge totalitaire* (Paris: Denoël, 1963), 26. See also Charbonneau's "Progrès et liberté," and P. Segaar, "Recherche biologique et foi chrétienne" in *Foi et Vie,* 55 (1956), 469–525. "Not true monist": M. Hudeczek, "De hominisatione," *Angelicum* 38/3 (July 1961), 356–370.

known. Every new thing we learn about the least known sends us scurrying back to reinterpret better the best known.[81]

"On a boat near St. Helena," poignantly recalling to us how closely triumph and exile were linked in the lives of two historic Frenchmen, in 1953 Teilhard wrote an essay called *The Stuff of the Universe*. In this essay he brings us nearer to the real roots of his discontent with conventional terminology about creation. *"It has accustomed us to a creator paternalism."*[82] This must be countered by "a functional completing of the One and the Multiple." He here suggests Christology rather than pantheism as the proper clue.

If, for the reasons indicated above, we try to leave in abeyance the Christological problem, we should be able to agree that for any Christian the world must somehow find its final completeness in God. He is the goal toward which the whole universe *naturally* tends. It tends even to *possession* of him and *absorption* in him, in proportion as these are possible to the respective created natures. There is nothing new or shocking in this. A good part of it was formulated long ago by Augustine, "You have made us, O Lord, for yourself, and our hearts are restless until they rest in you."

Meanwhile without ceasing to be a Christian, Teilhard observed that science alone, or a simple open-minded look at the wholeness of reality, shows the whole universe tending toward an ever more convergent and unified goal. Since the point of universal convergence cannot be multiple, and since no contradiction is involved, the goal of the physico-chemical operations of the universe is declared to be identical with the goal of men's thirsting spirit.

At some time in the future, at least, "God will be all in all." The whole universe will have been narrowed down into a single point and absorbed in the Being of God. Somehow that is the meaning of Omega Point. One of Teilhard's diagrams shows Omega as a Christic cone *inside* a cosmic cone, both revolving about a simultaneous *line* axis; but the *vertex* of the two cones is in fact a third thing, God, a *point*.[83]

---

[81] Teilhard, "Esquisse d'une dialectique de l'Esprit" (Paris: November, 1946), in Œuvres, 7, *L'activation de l'énergie* (Paris: Seuil, 1963), 149. In *The Divine Milieu* (Fontana edition), 116: *"The sojourner in the divine milieu is not a pantheist. At first sight, perhaps, the depths of the divine which St. Paul reveals to us may seem to resemble the fascinating domains unfolded before our eyes by monistic philosophies or religions. In fact they are very different, far more reassuring to our minds, far more comforting to our hearts. Pantheism seduces us by its vistas of perfect universal union. But ultimately, if it were true, it would give us only fusion and unconsciousness"; page 130, "The false trails of pantheism bear witness to our immense need for some revealing word."*

[82] Teilhard, "L'étoffe de l'univers" (1953) in Œuvres 7, *L'activation de l'énergie* (Paris: Seuil, 1963), 405.

[83] Teilhard, "Esquisse d'une dialectique de l'Esprit" (Paris: November, 1946), in Œuvres 7, *L'activation de l'énergie,* 156. There is a similar image of the cones

The very choice of a name like Omega Point implies that there is an Alpha Point to which it forms a counterpart. If, by eventual absorption into a point of utter unification and simplifying, God *will* be all in all, then God *was* all in all at the point of equal simplicity at which the whole creation "broke off from him," so to speak.

It did not really "break off," just as it will not really be "absorbed." Words fail us here; but we need not be ashamed to resort to the crutches of St. Thomas. We *affirm* what comes as close as we can get to what we mean about God. Then we *deny* that we meant by this anything incompatible with what we know about God's being or our own. Then thirdly we *heighten* the content of our affirmation by saying it is true in a degree and mode which are simply beyond our human competence to express adequately.

It is my conviction that we are not understanding correctly what creation meant to Teilhard until we have understood that Omega Point means to him the completion or restoration of Alpha Point. Before pursuing this problem in his own terms, let us insert here a recent Franciscan statement which without mentioning either Scotus or Teilhard sheds great light on the present problem and its biblical roots.

Universe and history are seen to have the same starting point, and to be converging towards the same end: the whole work is opened with the same alpha, and is closed with the same omega.

Man, therefore, by contemplating the gradual organization of the cosmos, can have some inkling of what is to be his own destiny, and the various aspects of the great act of creation will appear to him as the splendid prelude to the history of his salvation. . . . The inspired writers never evoked the creation for its own sake, independently of the Covenant which Yahweh had concluded with his people. The first page of Genesis, which always comes to mind when creation is mentioned, does not in fact claim to do more than suggest the great themes on which rests the whole history of Israel: the progress towards the light, the search for a refuge which the storms of the proud and raging sea will no longer smite. This is the first image with which the Bible opens, and it will be the last, when darkness and chaos will have at last given way to the mountain of peace where night is unknown (Apoc. 22:5), to the new land which will have no ocean to threaten its stability (Apoc. 21:1). Are the Christians of to-day truly aware that their faith implies this definite vision of the universe which encompasses them? [God is not merely a remote] agent who gave things their initial flick into existence; he is the master who, with the same gesture, in the pursuance of a single plan and the fulfillment of a

in *The Divine Milieu* (Fontana edition 114), where the divine milieu itself is called "however vast, a *center*" (as well as a vertex). Even when Teilhard turns from this "mediating supreme personality" as *goal*, to its activity as *outset-point*, he still calls it Omega rather than Alpha, says Bruno de Solages, "Les preuves teilhardiennes de Dieu," Mélanges H. de Lubac, *L'homme devant Dieu* (Paris: Aubier, 1963), 3, 129; 125–132; see there pp. 223–248, "La vision religieuse et cosmique de Teilhard" by Gaston Fessard.

single word, guides at one and the same time the universe and the course of history.[84]

Our interest in this passage focuses on the words "opened with the same alpha and closed with the same omega." As we have seen, the Omega Point envisioned by Teilhard is not unequivocally identical with Christ; even if it were, his terminology would no more exclude an orthodox interpretation than does that of Scotus or Paul. The Teilhard position involves two commitments: the eventual absorption of all reality in God, and the inevitableness of this absorption. Neither the absorption nor its inevitableness excludes sin and failure in the cosmic process, but the aim of nature is seen to be attained on a massive scale despite massive frustrations. The aim toward which nature itself is inexorably tending is seen to be "in" or "with" God.

Now if the point toward which the whole of Teilhard's evolution tends is a point of utter and divine unity at the top of the diamond, then to such an apex inescapably corresponds an Alpha Point at the bottom.

This Alpha Point must have exhibited a millionfold more intensely that "complexity latent in simplicity" which every ovum exhibits. Moreover, this Alpha Point must, like Omega, possess some special identifiability with Christ or God.

To one reflecting sympathetically on the rich horizons opened out by planetization, the conclusion which Teilhard would have drawn if he had consented to turn his gaze backward toward the moment of creation seems inescapable. The Alpha Point is no less inexorable and no less identified with divinity than Omega.

If this be so, how can we escape some sort of emanationism? Just as inevitably as the creation tends toward absorption in divinity, just so inevitably must it have arisen by a sort of sifting out from divinity. Or, at the very least, the "creation" by God would seem to be as necessary and inevitable as its eventual absorption in him.

True, one might say that God was utterly free either to set or not to set the first material particle in existence outside Himself, even though once it was set, the inevitableness of its inner structure would carry it toward reabsorption in divinity. But if with Teilhard we try to put down the data in a sort of physicist's graph, we should rather conclude that to the forward terminus of the graph there corresponds an outset point of equal inevitableness.

Not that Teilhard *taught* emanationism or the necessity of creation.

---

[84] Évode Beaucamp, *The Bible and the Universe: Israel and the Theology of History* (London: Burns Oates, 1962), 100, 99. See now his *Sous la main de Dieu* and *Israël regarde son Dieu* (Tournai: Casterman, 1964). It was from reflecting on the ideas of Teilhard while Beaucamp was serving in the army that he came to be attracted to the Franciscan life, as that which best exploits the relation of spirit and holiness to nature; so he told me.

"Emanation" is a word not congenial to him at all. "Monism," which is a sort of synonym, does in fact enlist his cautious sympathies to about the same degree as "pantheism." But it cannot be proved that by the slight glimmer of insight he attributed to either of these terms he meant anything other than the surface contradictoriness which reality itself exhibits.

Perhaps his defenders should be more audacious in admitting that his position left him with some unanswered questions, or even some unsolved dilemmas. The presence of paradox — which means nothing other than "apparent contradiction" — is a factor we have had to learn to live with, not only in a revealed religion based on mystery, but even in the "natural mysteries" of science itself.

In view of "the Analogy of Being," we should hesitate to claim that our certitudes about God are so univocal as to prevent a qualified expert from experimenting. It is just possible that from the microscopic or outer-space universe some genius may yet derive a more up-to-date framework for our awareness of the transfer of Being from God to things and its consummation again in Him.

It is unlikely that this Aquinas of the future will be any scientist not formed to philosophy — least of all one of Teilhard's relatively limited breadth of reading and competence. His originality is ultimately no greater than that of simple biology or astronomy manuals, though it strikes many as marvelous because it outspokenly links together what science and theology have been refusing to communicate upon.

If he has succeeded in asking even *wrong* questions about Being, or has given answers which an "adversary mentality" will conclude have to be condemned, his merit will be even greater for forcing on twentieth-century attention the fact that there *are* some questions to be answered which have not yet even been asked rightly.

We can appreciate Teilhard's "virile unswerving gaze," while lamenting his inadequacies of formulation. Significant is the comparison of his imperturbable end-of-the-world optimism to the "final apotheosis" of Origen. "Misunderstood, attacked, exiled, it is of him that Teilhard instinctively makes us think. . . . Origen has been a battlefield just like Teilhard. . . . The Church was disturbed and vexed by Origenism as she is now by Teilhardism, as is plain to see. And yet Origen . . . has remained one of the glories of Christian thought. His errors have not prevented us doing him justice and continuing to hold him in tender regard. We believe the same will be true of Teilhard . . . he will still be dear to our hearts because of his fine spiritual ambitions, his vast syntheses, his original ideas, and above all — for this above all he will survive — his *cosmic sense.*"[85]

---

[85] N. Corte [pen-name of Léon Cristiani], *Teilhard* (New York: 1957), 114.

SUMMARY OF THE FOURTH CHAPTER,
ON "OMEGA-ALPHA"

Teilhard has been charged with making visible reality depend insufficiently upon God. But the *eternity* of matter is neither opposed to true creation nor is it in fact in Teilhard's spirit. The *necessity* of creation is indeed suggested by him, but this rather pertains to the excess of divinity in creation; anyway, rather broad uses of the term "necessity" have always been indulgently tolerated within orthodox Christianity.

The notion borrowed from Bergson that "to create is to unite" does in fact seem to suppose that something is existing prior to God's creative act. Tresmontant's defense of Teilhard revolves about the claim that creatable potency itself resists the accepting of a perfection which God for his part could provide. But Teilhard explicitly says he never meant by "creative union" to postulate a preexisting substrate.

If his understanding of "nothingness" is rather elusive, he has this in common with Scripture itself. The main Old Testament accounts of creation borrow mythic terminology of a chaos or primitive ocean to describe what preceded creation. This was as near as human concepts could then arrive toward expressing "nothing." Nowadays we possess that notion, but recent existentialist philosophy can point to some difficulties in our understanding of it.

By excess, Teilhard is charged with pantheism, not only because he admits this very word occasionally with qualifications, but because for him all reality is destined to be absorbed in God much as it originated from God. The emergence of man meant precisely that the direction of evolution changed from centrifugal to convergence on an Omega Point.

Man's species has never divided, because he can prolong his bodily structure by tools separate from himself. And the very tools which men make to destroy each other quickly become a common possession forcing them together. Having occupied the whole globe, man is now turned in on himself and forced toward a higher unification.

Observance of nature itself suggests to Teilhard that the terminus of the coming union of the human race will be a super-being combining in himself the totality of mankind along with the transcendent and personal goal for which man was made. This claim seems to put human reason into contact with the Incarnation as a thing neither gratuitous nor supernatural.

Since such a charge rises not out of science or natural observation but out of a theology of revelation, Teilhard can counter it from sources of revelation, where Christ at least seems to be made the origin and goal of the whole creation. However, Teilhard never did really admit that the incarnate Christ was the Omega Point itself rather than "linked" to it.

Neither did he consistently hold that Omega Point is simply God. But in some sense the goal of all existing reality is absorption in God. To this goal corresponds a preceding Alpha Point, at which all reality emerged "from" God, by somehow sharing with God the one thing most fundamental to both, their "reality" or Being itself.

CHAPTER 5

THE SCOTIST COSMIC CHRIST

Not the least among the services of Teilhard de Chardin to twentieth-century religious thought is the revitalization of a classic controversy. Based largely upon thirteenth-century philosophical positions of the Franciscans as against the Dominicans, the "Motive of the Incarnation" came to form a part of the sixteenth-century Jesuit line on predestinating grace.

In an existentialist and communist world, the urgency of these historic contexts has given way to other problems, and our modern textbooks flit rather uninterestedly over the Scotist position, which being the heritor of a long tradition never impugned for its orthodoxy could not be simply omitted.

An appeal of the supreme Franciscan authority in 1933 resulted in numerous restatements of the Scotist position.[1] These in turn were met by Dominican restatements. In these researches, many valuable incidental clarifications have been turned up. But on the whole it can be said that nothing in the two basic positions has been altered by the change in world outlook due to the intervening contributions of Galileo and Darwin, to say nothing of Hegel or Marx.

---

[1] Leonardo Bello, *De universali Christi primatu atque regalitate* (Rome: Franciscan Curia, 1933). — In *Osservatore Romano* of July 24, 1966, appeared the message *Alma parens* of Pope Paul VI, commending the retention of "more Platonic-Augustinian Scotus at the side of Aquinas," on occasion of the Scotus centenary congress in England to which this chapter was submitted.

Now, however, says Karl Rahner,

The old question about the predestining of Christ is posed anew today as question of a Christ-centered cosmos. The issue is, whether the whole material cosmos too finds its meaning and fulfillment in the personal spirit, through its unity with the absolute reality of the infinite Being of God. By spirit is understood the individual, but also what is shared in common by all who possess spirit-reality. If the material cosmos does thus find its fulfillment, then Jesus Christ is the goal of the whole cosmos and of its "evolution." If he is that, then he is also its efficacious motive. This is in virtue of his hypostatic union, the highest spiritual unity between created spirit-nature and God.[2]

1. *The Scriptural Cosmic Christ*

When Teilhard's work began attracting attention, all theologians recognized that there was an affinity between his "cosmic Christ" and the Scotist "Christ as crown and origin of the material creation." Both Teilhard and Scotus in turn are observed to echo certain phrases of Saint Paul.[3]

Upon closer look, it will turn out that in neither case are these passages subjected to any sort of real exegesis.[4] Thus actually the basis in revelation is *supposed* rather than truly proved: the more so since both Teilhard and

---

[2] Karl Rahner, "Jesus Christus: Systematik der kirchlichen Christologie," *Lexikon für Theologie und Kirche*[2] (Freiburg: Herder, 1960), 5, 955; we have presumed to break up his long sentence into several. See further Rahner's *Christologie innerhalb einer evolutiven Weltanschauung* (Schriften zur Theologie, 5; Einsiedeln: Benziger, 1962); and Felix Malmberg, *Über den Gottmenschen* (Quaestiones Disputatae, 9; Freiburg: Herder, 1960), 25: "Many Catholic theologians do not sufficiently grasp [that salvation history forms a part of the metaphysical concept of the human nature of Christ itself, just as the spiritual 'ontic' completing of a spiritual nature belongs to it and to its very concept; nor, with due respect for the anti-existential reserves of *Humani Generis*] that this dynamic, historical, existential aspect of Christ's holy humanity belongs intimately and essentially to the metaphysical concept of Christ's human nature itself, and a fortiori to its speculative-theological concept."

[3] N. M. Wildiers, *Teilhard* (Paris: Presses Universitaires, 1960), 92.

[4] Georges Crespy, *La pensée théologique de Teilhard* (Paris: Éditions Universitaires, 1961), 197, is substantially correct in noting that Teilhard comes no closer to "explaining" Saint Paul than repeated fleeting mention of a couple of common places. However, C. Mooney in *Theological Studies,* 25 (1964), 596, cites one Teilhard footnote simply enumerating by chapter and verse some twenty-three passages; and Mooney also counts thirteen places where Teilhard says that God or Christ "will be all in all" (1 Cor 15, 28). Mooney's *Teilhard de Chardin and the Mystery of Christ* (New York: Harper, 1966), 240, holds that Teilhard's only mention of Scotus is in the 1946 *Esquisse d'une dialectique de l'Esprit*, Œuvres 7, *L'activation de l'énergie* (Paris: Seuil, 1963), 158. — For Leo Scheffczyk, "Die 'Christogénèse' Teilhard de Chardins und der kosmische Christus bei Paulus," *Tübinger Theologische Quartalschrift,* 143/2 (1963), 136 (−174), Teilhard and his supporters merely *claim* their accord with St. Paul. Scheffczyk concludes to a rejection of this claim. In 140/1 (1960), 19–37, "Die Idee der Einheit von Schöpfung und Erlösung," he does not deal with Teilhard, but see his "Sonnengesang . . . Schöpfungsfrömmigkeit," *Geist und Leben,* 35 (June 1962), 219–233.

Scotus are focusing upon what to them is a problem of *natural* knowledge or reality pattern.

Of course neither of them says or implies that the Incarnation is part of our natural knowledge of the world-process. But both of them are concerned with the legitimate and purely rational problem, *"Granted* that the Incarnation is known to have taken place, then what place if any must it vindicate in even the purely natural processes of cosmogenesis?"

Exegesis, therefore, and other researches in the sources of revelation are a little out of place here. The *fact* of the Incarnation can be known only from revelation, but there is no obscurity or disagreement about this fact among any of the parties to this intra-Catholic controversy. But whether the Incarnation *in the hypothesis* of its occurrence is pivotal to the natural material creation, is a problem in principle capable of solution without aid from revelation.

Hence if we seek for a basis in revelation it will be chiefly as an extrinsic or negative guide. And for the small amount of assistance we will get, it will turn out to be a lot of work. But no reader of Teilhard can escape an insatiable curiosity about just how well-founded theologically is that Scotist view which flits through his pages.

It may be admitted at the outset that the anti-Scotist position bases itself more firmly and frankly on Scripture. The statement of Luke 19:10, "The Son of Man came to seek and save that which was lost," seems to be adequately embodied in the formula of the Nicene Creed, "Jesus Christ was made man on account of us men and on account of our salvation."

In the whole of patristic literature, scarcely a single firm assertion maintains that the motive of the Incarnation was anything other than the Redemption.[5] From the Gospel and the earliest Creed it would seem to follow that apart from man's *fall* and need of redemption, the place of the Incarnation in the cosmic scheme of reality would simply not be posed.

We will examine first in the light of most recent exegesis those passages which may be regarded as justifying a different view. Then we will trace the Scotist hypothesis from its origins through the arguments of the theologians who have defended or adapted it, almost wholly without reference to Scripture as we shall see. Then we will conclude by an endeavor to follow and exploit those rare moderns who have tried to combine the scriptural and speculative data into a tenable synthesis.

If the synthesis is tenable, it may without further ado be called "the Teilhard position." Not that the French paleontologist had anything to do with elaborating it, or was even able to assent to it explicitly. But it forms

---

[5] Zeno of Verona (bishop in 370) "never speaks of a conditioned or dependent predestination; he sees Christ always in his own altogether proper and absolute hierarchical order": Ruggero Rosini, "Il primato di Cristo secondo S. Zeno Vescovo di Verona," *Studia Patavina,* 10/1 (Jan. 1963), 11, 3–36.

an indispensable theological grounding of much of what he claims for the evolutionary process, and thus for what we are concerned with, the mode of creation of the human soul.

In the Old Testament, "God created me 'as' the beginning of his ways," says Proverbs 8:22. The "me" refers to Wisdom, personified as recommending the pursuit of itself to the believer. This Wisdom suggests in some ways the Holy Spirit, and perhaps even more proximately the Son, to whom are more proper the Trinitarian functions of knowledge as distinct from love. But it is wholly unwarranted and today excluded that in this passage we have any assertion whatever regarding distinction of persons in the Trinity. Thus too the priority of Christ to creation is not taught here.

"God himself used [!] wisdom to construct the universe. . . . Wisdom is not now [as in 3:19] an abstraction; it is a concrete being, living and operating beside God. But it is not a creature; it is a divine being, because it existed before God created (verses 22-26), and concurred in the creation of everything (27–30). One would say that it is an essential attribute of God. But it is personified with such powerful vividness that from this description only a brief further step is required toward distinguishing more than one person in God. This step was taken when the divine wisdom became incarnate in Jesus."[6]

Similarly the deuterocanonical Sirach 24:9 says, "He created me from the beginning, before the world." These two references are linked in patristic tradition to the first chapter of Genesis: partly to verse 1 mentioning the "beginning" in which God created heaven and earth; partly to verse 26, in which man is created according to the "image of God," with reference to the sense in which we will find this term equated with Christ in Colossians 1:15. But the "Wisdom" in question is not really Christ.

2.   *Sighing of the Cosmos toward Liberation*

In a context closely connected both with original sin (Rom 5:12) and with the natural knowableness of God from material creation (1:20), Paul tells the Romans (8:18), "The sufferings of this present time are not to be compared with the glory which shall be revealed in us. (19) The expectation of the creation points toward the revealing of the sons of God. (20) Creation itself has been frustrated, not by its own will, but by reason of him who permitted this (21) in view of creation's eventual deliverance from the slavery of corruptibility into the glorious freedom of God's children. (22) We recognize that there is a groan and an anguish throughout the whole of creation up to now. (23) It is not merely the

---

6 Alberto Vaccari, *La Sacra Bibbia* (Firenze: Salani, 1961), 1080.

material creation, but also ourselves possessing the firstlings of the Spirit, who groan at the deferral of (sonly) redemption of our body. . . . (28) We know that all things work together for good for those who love God, those who are called according to his purpose; (29) because those whom he foreknew, he also predetermined to be in the same form as the image of his own Son, who was thus to be the firstborn among the many, his brethren."

Six key words in this passage are as interesting as they are controverted: creation, firstborn, frustration, the "permitter" (*hypotáxas*), predestination, deliverance.

1. The word "creation" occurs in five of these verses. In Greek it is in every case *ktísis* with the article. Strangely, *kósmos* as in Romans 1:20 does not occur here, but *ktísis* seems to have an equally cosmic meaning in both passages.[7]

Does this term mean the *material* creation only, exclusive of mankind? Many competent exegetes, with Chrysostom, think it does.[8] Others, in view of the personal attributes attributed to *ktísis,* hold that only mankind is meant, thus requiring a translation of verse 23 differing from ours.[9]

Other Fathers like Origen and Theodore of Mopsuestia thought that *only* the *angels* are the creation here envisioned: doubtless because of what we will see in Colossians about reconciling the things in the skies. But a recent research seems to show convincingly that the *ktísis* of Romans 8 means, and is now most widely held to mean, "all creation inclusive of men."[10]

2. Firstborn: This whole of creation, chiefly material yet including men, is in verses 28 f called simply "all things" or "the All," *pánta* instead of *ktísis,* and is loosely connected with "God's son" as its "firstborn." Thus

---

[7] Sasse, *"Kósmos," Theologisches Wörterbuch zum Neuen Testament* (Stuttgart: Kohlhammer, 1938), 3, 891: Scripture never really solves the fundamental paradox that the world is good as created by God (Alexandrian optimism, Hellenistic earth-joy), yet the world is under God's judgment and in need of redemption (Apocalyptic pessimism influenced by Persian dualism).

[8] Hermenegild M. Biedermann, *Die Erlösung der Schöpfung beim Apostel Paulus* (Sammlung Cassiciacum 8/3/2; Würzburg: Rita-Verlag, 1940), 70 f, rejects the patristic views that in *ktísis* are envisioned only the angels (Origen; Theodore of Mopsuestia) or only men.

[9] Augustine *ML* 40, 67; Gregory *ML* 75, 675; so recently Schlatter; A. Dulau, "Omnis creatura ingemiscit (Rom 8:22)," *Divus Thomas Piacenza,* 37/4 (July 1934), 390, 386–392; Walter Gutbrod, *Die paulinische Anthropologie* (Beiträge zur Wissenschaft vom Alten und Neuen Testament; Stuttgart: Kohlhammer, 1934), 13–17: *ktísis* in Colossians 1:15 is the created *individual* but in 1:23 all created *mankind,* as also in Romans 8:19 (in the light of 1 Corinthians 9:9 "does God care about oxen?"), but the *unregenerate* as distinct from "us."

[10] A. Viard, "Exspectatio creaturae (Rom VIII, 19–22)," *Revue Biblique,* 59/3 (July 1952), 340 f, noting as outdated the (Chrysostom and contemporary) view of M.-J. Lagrange, *Épître aux Romains* (Paris: Gabalda, 1916), 207.

we have a vague but unmistakable anticipation of *prōtótokos pásēs ktíse-ōs* below.[11] Since the object designated is plainly concrete rather than "the *act* of creating," the singular may have been chosen instead of the plural for euphonic or metrical reasons in the Colossians hymn which is held to be earlier than the epistle itself.[12]

The Son is not here in Romans said to *be* the image of God. Rather it is *in* the image of the Son that a *further* resemblance arises among men, only the "predestined," but not in so clearly exclusive a sense that *not all* men might be understood.

3. The *frustration* to which the whole creation has been subjected is capable of various explanations. It may be an abstraction used for the concrete "Fallen Mankind," to whom in fact the lower creation (not exclusive of man himself) has been made subject. It may mean also the abstract unbalance itself, announced in Genesis 3:17 as an alteration to 1:28. Either "fallen man" or "disorder" would seem to be an interpretation preferable to "the Evil Power" favored by Viard.

4. The frustration was due not to the will of the creation, but to a *hypotáxas*. "The one who permitted (or 'effected') this situation" may and in some sense must be understood of God, as was done by the capitalizing of "Him" by the editors of my *Theological Studies* article.[13] But the view there preferred is that the "him" refers rather to Adam.[14] As Viard observes: "it is clear how close appears the solidarity of the creation here mentioned with the sons of God and via them with the Son of God himself." A third and less likely view is that it was Satan who established the frustration of the *ktísis*.

5. The "predestination" of verse 29, delimiting "the many, the brethren" among whom Christ is "firstborn," is also vaguely supposed in the earlier verses. The "image" which this verse mentions will be taken up chiefly in Colossians; but it is explained in its present context as a new

---

[11] Pages 129–132 below; J. Kürzinger, "Symmórphous tēs eikónos toû huioû autoû (Rom 8, 29)," *Biblische Zeitschrift*, 2 (1958), 294–299.

[12] Charles Masson, "L'hymne christologique de l'Épître aux Colossiens 1, 15–20," *Revue de Théologie et de Philosophie*, 36 (1948), 141, 138–142; see below, p. 133, footnote 48.

[13] Robert North, "Teilhard and the Problem of Creation," *Theological Studies*, 24/4 (Dec. 1963), 590–595. So Franz-J. Leenhardt, *L'épître de saint Paul aux Romains* (Neuchâtel: Delachaux, 1957), 125: the *hypotáxas* is God, though *man's* fault is responsible for his doing it; page 129, man's solidarity with creation is a fact to which Paul alludes in a framework of reflections which we cannot quite grasp or necessarily approve, and regarding which a great sobriety is called for in the exegete.

[14] Foerster, "Ktízō, ktísis," *Theologisches Wörterbuch zum Neuen Testament* (Stuttgart: Kohlhammer, 1938), 3, 1030.

"pattern" to which the cycle being inaugurated by Christ must conform.[15]

The redemption of the lower creation seems to be presented as universal and unconditioned, though linked to a redemption of mankind which is presumably limited to a certain percentage, the predestined. As we have already noted, the interest of sixteenth-century controversialists in the cosmic Christ is largely in function of their preoccupation with predestinating grace; and in Chapter 9 we shall see that this preoccupation also dominates largely theologians' interest in the divine Concursus.

6. Finally, in what does this "redemption" or deliverance of the material creation consist? Many exegetes see the answer to this question in the "new heavens and new earth" of Isaiah 65:17 and 66:22; Acts 3:21; 2 Peter 3:13; and Apocalypse 21:1. However, the wording to the Romans envisions a "liberation" rather than a *renovation* of existing nature.

"Man is part of nature, and the whole 'nature' of which he forms part . . . will ultimately be redeemed."[16] "The various speculations on the way in which nature will eventually obtain her freedom from the curse of Genesis 3:17 cannot claim the authority of St. Paul. It is one of the mysteries not revealed to us."[17] Though it is not revealed, we may reasonably suggest that even for St. Paul the material creation is redeemed by the very fact that redeemed man is and remains completely bound up with materiality.[18] The soul is not a bird released from its cage to flit off to the happiness of its real life. Immortality and heaven are promised to the *man,* and not (even if it were possible!) to the form apart from its matter.

Is this redemption a kind of divine adoption? The word which we endeavored to render by the un-English "sonly" in parenthesis, is generally rendered "(we sigh, awaiting) our adoption as sons (the redemption of our body)." But a special research of Père Benoit finds that this

---

[15] A. Leaney, "Conformed to the Image of his Son (Rom viii, 29)," *New Testament Studies,* 10 (1964), 470–479; see G. Montague, "Progress in the Early Church," *The Bible Today,* 10 (1964), 640.

[16] F. F. Bruce, *The Epistle of Paul to the Romans* (London: Tyndale, 1963), 169. — See G. Schneider, *Neuschöpfung oder Wiederkehr* (Düsseldorf dissertation, 1961), and *Trierer Theologische Zeitschrift* 68/2 (1959), 257–270.

[17] A. Theissen, "Romans," in B. Orchard, *A Catholic Commentary on Holy Scripture* (New York: Nelson, 1953), 1065, citing Strack-Billerbeck, *Kommentar aus Talmud und Midrasch,* 3, 840–847.

[18] "The redemption of the universe is just a consequence of the redemption of man; more precisely a consequence of the redemption of man's body; nevertheless the universe is not merely the instrument of man's redemption, but is itself the object of redemption": Stanislas Lyonnet, "La rédemption de l'univers," *Lumière et Vie,* 9/48 (1960), 51; page 47 links the "alliance" underlying Paul with an alliance more ancient and universal concerning the natural universe in Genesis 8:21; 9:11 (so Paul in Acts 14:16 f).

word "adoption," *huiothesían,* is to be simply expunged, for both textual and exegetical reasons.[19]

Two other admirable Dominican scholars, the brothers Dominique and André-Maria Dubarle, have important light to shed on this as on most other teilhardian concerns with the relationship between spirit and evolving matter.[20] André claims that his own earlier belief that the sin of a free creature has put disorder into the material world was adopted by his brother.[21] But André has now reexamined the whole problem with very satisfying honesty and comes to the conclusion that it is not warranted *either* to read into the Pauline text, or to *exclude* from it, the idea that the sin of a free creature has put disorder into the material world.

"God has arranged for the realization of his plan in steps. All creatures must pass first through a painful condition lacking glory, but this will vanish. Man and the world around him are subject to the same law of vanity and corruptibility. Thus in nature can be seen gleams of man's destiny both in its sombre and in its hopeful aspects. Unlike man, nature has not been intrinsically altered by sin, though it can occasionally be utilized for guilty ends."[22]

When André Dubarle says that "man, unlike nature" has been intrinsically altered by sin, he does not of course assert that "man's nature has been altered by sin." And he does rightly imply that "man as he really was" has been changed by sin. Over and above that, he tends to imply that there is no such thing as man's "nature" distinct from "what he really was," a being created in a state of supernatural elevation; or distinct from what he became by the loss of a part of that endowment due to sin.[23] For those who do not fully grasp the de Lubac view of "the supernatural" as indicated above, the observations of Dubarle will not constitute a barrier to regarding the material creation as redeemed by the fact that redeemed man is material in his nature.

---

[19] Pierre Benoit, "Nous gémissons, attendant la délivrance de notre corps," *Recherches de Science Religieuse* 39 (Mélanges Lebreton 1, 1952), 267–280 = *Exégèse et théologie* (Paris: Cerf, 1961), 2, 41–52.

[20] André-Maria Dubarle, "Bulletin de Théologie Biblique," *Revue des Sciences Philosophiques et Théologiques,* 33 (1949), 196: "Before man, life did not enjoy that harmony willed by the creator. This privation was function of a sin which we could never locate in our scale of time." The view that man was neither carnivorous nor mortal before sinning is rejected.

[21] Dominique Dubarle, "La théologie du cosmos," in A.-M. Henry, *Initiation théologique*[2] (Paris: Cerf, 1961; [1]1952), 2, 319.

[22] A.-M. Dubarle, "Le gémissement des créatures dans l'ordre divin du cosmos (Rom 8:19–22)," *Revue des Sciences Philosophiques et Théologiques,* 38 (1954), 457, 445–465.

[23] See p. 105 above, and the documentation in chap. 8, footnote 21, p. 234 below.

3. Christ as Firstborn, Firstling, and Primate

The epistle to the Colossians is most characterized by its attack on distorted evaluation of spirit-realities by Gnosticism. It is called one of the "Pauline antilegomena" or controverted letters, as distinct from the "homologumena" or agreed ones: meaning that the distinctive least-common-denominator of Pauline style and thought is less perceptible here than in some others. Nevertheless it is most likely that the author is either Paul himself or a mouthpiece very directly under his guidance.

At the very beginning, even fused with the latter part of his salutation, the writer stresses that there is no power in the universe, spiritual or otherwise, which is not rooted in the man Jesus Christ.[24] (1:12) "We thank the Father, who has fitted us for our own special share of the holy things in the light, (13) and released us from the power of darkness, and effected the transfer into the kingdom of his beloved Son (14) in whom we have ransom, the remission of sins. (15) He is the image of the unseen God, the firstborn of all creation (16) because in him were created all things in the skies and upon the earth, the things seen and the things unseen, whether thrones or lordships or principles or authorities; all things have been created with him as their origin and goal. (17) And he is before all things, and all things have taken their stand in him, (18) and he is the head of the body, the chosen assembly. He is the principle, the firstborn from among the dead, in order that he may be in all things holding the primacy (19) because in him has been decided the lodging of all the fulness (20) to serve as principle of unification of all things, since he brings peace by the blood of his cross; he reunites all things whether upon the earth or in the skies."

We shall examine the terms here rendered as unseen, firstborn, origin-goal, primacy-principle, fulness, and unification. The "chosen assembly" is *ekklesía,* but without those implications of juridical structure which "Church" has today (verse 18).

1. *Unseen* is applied both to the Father and to the created things: those "in the skies," presumably, but by a reversal of order ("chiastically"). The Greek *aóratos* strictly may mean "not seen," but for practical purposes it implies "invisible."

The *image* of an invisible or unseen God is a paradoxical expression capable of opposite interpretations. Since an image is visually *like* the thing which it represents, one might logically say that the image of the

---

[24] Karl-Gottfried Eckart, "Exegetische Beobachtungen zu Kol 1, 9–20," *Theologia Viatorum,* 7 (1960), 87(–106).

invisible God is itself invisible, and that therefore Paul is speaking here of the preexistent Son as second person of the Trinity.[25]

But it seems more plausible to focus the fact that an image is something *to be seen* or to show forth the thing it represents. Most of the expressions immediately correlated with "image" here as predicates of the same subject refer to activities of Christ within the material creation.[26] Paul therefore meant to set up a *contrast* between the invisible God and the visible or incarnate Image.[27]

"The Invisible-in-itself becomes visible in Christ as its copy: not to be sure visible to the bodily eye [i.e. his divinity as such] but to the eye enlightened by the Spirit, as in 2 Corinthians 4:4."[28] It is even claimed that in the Pauline corpus "the invisible God" means always the Triune rather than specifically the Father.[29]

---

[25] Ernst Lohmeyer, *Der Brief an die Kolosser*[11] (W. Meyer's Kommentar, 13; Göttingen: Vandenhoeck, 1956), 54; the "unseen" is put in to detach the author's view from Old Testament *theophany* perspectives; the Image is first in *being,* but the Firstborn is first in dignity and activity.

[26] The "image" referred to Christ as man by José M. Bover, " 'Imaginis' notio apud B. Paulum," *Biblica,* 4 (1923), 176, prompts his exegesis of Colossians 1:15 in "Gratiae oeconomia per Christum, independens a peccato, secundum Pauli doctrinam" and "Dei Filius, homo factus, independenter a peccato, secundum Pauli doctrinam," *Verbum Domini,* 2 (1922), 79–87, 170–176.

[27] On the recurrence of this *eikōn* in Ephesians 4:24, "the new man, created in the image of God," see R. M. Wilson, "The Early History of the Exegesis of Gen 1, 26," in K. Aland, *Studia Patristica* (Texte und Untersuchungen 63; Berlin, Akademie, 1957), 1, 425, 420–437; Paul Althaus, "Das Bild Gottes bei Paulus," *Theologische Blätter,* 20/4 (Apr. 1941), 86: the image of God is the "(new) *life* which he gives" as Colossians 3:10. On Christ as image of God in 2 Corinthians 4:4, influenced by Plato's *Timaeus,* 92, see E. Preuschen, *"Eikōn toû theoû toû aorátou,* Kol 1:15," *Zeitschrift für die Neutestamentliche Wissenschaft,* 18/4 (1918), 243. According to David M. Stanley, "Paul's Interest in the Early Chapters of Genesis," *Studiorum Paulinorum Congressus, 1961* (Analecta Biblica, 17; Rome: Pontifical Biblical Institute, 1963), 250, Colossians 1:15 is one of those most characteristically Pauline ideas which echo Genesis; the adaptation of it to Christianity was probably his own doing, because it is suitable to his preoccupation with sin.

[28] Ernst Percy, *Die Probleme der Colosser- und Epheserbriefe* (Acta Litteraria 39; Lund: Gleerup, 1946), 68. On page 313 he holds it true both of Christ and of God in Colossians 1:19 "Everything has in Christ its goal; . . . the whole creation is made in view of Christ; and all the threads are destined to converge in him"; since in Philippians 2:6 Christ was "in the form of God," he partook in the relation of God to his creation; page 70 "Christ is not only the means and intermediary of all creation, but also its goal. Without him it has not only no possibility of existence but also no warrant for existing." Percy's earlier *Der Leib Christi in den paulinischen Homologumena und Antilegomena* (Lund Universitets Årsskrift, 1/38/1; Gleerup, 1942), 51 adds little except on *plērōma.*

[29] Ugo Lattanzi, *Il primato universale di Cristo secondo le sacre Scritture* (Rome: Lateran, 1937), 106, 84; Christ as man is firstborn "of *each* creature," meaning that each is a sort of younger brother to him, though the "birth" in question is Christ's Incarnation, in relation to which there could not be any actual *secundogeniti.*

2. *Firstborn.* This term is rather unexpectedly applied in this passage to Christ as firstborn "of the dead" as well as "of the whole creation."

As firstborn of the dead, or presumably of those risen from the dead, it would seem to echo the "firstlings" (*aparchē,* not *prōtótokos*) of the dead, in First Corinthians 15, 20. This "firstborn among those risen to newness of life" is doubtless part of the implication of *prōtótokos* in Romans 8:29, while in verse 23 of that passage *aparchē* seems to refer to the first Christian generation as sharers in this "risen life" even before their own bodily death, and this is the sense of *ekklēsía prōtotókōn* in Hebrews 12:23. But in Hebrews 1:6 "the firstborn" without explanatory nuance refers to the Old Testament figure found to be verified in Christ. This Hebrews "firstborn" has been found to refer to the Incarnation and/or Nativity of Jesus, in preference to the Second Coming or any other event envisioned as *future* to the time of writing the epistle.[30]

Going back to the context of Colossians 1:15, it seems to show that Christ *as man,* or rather as God-Man, is here spoken of as firstborn of creation. Exegetically, we take this to mean no more than that in the order in which creation actually came into being, the man Jesus Christ was somehow there first. Obviously he was not produced physically in time, or strictly "born," before any other creature. It doubtless goes beyond the writer's intention to tell the Colossians how this primogeniture means that an eventual union of all the material creation in Christ Incarnate was the goal implanted in the first elements of matter from the moment of their origin. But such a possibility is in fact left open, and better, if we regard the firstborn as man rather than as Preexistent God. It is important to aver that we do not favor this exegesis *because* it better fits the teilhardian perspective, but because of the context and the convergence of the various other controverted terms.

Research into the patristic tradition of the first five centuries shows that even then opinions about Christ as "firstborn of creation" were about evenly divided between the Preexistent and the Incarnate Word.

Various Fathers who considered that the Preexistent Word was "firstborn" explain this in three different ways. For some it refers to his eternal generation by the Father. For others it means simply that the divine generation occurred *before creation.* For still others it means "first in dignity," and is synonymous with the "primacy" held by Christ as firstborn "among the dead" in verse 18.

It is not quite accurate to say that the divine generation occurred *before* creation. God's eternity is equally *present* to each of the events which occur in time. However, our mind can scarcely fail to conceive

---

[30] A. M. Vitti, "Et cum iterum introducit Primogenitum in orbem terrae," *Verbum Domini,* 14 (1934), 306–312, 368–374; 15 (1935), 15–21.

as temporally prior to the Fiat of creation, that situation in which God was free either to pronounce this Fiat or to withhold it.

The question then becomes whether the genitive expression "of all creation" supports the sense "before all creation." First-of, or first-among, seems to imply *others* in series, all forming truly *part* of the word that follows; but of course this sense is not admitted by tradition relative to Jesus as "firstborn" of Mary in Luke 2:7. If the rendition "before" be admitted, then it is indifferent whether the Greek *pâsa ktísis* be rendered as "the whole of creation taken together" or "each creature taken individually." But we saw that the individual sense has been defended, the sense that Christ is the firstborn of *each* creature. It should be noted that the rendition *"before* any creature," though indispensable for defending the sense of Preexistent, is also favored by many in support of the primacy of Christ as man.[31]

The earliest Christian apologists, especially Justin, explained the Son as begotten or born for the sake of bringing creation into being. This sounds dangerously like the Platonic demiurge, or the similar neo-Platonic basis of Arianism. Nevertheless reserving the term *prōtótokos* precisely for this function with respect to creation gradually became common, whereas the term applied to the Divine Word in its own nature was rather *monogenēs,* "sole-born," as in John 1:14; 3:18. The relevance of this Johannine "creative role of the Word" to the Pauline cosmic Christ has been further studied and defended by Boismard.[32]

In the third century, when the Arian position became more widespread, it was natural that its opponents should steer clear of all misunderstanding; hence they preferred to see in Paul's *prōtótokos* an expression of Christ's human rather than his divine nature. The marvel is that the "Preexistent Firstborn" view managed to hold respect, and even to gain favor after the Arian scare had passed.

To show that this Preexistent Firstborn was not a creature in the Arian sense, Didymus the Blind (313-398, a younger contemporary of Athanasius), distinguished *prōtótokos* from *prōtóktistos.* Christ was not "created" *(ktistós)* first; he was "born (of the Holy Virgin! but) in the divine foreknowledge" first. As an alternative view, linked with Proverbs 8:22, Didymus admits the remote possibility of the interpretation *"salvation* was predetermined before the ages."[33] Really he ends up preferring "firstborn of every creature *reborn by baptism."* Nevertheless Cerny's research

[31] Joannes M. Bissen, "De primatu Christi absoluto apud Col. 1:13–20," *Antonianum,* 11 (1936), 3–26, 4, 16. This article mostly polemizes against Ferdinand Prat, *Theology of Saint Paul* (London: Burns Oates, 1933) 1, 289.

[32] M.–E. Boismard, *Saint John's Prologue* (London: Blackfriars, 1957), 112; *Prologue de saint Jean* (Lectio Divina 11; Paris: Cerf, 1953), 141, giving a reference to Viard which is suppressed in the English. To John 1:13 is added also 1:1 and Apoc 3:14; Heb 1:2.6; 2:10, in Julian Kaup, "Cur Deus homo?", *Franziskanische Studien,* 21/3 (1934), 236.   [33] On Proverbs 8:22, see above, p. 122, footnote 6.

concludes that the view of Didymus is in essentials identical with that of Scotus: Christ is made firstborn by God's advance decree.[34]

The demand to understand *prōtótokos* as something distinct from *prō-tóktistos,* and hence (with Luther) as "firstborn (in the Trinity) before *any* creation," is reiterated in several recent researches of Michaelis. The Romans 8:29 context seems indeed to make Christ as firstborn "one of many," yet upon closer look we have the paradox "the many are his brothers, but he is not without qualification their brother."[35] Taking into account the Greek usages, already influenced by the Bible, and especially the vexing implications of Mary's "firstborn" in Luke 2:7, Michaelis really comes around to giving to *prōtótokos* the rather generalized or metaphorical (or Hebrew *bekôr,* as Exodus 4:22) sense of "special, favored."[36]

Among other recent defenders of the Preexistent Firstborn, there is a trend to emphasize that relation to Old Testament Wisdom which we saw in Didymus. Christ's primogeniture has been equated with preexistent creative wisdom.[37] This would seem to form part of the really ultra-modern fervor for finding in Matthew 11:25 Jesus' own identification of himself with the personified Wisdom of Hebrew revelation.[38] But as for its relevance to our passage in Colossians, some rather negative conclusions are reached by a Benedictine research perhaps outdated now.[39] It holds with staccato bluntness that Wisdom is *not* in the Book of Proverbs an agent of creation; that Wisdom is nowhere in Paul a person or

---

[34] Edward A. Cerny, *Firstborn of Every Creature* (Baltimore: St. Mary's University, 1938), 61; Didymus, *De Trinitate* 3, 3 f; *MG* 39, 827.

[35] Wilhelm Michaelis, "Die biblische Vorstellung von Christus als dem Erstgeborenen," *Zeitschrift für systematische Theologie,* 23/2 (1954), 144, 137–157, also *"Prōtótokos,"* *Theologisches Wörterbuch zum Neuen Testament* (Stuttgart: Kohlhammer, 1959), 6, 872–883, 879 "[In Col 1:16] Christ is (firstborn as) the mediator in creation, to whom all creatures without exception owe their creation."

[36] W. Michaelis, "Der Beitrag der Septuaginta zur Bedeutungsgeschichte von *prōtótokos,*" Festschrift Albert Debrunner, *Sprachgeschichte und Wortbedeutung* (Bern: Francke, 1954), 313–320. The word occurs 130 times in the Septuagint. The oldest extrabiblical occurrence is not an alleged 200 B.C. text in which it is really accented *prōtotókos* "(an animal) giving birth for the first time," but at Yahudiyya in 5 B.C., very near to where the Septuagint itself was produced; it there refers to a woman who died giving birth to her firstborn: C. Edgar, "More Tomb-Stones from Tell el Yahoudieh," *Annales du Service des Antiquités d' Égypte,* 22 (1922), 9.

[37] Hans Windisch, "Die göttliche Weisheit der Juden und die paulinische Christologie," *Neutestamentliche Studien für Georg Heinrici* (Leipzig: Hinrichs, 1914), 220–234, 224 on Colossians 1:16.

[38] André Feuillet, "Jésus et la Sagesse divine d'après les Évangiles synoptiques," *Revue Biblique,* 62/2 (April 1965), 173, adding Sirach, 51, 23–30, with E. Norden, *Agnostos Theos* (Leipzig: Teubner, 1913), 277–308; Tomas Arvedson, *Das Mysterium Christi, eine Studie zu Mt 11:25–30* (Uppsala dissertation, 1937); "Phil 2, 6 und Mt 10, 39," *Studia Theologica,* 5 (1951), 49–51; Edvin Larsson, *Christus als Vorbild* (Lund: Gleerup, 1962), 174.

[39] D. B. Botte, "La sagesse et les origines de la christologie," *Revue des Sciences Philosophiques et Théologiques,* 21 (1932), 54–67.

substance, and that the letter to the Colossians contains no echo of any Old Testament sapiential book.[40]

"Firstborn of 'a' whole creation," rather than *the* whole creation, is the literal rendition of the Greek according to another fairly recent study. Thus "firstborn" seems to refer to a group or mass within the material-human reality: not explicitly reduced to "the saved" or anything like that; perhaps ultimately, like Paul's "the many," not excluding the totality. The author nevertheless seems to quote approvingly the view of Saint Francis of Sales, "All was created for this divine man, who therefore is called firstborn of all creation," and local councils at Sardica, Toledo, Milan, and Ephesus, pronouncing Jesus to be "firstborn" as man, "sole-born" as God.[41]

An article about the Firstborn Christ was written by one of Teilhard's Jesuit confreres in the theological seminary at Hastings, apparently while they were residing there together.[42] Durand firmly dismisses Christ's primogeniture as purely a metaphor of sovereignty. As he sees it, the firstborn of creation *probably* meant to Paul the same thing that it *certainly* meant in the Jewish Messianic tradition, "sovereign of the whole world" as man and mediator.[43] This perspective fits well enough the "primacy" of Paul's verse 18, which we will see to dominate the notion of "Scotist cosmic Christ" fostered by present-day Franciscans.[44] It is to be hoped that this emphasis on "sovereignty" would not lead to that kind of extrinsic and paternalist Christology which made Teilhard unhappy, as would be the case if Christ was "firstborn of creation" only because he is its boss and ruler.

3. Origin and goal. In verse 16 two prepositional phrases are used for what we have considered to mean "origin" and "goal" of creation. About *eis autón* as goal there can scarcely be any doubt, even though in *koinē* Greek the preposition "into" is often used carelessly for "in" without implying movement.

We must compare here 1 Corinthians 8:6, "For there is one God, the

---

[40] A connection of Colossians 1:15 with Psalm 89H:28 *bᵉkôr*, rendered *prōtótokon* in the Septuagint, is noted by Jean Hering, *Die biblischen Grundlagen des christlichen Humanismus* (Zürich: Zwingli, 1946), 7.

[41] P. Romualdus, "Christus, de eerstgeborene van de schepping?," *Studia Catholica*, 18 (1942), 155–171; Francis of Sales, *Traité de l'amour de Dieu*, 2, 4 (Œuvres; Annecy: 1892), 4, 99–104.

[42] Alfred Durand, "Le Christ 'premier-né,'" *Recherches de Science Religieuse*, 1 (1910), 56–66.

[43] T. K. Abbott, *A Critical and Exegetical Commentary on the Epistles to the Ephesians and the Colossians* (ICC; Edinburgh: Clark; around 1900), 211: the Jews understood *prōtótokos* as a Messianic title; Eadie and Hofmann take it to mean sovereignty, Alford and Lightfoot also though subordinatedly to priority; page 214, Abbott holds an exemplary cause, as maintained by the Schoolmen, cannot be meant, because *ektísthē* is "was *actually* created."

[44] See above footnote 1 and below footnotes 100 and 145; pp. 119, 146, 158.

Father, from whom (*ex hoû*) [ ] all things and we unto him (*eis autón*), and one Lord Jesus Christ, by whom (*di' hoû*) [ ] all things and we through him (*di' autoû*)." The twofold empty brackets are intended to call attention to a recent claim that the simple copula should not be supplied, as would normally be our tendency. Rather an active verb of movement like "we *are on the march* from God," would correspond to the dynamic movement expressed in *eis autòn.*[45]

The Corinthians parallel helps us to understand also the sense in which it is legitimate to render *di' autoû* as "Christ our Origin." God the Father too is our "origin," *ex hoû,* not as a "stuff out of which," but as the efficient cause. The Son, insofar as he is distinct from the Father in the work of creation, is the "Word" or image or pattern, expressing the whole of the creation-to-be-produced, and serving as design or blueprint to govern the production. In this sense the Word is just as truly at the origin of creation as is the (triune) efficient creator.

In Colossians 1:17 the Incarnate Son is moreover called "principle." The Greek *archē* may mean either "beginning" or "rule." Indeed, in the present context it has been found to have *all* the various senses (beginning, sum total, head, firstfruits) of Hebrew *rēšît,* which it is implicitly citing, from Genesis 1:1 via Proverbs 8:22 as recognized already by Epiphanius.[46] The link with Proverbs and Wisdom 7:26 is further pursued in a thorough study of the recently-much-reappraised "Christ as 'Model' for our Imitation."[47]

Since the *archē* of Colossians 1:17 refers proximately to "the (risen from the) dead," it seems to be a synonym of *aparchē* which we saw in Romans 8:23. In both cases we have a term whose vagueness is often reproduced in English by "firstlings," the earliest concrete examples of that "harvest" of New Life which Christ's redemptive act has brought.[48]

---

[45] F. M. M. Sagnard, "À propos de 1 Cor. VIII, 6," *Ephemerides Theologicae Lovanienses,* 26 (1950), 54–58, page numbers furnished inaccurately by me to *Theological Studies,* 24 (1963), 591.

[46] C. F. Burney, "Christ as the *archē* of Creation," *Journal of Theological Studies,* 27 (1926), 160–177; 173; Epiphanius, *Panarium adversus haereses,* 3, 1, 7, heresy 73, *MG,* 42, 415. *Archē* in *some cases* (1 Jn 1:1; 2:13; Heb 4:3) means Christ's part in creation, according to Gösta Lindeskog, *Studien zum neutestamentlichen Schöpfungsgedanken I* (Uppsala Universitets Årsskrift; Lundequist, 1952), 206; he refutes the effort to explain away the New Testament "protologisch" significance of Christ by M. Teschendorf, "Der Schöpfungsgedanke im Neuen Testament," *Theologische Studien und Kritiken,* 104 (1932), 337–372.

[47] Larsson as p. 131 *n.* 38 above, his p. 190; John Bligh, "Liturgical Mysticism," *Heythrop Journal,* 2 (1961), 341; C. H. Dodd, *Gospel and Law* (New York: Columbia, 1951), 40; E. J. Tinsley, *Imitation of God in Christ* (Philadelphia: Westminster, 1960); R. Thysman, "L'éthique de l'imitation du Christ," *Ephemerides Theologicae Lovanienses,* 42 (1966), 138–175.

[48] Friedrich W. Eltester, *Eikon im Neuen Testament* (Beiheft 23 to *ZNW;* Berlin: Töpelmann, 1958), 136, finds that the strophe division of C. Masson's *Épître de saint Paul aux Colossiens* (Neuchâtel: 1950) is invalidated by ignoring that *hós*

Though the *apó* of *aparchē* is a synonym of *ex*, "from," still we would not detect here an echo of the *ex hoû* in 1 Corinthians 8:6 describing the Father as "origin" of creation.

Archē is a synonym of *prōtótokos* itself in the Greek Genesis 49:3. The famous crux of John 8:25, "(I am) the *archē* speaking to you," is apparently just a misunderstanding for "Why do I speak to you *at all?*" But in Apocalypse 3:14 Christ is the *archē tēs ktíseōs,* which seems to be an equivalent of *prōtótokos pásēs ktíseōs,* rather than the *"auctor* or (efficient) cause" suggested by Zorell's New Testament dictionary.

4. Regarding the primacy of Christ expressed in verse 18 *prōteúōn,* we have noted the recent Franciscan emphasis on this as key to the sense of *prōtótokos,* and our fear of a too extrinsic and paternalistic notion of "sovereignty."[49] The word "primacy" as currently understood in Catholic hierarchical circles, *"primatus* of honor or jurisdiction," leaves too entirely out of account the *temporal* sense which is present in *prôteúōn* as a synonym of *prōtótokos.*

It is interesting to compare the original Jerusalem Bible Colossians notes by Benoit with the vest-pocket abridgment, where we read: "Primacy of Christ: in the creation, verses 15-17, then in the new creation which is redemption, verses 18-20. The preexistent Christ is regarded in the historical person of the Son of God made man (Phlp 2:5), perfect image of God (Rom 8:29; 2 Cor 4:4; Heb 1:3); firstborn of creation by a primacy of excellence and causality (Jn 1:3; 1 Cor 8:6) rather than by a primacy of temporal priority."

To this, Benoit's somewhat lengthier notes add: "Christ is clearly identified here with the eternally preexistent Logos. . . . For Paul, the Incarnation has placed the human nature of Christ at the head, not only of the whole human race, but also of the whole created universe, indirectly [!] concerned with salvation as it was with the fault."[50] If we are not mistaken, these formulations lay a discreet groundwork toward saving for the Incarnation that extrinsicism with regard to creation which we will presently see to be the Thomist position. In similar vein, the analysis of Romans 8:22 f by Feuillet suggests that the whole creation is interested in men's salvation only as consequence of the disturbance of creation wrought by men's fall.[51]

---

estin eikōn of verse 15 is parallel to *hós estin archē* of verse 18; see above, p. 124 *n.* 12. Eltester's page 138 reproves Percy and Michaelis for neglecting the cosmic role of Christ — linked by him with Philo.

[49] See above, footnote 42; and below, footnote 100; pp. 132 and 146.

[50] Pierre Benoit, *Épître aux Colossiens* (Paris: Cerf, 1949), 55 f.

[51] A. Feuillet, "Le plan salvifique de Dieu d'après l'épître aux Romains," *Revue Biblique,* 57/3 (July 1950), 381; see also 51 (1942), 58–79, "L'Homme-Dieu considéré dans sa condition terrestre de serviteur et de rédempteur"; p. 160 below.

5. Fulness, *plērōma*. It is chiefly this word upon which the attention of Père Benoit's several relevant researches is focused. Gewiess had held that the church includes only redeemed men, not the cosmos, and this "Church as fulness of Christ" takes precedence over the All.[52] A more recent volume claims that for Christ to be "Head of the Church" logically precedes his being "Head of the Cosmos." Benoit demurs: "Not in Saint Paul's view, whatever be the logic; Paul first conceived Christ as Head-Authority of the cosmic powers, then subsequently fused the themes of Vital-Principle Head and Body of Christ."[53]

Since then we have the claim of Eduard Schweizer that in the Colossians *hymn* taken over by the compiler of the epistle, Christ's body is the All or cosmos which he "reconciles"; but some insertions made by the compiler himself *alter* the notion of Body of Christ to mean the Church; and Christ's work as Head is consequently made out to mean to *defeat* the cosmic powers rather than "reconcile" them, so that the cosmic significance of Christ is not in his Ascension binding heaven with earth, but in the apostolate to all nations.[54]

Another line of thought would see in Christ's "fulness" simply a term for his divine nature. It has been noticed that the Targums on Psalms 68:17 and 3 Kings 8:27 use similar terminology to express that YHWH made his "Presence" (*šekînâ*) dwell upon men.[55]

For Benoit, the "fulness" of Colossians 1:19 was rightly seen by Theodore of Mopsuestia to mean neither (exactly) the Church nor the divine nature, but rather the cosmic extension of the work of Christ, as distinct from Christ's (mystical) "body." This *body* always means man as saved, or the Church, and is a figure borrowed not from pagan or Gnostic images but from Hebrew corporate solidarity.[56]

---

[52] Josef Gewiess, "Die Begriffe *plēroûn* und *plērōma* im Kolosser- und Epheserbrief," Festschrift Max Meinertz, *Vom Wort des Lebens* (Neutestamentliche Abhandlungen, Ergänzungsband, 1; Münster: Aschendorff, 1951), 139, 128–141.

[53] Pierre Benoit, *Revue Biblique,* 71 (1964), 459, reviewing Isak J. DuPlessis, *Christus as hoof van kerk en kosmos* (Eph/Col; dissertation under N. Ridderbos; Groningen: V.R.B., 1962).

[54] Eduard Schweizer, "Die Kirche als Leib Christi in den paulinischen Antilegomena," *Theologische Literaturzeitung,* 86 (1961), 245, 241–256; see in English his "Church as the Missionary Body of Christ," *New Testament Studies,* 8 (1961), 1–11. Col 1:15 is called a "first-rate missionary text" by Horst Bürkle, "Die Frage nach dem 'kosmischen Christus' als Beispiel einer ökumenisch orientierten Theologie," *Kerygma und Dogma,* 11/2 (Apr. 1965), 104, 103–115, citing G. Rosenkranz, "Die Rede vom kosmischen Christus innerhalb der indischen Geisteswelt," *Evangelische Missions-Zeitschrift* (1963), 159; and Allan D. Galloway, *The Cosmic Christ* (New York, 1951).

[55] Sverre Aalen, "Begrepet plērōma i Kolosser- og Efeserbrevet," *Tidsskrift for Teologi og Kirke,* 23/2 (1952), 58, 49–67.

[56] Pierre Benoit, "Corps, tête et plérôme dans les épîtres de la captivité," *Revue Biblique,* 63 (1956), 5–44 = *Exégèse et Théologie* (Paris: Cerf, 1961), 2, 136, 107–153. On page 131, Benoit finds exaggerated the claim that even among Old

For Gnosticism, "the whole cosmos is a great 'body,' and this even in its primary sense."[57] The alleged Gnostic influences on the Dead Sea Scrolls have been discussed largely in relation to echoes of the Essenes discerned in Lightfoot's commentary on the epistle to the Colossians.[58]

Testament and Hellenistic sources "head" implies salvation: José M. González Ruiz, "Sentido soteriológico de *kephalē* en la cristología de san Pablo," *Anthologica annua*, 1 (Rome: 1953), 185–224. The sense of *plērōma* as complement, i.e., the Church, is with Chrysostom preferred by Javier M. a Vallisoleto, "Christi 'Pleroma' iuxta Pauli conceptionem," *Verbum Domini*, 14 (1934), 49–55. Now Barnabas Ahern, "The Christian's Union with the Body of Christ in Cor., Gal., and Rom.," *Catholic Biblical Quarterly*, 23/2 (Oct. 1961), 200, favors Lucien Cerfaux, *Christ in the Theology of Saint Paul* (New York: Herder and Herder, 1959), 429–432, and J. A. T. Robinson, in their insistence (against Prat and Allo) that Christians belong not to a mystical Christ but to the organism of his risen person; see F.-X. Durrwell, *The Resurrection* (New York: Sheed, 1960), 108–150; M.-J. Scheeben, *The Mysteries of Christianity* (Saint Louis: Herder, 1946), 357–430. Ernest Best, *One Body in Christ* (London: SPCK, 1955), 115, notes Lohmeyer, Dibelius, Käsemann, and Knox holding that in Colossians the Body of Christ does *not* as in the earlier epistles consist only of believers united in Christ, but is now seen as embracing the entire universe; page 124, verses 19 f would indeed seem to give the reason, not for Christ's headship over the Church, but for the preeminence over all things [which] includes the Church but is not equivalent to it; page 126, the Church as Body consists of redeemed humanity, not including the heavenly powers or the whole creation. See further Victor Warnach, "Kirche und Kosmos," in Hilarius Emonds, *Enkainia* (Düsseldorf: 1956), 184–196; and M.-A. Wagenführer, *Die Bedeutung Christi für Welt und Kirche: Studien zum Kolosser- und Epheserbrief* (Leipzig: 1941).

[57] J. Dupont, *Gnosis: la connaissance religieuse dans les épîtres de saint Paul* (Theological dissertations, 2/40; Louvain: 1949), 432; page 423, on *plērōma/sōma* passages of Ephesians 3:19; Colossians 1:15, "Christ does not appear solely as 'head' of the Church, to the exclusion of those heavenly powers which are not part of it; the 'body' now extends beyond the Church and opens out cosmic perspectives"; page 175, Paul's antithesis of *psychikós/pneumatikós*, 1 Corinthians 15:44, is based on Genesis 2:7 as in Philo. — Martin Dibelius, *An die Kolosser, Epheser, an Philemon* (H. Lietzmann, Handbuch zum Neuen Testament 12; Tübingen: Mohr, 1953), 11, sees Christ of Colossians 1:16 as the Gnostic *Urmensch*, and as World-Soul and Creator; this otherwise un-Pauline Christology becomes intelligible when we take into account the Colossae adversaries. Walter Schmithals, *Paulus und die Gnostiker: Untersuchungen zu den kleinen Paulusbriefen* (including Romans 16 but not Colossians; Theologische Forschungen, 35; Hamburg: Reich, 1965). Günther Bornkamm, "Die Häresie des Kolosserbriefes," in *Das Ende des Gesetzes: Paulusstudien* (Beiträge zur evangelischen Theologie, 16; Munich: Kaiser, 1952), 139–156, holds on pages 147 ff a fringe-Jewish redemption Gnosis. Stanislas Lyonnet, "Les adversaires de Colosses" as part of "L'étude du milieu du Nouveau Testament," *Biblica*, 37 (1956), 27–32, commends Dupont; and in "L'hymne christologique de l'Épître aux Colossiens et la fête juive du Nouvel An (Philon, Spec. Leg. 192)," *Recherches de Science Religieuse*, 48 (1960), 93–100, finds at Colossae a syncretism of largely Jewish inspiration. But Gnosis is not mentioned, and the adversary-syncretism is hard to name and pertains to no recognizable system, for Karl Staab, *Briefe an die Epheser . . . Kolosser* (Würzburg: Echter-Bibel, 1954), 47; see his *Pauluskommentare aus der griechischen Kirche* (Neutestamentliche Abhandlungen; Münster: Aschendorff, 1933).

[58] J. B. Lightfoot, *Saint Paul's Epistles to the Colossians and to Philemon*,[3] (London: Macmillan, 1879), 349–419, has been a valuable mine for linking the

Again the inquiries of Martin in the wake of Norden find Colossians 1:15-20 to be "a gnostic myth of primal man adapted to pure Christian theology."[59] Depending on how well it was "adapted," we may or may not be disposed to admit that the Pauline firstborn Christ is an image borrowed from a creation myth.

Plērōma is indeed in Ephesians 1:23 linked with the Body, of Ephesians 4:16 and 1 Corinthians 12:27; but "the *plērōma* declarations of Colossians set forth the full unity of operation between God and Christ in such a way as to safeguard their personal being and safeguard also monotheism: God works through Christ in his whole fulness (1:19), his whole being-God (2:9)."[60]

Mussner's failure to find a cosmic nuance in *plērōma* is called by Benoit "too timid, not to say inexact."[61] There is cogency in Goguel's claim that Ephesians 1, 10.22 depicts "a restoration" in Christ which engulfs the whole universe, so that redemption is no longer merely personal but cosmic.[62] However, Benoit adds that "recapitulation" is a more accurate

Essenes with the Qumran Dead Sea community; see our "Qumran 'Sadducees,'" *Catholic Biblical Quarterly,* 17/2 (O'Hara Festschrift, April 1955), 57. On pages 73 to 113 Lightfoot maintains that "the Colossian heresy" was Essene with a Gnostic turn. Pleroma is a Gnostic term for "the totality of divine powers and attributes" (pp. 102, 159). "A perverted view respecting the nature of the mediation [of the Logos between God and creation] lay at the root of the heretical teaching of Colossae" (p. 101). "The history of the patristic exegesis of [*prōtótokos,* chiefly meaning priority and secondarily sovereignty: above, footnote 43] is not without a painful interest," namely its referral to the Incarnate Christ as an *ad hoc* expedient against Arius (p. 148). But our Colossians passage is a baptismal liturgy containing *none* of the alleged allusions to heresies rampant at Colossae, according to Ernst Käsemann, "Eine urchristliche Taufliturgie," in the (1949 not 1954!) *R. Bultmann Festschrift* (Stuttgart: Kohlhammer, 1949), 143.

[59] Ralph P. Martin, "An Early Christian Hymn (Col 1:15–20)," *Evangelical Quarterly,* 36/4 (Oct. 1964), 195–205. According to James M. Robinson, "A Formal Analysis of Col 1:15–20," *Journal of Biblical Literature,* 76 (1957), 270–287, 279, this passage like Heb 1:3 "moves from the *imago Dei* and *tà pánta* concepts of preexistent, to the victory over the spirit world at the exaltation"; similarly H. Hegermann's Halle dissertation reported in *Theologische Literaturzeitung,* 85 (1960), 468.

[60] Gerhard Delling, "*Plēróō,*" *Theologisches Wörterbuch zum Neuen Testament* (Stuttgart: Kohlhammer, 1959), 6, 302. There is no article on pleroma in *Religion in Geschichte und Gegenwart.*3 M. Bogdasavich, "The idea of *Pleroma* in the Epistles to the Colossians and Ephesians," *Downside Review,* 83/271 (Apr. 1965), 118–130, concludes that it is a term to "build with" rather than to define.

[61] Franz Mussner, *Christus, das All und die Kirche: Studien zur Theologie des Epheserbriefes* (Trierer Theologische Studien, 5; Trier: Paulus-Verlag, 1955); Benoit, *Exégèse et Théologie* 2, 164.

[62] Maurice Goguel, "Esquisse d'une solution nouvelle du problème de l'épître aux Éphésiens," *Revue de l'Histoire des Religions,* 111/3 (May 1935), 254–284; 112/1 (July 1935), 73–99; page 98, the imitations of Colossians in Ephesians are an interpolation rather than as Benoit claims a development within the Pauline corpus; proved page 83 from *prōteúon* of Colossians 1:18 expressing fleetingly the whole Christological preoccupation of the author, as in Ephesians [1:22]. In "Le caractère et le rôle de l'élément cosmologique dans la sotériologie paulinienne,"

term than restoration, and "the redemption of the [infra-human] creation is not primary but in spite of itself. . . . In Ephesians one is conscious of penetrating, at the side of the truly Pauline idea of vanquishment of the celestial powers in a redemptive triumph, to the new concept of a redemption engulfing them in a vast cosmic salvation of which human salvation is [an aspect]."[63]

Benoit's view of Christ's cosmic functions approaches the "paternalistic and extrinsic" by focusing on the *defeat* or management of the "spirit-powers" by Christ. This is faithful to the *ad hominem* character of Paul's attack on actual gnosticizing adversaries at Colossae. This approach to one special threat against Christ's primacy is not opposed to, or even ultimately explainable otherwise than as, a function of Christ as firstborn of creation to the exclusion of such mythic cosmic powers.

The "recapitulation" of all things in Christ, of Ephesians 1:10, is specially considered here by Mooney,[64] in his article which concludes with this citation:

> It would not be extravagant, as long as it was done with prudence, to conceive the evolution of the world as an orientation *toward Christ*. . . . The only danger to be avoided is the suggestion that such evolution is an ascent which the world accomplishes by forces which are wholly its own. If what St. Paul says in Col 1:15 is true and not softened by some moralistic interpretation, if furthermore the world as a whole, including therefore its physical reality, is actually in process of reaching in and through Christ that final state in which God is all in all, then the line of thought we are developing here cannot be entirely false.[65]

6. Finally we have rendered as "principle of unification of all things" the term of Colossians 1:20 "to reconcile all things in (-to) him." The Greek *katalláxai* is literally "readjust." It is in fact used by Paul for reconciliation, for example of a woman with her deserted husband (1 Cor 7:11);

Revue d'Histoire et de Philosophie Religieuses, 15/4 (July 1935), 335–359; page 349, Christ is superior to the "elementary cosmic powers" (*stoicheîa* = the stars) because he created them; this is the sense of *prōteúōn* in Colossians 1:18 as *contrasted* with *prōtótokos;* page 345 rejects the view of H. Lietzmann, *An die Römer* (Tübingen: Mohr, 1933), 85, that the "corruption" of Romans 8:21 means servitude of demons.

[63] Pierre Benoit, "L'horizon paulinien de l'épître aux Éphésiens," *Revue Biblique,* 46 (1937), 351, 342–361, 506–525, *Exégèse et Théologie,* 2, 53–96, 62.

[64] Christopher F. Mooney, "The Body of Christ in the Writings of Teilhard de Chardin," *Theological Studies,* 25/4 (Dec. 1964), 576, 610. In reviewing *Le premier Teilhard: le Christ et le Monde* in *Études* (May 1965), 658 f, on Colossians 1:15, Christian d'Armagnac observes, "Teilhard insisted greatly on the continuity between the creative action of God and the unifying work of the Incarnate Word, the second harmoniously prolonging the first through showing God's gratuitous love," citing Pierre de Lorea, "the Incarnation was profitable to the entire universe."

[65] Karl Rahner, *Theological Investigations* (Baltimore: Helicon, 1961), I = Probleme der Christologie von heute," *Schriften zur Theologie* (Einsiedeln: Benziger, 1958), 1, 187 f.

and also for men's reconciliation with God after he has become offended
by sin (Rm 5:10). In 2 Corinthians 5:18, God is said to have "readjusted
us to himself through Christ and given us a ministry of readjustment," but
Paul goes on "in the same way that God has been readjusting the cosmos
to himself in Christ."

How does Christ reconcile the things which are "in the skies" or in
Heaven? This is referred to the *Angels'* "need of the grace of Christ," in an
article written by the present Secretary of the Biblical Commission.[66] But
it is doubtful that Paul could have been thinking of the "reconciliation" of
any real Spirits, either the good, who did not need any, or the evil, whose
redemption is unknown to Christian tradition.[67]

Actually any reconciliation among individual intellectual beings is a
"unification," a breaking down of barriers and divisions. However, in
choosing "unification" to express such root senses of *kat-alláxai* as "reduced
otherness" or "redirected alteration," we have admittedly drawn Paul's
text a step closer toward the teilhardian vision of creation itself as a continuing cosmic process tending through multiplicity toward unity.

4. *Pre-Thirteenth-Century Posing of the Problem*

The Fathers of the Church do not discuss whether Christ is head of the
material creation even to the extent that he would have become incarnate
if there had been no sin. Not long ago there was discovered such a declaration in the works of Isaac of Nineveh A.D. 700.[68] This is a surprising
anticipation, outside the stream of Latin theology, of a doctrine which
became discussed only in a much later setting. More surprisingly still
the statement was somehow omitted in the English translation by
Wensinck.[69]

ANSELM OF CANTERBURY finished his course in 1109. "Why did God
become man?" the title of his major work, seems an obvious step toward
answering the question as posed above.[70] To have no rational answer to

---

[66] Benjamin N. Wambacq, "Per eum reconciliare . . . quae in coelis sunt (Col
1:20)," *Revue Biblique,* 55/1 (Jan. 1948), 35–42; see now C. Maurer, "Die
Begründung der Herrschaft Christi über die Mächte nach Kolosser, 1, 15–20,"
Wort und Dienst, Bethel-Jahrbuch, 4 (1953), 79–93. See below, p. 156, n. 137.

[67] Johann Michl, "Die 'Versöhnung' (Kol 1, 20)," *Tübinger Theologische
Quartalschrift,* 128 (1948), 442–462; what is reconciled is "the whole order of
creation," disturbed by men's sin.

[68] Isaac de Ninive, *De perfectione religiosa,* edited by Paul Bedjan (Paris: 1909),
583–586; Irénée Hausherr, "Un précurseur de la théorie scotiste sur la fin de
l'Incarnation," *Recherches de Science Religieuse,* 22 (1932), 316–320.

[69] A. J. Wensinck, *Mystic Treatises by Isaac of Niniveh* (Amsterdam: 1923).

[70] Rudolf Haubst, "Das hoch- und spätmittelalterliche 'Cur Deus homo,'" *Münchener Theologische Zeitschrift,* 6/4 (1955), 302–313.

Anselm's question, "Why a God-man?" would show up badly the alleged "reasonableness" of Christian dogma, though of course what is a mystery cannot be "proved" or even "adequately explained."[71]

It has been pointed out that authors such as Josson are anachronistic in looking to Anselm's essay for the answer to a question raised later about the motives of the Incarnation.[72] He nowhere shows concern over whether Christ was incarnate only to repair the original fault; his viewpoint is only after the event: *if* man is to be restored, the Incarnation is necessary. "His aim was, to present to the faithful as well as to 'unbelievers' one single same 'demonstration' of the 'necessity' of the redemptive Incarnation, which would be valid for all."[73]

Anselm attacks those who say the Incarnation and Passion were unnecessary. But his own *rationes necessariae* mean not merely the conclusion of a deductive process, nor do they deny God's freedom; they express only men's "need of salvation."[74]

Anselm's inquiry marks a step beyond the previous perspectives. Even though it is still far off from the inquiry about whether the Incarnation would have happened without the fall, still its hinting at the shape of things to come is admitted in Haubst's Thomist-slanted research by severely calling Anselm's position "a novelty abandoning the concrete salvation-history situation for an unreal hypothesis."

RUPERT OF DEUTZ is the first (apart from Isaac) to have asked the question in that "contrary-to-fact" form, around 1100 or during Anselm's last years. Rupert proceeds to cite various evidences supporting really a negative answer. Still he adds, "the real question is whether it was in some way necessary for the human race that the God-man should become lord and king of all. Certain it is that the saints and elect would have been born if there was no sin."[75] The conclusion seems to be that their sanctity would still have had to be grounded in the Incarnation.

ALEXANDER OF HALES, the Franciscan leader one century later in 1200, takes up Rupert's question, but gives it an evasive answer. "Even if human

---

[71] Anselm, *Cur Deus Homo?* 1, 1; *ML* 158, 361; dated about 1095; see B. Geyer, "Zur Deutung von Anselms Cur Deus homo," *Theologie und Glaube,* 34 (1942), 205.

[72] J. Josson, *Saint Anselme: sa vie et son traité des Motifs de l'Incarnation* (Charleroi: 1872).

[73] René Roques, *Anselme: Pourquoi Dieu s'est fait homme* (Sources chrétiennes 91; Paris: Cerf, 1963), 47; on Josson 66.

[74] Anselm, *Cur Deus homo?*, 2, 5; *ML* 158, 361; *De Incarnatione Verbi,* 6, ed. S. Schmitt (Florilegium patristicum 28; Bonn: Hanstein, 1931), 2, 70. See also A. Dondaine, "La question 'De necessitate Incarnationis' de Robert Kilwardby, O.P.," *Recherches de Théologie Ancienne et Médiévale,* 8 (1936), 97–100.

[75] Rupert of Deutz, *De gloria et honore filii hominis, ML* 168, 1628. On the other hand, in his *De operibus Spiritus Sancti,* 2, 6; *ML* 167, 1610, are given reasons why the Incarnation would not have happened apart from sin.

nature had not fallen, there would still be a certain suitableness in the Incarnation."[76] This answer, by accentuating the positive, rather favors the eventual Scotus reply. The term "suitableness" recalls to us how the reliance of Scotus on his "argument from suitableness" was to give a decisive boost to the theology of the Immaculate Conception.

However, the successor of Alexander was Odo Rigaldi; and he refuted Alexander's teaching on the ground that God cannot be held to do everything best.[77]

ALBERT THE GREAT, in his early Summa on the Incarnation around 1200, set down as the sole motive of God's becoming man "the relief of misery." But in his later commentary on Peter Lombard he declares expressly, though as a mere personal opinion, that the Son of God would have become man even in case there had been no sin. His reasons for this include God's love and goodness, but more basically the old "suitableness." Creation comes from God and goes back to God in a sort of cycle, which can only be tapered off by the union of God and man, saving always God's freedom and the supernatural mystery of such a union.[78]

Robert Grosseteste agreed with Alexander and Albert.[79]

5. The Positions of Aquinas and Scotus

When BONAVENTURE succeeded to the Franciscan leadership after 1250, he was confronted with a choice between the views of Alexander and Odo. Instead of merely giving his personal opinion, he is the first to outline *proofs* of the respective positions, both of which he qualifies as orthodox. He deals with the difficulty of how "the lesser can cause the greater," as would happen if Christ's keystone position in the universe is held due to

[76] Alexander of Hales, *Summa Theologica*, 3, 1, 2, 2 (Quaracchi near Florence: St. Bonaventure's College, 1948), 4, 42. But in 2, inq. 1, tr. 2, q. 3, c. 6, a. 4 [as cited by Haubst in *Münchener Theologische Zeitschrift*, 6 (1955), 304], he says that the Incarnation would have added nothing to the beauty of the universe in a state of innocence; whence Haubst concludes it is hard to know on which side Alexander really was.

[77] Odo Rigaldi, *Quaestio de motivo Incarnationis*, edited by John M. Bissen in *Antonianum*, 7 (1932), 334–336. Bissen's interpretation is challenged by F. M. Henquinet, "Eudes de Rosny, O.F.M., Eudes Rigaud et la Somme d'Alexandre d'Halès," *Archivum Franciscanum Historicum*, 33 (1940), 3–54.

[78] Albert, *In Sententias*, 3, 20, 4; 3, 1, 1 (Auguste Borgnet edition; Paris: Vivès, 1894), 28, 360; 28, 6. The citation from *Summa de Incarnatione* is given by Haubst from a manuscript prepared for publication by I. Backes. See Ferd. Haberl, *Die Inkarnationslehre des hl. Albertus Magnus* (Freiburg: 1939), on Third Sentences, 20, 4.

[79] Dominic J. Unger, "Robert Grosseteste Bishop of Lincoln (1235–1253), on the Reasons for the Incarnation," *Franciscan Studies*, 16 (1956), 1–36: a newly available manuscript, containing relevant statements from *De cessatione legalium* and from *Hexaemeron*.

man's fall. But he opts firmly for the prevalence of patristic tradition over theological reasoning and concludes that redemption from sin was the chief motive of the Incarnation.[80]

THOMAS AQUINAS, "early in his career and long before Scotus, had considered it probable that the Incarnation would have taken place apart from men's sin. At the end of his life, he puts himself definitely back into accord with the word of God [!], which knows only the Redemption, and he holds this is the motive, not exclusive but determinant, of the Incarnation."[81]

With another recent Thomist we might more moderately say that Aquinas in his mature life declared that whether the Incarnation would have taken place apart from men's sin "is not a matter of great importance; simply a thing we cannot know"; so that on the dialectical consequences to be drawn from revelation he does not set himself in opposition to Albert.[82] In his commentary on Lombard, Aquinas still allows as probable Albert's conclusion from the needed cyclic fulness of the universe.[83]

But the *Summa Theologiae* reaches this view: "Since in Scripture everywhere the reason of the Incarnation is assigned as the sin of the first man, it is more suitably (*convenientius*) held that the Incarnation was ordained by God for a remedy against sin. Thus if sin had not existed, neither would there have been an Incarnation."[84]

As basis for this judgment, Aquinas makes his own the gloss which really adds nothing to the wording of 1 Timothy 1:5, "Jesus Christ came into the world to save sinners." The more authoritative gloss of Augustine

[80] Bonaventure, *In Sententias* (Florence-Quaracchi edition; 1887), 3, 23. See now Alexander Schaefer, "The Position and Function of Man in the Created World According to Saint Bonaventure," *Franciscan Studies*, 20 (1960), 261–316; 21 (1961), 233–282.

[81] Maurice Corvez, "Le motif de l'Incarnation," *Revue Thomiste*, 49 (1949), 110.

[82] H.-M. Féret, "À propos de la primauté du Christ," *Revue des Sciences Philosophiques et Théologiques*, 27 (1938), 70; 30 (1941), 101: the Thomist view is just a statement of revelation, almost without dialectic; page 132: the Church chose this least dialectical of her theologians as her *doctor communis;* if he had not fallen under a cloud in 1270–1277 the Church would have been spared the sterile wrangling which prompted Luther to exclaim, "It would have been a good thing for the Church and its theologians if there had never been born a Porphyrius with his universals."

[83] Aquinas, *In Sententias*, 3, 1, 1, 3 (Maria-Fabian Moos edition; Paris: Lethielleux, 1933), 22: "Most of the Fathers say only because of sin. But some [contemporaries] say God's aim was the exaltation of the race, so that the Incarnation would have happened apart from sin. That too is probable."

[84] Aquinas, *Summa Theologiae*, 3, 1, 1, 2. See now Reginald Garrigou-Lagrange, "De motivo Incarnationis: examen recentium obiectionum contra S. Thomae III, q. 1, a. 3," *Acta Academiae Romanae S. Thomae*, 10 (1945), 7–45; and "Motivum Incarnationis fuit motivum misericordiae," *Angelicum*, 7 (1930), 289–302.

is further cited: "There was no cause for the coming of Christ except to save sinners. If you postulate the nonexistence of the disease and wounds, then there is no reason for the medicine. 'The Son of Man came to save what was lost' (Lk 19:10). Therefore if man had not sinned, the Son of Man would not have come."[85] The maxim here quoted is perhaps what prompted Henri Marrou to accuse Augustine of having caused "that atrophying of the cosmic bearing of Christian salvation" which Teilhard after a long time remedies.[86]

Aquinas, however, elsewhere in the *Summa* strongly vindicates for Christ a preeminence in the whole of creation which [was existing "already" and therefore] was not lost to him in his being handed over to death by God for men's sin.[87] Our inserted word "already" hints at the distinction of successive acts in God, either according to their term or according to our mode of conceiving, which with some later Scholastics will become paramount. The *Summa* itself insists on the unicity of the act by which God predestined both the Incarnation and the saving of the elect.[88]

Despite the influence of Aquinas, the half-century between him and Scotus saw a universal acceptance of the Alexander-Albert thesis.

MATTHEW OF AQUASPARTA in 1282, dissenting from his admired Bonaventure, maintained that for the perfecting of the natural order the Incarnation was to be supposed.[89] RAYMOND LULL in 1289 affirmed that the primary aim of the Incarnation was not our redemption but the showing forth and love of God.[90] Even the Thomist PIERRE OF AUVERGNE in 1298 distinguished God's first intention as the elevating of human nature, from the redemption as his second intention.[91] Meanwhile at Oxford, following Roger Marston, WILLIAM OF WARE held that "the Incarnation without

---

[85] Augustine, Sermon 175 on Scripture, *ML* 38, 945; Walafrid Strabo, *Glossa Ordinaria, ML* 114, 626.

[86] Pierre de Boisdeffre, "Problèmes actuels et pensée teilhardienne," *Revue Générale Belge* (Jan. 1961), offprint p. 3; see now E. Scano, *Il cristocentrismo e i suoi fondamenti dommatici in sant' Agostino* (Turin: 1951); F.-J. Thonnard, "Philosophie augustinienne et phénomène humain," *Revue des Sciences Religieuses,* 31 (1957), 275–289: page 285, Augustinianism is more suited to Teilhard's worldview than Thomism; but (p. 288) Augustine first lays down the Catholic faith and then fits science in; Teilhard starts from facts and finds they demand faith.

[87] Aquinas, *Summa Theologiae,* 1, 20, 4, 1.

[88] *Summa Theologiae,* 3, 24, 3 f; also *Contra Gentes,* 1, 66.

[89] Matthew of Aquasparta, *Quodlibeta,* 5, 2, 1.

[90] Raymond Lull, *Quaestiones per artem demonstrativam seu inventivam solubiles,* 29.

[91] Peter of Auvergne, *Quodlibeta,* 3, 2, cited from the Paris manuscript by Haubst in *Münchener Theologische Zeitschrift,* 6 (1955), 309.

passibility" (a distinction borrowed from Bonaventure, later to prove important) would have taken place apart from sin.[92]

DUNS SCOTUS will perhaps mean most to the religious thinkers of our generation as the man around whom Martin Heidegger built his doctoral formation.[93] Many of us also, too many, have learned to stereotype Scotus as the inventor of a glib formula, *formalis a parte rei,* for slipping between hammer and anvil in the Thomist controversy on real distinction between essence and existence. It seems somewhat less than fair to take up any theological insight linked to his name without locating it in the perspective of that whole system of formal-real distinction. But the compartmentalization of science forces us to leave our findings open at this point for that technical treatment which only a philosopher can undertake.

As part of his Oxford lectures, Scotus wrote but did not finish a work called *Ordinatio.* In it he asserted that the Incarnation was not necessarily bound to man's fall as a *conditio sine qua non,* because Christ *could* also in other conceivable situations have become man. In this there is no dissent from the teachings of Bonaventure and Aquinas. And, according to the recent Franciscan editor of his works, this is the *only* declaration on the subject which we have from Scotus himself, as distinct from class notes edited by his pupils.[94]

The *Opus Oxoniense,* apparently as a disciple's continuation of the *Ordinatio* on the basis of lectures given in 1302, distinguished a series of five acts in God. First he recognizes himself as supreme good. Secondly he recognizes all creatable things. Thirdly he predestines to glory and grace. Fourthly he foresees those who will fall in Adam. Fifthly he foresees his means of rescuing them.[95]

In this series, Christ as man takes his place in the *third* step, among the elect, before the foreseeing of sin.[96]

These *signa rationis* undoubtedly betray a kinship to the sixteenth-century Nominalism threatening on the horizon. However, they are to some extent inseparable from any "analysis" of the many facets of the-

---

[92] J. M. Bissen, "Une question inédite de Guillaume de Ware, O.F.M., sur le motif de l'Incarnation," *Études Franciscaines,* 46 (1934), 218–222; on Roger Marston, *Quodlibeta,* 2, 5, see Jean-F. Bonnefoy, "La question hypothétique: Utrum Si Adam Non Peccasset . . . au XIIIᵉ siècle," *Revista Española de Teología,* 14 (1954), 352.

[93] Martin Heidegger, *Die Kategorien- und Bedeutungslehre des Duns Scotus* (Tübingen: Mohr, 1916). See too Béraud de Saint Maurice, *John Duns Scotus: a teacher for our time* (translated by C. Duffy; St. Bonaventure, N. Y.: Franciscan Institute, 1955), 239–275.

[94] Karl Balič, "Duns Skotus' Lehre über Christi Prädestination im Lichte der neuesten Forschungen," *Wissenschaft und Weisheit,* 3 (1936), 21.

[95] Duns Scotus, *Opus Oxoniense,* 3, 19; Vivès edition, 14, 714.

[96] See Scotus, *In Sententias,* 4, 3, 7, 3.

odicy which are all in God's one simple indivisible act. Perhaps we can detect behind the naiveté of student reporters an acceptable grain within the "vital situation" of Scotus' lectures themselves.

In the similar reports of his Paris lectures around 1307, the conclusion was reached that Christ did not enter into the system of either the natural or the supernatural world "by accident." God's sovereign work could not have been the result of an "occasion" or incidental event that might not and indeed *should* not have happened.[97]

Six Reserves about the role of Scotus. The above well-sifted facts seem to connect the "Scotist theory of the motive of the Incarnation" ineluctably with Duns Scotus. And really, this situation is not essentially changed by six important qualifications which have now to be made.

1. In preparing a definitive edition of the Scotist corpus, Balič came up with a dramatic proof that the "Scotist" thesis is found only in notes edited by pupils, and nowhere in Scotus' own work.[98] In the work called *Ordinatio,* or also *Opus Oxoniense,* Scotus himself denied that the fall was *conditio sine qua non* of the Incarnation, but did not say explicitly that the Incarnation would have taken place if man had not sinned. The *Reportationes* taken down by students in Paris state categorically that the Word would have become man even if Adam had not sinned. In setting forth Balič's discovery in English, Rabbitte claims that this last is "quite a different doctrine."[99]

Not all will agree that it is so altogether different. To deny that the Fall conditioned the Incarnation may well seem to anyone but a *doctor subtilis* equivalent to saying that the actuation of the Incarnation was independent of the foreseen fall. Moreover, the fact that the more explicit form attributed commonly to Scotus escaped detection and outcry for so long would seem to leave a presumption in favor of his having really taught it, whether

---

[97] Scotus, *Reportata Parisiensia,* 3, 7, 5; P. Raymond, "Duns Scot," *Dictionnaire de Théologie Catholique* (Paris: Letouzey, 1939), 4, 1891. — According to A. Pelzer, "Le premier livre des Reportata Parisiensia de Jean Duns Scot," *Annales de l'Institut Supérieur de Philosophie de Louvain,* 5 (1923), 449, the Vienna codex was checked by Scotus himself. — Theophilus Harapin, "De praedestinatione Christi iuxta doctrinam B. J. Duns Scoti," Latin summary of "O predestinaciji Kristovoj po nauci Bl. Ivana Duns Skota," *Collectanea franciscana slavica* (Zagreb congress, 1935; Sibenik, Jugoslavia: Kačič, 1937), 267 =310, brings out that Scotus nowhere appealed to revelation to establish his view; and that despite de Basly and though avoiding the "purely hypothetical," he really held the Incarnation would have happened even if Adam had not sinned.

[98] Karl Balič, "Duns Skotus' Lehre," *Wissenschaft und Weisheit,* 3 (1936), 19–35; see also Dominic J. Unger, "Select Questions on the Final Cause of the Incarnation," *Franciscan Educational Conference,* 38 (1957), 46–76.

[99] Edwin Rabbitte, "The 'Motive' of the Incarnation: was Scotus a Scotist?," *Irish Ecclesiastical Record,* 65 (1945), 117–125; see also 70 (1948), 878–889.

he wrote that particular page or not. At the very least it leaves us fairly sure that Scotus never squarely posed the question with the intention of *dissociating* himself from the view which bears his name.

2. Long before Balič's discovery, there had already been advanced by other Franciscans a claim that in this discussion "Scotus was as remote from the Scotists as from the Thomists."[100] This school sees paramount importance in the fact that Scotus never posed an *unreal* hypothesis, "what *would* have happened *if*. . . ." Among those who commented on Scotus, the earliest to formulate the question in such a way as to return from unreality to historical reality was Dupasquier.

> We inquire here whether in the eternal decree of the Incarnation God regarded man's redemption by the death and blood of Christ in such wise that if Adam had not sinned nor thus needed redemption, *in virtue of the existing decree* Christ would not have come.[101]

The position of Dupasquier and de Basly bears a similarity to the reformulation made by the Jesuit Billot in order to favor the Thomist solution:

> The proposition, "If man had not sinned, the Word would not have become incarnate," is nothing other than a circumlocution to express the adequate end toward which God in fact foreordained the Incarnation. . . . The whole assertion is limited to the decree now existing. It is asserted to be such that with sin removed its reason and end would no longer be there.[102]

In spite of the emphasis laid by recent polemics, it would seem to me that the posing of the unreal hypothesis is an altogether legitimate reframing of the question at issue. Or at worst it could be called an inescapable deduction from the basic position. As often happens in mastering the fine points of *moral* theology, a norm of profound importance and wide applicability can best be grasped as exemplified in an oversimplified and implausible border-line case. I believe that with this claim I rejoin the essential conclusions of Carmelite Xiberta's elaborately documented research.[103]

---

[100] Deodatus M. de Basly, "Le vrai motif de l'Incarnation: Scot aussi loin des Scotistes que des Thomistes," *Revue Duns Scot,* 9 (1911), 149; cited by E. Caggiano in *Antonianum,* 32 (1957), 312, 317.

[101] Sebastien Dupasquier, *Summa theologiae scholasticae* (Padua: 1706), 5, 153; so also Bartholomaeus Durandus, *Clypeus scotisticae theologiae* (Venice: 1709), 4, 74; Bartholomaeus Mastrius de Meldula, *Disputationes in 3 Sent.,* 4, 1 (Venice: 1719), 206; Crescentius Krisper, *Theologia scholae scotisticae* (Innsbruck: 1748), 3, 237.

[102] Louis Billot, *De Verbo Incarnato*[4] (Rome: Gregorian, 1904), 33.

[103] Bartolomeo M. Xiberta, *Tractatus de Verbo Incarnato 2. Soteriologia* (Madrid: Instituto Suárez, 1952), 659 f: the only reasonable way to pose the question is in view of arriving at "a motive of such a kind that apart from it the Incarnation would or would not have taken place"; in this sense we must say that man's Fall

3. A third avenue for cutting out the ground from under the objections to the Scotus view is represented by an article of Assouad. The sin of Adam is not the motive of the Incarnation itself, but of its *modality* in "passible" form.[104]

4. The manner in which many modern Franciscans seem to equate our present question with that of the Primacy of Christ in the existing creation seems to me of dubious validity. No party to the discussion has ever shown any inclination to deny that once his coming has been actuated or even decreed, Christ is the king and acme of creation. But there would seem to be a danger of inverting the question "whether sin or rather creation itself is the motive of the Incarnation" into "whether the Incarnation or God's own Being is the motive of *creation.*" This would head us toward a position basic to Malebranche, but really quite different from the one with which we are concerned:[105]

> Without the Incarnation, creation would not adequately have served its purpose, viz. to give the greatest possible glory to God. . . . For God to have created the material universe without any ulterior end would not have been an act worthy of Himself.[106]

This article of one American Franciscan, despite the title which the above words belie, is rejected by another as "a reversal of the genuine, traditional Scotistic view."[107] The charge would seem to be warranted, but also to be valid against the many treatises which more eruditely and more

---

is the motive of the *execution* of the Incarnation-decree (as all would admit) but not of the decree *itself.* Xiberta's bibliography, pp. 735–739, is supplemented by patristic sources in his *Enchiridion de Verbo Incarnato* (Madrid: 1957), 801.

[104] Nicola Assouad, "Necessarium Adae peccatum," *Studi Francescani,* 7 (1935), 217. As noticed by Egidio M. Caggiano, "De mente Joannis Duns Scoti circa rationem Incarnationis," *Antonianum,* 32 (1957), 311–334, Honorius of Autun was holding as early as 1130 in *De angelis et homine, ML* 172, 1186, "Tradition indeed says that sin was cause of the Incarnation, but this is not evil causing good; sin really was only the cause of the *passible state* of Christ." Caggiano on page 329 concludes, "Scotus does not skirt the *problem* posed by the question 'Would the Son of God have become incarnate even if men had not sinned?,' though he does skirt the *formulation* itself." See above, p. 87 on Adam's necessary sin.

[105] Jean-Joseph Maydieu, "La création du monde et l'Incarnation du Verbe dans la philosophie de Malebranche," *Bulletin de Littérature Ecclésiastique,* 36 (1935), 73: "Without the Mediator and his taking charge of *matter,* the world was unintelligible, impossible, inconceivable, and pure nothingness."

[106] Father George, "Incarnation is Complement of Creation: the Duns Scotus View," *American Ecclesiastical Review,* 88 (1933), 523 f. It is fair to remark that we have here basically a sermon for the feast of Christ the King.

[107] Michael D. Meilach, item 218 of the mimeographed bibliography prepared in continuance of his work on the popularizing volume *Firstborn Son* (Chicago: Franciscan Herald, 1962). I have also been greatly helped by the use of the mimeographed bibliography and class-notes of Father Camillus Hay of the Franciscan theology seminary of Melbourne.

guardedly set the actual primacy of Christ in the center of the discussion.[108]

Before leaving this topic we may call attention to the high-caliber disagreement between two Dominicans about the impartial exposition of Scotus' view. In a recent volume of Bouëssé the relevant pages contributed by Jerusalem exegete Lemoine pose the question, "What is the motive, or rather the finality, of the Incarnation? . . . Is it willed for itself, for its own value as supreme communication of Being and perfecting of the universe? . . . Rather it had as it motive man's sin, or more accurately God's will of saving man from his sin. Otherwise we would have no answer to the objection of John of St. Thomas, 'So then God willed the evil for the sake of the remedy.' "[109] To all this Nicolas replies, firmly holding the Thomist position in essentials, but calling for greater fairness to Scotus on several details. Scotus proves that Christ *cannot* NOT have been, if he is the head of the natural universe. "Scotus did not say, as Bouëssé and many Scotists today make him say, 'The world with Christ is more worthy of being willed than the world without Christ.' "[110]

Whether Scotus said that or not, what's wrong with it? Surely some worlds God could have chosen are better than others, and are better than the one he actually chose. Surely a world with Christ in it is *in some sense* more pleasing to God.

Nicolas' scruple lies at the basis of similar charges which have been leveled against Teilhard.[111] In defending him, recourse is had to some astonishing declarations of the Greek Fathers. "We are God outside of God," attributed to Gregory of Nyssa, is paraphrased to mean, "only in

---

[108] Dominic Unger, "Franciscan Christology: Absolute and Universal Primacy of Christ," *Franciscan Studies*, 2 (1942), 430: "God predestined Christ Jesus to be the Son of God absolutely and primarily for Christ's own glory, and that in the present economy of divine providence."

[109] F.-M. Lemoine, "La pensée 'scotiste' et la pensée patristique," in Humbert Bouëssé, *Le Sauveur du Monde 1. La place du Christ dans le plan de Dieu* (Doctrina Sacra 4; Chambéry: Collège Dominicain, 1951), 171–308. — In a more recent compilation of Bouëssé, *Problèmes actuels de Christologie* (Paris: Desclée, 1965), the article of Jesuit G. Martelet, "Sur le motif de l'Incarnation," is favorable to the Teilhard position, at least from where the reviewer in *Études* (May 1965, p. 659) is sitting.

[110] Marie-Joseph Nicolas, "Christologie," *Revue Thomiste*, 51 (1951), 665 f.

[111] The semi-official *Osservatore Romano* comment on the Holy Office *Monitum* of June 30, 1962, objects that for Teilhard God becomes somehow more perfect [or "gets more satisfaction"] by the assimilation of the cosmos. Perhaps the danger is seen to lie in such passages as *L'avenir de l'homme* (Œuvres 5; Paris: Seuil, 1959), 403; *"Paul teaches us* (1 Cor 15:23) *that when Christ has finished emptying selfishness out of all created forces (rejecting what dissociates and reanimating what unites), he will complete the universal unification by delivering himself in his total adult Body with capacity for Union definitively complete, to the embraces of the divinity. Thus will be constituted the organic complex God and the World, the Pleroma. It is a mysterious reality which we cannot claim to be more beautiful than God all alone, since God could have got along without the world. But neither can we think of it as absolutely incidental, without making Creation meaningless, the Passion of Christ absurd, and our own effort unappealing."*

us can God grow (*grandir*), and this is a formula used by the most orthodox theology."[112]

5. A detail which so far has played no real part in the discussion just might turn out to yield an important clue. According to Lennerz, the principle "every reasonable willing of means to an end must involve prior willing of the end itself," was *never* applied by Albert or Aquinas or Bonaventure toward proving the gratuitousness of predestination to glory. But it *was* so applied by Scotus. His disciples followed his example, and this view came eventually to be merged with one of Henry of Ghent which in its origins had been altogether contrary.[113]

6. Our final quibble about what Scotus really held concerns the claim that it was no different from what Aquinas held, at least not irreconcilably.[114] This will turn out to underlie the positions which we will examine in both Suárez and Molina. But even after them, there has been registered in our time a certain impatience for this alleged needless multiplying of entifications.

An article and then a book by the Marianists Rocca and Roschini find the controversy irksome and readily dissolved; they class pretty much everything which has been written on our subject during these seven centuries as sterile diatribes.[115] One has an uncomfortable impression that their real impatience is against metaphysical obstacles to drawing the mother of Jesus into the forefront of the discussion, though in what regards this perspective the Marianist authors have been anticipated and outstripped by their critics.[116] Roschini has been claimed to assert that he is a Thomist

[112] Roger Leys, "Teilhard dangereux?," *Bijdragen,* 24/1 (Jan. 1963), 9.

[113] Heinrich Lennerz, "De historia applicationis principii 'omnis ordinate volens prius vult finem quam ea quae sunt ad finem' ad probandam gratuitatem praedestinationis ad gloriam," *Gregorianum,* 10 (1929), 243, 246, 258.

[114] Carmelo de Iturgoyen, "De incarnationis motivo ac de Christi Domini primatu," *Collectanea Franciscana,* 7 (1937), 161–178, 341–356; Giacomo Biffi, "Fine dell' Incarnazione e primato di Cristo," *La Scuola Cattolica,* 88 (1960), 241–260; so also Féret, *RSPT,* 30 (1941), 96–132 in footnote 82 above. "Theological questions of first importance lie behind the motive of the Incarnation," according to A.-M. Knoll in a Karl-Adam-Festschrift, *Abhandlungen über Theologie und Kirche,* (Düsseldorf: Patmos, 1952), (not *Vitae et Veritati* published for his eightieth birthday at Düsseldorf in 1956) entitled "Thomismus und Skotismus als Standestheologien: die soziologische Bedeutung der thomistisch-skotistischen Kontroverse: Cur Verbum caro factum," 225–239; p. 228, the Thomist view is evolutionist; the Scotist cosmic-Christ grows out of the *anti-evolutionist* assumption that the better cannot come out of the inferior; p. 234, Thomism is pastoral, Scotism gives *secular status* to Church scholarship!

[115] Gesualdo Rocca and Gabriele Roschini, "Intorno alla ragione primaria dell' esistenza di Cristo e della Madonna," *Marianum,* 3 (1941), 301–371; *De ratione primaria exsistentiae Christi et Deiparae: novum tentamen conciliationis sententiae Thomisticae cum sententia Scotistica circa sic dictum motivum Incarnationis* (Rome: 1944), 133.

[116] Dominic Unger, "The Absolute Primacy of Christ Jesus and his Virgin Mother

and yet to defend the essential Scotist theses.[117] At any rate the pair held that the primary motive of the Incarnation is the divine choice of the present order in such wise that no certain conclusion can be drawn as to whether Christ would have become man if Adam had not sinned. The alternative to their position is this preliminary admission of Brinkmann, "From what Paul does say about Christ's status, it may well be that conclusions *can* be drawn."[118]

6. *After the Thirteenth Century*

Whatever Scotus himself, as distinct from his students, may have intended to maintain, the view attached to his name is not unworthy of him and was unanimously regarded as tenable by the unity of Christendom up through the Reformation. This is the major point at issue in the cross-examination of Teilhard.

JOHN OF SAINT THOMAS and CAJETAN were the most eminent continuing defenders of the Thomist view. They were well grounded in Scripture, patristic tradition, and the authority of St. Thomas, and do not seem to have added to the discussion any elements that call for mention here.[119]

NICHOLAS OF CUSA (1401-1464), despite the reserves of his "educated ignorance," puts great stress on the centrality of Christ in the universe, really in the tradition of Raymond of Lull.[120] Nicholas "unfolds the natural and supernatural uniqueness of the hypostatically united sacred humanity of Jesus. It realizes in itself all possible human and spiritual perfections, contains mediatorially within itself all redemptive grace and supernatural perfecting. It is not only *de facto,* but also in the one sole eternal divine plan of providence and salvation, the culmination and goal for which God made the whole universe. Does not this amount to an 'absolute' predestination anterior to the Fall? [Not really, because] God's providence does not reckon after the fashion of human hypotheses and thought sequences."[121]

According to St. Lawrence of Brindisi," *Collectanea Franciscana,* 22 (1952), 117 ff: "In this matter, whatever is said of Christ holds of Mary too, always observing, of course, the principle that Mary is under Christ. In other sermons, St. Lawrence himself puts Mary on a par with [? no longer under] Christ in this matter. . . . [In his *Opera* 9, 639, the foster-father of Jesus *shares* the Absolute Primacy], so we could have included St. Joseph in our study."

[117] Dominic Unger, "The Primary Reason for the Incarnation According to Father Roschini," *Antonianum,* 34 (1959), 445.

[118] Bernhard Brinkmann, "Die kosmische Stellung des Gottmenschen in paulinischer Sicht," *Wissenschaft und Weisheit,* 13 (1950), 7; see below, p. 160, n. 150.

[119] See the citation documented by footnote 109 on page 148 above.

[120] Rudolf Haubst, *Die Christologie des Nikolaus von Kues* (Freiburg: Herder, 1956), 191.

[121] Rudolf Haubst, "Das . . . 'Cur Deus homo,'" *Münchener Theologische Zeitschrift,* 6 (1955), 312.

BERNARDINE OF SIENNA (1380-1444) may also be reckoned as a step in the development of the Christocentric world view, be it only because of the influence his work had in rendering more prominent the *name* of Jesus.[122]

AMBROSE CATHARINUS is a colorful scholar who in 1542 published an *Opusculum de Christi praedestinatione*. He was a Dominican, but a rather difficult character who "turned far away from the traditions of his order in holding that the redemption was not the motive of the Incarnation."[123] For this or similar deviationism, the Dominican editor Mandonnet did not wish any account of him to appear in *DTC* under his religious name, so he has to be looked up there as "Lancelot Politi."

GIACOMO NACCHIANTI was also a Dominican, who became Bishop of Chioggia. Before detailing his relevance to the Scotist controversy, it may be well to outline here his monumental importance for one of the most agitated issues of the mid-twentieth century.

It was he who at the Council of Trent protested against the formula that God's revelation was contained *partly* in Scripture and *partly* in tradition. History has recently vindicated the importance of this single-handed resistance to the inclination of his fellow bishops to drive a wedge between Catholics and Lutherans. Intriguingly, that partly-partly formula seems to have first crawled into the Catholic stream from the researches of a defender of the faith named Henry VIII.[124] Whatever may have been the reason, or whatever the influence of Nacchianti, the final redaction of Trent's decree replaced the *partim-partim* with a less intransigent formula, capable of the interpretation "God's revelation is wholly in Scripture *and* wholly in tradition": it is wholly in Scripture in the sense in which it is anywhere in Scripture, not as an encyclopedia or abstract synthesis, but as the vital and somewhat random historical expression of a wider living faith. Such at least is the interpretation promoted by Geiselmann and popular in recent ecumenical circles.[125]

This same Nacchianti, although he was a Dominican, was also the

---

[122] F. Vernet, "Bernardin de Sienne," *Dictionnaire de Théologie Catholique* (Paris: Letouzey, 1923), 2, 787–791.

[123] M.-M. Gorce, "Politi," *DTC* (1935), 12, 2427; F. M. Paolini, *De eximia praedestinatione Christi fratris Ambrosii Catharini Politi, O.P.* (Bastia: 1937).

[124] Georges Tavard, *Holy Writ or Holy Church* (New York: 1960), 132.

[125] My survey of Geiselmann and his critics has been incorporated into the paper of my colleague, Gerald Van Ackeren, "Is All Revelation in Scripture?" *Proceedings of the Catholic Theological Society of America,* 17 (1962), 254; now carried forward by P. Joseph Cahill, "Scripture, Tradition, and Unity," *Catholic Biblical Quarterly,* 27/4 (Oct. 1965), 315–335.

Trent era's most vigorous defender of the view that the primary motive of the Incarnation was Christ's uniqueness rather than the redemption.[126]

With Trent we are brought to the era of the Jesuit counter-reform theologians and their challenge to the Thomist explanation of God's governance utilizing men's free acts. The Salamanca Carmelites, as noticed above in the formulation of Xiberta, claim already to have found that reconciliation of Thomist and Scotist positions which we will now take up in some Jesuits.

7. *Suárez: Bivalent Motivation*

FRANCIS SUÁREZ (1548-1617) claims to have found a mid-ground between Scotus and Aquinas. He sets out from the norm "no sin — no Incarnation," grounded by Aquinas on First Timothy and Augustine. For this solution, Suárez seems at first to have nothing but praise. He does indeed express some reserves about Thomas' reasoning that we can know *nothing* of God's free acts except what is revealed. We can with the help of reason draw *some* conclusions, and even those here said by Suárez to be "the more probable" are thus drawn by Aquinas.

Also, concerning the Bible, Suárez voices two modern-sounding reserves. He shows that by the term Scripture St. Thomas means the same as revelation, and includes the whole infallible rule of faith, whether written or tradition or definition of the Church. Secondly, when Thomas says that "everywhere" in Scripture the Incarnation is presented as motivated by the redemption, this is a loose way of speaking inasmuch as it does not apply to Ephesians 1:5, "God predestined us to be his sons in Jesus Christ."

Here now is the Thomist insight which Suárez most approves:

> By his question Thomas does not ask, "What could God do if man had not sinned?" nor "What would he have done in instituting a new mode and order of predestination?" but simply, "From the knowledge we have of that mode and intention by which God in fact has willed the Incarnation, can we conclude that it would have taken place even if man had not sinned?"

After apparently assenting to the answer "No," Suárez subjoins several long disputations. The problem, "Whether from the primary predestination of Christ it follows that the Word would have been made flesh even if man had not sinned," is made dependent upon another, "Which was God's primary reason, or motive of effecting and decreeing the

---

[126] Columban Fischer, "Jacques Nacchianti, O.P., évêque de Chioggia † 1569, et sa théologie de la Primauté absolue du Christ," *La France Franciscaine*, 20/1 (1937), 97–174; cf. 19/1 (1936), 38–49, "La place du Christ dans le plan de la création pour . . . Scot," by R. Hercedez.

Incarnation?" And this in turn depends upon, "Whether in God the willing of the Incarnation preceded or followed the foreknowledge of original sin."

Suárez ends up with two assertions by which he himself claims to have reconciled all diverging opinions of self-styled followers of Aquinas. On the one hand, even if man did not sin, God's intention of effecting the Incarnation could nevertheless persist such as it was, and have its effect. In support of this view are cited several contemporaries, as well as the relatively few who before Thomas constituted in fact a kind of consensus among those who had ever put the question. On the other hand, in the supposition that in making his decree God foresaw that sin *would* be intruded, *that* decree could not be made apart from foreknowledge of sin.[127]

Thus Suárez is commonly understood to claim that the manifestation of the perfection of the divine works, independently of the restoration of fallen humanity, is a complete, sufficient, adequate motive for the Incarnation. At the same time he tries to maintain that the restoration from sin was another and *equally* adequate motive. Apart from the problem of whether there *can* be more than one "equally determinant motive," it would seem that in the essential question Suárez has not really discovered a third approach but has approved the Scotist position.[128] "That [Scotist] position is probable; the opinion of Thomas is just more probable. Or, Scotus is more satisfying from the point of view of reason; but Thomas is inescapable from the point of view of faith founded on revelation."[129] No one is being called a heretic.

Suárez tried to be a "third force" between Scotus and Thomas, but failed. A similar effort made by Molina is called a "fourth force," in Spindeler's rather lucid delimiting of the issues.

8. *Molina: Exterminate the Steps*

The life-span of Luis de Molina (1535-1600) is a half-generation earlier than that of Suárez, but their inquiry into this question seems to have been independent. Molina's fame rests on a work reconciling God's universal governance with man's free will via what is called midway foreknowledge. It is in this work, not in any direct treatment of the Incarnation, that he embodies strictures that affect Scotus relevant to the motivation of God's acts.

---

[127] Francis Suárez, *De Incarnatione* (Opera Omnia 16; Venice: Colet, 1745), 139 ff; sections 2, 4, and 5 of Disputation 5 on Aquinas *Summa Theologiae*, 3, 3, 3; also p. 101 ff on *Summa*, 3, 1, 1.

[128] Aloysius Spindeler, *Cur Verbum caro factum?* (Forschungen zur christlichen Literatur- und Dogmengeschichte, 18/2; Paderborn: Schöningh, 1938), 34.

[129] A. Michel, "Incarnation: cause finale," *Dictionnaire de Théologie Catholique* (Paris: Letouzey, 1923), 7, 1506 and 1496.

The final chapter of this tome purports to deal with Question 23 on Predestination from the First Part of the *Summa Theologiae* of Saint Thomas. The fourth and fifth articles of that question are considered together, not by way of commentary, but as basis of four "disputations." The first of these is "whether there is any cause of predestination in the one being predestined," and is so complex that it is divided into fourteen "members."

Molina first examines several alternatives to his own view, and among these in Member 8 he takes up Scotus, under the anonymous title, "Examination of the procedure which some imagine God went through in predestining men to salvation or doom: the question being whether the foreknowledge of sins or any kind of choice precedes this predestining act."

Molina thereupon attributes to Scotus only four steps, instead of the five we described above.[130] Really *three* of ours are contained in Molina's first, "God efficaciously willed beatitude for Christ and certain others." However in the following paragraphs Molina will explain that the "four instants" of Scotus are subdivided into several others. Thus he says the first includes God knowing himself, knowing creatures, and predestining Christ the head of creatures. Molina's *second* Scotus step is really a subdivision of our third, the decree of grace as distinct from the decree of glory. In the third place, as Molina interprets Scotus, God *wills permitting* Adam's sin. This was our fourth step, but focusing the foreknowledge rather than the decree. The final step is repair of the Fall by sufferings on the part of Christ, "who, as Scotus thinks, would have been there anyway even if Adam had not sinned."[131]

Augustine frequently insists that God's foreknowledge of the *massa damnata* infected by sin was prior to any decree of predestination.[132] But, continues Molina, Augustine got into deep water in trying to link reprobation with original sin. Anyway, God's will that *all* men should be saved is asserted in 1 Timothy 2:4 and Ezekiel 18:23 expressly regarding the state of *fallen* nature. The ambiguous opinion of Aquinas that predestination supposes foreknowledge was restricted by Cajetan to those future actions which do not originate in the predestined order but are supposed by it.

Molina thereupon outlines his own analysis of what took place. Rather

---

[130] Paragraph of p. 144 documented in n. 95 above.

[131] Luis de Molina, *Liberi Arbitrii cum gratiae donis, divina praescientia, providentia, praedestinatione et reprobatione Concordia* (1595; J. Rabeneck edition; Madrid: Sapientia, 1953), part 7, articles 4–5, disputation 1, member 8, #1–2, p. 510 f.

[132] Augustine, *To Simplician* 8, *ML* 40, 115; Letters 190 and 194 to Optatus and Sixtus, *ML* 33, 857 and 874; *Predestination and Grace, ML* 45, 1667. But see footnote 85 above, and Martelet's essay cited in footnote 109, pp. 143, 148.

uncautiously he speaks of one knowledge *preceding* another in the mind of God. "God did not wish to permit the fall of the human race unless he also wished the fortunate remedy of this by Christ. God did not wish the Incarnation unless adjoined to the restoration of the human race as a part of his total aim. . . . From eternity God willed whatever he willed with one utterly simple act of his will, and full advance deliberation or knowledge of relevant factors. Therefore the steps of Scotus must be eliminated."[133]

Sane exterminanda omnino videntur instantia Scoti! This harsh sentence doubtless closed the minds of many to a calm consideration of whether ultimately Molina was more in the Scotist than the Thomist camp. It is no mere question of the choice of one unfortunate term. The sentence continues, "Making God will one thing before another, or foreknow one free action before another, are surely steps so obfuscating the issue that they make no sense at all."

Intriguingly, we possess the Jesuit censors' unfavorable verdict on this broadside of Molina. Not only the harshness of *exterminanda,* but the fact that he blames in another what he himself does, rightly prompts their admonition. "The author insists that the totality of God's willing is effected by a single utterly simple act, and yet he himself cannot escape postulating some kind of sequence in the divine acts in order to evade further difficulties."[134] To acquit himself of this charge, Molina added a long appendix to this Member 8 in some later editions.

However, even in the original edition there had been subjoined a few remarks in milder vein. "Scotus based himself on this principle: Whoever wants an end and the means thereto, in an orderly order one after another, of course wills the end before the means. And that is true. God however wills the end and the means simultaneously. . . That same principle is what Scotus applies in order to prove that the Incarnation would have happened even if Adam had not sinned. Christ and his predestination are thus seen as the goal of the predestination and benefits of all men and of the whole universe as well. The willing and foreknowledge of the end in its future realized entity is made to precede in God the willing and foreknowledge of what leads to that end."[135]

Here too Molina denies that the ordinary relation of priority between means and ends holds in the special case of Christ's predestination. He then takes up the reasons which led Aquinas to deny that the Incarnation would have taken place apart from sin. Thereupon he gives six arguments

---

[133] Molina, *Concordia* disputation 8/1, #15, Rabeneck edition, p. 516.

[134] Preface to the Rabeneck *Concordia* (1953), p. 47".

[135] Molina, *Concordia* disputation 8/1, #16 f, Rabeneck edition, p. 517 f; as evaluated by Lennerz, see footnote 113 above, p. 149.

to prove that foreknowledge of *actuated* sin did not precede the decree of predestination and hypostatic union. The position of Cajetan is rejected as not sufficiently safeguarding the primacy of Christ among the predestined.

Molina's final conclusion: By a single act God chose that order in which the Incarnation and the Redemption are contained in the proper subordination of dignity and influence with regard to one another. In this act Christ was in fact willed as redeemer. But he was also willed as Son of God and first among those predestined to glory, head of men and angels and of the universe.

"God simultaneously ordained everything natural and supernatural toward Christ as its goal. At the same time he willed that the Incarnation and Christ himself, though superior in dignity to everything created, should serve for the restoration of the human race as a part of that *total* aim without which probably the Incarnation of Christ would not have taken place."[136]

9. *Some Modern Efforts at Synthesis*

What must strike us most about all these last dozen pages is how irrelevant anything scriptural seems in their perspective. It will now be no easy chore to try to find a way of combining all our available theological and scriptural information into one overall evaluation of the Scotist thesis as it relates to the world view of Teilhard.

We may begin by acknowledging that our analysis of Molina left completely out of account an approach to the problem which many commentators consider basic to him. This is his contention that the *angels* owe their grace to Christ, and that *therefore* Christ cannot be regarded as altogether subsequent to men's foreseen sin. This in fact echoes the interpretation which we saw in Wambacq and some others regarding those things "in the skies" which in Colossians 1:20 are declared to be "reconciled" by Christ.[137] Not specially for this exegetical reason, the approach to our problem via the angels has appealed to de Lugo, Billot, and Galtier, as well as to the Dominican Hugon.[138]

But this avenue of inquiry involves endeavoring to explain the unknown by the more unknown. The status of the angels is a matter on which we are only indirectly and imperfectly informed. Our dogmatic and scriptural

---

[136] Molina, *Concordia* disputation 8/1, #29; Rabeneck, p. 523.

[137] See above, footnote 66 to p. 139.

[138] Aloysius Spindeler, *Cur Verbum caro factum?* (Paderborn: 1938); Édouard Hugon, *Le mystère de l'Incarnation* (Téqui: 1931; ²1946), 63–108; Guglielmo Calà Ulloa, "Il motivo tomistico dell' Incarnazione e la critica del P. Delft," *Sapienza,* 9 (1956), 456, rejecting the claim of Delft in *Collectanea Franciscana,* 26 (1956), 266–273, that because "all" grace comes from Christ, therefore also that of the angels.

data are far less assured than was imagined by medievals who ascribed to Denis the Fake-Areopagite an authority greater than he deserved. In the material and spiritual creation of which man forms an observable part, we find more suitable data for determining the relation in which the Incarnate God stands to the rest of it.

The position of Molina has been revived in our century chiefly by his fellow-Jesuit Galtier.[139] And one of the most emphatic steps in the reviving Franciscan defense of the Scotist view has revolved largely about refuting Galtier, together with remedying certain weak points in the Scotist position to which the controversy has shown it to be exposed.[140]

That zealous energetic output may be regarded as finding its summation in a posthumous work of Bonnefoy.[141] He naturally makes capital of the Concordia's discordant "exterminating," but apparently does not recognize how far he is echoing Jesuit censors when he says Molina himself no less than those he combats fell into the snare of letting imagination introduce either time or space into their notion of priority.

Bonnefoy has enjoyed a rather deserved standing as a twentieth-century exponent of the Scotist view. He would therefore be a natural ally in the defense of what is defensible within Teilhard's Christocentrism. Hence it seems all the more necessary, though doubtless ungracious, to scrutinize narrowly here some of Bonnefoy's norms for the use of Scripture, which might otherwise vitiate a plausible case.

He declares that he is a former professor of exegesis. Moreover, he had

---

[139] Paul Galtier, "Le vrai motif de l'Incarnation," *Nouvelle Revue Théologique*, 43 (1911), 44–57, 104–124. In *De Incarnatione et Redemptione*[2] (Paris: 1947), 456–482, Galtier sets forth Molina's view that the goal of creation was the excellence of the Redeemer. The terms in which on page 468 he claims for this view also de Lugo, Gonet, Billot, Hugon, and L. Janssens (to which Spindeler adds Kleutgen and Scheeben) are sufficiently circumspect to fit also the Thomist view. In *Les deux Adam* (Paris: Beauchesne, 1947), 121, he rejects those peacemakers who maintain *equal validity* of the Thomist and Scotist motivations of the Incarnation; as in his example of a man who buys a good field *for* his family but *because of* the excellence of the field, "If the Incarnation is *for* fallen man, then Christ does not really hold the primacy."

[140] Chrysostome Urrutibéhéty, "Le vrai motif de l'Incarnation," *Nouvelle Revue Théologique*, 43 (1911), 367–382, 389–404, 682–696; Galtier's rejoinder, 503–507. Chrysostome's position in book form, *Christus Alpha et Omega*, is cited by Longpré in *Studi Francescani*, 6 (1933), 171–177; finally *Le Motif de l'Incarnation et les thomistes contemporains* (Tours: 1921). Lemoine-Bouëssé following Michel [footnotes 109 and 129 above] reduce the contentions of Chrysostome to eight, of which they then assert: (a) none is incompatible with the Thomist view; (b) the assertions are not proved to be found in the Fathers; (c) even if they were, they would not prove the Scotist thesis. See also L. Ciappi, "Il motivo dell' Incarnazione e 'Les deux Adam' di P. Galtier," *Sapienza*, 3 (1950), 92–107; Maurice Corvez, "Le motif de l'Incarnation," *Revue Thomiste*, 49 (1949), 110.

[141] J.-F. Bonnefoy, "La place du Christ dans le plan divin de la création," *Mélanges de Science Religieuse*, 4 (1947), 257–284; 5 (1948), 39–62; see above, footnote 92 to p. 144.

cultivated a lifelong interest in the nascent science of *semantics,* which he finds has been deplorably neglected in the teaching of biblical hermeneutics.[142] When, as firstfruits of this preoccupation, Bonnefoy goes on to reject categorically the "plenary sense," the present writer can only applaud.[143] Bonnefoy also laudably acknowledges that in a four-volume work by which Risi had anticipated Bonnefoy's own orientations, the use of Scripture is somewhat vitiated by a tendency to use scholastic syllogisms for deducing the meaning of the sacred text.[144]

Bonnefoy is at pains to safeguard both himself and his readers from the error of imagining that we can find in Scripture answers to questions which its authors never asked. However, he feels that he must prefix to his scripture inquiries a scholastic survey of what that problem *is,* concerning which we wish to ascertain *whether or not* the Bible furnishes elements for a solution. "It would be a bad method to want to find at any cost a thesis in the Bible; but it would be still more inept to seek something there without knowing what is sought."[145]

Our objections to this program begin to arise only when we see that in the "speculative preview" some key steps already involve scripture texts, whose interpretation is thus taken for granted, or at any rate worked out as part of those very processes of deduction which he had said were not suitable for exegesis.

Much more disquieting is the use to which this "preliminary survey" puts the texts of Proverbs 8:22–9:16 [Sirach 24:1–31] and their citation in the bull *Ineffabilis* by which Pius IX in 1854 defined the Immaculate Conception. Bonnefoy's argument seems to run, "These sapiential texts are somehow relevant to *Mary,* because the bull says so. But this cannot be in any mystical or accommodated sense, which is always a spiritualizing of concrete *material* data: whereas the 'wisdom' in question here is something not perceptible to the senses. Therefore the *literal* sense of the passage must be as an allegory, and it is Christological."

The abrupt transit to Christ from what Pius IX said about Christ's mother is accounted for by the fact that the same decree of God predestined both Christ and his mother. Is this exegesis? And even if it is, surely

---

[142] On this see now Luis Alonso-Schökel, "Hermeneutics in the Light of Language and Literature," *Catholic Biblical Quarterly,* 25/3 (July 1963), 371–386.

[143] R. North, "Scripture Trends in 1964," *American Ecclesiastical Review,* 152/6 (June 1965), 371 f.

[144] Francisco M. Risi (of the Order of St. John of God), *Sul motivo primario dell' Incarnazione del Verbo* (Rome: Desclée, 1898). Volume 4 gives the pro-Scotist proof from Scripture, in 390 pages. Volume 1 is the state of the question, in 514 pages; volume 2, St. Thomas' view, 298 pages; volume 3, pro-Scotist proof from tradition, 444 pages. Of this work, Xiberta's *Soteriologia* [footnote 103 above] says on page 737: "2 volumes. Defends, against the Scotist theory, that the redemption in passible flesh is a merely occasioned finality."

[145] Jean-François Bonnefoy, *La primauté du Christ selon l'Écriture et la Tradition* (Rome: Herder, 1959), 6; 34.

every exegete will feel some perplexity about the manner in which the authority of the Church is being invoked in the above procedure. "Since there is no doubt about the sense which Holy Mother Church has held and holds, it remains for us to prove that it fulfils the requirements of a scientific exegesis." But actually there is *plenty* of doubt as to what Pius IX meant to be the *exegetical* binding force of his Old Testament citations in relation to his pronouncements about Mary.

And even if that doubt could be solved, it hardly seems approved theological method to repose our assurance about basic Christological doctrines on some casual and presumptive inference from texts applied to Mary. Actually the exegesis here given by Bonnefoy fits rather the Second Person of the Trinity, and seems to be put forward as an exposition and proof of Trinitarian doctrine. But then he tries to limit its relevance to the Word as Incarnate, though admitting that he here parts company from the competent exegete whom he had been following, really too exclusively, throughout these pages.[146]

We must also register some reserve about the exegete's alleged function of proving that passages of Scripture really mean what the Church says they do. There are comparatively few passages, less than a dozen, whose sense has really thus been defined.[147] Even in their case, it would seem that the meaning of the scripture passage dictated the view of the Church, rather than vice versa.

This is not to deny that one of the most reliable aids on which we may fall back for determining the sense of controverted passages in Scripture is our assured knowledge from other sources. These utilizable certitudes can come from some other branch of human science, or from what is called "the analogy of Faith," the truths of revelation. But even when an apparent teaching of the Church or its scriptural basis is seen to *conflict* with truths reliably known from elsewhere, the First Vatican Council prescribed that the theologian should reexamine whether those texts really mean what he has taken them to mean.[148] At any rate, in situations in which the mind of the Church regarding the scripture text itself is by no means unequivocal, the method of starting out from certitude that "proofs" can be found for one particular exegesis seems questionable.

Our disquiet is not allayed in reading that the Wisdom texts "fit" the

---

[146] Bonnefoy, *Primauté*, page 37 f; André Robert, "Les attaches littéraires bibliques de Prov. I–IX," *Revue Biblique*, 43 (1934), 190: the evangelical and Johannine overtones of the book of Proverbs reduce to "seek and you shall find," a fundamentally Old Testament idea; further 42–68, 172–204, 374–384; 44 (1935), 344–365, 502–525.

[147] H. Kruse, *Die heilige Schrift in der theologischen Erkenntnislehre* (Paderborn: 1964).

[148] DS 3017 = DB 1797 [footnotes 2 and 3 to p. 206 below].

scholastic formulas, at least with the help of fewer subtleties than go into the "current Pentateuch-authorship theory"!

> Lagrange estimated that "Judaism had brought the doctrine of Wisdom up to the term of Son of God." This effort was meritorious; and it is understandable that the illustrious exegete could not go beyond these conclusions in view of his definition of literal sense. But we hold this concept of literal sense to be erroneous, and we believe one can and must go further. Instead of attributing these expressions to the Word as such, we attribute them to the future Christ speaking as God.[149]

It would be difficult for most exegetes to take these norms in stride and conclude that Bonnefoy's work has furnished any substantial scriptural underpinning to the Scotist position.

*   *   *

More help would seem to be available in a rather satisfyingly exegetical essay of Brinkmann with which we will conclude. He takes up Suárez, and shows that it is the exegesis of Saint Paul which warrants the support Suárez gave to the Scotus view that Christ would have become man even if mankind had not sinned in Adam. He takes up the objection that we cannot find the answer to this question as long as it is not explicitly revealed, and answers that we can legitimately *conclude* to an answer from what is in fact revealed.

> "If Christ precisely as God-man is image of (the invisible) God (Col 1:15; 2 Cor 4, 4) or a gleam of his glory (Heb 1:3), and on the other hand according to 1 Corinthians 11:7 man too is an image of God [Gn 1:26; 1 Tim 2:13], then the conclusion suggests itself that Paul sees man's exemplary cause in the God-man as such. And that means that the Incarnation of the Son of God fits into God's plan of creation and salvation independently of Adam's sin."[150]

---

[149] Bonnefoy, *Primauté*, p. 143 f; p. 116 referring M.-J. Lagrange, "La paternité de Dieu dans l'Ancien Testament," *Revue Biblique*, 17 (1908), 496; 481–499. See Vaccari above, footnote 6 to p. 122.

[150] Bernhard Brinkmann, "Die kosmische Stellung des Gottmenschen in paulinischer Sicht," *Wissenschaft und Weisheit*, 13 (1950), 11; see 14 (1951), 133: in Genesis 1:26 God created man according to some pattern distinct from himself (so Hilary on Psalm 118; *ML* 9, 566), and this was the Christ of Philippians 2, 6 though the fact was not known to the author of Genesis — A. Durand, "Incarnation et Christocentrisme," *Nouvelle Revue Théologique*, 69 (1947), 485: "Because precisely by the Incarnation the whole creation, which is natural and supernatural, is completed, it thereby constitutes the heart of reality and of intelligibility; Pascal, 'Without Jesus Christ, the world would not subsist.' " According to Abel Jeannière, "Approches christologiques," in *Recherches et Débats du Centre Catholique des Intellectuels Français* 40, *Essais sur Teilhard de Chardin* (Paris: Fayard, Oct. 1962), 79–95, what makes Teilhard's claim *look* radically different from that of Scotus

And *that* means it is not so altogether intolerable to work toward a new synthesis of scientific and theological data concerning God's mode of creating the material-spiritual being which is man, in such a way that Christ will in fact be seen as somehow the term of biological evolution.

is ultimately the Thomist-Scotist background of a static universe, with scarcely any recognition of the molecular structure by which the whole universe is kept in motion toward its goal; page 91 comments that we will neither take up time posing "unreal questions" [footnote 100 above], nor believe that the medieval theologians were as unreal as all that; page 95, the basic datum is that "all things are yours, and you are Christ's, and Christ is God's" (1 Cor 3, 22), "recapitulating all things in Christ" (Eph 1, 10).

SUMMARY OF THE FIFTH CHAPTER,
THE COSMIC CHRIST

Teilhard threatens the separateness of the supernatural order by making Christ the term of biological evolution. Against the charge that he thus opposes Christian revelation and tradition, his best defense lies in comparing the implications of his view with those of Paul and Scotus. The three have very little in common and are scarcely linked by any traceable lines of dependence. Yet since objectively "Christ the goal of creation" is specially characteristic of all three, it seems indispensable even if not "useful" here to analyze fully the relevant texts and their commentaries.

Romans 8:21 asserts that the non-human cosmos also will be redeemed and that Christ is firstborn among the many. We take this to mean that the material creation is redeemed by the fact that redeemed man is material in his nature.

Colossians 1:15 again calls Christ the firstborn of all creation, in a passage which makes him image of the unseen God, fulness of reality, and unifier of all things of earth or sky. We find it at least optional and orthodox to take Christ *as man* to be the first-decreed of all creation, from whom and for whose sake the rest was created (1 Cor 8:6), in echo of Proverbs 8:22.

Before Scotus, Anselm's similar-sounding phrase had really not been concerned with the "motive" of the Incarnation, always assumed from Luke 19:10 and the Nicene Creed to be men's need of redemption. But apart from aberrant anticipations recently recovered in Isaac and Zeno, Alexander of Hales and more explicitly Albert the Great held the economy of the Incarnation to be such that it would have taken place even if man had not sinned. Thomas Aquinas at first espoused that position but later rejected it.

Scotus in his own writings holds that the Incarnation does not of its nature require men's sin as an occasion. In notes edited by disciples from his lectures it is said more clearly that God's sovereign work could not have been due to an "accident," or rather incident, that might not and should not have happened. Whether Scotus said it or not, it seems true that a universe with Christ seems somehow more worthy of being willed by God.

Though most Dominicans firmly backed the late-Aquinas opposition, the Scotus view was defended by Catharinus and Nacchianti. The Salamanca Carmelites, and the Jesuits Suárez and Molina, endeavor to "reconcile" Scotus with Aquinas; but really all such views grant the *essential* that in the present concrete order the preeminence of Christ and not the fall of man is the motive of the Incarnation.

Recent efforts have been made to link this view with Scripture. Less felicitous is the emphasis on Proverbs 8:22 as cited in Papal Mariological documents. More valid is the claim that St. Paul sees man's exemplary cause in the God-man as such, so that the Incarnation fits into the creation plan independently of sin.

CHAPTER 6

SCRIPTURE PROOF-TEXTS FOR THE CREATION OF SOULS

Up to now we have shown that Teilhard is not to be charged with any disposition to diminish the role of God as Creator.

Even in his passion for evolution and his leanings toward polygenism, he does not diminish but merely *relocates* the indispensable and utter dependence of the whole creation on the personal being outside it giving it orthogenetic finality.

In his insistence upon the Cosmic Christ as firstborn and goal of creation, he has not altogether unwillingly, and not provably more than Paul's epistles, given ground for being taxed with a certain kind of "pantheism" — a *special* kind, of which the worst that can be said is that it is not truly *proved* to be the revealed doctrine of Scripture; but neither has this been disproved.

1. *Why Turn to Revelation Instead of Philosophy?*

Just as Teilhard insists on the need of creation, or at least the need of God and of orthogenesis, so also he insists that creation "once for all, in the beginning" is not enough. Creation is a *continuing* procedure. Our cosmogenesis, our evolution, *is* our creation. As such, its dependence upon God is continuous and now, not just the relic of some event that took place in the far-off past.

God's dynamic and creative power in the evolutionary process is manifested most of all at the "critical thresholds," where matter is observed to "surpass itself" and leap to a higher stage. Actually every *production* of whatever kind is a sort of self-surpassing by the agent, in which whatever can truly be called new *being* has the same direct and immediate dependence upon God as did the initial step in such a chain of causalities.

Of all the threshold leaps attested in the evolving reality around us, none is so exciting and so baffling, even for the scientist, as the emergence of the human spirit. Here if anywhere the most impassive observer would be inclined to admit the need of a further injection of creative power from outside the system itself.

Teilhard in fact not only emphasized this uniqueness of the phenomenon of man. He even explicitly spelled out in several footnotes the appropriateness of linking this nature observation with what Revelation teaches about the immediate creation of the human soul by God.[1]

In indicating this apparent correspondence, he did not purport to claim either that science proves by its experimental techniques a truth hitherto known to mankind only by revelation; or that revelation provides some fundamentally missing link in what reason can know about the relation between man's spirit and its material antecedents.[2]

In other words, he kept "hands off" what he rightly conceived to be the domain of the theologian and the exegete: to determine exactly *what* doctrine about the origin of the human spirit is either *revealed* directly and supernaturally, or *inferred* as an inescapable premise or conclusion from some revealed doctrine in its relation to truths solidly established by other branches of human scholarship.

But is it only toward the sources of revelation that Teilhard does or ought to show this respect? What about philosophy? He claimed not to be giving us a metaphysics, and thereby he seemed to acknowledge that there is such a legitimate domain of knowledge, whose firm conclusions ought to guide and warn him no less than those of revelation.

In principle, yes. But he precisely felt, as many other twentieth-century Catholics feel, that our traditional metaphysics is too much bound up

---

[1] Teilhard, *The Phenomenon of Man* (New York: Harper, 1959), 29, 169, 185, 298.

[2] On Teilhard's reserve in touching questions of exegesis, see in Chapter 1, p. 4, note 9, above. The first issue of the *Revue de la Société Teilhard de Chardin* (June 30, 1960), on the inside back cover notes a lecture of that same date by Robert Aron on "Teilhard and the Old Testament"; he communicated to me that the title was not of his choosing, and his theme was "a basic congeniality of outlook," as in Tresmontant, p. 89, notes 15–18 in Chapter 4, above. — According to Michael Polanyi's review of *The Phenomenon* in the *Saturday Review* (Jan. 30, 1960), 21, "Teilhard's purpose is to rewrite the book of Genesis in terms of Evolution," using scientific knowledge as factual imagery and thus bypassing many decisive issues, "an epic poem that keeps closely to the facts."

with a world view which is untenable. The word metaphysics means "what comes next after physics." It is unhistorical and unreal to pretend that we can leave unchanged the metaphysics, while replacing almost completely the physics which served as its scaffold.

Specifically Teilhard does not consider what is universally given in theology textbooks as an apodictic proof from reason alone that every human soul is intrinsically independent of matter, therefore immortal, therefore immediately created out of nothing by God in a way different from any other production in the observable universe.

The following formulation, though not in the exact words of Saint Thomas, may be said to indicate the major line expressed in the First Part of his *Summa Theologiae,* chiefly the body of Article 2 of Question 90, "Whether the soul is produced into being by creation," and its cross-reference in Articles 2 and 6 of Question 75, "Whether the human soul is something subsistent . . . incorruptible":

> The human vital principle possesses certain operations (chiefly its own self-awareness of identity) intrinsically independent of matter; and is shown (chiefly by ethical factors) to be destined to an existence (at least temporary and unconnatural, not ever in any sense as a "pure" spirit) in complete severance from matter.
>
> But that which in any of its operations, and in its continuation in existence, is intrinsically independent of matter, cannot have originated in any dependence upon matter.
>
> Therefore the production of the first and every other human soul is due to a non-material cause, not an angel but God.

Actually in both the second and the third articles of his Question 90, Thomas leads over into his rational proofs by asserting that the creation of the soul is revealed in Genesis 1:27, "God created man to his image,"[3] and its immediacy in Genesis 2:7, "God breathed the breath of life into the face of man." But a comparison with the *Sed contra* device elsewhere throughout his works will show that he did not intend this piece of exegesis for itself, nor even as a step toward establishing a revealed dogma, but as a sort of cue-word for the speculative reasonings which are to follow. And in fact Catholic philosophers today feel so completely assured that the reasonings which Aquinas gives are "from reason alone," that Grenet can protest about Teilhard's obstinately refusing to acknowledge what is part of the observable evidence:

> To say we are in presence of a being capable of reflection, is philosophy. Not to go on and say we are in presence of creation of a pure spirit, is bad philosophy. . . . Either it is philosophy if you affirm difference of nature, so go ahead and affirm intervention of a Cause; or if you refuse

---

[3] See below, footnote 33 and pp. 180–181.

to philosophize by postulating intervention of a Cause, then how can you philosophize by affirming difference of nature?[4]

It is not our aim here to evaluate any positive philosophical affirmation on the nature or origin of the human soul. We are only concerned to evaluate whether what Teilhard says or implies on the subject is incompatible with the revealed dogma of the Catholic Church. We will not fail to consider (in Chapter 7) the extent to which pronouncements of Catholic authority claim to be affirming or "canonizing" positions which in themselves are purely tenets of human reason or philosophy, but whose maintenance is seen as an indispensable support for relevant revealed doctrines.

What we will *not* presume, however, is that any particular philosophy or tenet of philosophy enjoys some kind of untouchableness *apart* from what revelation may have to say about it. Specifically regarding Grenet, we will say that there is in his stress on Aquinas and papal documents a sort of implication that all further progress of knowledge can consist solely in a sort of exegesis of these two sources, as if they possessed a divine inspiration which they do not.

Teilhard had some things to say which traditional Christian philosophy finds unacceptable. It is no reasonable answer to say that *he* must *first* create a philosophy which will adequately make room for his new insights alongside all other known truths. That is not *his* job. That is the philosophers' job; and they have no choice about consenting or refusing to do it, *if* the insights offered by Teilhard do in fact correspond to the real order, and express a real convergence among the known facts of science.[5]

Well then, Teilhard affirms an observable continuity and proportion between growth of complexity and of consciousness. He also affirms that the observable upbuilding of the universe despite the destructive momentum of entropy comports a quasi-observable "inner face" of matter compensating the incomplete energy quotient of its outer face. From these two relatively observable truths, he goes on to propose as a *working hypothesis* that the ultimate units of this interior energy coalesce with the ultimate units of consciousness, and that when these are built up into sufficiently complex structures they progressively reach (by suitable threshold leaps) the highest type of consciousness proper to man.

From this it seems to follow either that man's highest operations do not require any spiritual principle at all different from increasingly com-

---

[4] Paul-Bernard Grenet, *Teilhard de Chardin ou le philosophe malgré lui* (Paris: Beauchesne, 1960), 21; see p. 29, n. 68 and p. 88, n. 14 above.

[5] Quite fair is the challenge of Olivier A. Rabut, *Dialogue avec Teilhard de Chardin* (Paris: 1958), 207 [= *Teilhard de Chardin: A Critical Study* (New York: Sheed, 1961)]: "If anyone does not like the way Teilhard has done it, let *him* do better." See on this work Bernard Towers, "Significance of Teilhard de Chardin," *Blackfriars*, 40 (1959), 126–129.

plexified matter; or that man's spirit is a mere summation of spirit-units which are found less amply in plants and animals, and in a diffused and rudimentary form in even the tiniest particles of matter.[6]

Thus among the "confused concepts" which we are told the Holy Office Monitum warns against, "Teilhard says that concretely there does not exist Matter and Spirit, but there exists only Matter which becomes Spirit. . . . The World-Stuff is Matter-Spirit."[7]

He says that, all right; and it is the sort of thing that insufficiently prepared manipulators of philosophical concepts have to be "warned" about. According to Teilhard, the operations of the human intellect not only correspond fully to the material complexification of the brain, but give ultimate meaning to the whole process of animal and material evolution itself. Is it reasonable to postulate God "intervening" to create out of nothing that proportionate principle of human activity which Nature was on the point of producing anyway?

It is my intention to show that Teilhard's bold contentions are *not* in fact incompatible with the Catholic doctrine of the immediate creation of each human soul by God. But they require a revised understanding of what our Catholic dogma itself means and has meant as it is traceable through the centuries. In order to show this, we will begin with the exegesis of those passages of Scripture which have been traditionally held to afford some ground for the Christian belief in the immediate creation of the human soul.

2. *Qohelet's Return of the Spirit to Its Giver*

Contrary to what we might expect, the patristic tradition does not seek the immediate creation of the soul primarily in Genesis. It finds this doctrine more explicit in Ecclesiastes 12:7: "(Remember your Maker in the days of your youth, before the darkness comes) and the dust returns to the earth as it was, and the 'spirit' returns to God who gave it."

"Spirit" of the Vulgate, following Septuagint *pneûma* for Hebrew *rûaḥ,* is retained by the Revised Standard Version. But the American Catholic translation substitutes "life breath." The other words of the pas-

---

[6] Philip G. Fothergill, "Teilhard de Chardin and the Attenuated Consciousness," *Newman Association Philosophy of Science Group, Bulletin,* 38 (London: 1960), 4–22; E. Borne, "Matière et esprit dans la philosophie de Teilhard," *Recherches et débats CCIF,* 40 (Paris: Fayard, 1962), 45–65; Michael Wrede, *Die Einheit von Materie und Geist bei Teilhard de Chardin* (Glauben-Wissen-Wirken, 3; Limburg: Lahn, 1964) 23; Georges La Fay, *La montée de conscience: essai de synthèse de la pensée de Teilhard de Chardin* (edited posthumously by M. Barthélemy-Madaule); (Paris: Éditions ouvrières, 1964) 49; see footnote 28, p. 11, above.

[7] Andrés Avelino Esteban Romero, "El Padre Teilhard de Chardin ¿Científico optimista y teólogo pesimista?", *Crisis,* 9 (1962), 175.

sage are quite literally rendered in the Greek, and also in the Vulgate except that it substitutes "(the earth) from which (it was)."

Thus in his translation Jerome does not choose to say that the body will "become *as* it was," but only that it will "go back to *where* it came *from.*" He may be here retaining an earlier Latin; or he may have feared that the Hebraic parallelism would make it seem that *as* the body had a previous existence, so also did the soul. More likely he meant to express nothing at all other than the Hebrew and Greek; at any rate it is hard to understand why a twentieth-century theologian says Alexander of Hales cited this verse in the Vulgate because the original has a different sense.[8]

But Jerome has a comment on this verse more direct than whatever may be latent in his Vulgate rendition. He says, with a cantankerousness not rare in him, "From this we can get plenty of laughs — *satis ridendi* — at those who think souls are sown with bodies and generated not by God but by the parents' bodies."[9] Jerome seems to imply here that he gets this information directly from the Hebrew text, rather than that he uses the biblical terms as a point of reference for some dogmatic truth known to him independently.

The most immediate content of our chapter is that the earth's recurrences of pleasure or pain will have no importance for a man on the day when he is called upon "to walk to the house of his longlastingness."[10] Then mourners shall roam in the marketplace, "until the time when . . . the pitcher is broken at the fountain . . . and the dust returns to the earth as it was, and the spirit returns to God who gave it. Vanity of

---

[8] A Michel, "Traducianisme," *Dictionnaire de Théologie Catholique* (Paris: Letouzey, 1946), 15, 1356.

[9] Jerome on Ecclesiastes 12:7, Migne *Patrologia Latina*, 28, 1112; *Corpus Christianorum*, Series Latina, 72 (Turnhout: Brepols, 1959), p. 357. In ML 23, 1106, Jerome outlines four traditions of interpreting this passage. The one which he calls "historicizing" is really the most allegorizing, i.e., "all this happened to Israel in its history." Then there is the eschatological: all this *will* happen, either to the whole world or to the individual. The third approach is "astral or angelic." The fourth, called physiological, is also highly allegorical, linking the various experiences here noted to the several parts of the body; this interpretation is strangely fashionable among such moderns as Crampon, Podechard, Vaccari, Tobac. As against all four of Jerome's alternatives, the "literal" sense is preferred by Denis Buzy, "Le portrait de la vieillesse (Ecclésiaste XII, 1–7)," *Revue Biblique*, 41/3 (July 1932), 329–340; in 43/4 (Oct. 1934), 494–511, "La notion du bonheur dans l'Ecclésiaste," Buzy finds that the author reproaches excessive straining toward being happy.

[10] The Egyptian notion of the "house of eternity" (or tomb) comes to Qohelet mediately via Phoenicia, according to Mitchell J. Dahood, "Canaanite-Phoenician Influences in Qoheleth," *Biblica*, 33 (1952), 216: not immediately, as S. Morenz, "Die ägyptische Literatur und die Umwelt," *Handbuch der Orientalistik*, 2 (Leiden: 1952), 199. See Rudi Kroeber, *Der Prediger* (Schriften und Quellen der Alten Welt 13; Berlin: Akademie, 1963), 156.

vanities, says Qohelet, and all is vanity"; and thus the book closes with the same words with which it opened.[11]

The passage is highly moving and poetic, and perfectly intelligible in a general way. Naturally, as always in poetry, the imaginative figures replace each other so rapidly that it is not easy to recapture the logic or exact force of each.

Surely, though, in the context it is implied that our life on earth in whatever stage is not without relation to God. By God's will and decree, life was given to us, and will be taken away. Certainly the *primary* emphasis of "the spirit returning to God who gave it" is that the Life which Qohelet is describing comes to a *stop*.

The "return" of the soul to God does not of itself indicate more than that human *life* owes its being to God in the first place, with no more implication of some "principle" of that life *continuing* in existence afterwards than of its *preexisting*. Precisely this is said in the note of the abridged Jerusalem Bible, though with an inserted motive clause which seems to be smuggling in some rather recent philosophy: "That which in man is from the earth, returns to the earth. But *since nothing here below can give him satisfaction,* not everything in him comes in fact from the earth, and that which is from God returns to God."[12]

The real point at issue is whether this passage of Qohelet can be discerned as saying that there is a *difference* between the termination of the life of man and of other living things, corresponding to a difference in the manner in which they were respectively produced by God. "Life" itself, the precious gift upon which Qohelet 12 is really musing, is truly a gift of God also in animals and plants, and by his decree is initiated and terminated. But in saying that (man's) "spirit returns to God who gave it," is Qohelet implying that it returns to God *to continue in life apart from the body?* or that therefore it was *produced by God* in intrinsic independence of the body?

---

[11] An appendix of six verses speaks of the work of Qohelet in third person. The name, which is rendered in Greek as Ecclesiastes, has come to be understood as "the Preacher." Really both Hebrew and Greek are a noun-form of a verb made up from the noun meaning "the Congregation, people of God, *qāhāl/ekklesía*." The true sense seems to be "the one who calls the people together." In the Greek this noun is masculine; in Hebrew too it is construed with masculine verb-forms. But the form of Qohelet itself is unmistakably a *feminine* participle, and I venture to propose that it means basically "(the voice of) the *community* calling (*itself*) together."

[12] *La sainte Bible . . . de Jérusalem, édition de poche* (Paris: Desclée de Brouwer, 1955), 1516. — The "spirit" of 12, 7 is not a divine spark which returns to God, but the animation of the body through God's act, which ends when God so determines, according to R. B. Y. Scott, "Proverbs, Ecclesiastes" (Anchor Bible: Garden City: Doubleday, 1965), 255. Scott on p. 204 holds as Qohelet's teaching, *"One must face facts,* and not go on asserting or accepting as true what will not stand up under examination in the light of the evidence."

We might say that these are questions posed by modern dogma, and that since Qohelet did not pose them, we cannot expect from him an answer to them. But the fact is that he *did* pose these very questions, in 3:19: "There is an encounter of the sons of men, and an encounter of the cattle; and the encounter is the same for both. As the death of one, so the death of the other. And there is one spirit (breath, *rûaḥ*) for all. And there is no superiority of man over cattle, because all is emptiness. (20) All is heading toward one place. All had its being out of the dust, and all is tending back toward the dust. (21) Who knows the spirit of man? does it mount upward? and the spirit [!] of cattle, does it descend downward unto the earth? (22) And I concluded that there is nothing better than that a man should be joyful in his activities, because that is his role; who will conduct him to gaze upon whatever there will be after him? (4:1) Praise have I for the dead, dead as they are already, rather than for the living who are still alive; but I praise as better than both the one who never yet came into being. . . . (9:4) It is better for a living dog than a dead lion. (5) The living know they shall die, but the dead do not know anything. They have no longer any recompense, because their very remembrance is forgotten. . . . (9:10) Whatever you find to hand to do, do it with all your heart. There will be no work, or enterprise, or knowledge, or philosophy in the grave you are headed for."

These utterances are pessimistic, but not consistently.[13] More plainly they are agnostic, or a downright defense of crass materialism. Podechard finds his solution of the enigma in his contention that the "spirit" spoken of by Qohelet is *rûaḥ,* which means merely "vital force," as distinct from *nepeš,* "personal individual soul," as we shall see below.[14] He also pro-

---

[13] According to Roland E. Murphy, "The *Pensées* of Coheleth," *Catholic Biblical Quarterly,* 17/2 (O'Hara Festschrift, April 1955), (184–) 194, the author's pessimism is only a literary device; he really enjoys life. For André-M. Dubarle, "La conception de l'homme dans l'Ancien Testament," *Sacra Pagina* (Louvain Congress 1958; Paris: Gabalda, 1959), 1, 522–536, Qohelet experienced that man can find joy only in activity, but he was disillusioned (p. 534). Hinckley G. Mitchell, " 'Work' in Ecclesiastes," *Journal of Biblical Literature,* 32 (1913), 137 f, holds against J. Genung that the author had no "gospel" of work or anything else, but only the shallow philosophy that work was "a folly to be shunned when it was not a misfortune to be endured." See further E. Wölfel, *Luther und die Skepsis: eine Studie zur Kohelet-Exegese Luthers* (FGLP: 1958).

[14] E. Podechard, *L'Ecclésiaste* (Études Bibliques; Paris: Gabalda, 1912), 311 f. More concretely, Paul Humbert, "Qohéleth," *Revue de Théologie et de Philosophie,* 3 (1915), 253–277, holds that for the author of 3:19 the *nepeš* survives in Sheol; but against this the *rûaḥ* (of man and beast) is "gathered" to God. J. van der Ploeg, *Prediker* (A. van den Born, De Boeken van het OT 8/2; Roermond: Romen, 1953), 69, also finds "the soul returning to God the giver" of 12:7 rather in conflict with 3:21; his solution is that 12:7 just takes over *rûaḥ* in the sense it had in a current expression, whereas 3:21 poses an original problem and uses *rûaḥ* in a special sense.

tests against the tendency of commentators to link 3:19 unduly with 3:17 and thereby with some notion of a moral sanction, which he asserts is utterly beyond the scope of that chapter.

Qohelet 3:19 doubtless does not mean that the destiny of man is from start to finish no less miserable than that of the beast, but only that whatever advantages man may have disappear at death [!!]. It is evident that if Qohelet had known about a glorious immortality, he would never have written his book. On the other hand, it would be childish to claim that at the end of his reflections he hits upon and expresses propositionally a truth which would have to change the face of the religious world and displace the pole of human life by deferring to eternity the motives for living. If he had received such a revelation, he would have expressed it far more triumphantly instead of following it up with his old "vanity of vanities."[15]

More evasive is the claim that 3:21 means merely "there is no proof that there will be a difference between the breath of man and of beast after death."[16]

Recent exegesis seeks the key to the meaning of the Wisdom books more proximately in the Egyptian tradition which influenced their composition. Thus for Gese, Qohelet intends to contradict and cast off the "old" wisdom of the Hebrews borrowed from Egypt. The "new" outlook is that man will perforce be hostile to his environment in proportion as his authentic individuality is allowed full play; and that *death* as a factor in his development is an intrusion not dependent on the subject's own activity.[17] If all this is really what Qohelet was thinking, then

---

[15] Podechard, *L'Ecclésiaste*, p. 470. See below, footnote 96 to p. 198.

[16] Oswald Loretz, *Gotteswort und menschliche Erfahrung: eine Auslegung der Bücher Jona . . . Qohelet* (Freiburg: Herder, 1963), 143; in his "Zur Darbietungsform der 'Ich-Erzählung' im Buche Qohelet," *Catholic Biblical Quarterly*, 25/1 (Jan. 1963), 46–59, with ample documentation, Loretz concludes we cannot distinguish the author's "own inner convictions" from the fact that they are introduced by "I." H. Hertzberg, *Der Prediger* (KAT 17/4; Gütersloh: Mohn, 1932; 1963 edition by H. Bardtke) 185, sees no contrast between 12:7 and 3:20; Qohelet doubts recent views that the soul goes "up" (to Heaven), but has no doubt it will be "with God"; on p. 94 Hertzberg rejects D. I. Macht, *Jewish Forum* (Nov. 1926), 1–3 on Qohelet 3:21: "He who useth his intelligence will know that the spirit of man tendeth upwards, while that of the beast tendeth downwards" — on the basis that in general the root goes down but the outcome goes up! — George A. Barton, *Ecclesiastes* (International Critical Commentary; Edinburgh: Clark, 1908), 110: "In his mood of despondent pessimism, [3:21] seems to deny what we know from 12:7 he holds: that the breath of man goes back to God, unlike that of animals which goes to the earth."

[17] Hellmut Gese, "Die Krisis der Weisheit bei Koheleth," *Les Sagesses du Proche-Orient Ancien* (Colloque de Strasbourg 1962; Paris: Presses Universitaires, 1963), 142 f. So Charles C. Forman, "The Context of Biblical Wisdom," *Hibbert Journal*, 60/237 (Jan. 1962), 125–132; p. 131: "Koheleth is pessimistic because of the inherent weakness he encountered in the postulates of orthodox *ḥokmah*"; H. H. Blieffert, *Weltanschauung und Gottesglaube im Buche Koheleth* (Rostock: 1938),

it was "new" indeed; in fact it surprisingly anticipated existentialism. Or may we not rather suspect that Gese in his effort to release biblical thought from scholastic shackles has found for it others more congenial to him but not necessarily to it?

A different aspect of existentialism, its *angst,* is more cautiously discerned by Ellermeier. He proceeds from an assumption to be queried below, namely that *nepeš* really means "throat"; and concludes that it would be unwise to draw any *moral* lesson. Really (by chance) the English "lump in one's throat" comes close to the sense he prefers, "the sort of *disquiet* or yearning which a being experiences," along the lines of that *curiosity* which distinguishes a Wise Man.[18]

Power's recent commentary dismisses completely our whole verse 12:7, or at least the part about the spirit, as "the addition of a pious commentator."[19] For him the sense of the passage is recaptured by the translation made in 1918 by W. B. Forbush in Khayyam-FitzGerald style:

So man unto his House Eternal goes:
The portals once for entrance ope, then close.
  Along the sodden street the mourners trudge —
But what is done behind those Doors, who knows!

In similar vein, the major German commentary emends "Think of your creator" in 12:1 ("an unusual idea and expression") to "think of your *grave";* in this perspective verse 7, like Psalm 104H:29 and Job 34:14 "means the great anonymity in which a man's individual existence ends; it is not a declaration of resurrection."[20]

It would seem that none of these interpretations puts us as well on the right track as Cardinal Bea's little booklet with its insistence that Qohelet was written under the influence of Greek philosophy and as a reaction to it.[21]

---

107 ff: he experienced an inward struggle between the faith of his fathers and the ideas of his time; see W. Zimmerli, *Das Buch des Predigers Salomo* (Göttingen: 1962), 131.

[18] Friedrich Ellermeier, "Die Entmachtung der Weisheit im Denken Qohelets," *Zeitschrift für Theologie und Kirche,* 60 (1963), 16 ff, 1–20. On *nepeš* see below, footnote 77 to p. 194.

[19] A. D. Power, *Ecclesiastes or The Preacher* (London: Longmans, 1952), 129 f.

[20] (Max Haller-) Kurt Galling, *Die fünf Megilloth . . . Prediger Salomo* (HAT 18; Tübingen; Mohr, 1940), 88. — On the heterodoxy of Qohelet alleged by Ginsberg, see Alejandro Diez Macho, "La Kallah de Omaha," *Estudios Bíblicos,* 13/4 (1954), 434–439; in 7/4 (1948), 369–406, Serafín de Ausejo, "El género literario del Eclesiastés," holds it a Hellenistic diatribe.

[21] A. Bea, *Liber Ecclesiastae qui ab Hebraeis appellatur Qohelet* (Rome: Pontifical Biblical Institute, 1940). Bea shows that the author's identifying himself as "son of David, king in Jerusalem," does not preclude composition after 300 B.C. A date nearer to 150 is preferred by many. On page 26, Bea's rendition of 12:5c differs from ours in making man's long road and the mourning a parenthesis. Now

In fact the whole book constitutes a passionate *rejection* of Greek philosophy as a norm for concrete action. Thus it is partially a *return* to the "old" Egyptian-Hebrew wisdom as against new thought currents mushrooming around it in Greek-Egyptian-Jewish Alexandria.[22] But more than that, it is a return to that good old man-in-the-street "common sense" which in every age is mistrustful of will-o'-the-wisp philosophizings.

Common sense shows us what our human nature and its concrete situation impose upon us to do here and now. Whether Pythagoras is right and the soul will be reincarnated after death; or whether Plato is right and the soul will be released from its bodily cage; or as Aristotle says there is only a single world-soul functioning in humans as long as they breathe; or as Democritus claims there is nothing but interchanging atoms: the answers to these ethereal questions change nothing of the fact that man has his job cut out before him. From dawn when he gets up, be he prince or slave, he has to go through a round of chores until he stumbles home tired to get what nourishment, relaxation, and self-fulfilment he can before falling asleep and starting the cycle of another day.

Says Qohelet virtually, "Ours not to reason why; ours but to do and die" — at least in the sense that we will never do our elemental duty in life, nor secure the pleasure it is bound up with, if before acting we require assurance as to which of the conflicting systems of Greek philosophy is best.

Thus the book emphasizes the inadequacy of speculation: (12:12) "Of making books there is no end, and much study wears out the flesh";

Alexander A. DiLella, "Conservative and Progressive Theology: Sirach and Wisdom," *Catholic Biblical Quarterly* 28/2 (April 1966), 139–154, 150, finds that Qohelet accepts neither the traditional Hebrew view of retribution on this earth, as Sirach; nor the Greek view, as Wisdom; he refers P. W. Skehan, *The Literary Relationship between the Book of Wisdom and the Protocanonical Wisdom Books* (Washington: 1938), 3; J. Reider, *The Book of Wisdom* (New York: 1957), 11; and M. Baily, "Biblical Man and Some Formulae of Christian Teaching," *Irish Theological Quarterly* 27 (1960), 173–200.

[22] Harry Ranston, *Ecclesiastes and the Early Greek Wisdom Literature* (London: Epworth, 1925), 11, notes as the view of Driver, Peake, Wellhausen, Kuenen, "While Koheleth never adopted the tenets of any particular school, he was influenced by an atmosphere of Greek thought"; so now Robert Gordis, *Koheleth — the Man and his World* (New York: Jewish Theological Seminary, 1951), 50. Ranston himself holds that the author of the Book of *Wisdom* set himself to *correct* Ecclesiastes; on his claim of page 142 that the echoes of Theognis may be due ultimately to Babylon, there is no noticeable corroboration in W. E. Lambert, *Babylonian Wisdom Literature* (Oxford: 1960). But now A. F. Rainey, "A Study of Ecclesiastes," *Concordia Theological Monthly,* 35 (1964), 148–157, finds that the book is a balance between contrasted proverbs, from pre-Alexander Achemenid Mesopotamia. — Qohelet's God is remote and impersonal, says Egon Pfeiffer, "Die Gottesfurcht im Buche Kohelet," H.-W. Hertzberg Festschrift, *Gottes Wort und Gottes Land,* edited by H. Reventlow (Göttingen: Vandenhoeck, 1965), 136; 133–158, following G. von Rad, *Erwägungen zum Prediger Salomo* (1941).

(1:18) "in much philosophy there is much grief; to increase knowledge increases sorrow"; (1:9) "there is nothing new under the sun"; (2:14) "the wise man's eyes are in his head, and the fool walks in darkness; and yet even I know that a single encounter will befall them all"; (3:2 ff) "There is a time to be born, and a time to die . . . a time to laugh and a time to weep; (3:10) I have taken note of the object of attention which God has given to the sons of men to be occupied with; (3:11) he has made everything fine for its own time: both this world and the next ['*olam* means both!] he has placed within their heart without man's being [*b*e*lî* + *lō* = ? un]able to discover the effect which God has produced from start to finish. (3:12) I know that there is nothing better for them than to be joyful in the performance of good in their lifetime; (3:13) the fact that every man has to eat and drink and see some good amid his toil, that too is a gift of God."

In other words, our failure to solve definitively the problems of the universe must not be made a pretext either for leaving our duty undone or for renouncing the pleasures which are just as much a part of "Nature's Law" as duty itself. Hence the apparent pessimism — or rather cynicism — turns out to be a wholehearted and well-founded optimism. Not the *existence* of future rewards is rejected, but only the fumbling which would result from requiring exaggerated advance assurance in their regard. (11:9) "Rejoice, O young man, in your youth; let your heart cheer you, and walk in the ways of your heart." (9:10) "Whatever you find to hand to do, do it with all your heart. There will be no work, or enterprise, or knowledge, or philosophy, in the grave you are headed for; (9:11) the race is not to the swift, nor the battle to the strong or strategic . . . time and chance have the last word."

Even the arch-materialism of 2:24, "There is nothing better for a man than to eat and drink and enjoy life," is at base a reformulation of the supreme norm of morality, *ordo rerum in finem*. It is only by acting according to his *nature*, that is to say by observing the natural law, that man can hope to achieve happiness or "know, love, and serve God."

In this context we may conclude that Qohelet at no point denies the immortality of the soul; but he at all points warns against making its rational proof a stipulation for following the course of action plainly dictated by our nature here and now. In this outlook, and in the more immediate "funeral sermon" context, the dictum of 12:7 means primarily that we should do *now* what we have to do, because "the night cometh in which no man can work" (Jn 9:4). A significant difference is indeed established between the materiality which we have in common with the clod, and the vitality which is God's special gift. Whether this special gift of God applies only to humans as distinct from animals is unmentioned in 12:7. In 3:21 it is hinted to be so, yet this is regarded as a speculation more apt to be harmful than helpful.

Finally we must notice that Qohelet 12:7 is an echo of Psalm 104H:29 as here underlined in its larger context. (23) "Man goes forth to his toil, and to his labor until evening. (24) How ample have your works become, O yhwh. All of them you have made in wisdom. The earth is full of your output. (25) Take for example the sea, deep and vast in extent. It teems beyond counting with living things small alongside great. (26) There ships ply, like fabled Leviathan made by you for sport. (27) Whatever there is waits upon you to give its food in due order. (28) You give them, they gather; you open your hand, they are fed well. (29) You hide your face, they are aghast; *you collect* THEIR *spirit* (*rûaḥ*), they expire and *to their dust they return*. (30) You send YOUR spirit, they are created, and you freshen the face of the earth."

Christian theology has been so absorbed by this last verse, and by resisting the urge to find here a revelation of the Third Person of the Trinity, that it has never exploited the preceding verse as a confirmation or explanation of what Qohelet says about the soul's origin from God. Perhaps it is just as well, because it is plain that the spirit which God "gathers" — and this can hardly mean less than "takes *to himself*" is something common to all the *animals* along with man; and their return to dust, no less than his, is a consequence of their loss of this *rûaḥ*. However, it is not said as explicitly as in Qohelet that this *rûaḥ* comes "from" God.

3. *The Mud and Breath of Genesis*

Already in Chapter 2 we have been forced to stress that the whole Christian resistance to evolution was based on an alleged exegesis of the one verse of Genesis 2:7 in defiance of the sound norms laid down by Augustine and Aquinas.[23] We further pointed out that when Pius XII sanctioned evolution, dogmatic exegetes were forced to abandon what had been claimed to be the literal sense of *half* of that verse. They thereupon stiffened their lines of resistance to maintain this kind of literalness for the *other* half, as proof that God creates the soul immediately out of nothing.

Now we must examine with all possible care and objectivity the problem of what really is *asserted* in both halves of Genesis 2:7, and in what terms. Or to put our question in a more concrete way, is the word generally translated "soul" in that verse really applicable to the human soul in the sense which Christian philosophy gives to that word?

---

[23] See above, footnotes 68 and 69 to p. 59; and on Teilhard's own use of the Old Testament, footnote 9 in chap. 1 and footnote 2 above, pp. 4 and 164.

And if not, does any other term or implication of the verse convey to us what the modern Christian means by saying "the human soul is created immediately by God." Note that we are here not yet concerned directly with establishing the meaning of *nepeš* or *rûaḥ,* a problem which we will take up systematically only after having scrutinized the principal concrete uses in their context.[24]

"God formed man dust from the earth, and breathed into his nostrils the breath of life; and man became a living soul" (Gn 2:7).

How pleasingly simple and clear this passage is at the very first look! Man is a strange mixture of the earthy and the divine; and his *life,* though it is a thing he somehow shares with the animals, is the very quality which most expresses the loftiest endowment of his nature. Or in scholastic terms, the same identical principle which makes man *live* in the way animals and plants live, also sets him apart from them as possessing a reality more akin to that of God as a pure spirit.

This interpretation is on the whole solid, and must stand. But when it comes down to attaching all or any part of these paraphrases to specific terms such that we can really grasp and identify what the author intended to convey, then we at once find the obscurities multiplying the more we look at them.

First there is the fact that "man" is grammatically anticipated in the sentence. To say "God made man clod from the earth" is a perfectly understandable way of saying "God took a clod from the earth and *out of it* made man," leaving open the question of whether this is imagery for a more subtle kind of causation. But when the verse goes on, "and man became soul of life," it puts a bit more strain on the grammar to take this as meaning "God took a clod from the ground and out of it formed something which, after he had breathed into it the breath of life, became a living being, namely man."

Secondly, *if* we are to adopt this understanding of the passage, and at the same time admit the legitimacy of bodily evolution, then an impression is somehow created that we are taking the *first* half of the verse as metaphorical, while retaining a *proper* or non-metaphorical sense for the second half. Only upon reconsideration it becomes obvious that God's "breath" is even *more* metaphorical than his "taking mud"; and his breath was *never* in fact claimed by patristic exegetes to be an unmetaphorical expression, as his taking mud was in fact through many centuries claimed to be. Nevertheless, making all possible effort not to read our own thoughts into what the biblical writer was saying, it seems inescapable that by the terms mud-breath he was trying to indicate our

---

[24] For those who would prefer, that treatment on pages 188–199 can be examined first.

dependence upon God both for our *invisible* or spiritual being which is infused by him directly, and for our perceptible matter which we share with the inferior creation. Since however the scientific teaching on evolution makes it improbable that God did in fact form the body of man directly from inorganic elements, there seems to be ultimately a kind of diminishing of the literalness with which we may take the first half in comparison with the second half.

Thirdly, the real enigma of the verse is one that does not become apparent at first reading at all. Namely, the special gift called "his own breath" which God puts into the thing called by anticipation "(living) man," may mean one of two things. It may mean something by which living man is distinguished from all *inorganic* matter and even from all living matter possessing no principle of its life other than the purely material. Or it may mean simply that man possesses "life," a thing which in fact he has in common with the lower orders of living things, not only because these are not simply "dust of the earth" but because they are expressly called by the same name "soul of life, *nepeš ḥayyâ*" in 2:19. Really verse 2:7 does not say that by God's action either "the non-living became living" or "the merely living became spiritual." But it does say that *something* (not clearly qualified as either human nonliving or living nonhuman or neither living nor human) became a living human being.

Nepeš ḥayyâ, the final term of God's *special* action in producing man, is in fact a term which is applied also to animals in 2:19. Therefore the term of itself can mean no more and no less than "a living being." Moreover there can be no doubt that *ḥayyâ* means "living," though we have no way of deciding whether it is a feminine adjective, or an abstract genitival noun which in Hebrew often or even preferably expresses the adjectival relationship.[25] Subtracting *ḥayyâ* from *nepeš ḥayyâ* and "living" from "a living being" seems to leave us with the sense of "a being" or "a being apt to be connected with life" for *nepeš*. And this sense we will later see corroborated.

But though living animals are called *nepeš ḥayyâ,* they are *not* said either in Genesis 2:19 or elsewhere to be formed by a *double* action of God, or related to his "breathing." Moreover in Genesis 1:24 the *earth* is commanded to produce all the animals; really this is in a narrative which is not *part* of that containing 2:19, but parallel and written from a different viewpoint. From these divergences concerning the animals, it is maintained that 2:7 is a proof of the immediate creation of the

---

[25] Aubrey R. Johnson, *The Vitality of the Individual in the Thought of Ancient Israel* (Cardiff: University of Wales, 1949), 23 *n* 2: we cannot be sure *ḥayyâ* is noun rather than adjective unless it is preceded by the article as in Genesis 1:21.

spiritual soul, not because a *nepeš ḥayyâ* results, but because it results from an action more *composite* and more *intimate* on God's part.[26]

As formulated by van Imschoot, the difference between Genesis 2:7 and 2:19 "doubtless insinuates that man is composite, and has a relation to Yahweh different from that had by animals."[27] The innocent word "composite" is apt to be taken without further ado as signifying "composed of body and soul," but this is in no way hinted by the text or by van Imschoot. It may equally well mean "composed of inert matter and of life."

The formulation of Vollert seems to go more notably beyond the evidence. He denies that *nepeš ḥayyâ* of verse 7 proves or depicts the immediate creation of the spiritual soul, yet adds "all we need to conclude is that the divine breath imparted something which animals lack."[28] About animals there is nothing at all in verse 7; in its context two things are juxtaposed, plant life and man the tiller; and the comparison with verse 19 warrants concluding no more than that man is composite and has a special relation to YHWH.

Even more is read into the text by the words which we here italicize in Clamer's observation: "Elsewhere animals too are shown to possess a living soul 'dependent upon the divine breath.' But nowhere else do we encounter as here a *divine participation properly so called,* from which results the incomparable superiority of man over the animal, because *he possesses not only physical life but also the higher life which is that of the soul.*"[29] These congenial Christian notions about "participation" and "higher life of the soul" are simply not in the text at all. On the other hand, his admission that animals possess the living soul "equally" is not borne out by his claim that the "divine breath" is assigned to them in three verses he cites. Job 34:14 says "If (God) turns his attention toward (man!), his spirit and his breath will be gathered to him." Genesis 7:22 says that in the nostrils of all animals is "the breath of the spirit of life," *nišmat rûaḥ ḥayyîm,* but it is *their breath,* not God's. Psalm 104H:29 also and more explicitly says it is *their* spirit which is taken away by God when the animals return to the dust, as we saw above.

Only the transit to a living human state, on the part of what is by

---

[26] Benedetto Prete, "L'origine dell'uomo nel racconto biblico," *Sacra Doctrina,* 4 (1959), 207–237; 221: "Man appears here in his concrete unity, which supposes both physico-spiritual unity and also the vital perfection of his being; in fact Genesis 2:7 affirms with terms of eloquent realism that by the breath of God 'man became a living being.'"

[27] P. van Imschoot, *Théologie de l'Ancien Testament,* 2. *L'Homme* (Paris: Descleé, 1956), 4; cf. 13.

[28] Cyril Vollert, "Evolution and the Bible," in B. Boelen, *Symposium on Evolution* (Pittsburgh: Duquesne, 1959), 104; 95.

[29] A. Clamer, *La Genèse* (L. Pirot Sainte Bible 1/1; Paris: Letouzey, 1953), 117.

anticipation called man, is dealt with in Genesis 2:7. There are no further implications *here* on the difference of his life from that of animals. This is perhaps compatible with Vollert's further guarded formulation, "The only inference we can draw is that the substance marked out to be the body of Adam was not a human body until a rational soul animated it." If by "rational soul" he means no more than "the vital principle which is in fact characteristic of the rational animal," this is not even an inference, but a *restatement* of "transit to a living human state." Van Imschoot says, "The man fashioned by Yahweh was not yet alive, because he did not have the life-breath. . . . By getting the life-breath into his nostrils, man becomes a living being, or rather a living person." Here again, "person" is acceptable if it means merely a living being that happens to be human. But there is danger that by *correcting* "living being" to "living person," the impression may be created in readers not accustomed to theological exactitude, that terms like "person" or "rational" conveyed to the Hebrew writer the sense which has come to be elaborated with the help of Greek philosophy.

> Highly philosophical ideas cannot be drawn from this text, for example the creation of the body and of the spiritual soul. . . . The Hebrews do not conceive either a man or a soul without body, and they always consider the man as a whole. Hence they say without appreciable difference of sense that the man or flesh or *nephesh* reflects, wills, experiences feelings or sensations, lives, dies. They doubtless distinguish soul from flesh, and spirit from flesh; but they do not oppose the flesh to the soul or spirit within man. . . . Opposition between man's spirit and flesh is encountered only in the books where Greek influence penetrates and [!] in the New Testament.[30]

The biblical passages in which an antithesis between flesh and *nepeš* is alleged to prove the spirituality of the *nepeš* are either synonyms, as Isaiah 10:18, soul and body; or parallels, as Psalm 63H:2; or quite irrelevant, as Job 14:22, pain is felt in the flesh. Van Imschoot adds, "Man is totally flesh, i.e., weak, and totally *nepeš*, i.e., alive." He concludes that in Genesis 2:7 nothing is said of flesh, and certainly nothing of body (for which there is not even a word in Hebrew), but of man non-living and living; to make out this difference to be due to presence or absence of a spiritual soul is pure Greek speculation.

Thus we cannot accept an interpretation proposed in 1936 along with distinguishing of priestly and Yahwist contributions, a thing which then required considerable insight and courage in a Catholic: "We have no hesitation in understanding the deep truth which is hidden under the figure of speech, 'God breathes on the face of man' [to mean] the human soul is produced solely by divine power without any concurrence of sec-

---

[30] P. van Imschoot, *Théologie de l'AT*, 2, p. 4.

ondary causes."[31] This seems to imply notions of concursus and causality which are too specialized for the Hebrew writer's outlook.

Similarly in the following passage, along with some valuable insights, the term "soul" which renders *nepeš* is not taken in its proper sense of "(living) being"; and "breath" is unwarrantably equated with a "special act of creation" different from God's type of activity in the molding of mud. Moreover there is added a new element to the discussion, the "Image":

> The Paradise account, which abounds in anthropomorphisms, tells how Yahweh fashioned the body of man from earth and breathed into his nostrils the breath of life. . . . Man's soul is something essentially different from the body; it is of divine origin, brought forth by a special act of creation; and because man has a reasoning soul he is in God's image. . . . The spiritual element has various designations in the Old Testament [including] breath. . . . The image of God in man can refer only to the soul.[32]

It is true that St. Thomas formulates a rigorous syllogism to prove from the likeness of man to God (Gn 1:27) the immediate creation of the soul. But this is rather incidental to what he is at that point concerned with showing. The body of the article, *Summa Theologiae* 1, 90, 2, deals with the soul as a substance rather than an inhering characteristic.[33] But in his customary way, Aquinas gives this positive doctrine only after first listing proofs for the alternative view, then interposing a "bridge" over to his own doctrine. This bridge usually takes the form of a well-known slogan cited from Aristotle or Augustine or Scripture, often with the undisguised intent of *modifying* the sense which had been previously given to it.

In the present case he says, "It is written [Gn 1:27] God created man to his own image. But man is like to God in his soul. Therefore the soul was created." In the preceding article, in answer to the first objection, Thomas had said, "The term 'breathe,' as regards the act of God [Gn 2:7], is the same as 'to make a *spiritus*' [which in Latin may mean either 'a breath' or 'a spirit']. Moreover, in the material sense, man by breathing does not send forth anything of his own substance, but an extraneous thing." Perhaps this passage suggested or may excuse this Dominican author's characterizing the human soul as "the very breath of God":

[31] P. M. Périer, "L'origine de l'homme," *Revue Apologétique,* 62 (May 1936), 518 f; these essays appeared posthumously as a book, *Le transformisme: l'origine de l'homme et le dogme catholique* (Paris: Beauchesne, [3]1938).

[32] Paul Heinisch, *Theology of the Old Testament,*[2] translated by William Heidt (Collegeville, Minnesota: Liturgical Press, 1950 = 1940), 156, 159, 161.

[33] See footnote 3 above on p. 165.

God is depicted after the manner of a sculptor [in Gn 2:7]: he moistens a lump of clay and artistically fashions it into the shape of a body. Then he breathes life into the finished product, and a man is made. . . . But man, unlike the brute, has a spiritual side to his nature, which is also produced by a special act of God. The human soul, it is absolutely clear, was not made out of any pre-existing matter. The soul was *immediately* and *directly* created by God. This is a unique event: the recital of the separate production of soul and body occurs only in the production of man. . . . His soul is immaterial, created out of nothing, the very breath of the infinite, eternal, and omnipotent God.[34]

To return to the claim of Aquinas that the Image of God is in the soul: his interpretations of Scripture are remarkably common-sense and well-founded in comparison with those of his contemporaries. But research into "God's Image" has made considerable strides since his time. The view that the image of God is chiefly in the soul has been traced as far back as Ambrose, and was still enshrined in the Baltimore Catechism. But it also became a distinctive teaching of Calvin. And yet to one of the most loyal and enlightened Calvinists of our century we owe a thorough and apparently definitive refutation of this view.[35]

Analysis of the various other possibilities shows that there is a measure of truth in several of them. The image of God's majesty is man's whole being, dominating the lower creation both by his erect stature and by the creativity of his bodily and intellectual powers.[36] To the considerable bibliography on which we have already drawn, a veritable flood of continuing interest in the subject would now have to be added.[37] It is espe-

---

[34] William B. Murphy and others, *God and His Creation* (Dubuque: Priory, 1958), 392. More acceptably B. Hansoul in *God and His Creation,* volume 2 of *Theology Library* edited by A. M. Henry (Chicago: Fides, 1955): "There is nothing, in function of the text itself [Genesis 1, especially verse 26, which] can make us conclude to an explicit affirmation of spirituality and immortality such as we conceive them today." See the woefully unrealistic presentation recommended by James Nist, *The Practical Catechist* (Herder: 1913), 46 ff, pilloried by Ernest Messenger, *Theology and Evolution* (Westminster, Maryland: Newman, 1949 = London: Sands, 1949), 47, 194.

[35] Paul Humbert, *Études sur le récit du Paradis et de la Chute dans la Genèse* (Neuchâtel: University, 1940), 153 ff.

[36] Robert North, "The Genetic Image of God," *Spiritual Life,* 8/4 (Winter 1962), 224–233.

[37] Arnold Struker, *Die Gottebenbildlichkeit des Menschen in der christlichen Literatur der ersten zwei Jahrhunderte* (Münster: Aschendorff, 1913), 131 f: ignored or neglected until Gnosticism gave it a push, the image of Genesis 1:26 consists chiefly in spirituality and freedom; A. M. Rohner, "Thomas von Aquin oder Max Scheler — Das Ebenbild Gottes," *Divus Thomas Fribourg,* 1 (1923), 342; P. Paluscsák, "Imago Dei in homine," *Xenia Thomistica* (Rome: 1925), 2, 119–154; Amedeo Rossi, "Similitudo Dei in creaturis," *Divus Thomas Piacenza,* 31 (1928), 417–448; Philipp Bachmann, "Der Mensch als Ebenbild Gottes," Festschrift L. Ihmels *Das Erbe M. Luthers* (Leipzig: 1928), 276, linking Genesis 1:26 to 1 John 1:32 "we will be like him because we will see him as he is"; Franz Dander, "Gottes Bild und Gleichnis in der Schöpfung nach der Lehre des heiligen Thomas von

cially reassuring to find Catholic experts like Gross and Burghardt rejecting no less emphatically than Humbert the notion that God's Image is chiefly in the soul.[38] So we must regretfully part company with Aquinas and other esteemed exegetes who would find in that interpretation an even

Aquin," *Zeitschrift für Katholische Theologie*, 53 (1929), 1–40, 203–246; J. Wendland, "Die Lehre vom Ebenbilde Gottes und von der religiösen Anlage im Menschen in der neueren Theologie," *Zeitschrift für Theologie und Kirche*, 17 (1936), 67–82; Adolf Hoffmann, "Zur Lehre von der Gottebenbildlichkeit des Menschen in der neueren protestantischen Theologie und bei Thomas von Aquin," *Divus Thomas Fribourg*, 19 (1941), 3–35; Ludwig Köhler, "Die Grundstelle der Imago-Dei-Lehre, Genesis 1:26," *Theologische Zeitschrift*, 4 (1948); J. Giblet, "L'homme image de Dieu dans les commentaires littéraires de Philon d'Alexandrie," *Studia Hellenistica*, 5 (1948), 93–118; F. Michaeli, *Dieu à l'image de l'homme: étude sur la notion anthropomorphique de Dieu dans l'Ancien Testament* (Neuchâtel: Delachaux, 1950); H. van den Bussche, "L'homme créé à l'image de Dieu (Gen. 1:26, 27)," *Collationes Gandavenses*, 31 (1948), 185–195; G. Söhngen, "Die biblische Lehre von der Gottebenbildlichkeit," *Münchener Theologische Zeitschrift*, 2 (1951), 52–76; B. Brinkmann, "Geschaffen 'nach dem Bilde Gottes,'" *Wissenschaft und Weisheit*, 14 (1951), 129–134; Walter Dürig, *Imago: ein Beitrag zur Terminologie und Theologie der römischen Liturgie* (Münchener Theologische Studien: Systematische, 2/5; Munich: Zink, 1952); Wilhelm Rudolph, "Das Menschenbild des Alten Testaments," Festschrift H. Schreiner *Dienst unter dem Wort*, ed. K. Janssen (Gütersloh: Bertelsmann, 1953), 238–251 (248 upright posture is involved, to the extent that the image involves no belittling of the material); H. Crouzel, *Théologie de l'Image de Dieu chez Origène* (Paris: Aubier, 1956), on which see P. Th. Camelot, "La théologie de l'Image de Dieu," *Revue des Sciences Philosophiques et Théologiques*, 40/3 (July 1956), 443–471 (p. 445: Colossians 1:15 takes precedence over Genesis 1:26; "it is first Christ who is the image of God"); B. de Géradon, "L'homme à l'image de Dieu: approche nouvelle à la lumière de l'anthropologie du sens commun," *Nouvelle Revue Théologique*, 80/7 (July 1958), 689–695: the image consists in the fact that man like God can think, speak, act: all three *bodily* actions described anthropomorphically of God; Othmar Schilling, "Ebenbild," in J.-B. Bauer, *Bibeltheologisches Wörterbuch* (Graz: 1959), 121–127; R. M. Wilson, "Genesis 1:26 and the New Testament," *Bijdragen*, 20/2 (1959), 117–125; also 126–145, "L'homme, image de Dieu: origine du thème" by H. Somers, anthropological parallels largely from Frazer; image = "blueprint"; Olaf Linton and Nils Dahl, "Imago Dei: Opposisjonsinnlegg ved Jervell," *Norsk Teologisk Tidsskrift*, 61 (1960), 65, 71, 94; Anton Burkhart, *Der Mensch: Gottes Ebenbild [bei] F. Staudenmaier* (Freiburg: Herder, 1962), 443; Stanis-Edmund Szydzik, "Die geistigen Ursprünge der Imago-Dei-Lehre bei Ambrosius von Mailand," *Theologie und Glaube*, 53/3 (1963), 161–176; John E. Sullivan, *The Image of God: the Doctrine of St. Augustine and its Influence* (Dubuque: Priory, 1963).

[38] H. Gross, "Gottebenbildlichkeit," *Lexikon für Theologie und Kirche*[2] (Freiburg: Herder, 1960), 4, 1087; Walter J. Burghardt, *The Image of God in Man According to Cyril of Alexandria* (J. Quasten, Catholic University Studies in Christian Antiquity 14; Washington: 1957), 24: Cyril reads the New Testament into the Old by putting the image in the soul and not the body; this is not Hebraic. But G. Duncker, "L'immagine di Dio nell'uomo (Gen. 1:26–27); una somiglianza fisica?", *Biblica*, 40 (1959), 384–392; 387, basing himself on an unpublished manuscript of Lagrange (Genesis 5:1 must be explained by 1:26 and not vice versa) and H. Rowley, *The Faith of Israel* (1956), 75, holds it impossible to set the image in a physical likeness as does Humbert. See below, footnote 19, chap. 7, p. 212.

partial or confirmatory proof of the immediate creation of the soul in Genesis 2:7.[39]

Whatever be the extent or content of metaphorical usage in the two halves of Genesis 2:7, it nevertheless and always remains true that in both halves an *equal* immediacy is attributed to God's activity in the formation of the first man. Whatever immediacy is expressed regarding God's production of that nobler part of man symbolized as "God's breath" must also be acknowledged here regarding the remainder of man's being.[40] Conversely, if by "molding mud" is to be understood no immediate intervention of God at all, then there is in this text no proof of the immediate creation of the soul either. Or rather let us say, in an effort to keep fully before us the whole complexity of the exegetical problem, our goal should be to find in this text a formula to express the *equal* immediacy of the dependence of the whole man, in his body and his soul, upon God.

In this effort the situation is easiest for the opponents of transformism. "*Since* Genesis 2:7 teaches the immediacy of God's creation of the soul, and *since* an equal immediacy is asserted in the two parts of the verse, *therefore* Genesis 2:7 teaches the immediacy of God's creation of the body." This, though restated in my own words, is ultimately the position of some textbooks very up-to-date in their presentation and published in the second half of our century.[41] But to understand why they are saying what they do, we must examine the slow and subtle transformation which this position has been undergoing since the beginning of the century. Hurter in 1903 put the state of the question with unmistakable clarity. "After we have vindicated the Catholic doctrine on the origin of the human race . . . at a date no earlier than that assigned by Moses between 6984 and 3761 B.C.," and excluding bodily evolution, "our next step is to show that the immediate creation of the soul too

---

[39] Ghislain Lafont, "Le sens du thème de l'image de Dieu dans l'anthropologie de saint Thomas d'Aquin," *Recherches de Science Religieuse,* 47/4 (Oct. 1959), (560–), 569: the image as treated in proximity to Summa, 1, 93, follows the lead of Genesis and is centric to Thomas' theology, *more* than is apparent in other parts of the Summa. See M. J. de Beaurecueil, *L'Homme et l'Image de Dieu selon Saint Thomas d'Aquin* (Études et recherches 8; Ottawa, 1952–1955); P. M. Matthijs, *De imagine Dei in homine secundum doctrinam S. Thomae Aquinatis* (Rome: Angelicum, 1952).

[40] This seems to me overlooked in José M. González Ruiz, "Contenido dogmático de la narración de Génesis 2:7 sobre la formación del hombre," *Estudios Bíblicos,* 9/4 (1950), 438. I should express my indebtedness to colleague James Quigley for stimulating re-appraisal of my analysis here and at other key points.

[41] So J. Sagüés, *De Deo creante* (Madrid: Biblioteca de autores cristianos, 1952), 2, 719; Gabriel Huarte, *De Deo creante et elevante*[2] (Rome: Gregorian, 1935), 203.

is altogether Catholic teaching and genuinely universal."[42] For the wide-spread area of thought which Hurter represented, the historicizing inter-pretation of Genesis 2:7 demanded on one and the same ground the negation of transformism and the immediate creation of the human soul out of nothing.

Whether or not because Catholic denials of evolution in the past thirty years have been pretty much a façade, there are very few text-books still in use today which find it contrary to Scripture, and very few which allow to Genesis 2:7 any genuinely probative force in the thesis on the creation of the soul. That verse is limited to "supplying the foundation" or "giving a sufficient hint" in Garrigou-Lagrange and Hugon.[43] Van Hove puts Scripture proofs in first place but acknowledges they are not apodictic.[44]

Genesis 2:7 has been excluded from the Scripture proof offered by Pesch, Daffara, and van Noort.[45] The latest Lercher says there is "nothing direct and convincing" in Scripture, and at any rate Genesis 2:7 proves nothing about any human soul after Adam's.[46] No Scripture proof at all is attempted by Pohle-Gummersbach, Beraza, Pignataro, or Moran.[47] Diffidence is shown by Mors, Bozzola, and Reany.[48] The quite up-to-date approach taken by Schmaus does not involve any reinterpretation of the Genesis text.[49]

To attempt to draw from Genesis 2:7 the *nature* of the vital principle given by God can scarcely fail to *presume* this rather subtle tenet of scholastic speculation, "A substance which possesses some operations in-trinsically independent of matter, cannot have arisen in dependence upon

---

[42] H. Hurter, *Theologiae dogmaticae compendium*[11] (Innsbruck: Wagner, 1903), 2, 239. Cf. C. Boyer, *De Deo creante*[4] (Rome: Gregorian, 1948), 104: "Our first step will be to show that no one of the Fathers ever taught the origin of a species from a diverse species."

[43] Reginald Garrigou-Lagrange, *The Trinity and God the Creator* (St. Louis: Herder, 1952), 613; Édouard Hugon, *De Deo uno et trino, creatore et gubernatore* (Paris: Lethielleux, 1933), 769.

[44] Aloysius van Hove, *Tractatus de Deo creante et elevante* (Malines: Dessain, 1944), 219.

[45] Christian Pesch, *Praelectiones dogmaticae 3. De Deo creante* (Freiburg: Herder, 1895), 66; Marcolino Daffara, *De Deo creatore* (Turin: Marietti, 1947), 223; G. van Noort, *Tractatus de Deo creatore*[3] (Bussum: Brand, 1920), 189.

[46] Ludwig Lercher, [3]F. Schlagenhaufen, *De Deo uno et trino creante et elevante*[4] (Barcelona: Herder, 1945), 317.

[47] Josef Gummersbach, *Pohle: Lehrbuch der Dogmatik*[10] (Paderborn: Schöningh, 1952), 1, 560; Blasio Beraza, *De Deo creante* (Bilbao: Eléxpuru, 1921), 509; Felice Pignataro, *De Deo creatore* (Rome: S. Giuseppe, 1904), 245; John Moran, *Alpha et Omega: theses quaedam selectae* (Worcester: Harrigan, 1935), 110.

[48] José Mors, *De Deo creante* (Petropolis: Vozes, 1940), 101; Carlo Bozzola, *De Deo uno et trino creante et elevante* (Naples: d'Auria, 1948), 205; William Reany, *The Creation of the Human Soul* (London: Ouseley, 1929), 61.

[49] Michael Schmaus, *Katholische Dogmatik B 2: Gott der Schöpfer und der Erlöser* (Munich: Hueber, 1954), 295, 323 f.

matter." But this is precisely the assertion which is questioned by Teilhard and modern science. Whether or not it will emerge an unshaken truth of reason or revelation, it cannot be presumed or declared to have formed part of what the author of Genesis 2:7 was trying to convey.

Holding with Pius XII the legitimacy of bodily evolution, we are forced to leave the *immediacy* of God's activity in the first half of Genesis 2:7 open to a symbolic interpretation. His *concern* with man's emergence was so great that it is depicted under the form of molding mud directly, though this expression does not dogmatically exclude that the body of man had developed otherwise. But there is no indication within the text that the immediacy of God's breathing is not capable of a similar interpretation. Whether, *apart* from this text, *Church authority* precludes such an interpretation will occupy our whole next chapter. But in Genesis 2:7 what the text itself expresses is that God's *concern* with man's emergence was so great that it is depicted under the form of directly breathing upon something in such a way that it becomes a living human being.

4. *Maccabees and Related Texts*

As his *first* proof of the thesis that the human soul is created immediately by God, van Noort puts the single half-verse of Psalm 33:15. This says in the Hebrew "(God), the one fashioning (al)together their hearts." Via the Vulgate can be proposed a rendition more like "he fashioned their hearts singly." It should be noted that "heart" in Hebrew, *lēb* or *lēbāb,* is the organ symbolizing intelligence, rather than love or emotion *contrasted* to intelligence as with us.[50] This does not strictly bring us any closer to our goal, since human love no less than human thought is a spiritual operation; only for the Greco-modern there is danger of conceiving love as a refractory urge of some subspiritual faculties, more than thought is. Perhaps for this reason, or because of "God's creative word" in verses 6 and 9 of this psalm, this verse 15 may deserve consideration as showing that God created the "soul" at least as much as he created the body. More fairly in its context this verse seems to mean "God knows what's going on." He forms the thoughts of man: that is, his providence presides over men's planning; as the second half of the verse continues, "he has understanding of all their doings." Yet perhaps here, as in the verses 14 and 2 of Psalm 139H, it was the Psalmist's intention to say God knows my thoughts because he made the principle from which they proceed.

Van Noort argues also from Hebrews 12:9, "shall we not rather obey

---

[50] R. North, " 'Humilis corde' in luce Psalmorum," *Verbum Domini,* 28/3 (May 1950), 153–161.

the father of spirits and live?" It is understandable that the Christian theologian would want to draw at least some tenuous support for his case from somewhere in the New Testament. It is rather humiliating to be left with the impression that for so sublime and advanced a doctrine as the Spirituality of the Soul we are left wholly without resource in Christian revelation, or at least our traditions are overwhelmingly connected with what God communicated to that stiff-necked people of flesh and stone. Alas, even the Hebrews passage is primarily an unmistakable echo of the passages we will see in Numbers 16:22 and 27:16.[51] Their formula *"God* of the spirits" is retained even in the Septuagint translation and as taken up in the apocalyptic Henoch 37:2 (cf. Jubilees 10,3). In this light, "father" in Hebrews 12:9 doubtless means "ruler over" rather than "creator of."

"The basis of such an expression relates to the ruler over the angelic powers, as apocalyptic usage shows. The same liturgical tradition is further attested in votive inscriptions of Rheneia and in the epistle First Clement 59,3. It is important to observe that this verse of Hebrews speaks of [the fathers, i.e. educators, of] 'our flesh' but not of 'our spirit.' Flesh and spirit are thus not quite parallel here."[52] From what this expert has thus far said, to find in what continues the words we italicize is at least perplexing: "The expression 'father of spirits' serves to recall *first of all* that God puts the spirit *and the soul* in men (Targum to Numbers 16:22; 27:16; Mishna Nidda 31a); secondly that above all it is the prophetic word which stems from the 'father of spirits' (Henoch 37,2.4; 39,7; Apc 22:6); and thirdly that especially the dead (Henoch 40,5; 61,12; 70,4) and the angels (Henoch 60,16; 61,10) *become* spirits. . . . The rabbinical exegesis focuses on man ['s spirit: *ist anthropologisch*]." In short, the exegesis required to make this passage a proof of soul creation is well rooted in Jewish tradition, but does not so well accord with an objective evaluation of the sources of this concept.

Adam says of Eve in Genesis 2:23, "This is bone of my bone, flesh of my flesh." Augustine finds this sufficient proof that her soul, and therefore that of all other humans, did *not* come from the body of Adam, and therefore came immediately from God! Incredibly, in the year A.D. 1947 Daffara agrees with this exegesis.

"He who lives forever, fashioned everything in common," says Sirach

---

[51] See the portion of page 195 below, from which footnote 84 refers to here.

[52] Otto Michel, *Der Brief an die Hebräer*[11] (H. Meyer, Kritisch-exegetischer Kommentar zum NT; Göttingen: Vandenhoeck, 1960), 299. Adolf Deissmann, "Jewish Prayers for Vengeance found at Rheneia," Appendix I of *Light from the Ancient East* (London: Hodder Stoughton, 1910) [= *Philologus*, 61 (1902), 253–265], 427, 431: "Lord of spirits and all flesh"; J. Carmignac, *Textes de Qumran* (Paris: Letouzey, 1961), 1, 249, *Hodayot*, 10, 8 "lord of every spirit"; H. Strack, P. Billerbeck, *Kommentar zum Neuen Testament aus Talmud und Midrasch* (München: Beck, 1926), 3, 747.

18:1 in the Greek text which has been preserved for us. The Vulgate substitutes "simultaneously" for the Greek *koinêi* "in common." This verse would seem utilizable chiefly by those who seriously maintained that the souls were all created in the beginning and stored up for the day when a body would be ready for each.[53] But in fact this is the only Scripture text cited, along with Augustine, in the important dictum of Anastasius II relevant to soul creation which we will treat in Chapter 7.[54]

Two deuterocanonical passages merit attention, though rarely invoked by the authors. This is the more surprising since the proof of creation of the *world* out of nothing in 2 Maccabees 7:28 is generally recognized as the most explicit. In verse 22 of the same chapter, the mother of the seven martyrs says, "I do not know how you appeared in my womb; at any rate I did not favor you with spirit and life, and the structure of each I did not adjust. (23) Therefore the creator of the cosmos, fashioner of men's coming to be, and inventor of all things' coming to be, gives you in turn both spirit and life mercifully."

Three things may be noted: (1) The mother claims to be no more responsible for her son's body than for his spirit, if we have rightly rendered *stoicheíōsin ou dierýthmisa* as "structure or elements I did not harmonize or adjust." (2) As in Genesis 2:7, she is concerned with life as opposed to inertia or death, rather than soul as opposed to matter. (3) Her point seems to be that God can give *again* life, by which is meant an animated body. Our rendering "gives you in turn," *apodídōsin pálin,* really means "gives you back again." Either this has to be understood as a future, referring to resurrection and reward of valor; or the sense "gives *away* to you in *turn* (in the *past*)" may be preferred as fitting better the creation context.

The Wisdom of Solomon 15:11 pities the manufacturer of utensils, "because he ignored his own fashioner, the one who breathed into him an activating soul, and blew the vivifying spirit in." The word for soul, *psychē,* and not "spirit," *pneûma,* is here paired with a verb cognate of *pneûma.* Either the last stich alone, or perhaps the last two in combination, seem to be a maximally faithful rendering of Genesis 2:7, "God breathed into his nostrils the breath of life, and he became a *nepeš ḥayyâ.*"

"I was a well-favored child, and got a good soul; or rather it was I who was already good when I came into a blameless body" is not merely

---

[53] H. de Leusse, "Le problème de la préexistence des âmes chez Marius Victorinus Afer," *Recherches de Science Religieuse,* 29 (1939), 197–239; on the notion that souls are called *psychē* in Greek because they were preexistent and kept in cold storage ("cooled off," *apo-psygeísas*), condemned by Justinian and Pope Vigilius (DS 456 = DB 236), see W. Reany, *Creation of the Human Soul* (London: Ouseley, 1929), 54.

[54] See below, footnote 21 to chapter 7, p. 213.

an amusing smugness by which the author of Wisdom 8:19 f characterizes himself. Rather it affords us an intriguing perspective on Platonic notions of the soul.[55] Its preexistence is hinted here. This was an irresistible snare for some early Christian fathers, as noted above.[56] We must honestly face the extent to which the separate existence of the soul and its imprisonment in a sluggish body were Platonic notions read by Christians into the formulations of Genesis or later books. Beauchamp finds that 8:20 rather rectifies 8:19 by indicating that where body and soul are in question, it is rather "soul" which would be the subject of the verb "receive": if this fits the case, it is only by emphasizing that for the author the soul is identical with the ego, which somehow already exists before it comes into a body.[57]

5. *Nephesh, Ruach, and Neshama*

In the passages which we have been considering, our English translations contain the words "soul" and "spirit" with various assertions about them.[58] It might well have seemed that we should *first* determine the exact meaning of these key words, and then go on to draw further conclusions from their varying contexts.

The fact is, we made an unsuccessful attempt to do exactly that. After first setting forth our information more or less in the form of this chapter, we found that it was rather unfavorably received by professional exegetes.[59] Notably Père Roland de Vaux, both by his stimulating reaction to the oral presentation and in later amiable conversation, made clear

---

[55] Frank C. Porter, "The Pre-Existence of the Soul in the Books of Wisdom and in the Rabbinical Writings," *American Journal of Theology,* 12 (1908), 53–115: "To the Greek the soul that pre-exists was or tended to be the personality, the man's real thinking self; while to the Jew it was only a part of the coming man, the divine breath or spirit which was to make him alive" (page 57); the writer of Wisdom 8:19 f, "first and most naturally thinks of the body as that pre-existing part of man with which the personal pronoun could connect itself; but then he thinks of the *psychē,* the other part of the coming man, that which God breathes into him or lends to him, as better deserving to be called 'I' " (page 70).

[56] Letter of Diognetus, Migne *Patrologia Graeca,* 2, 1176: "The soul has been shut up in the body, and itself restrains the body."

[57] Paul Beauchamp, "Le salut corporel des justes et la conclusion du livre de la Sagesse," *Biblica,* 45/4 (Oct. 1964), 495.

[58] In the subtitle we used a popular spelling of the Hebrew *nepeš, rûaḥ, nᵉšāmâ,* which indicates their pronunciation in English; we may be pardoned for retaining the scientific transcription elsewhere.

[59] This volume grew out of papers given at the Catholic Biblical Association meetings at Maryknoll in 1962 and at Flushing in 1964; see *Catholic Biblical Quarterly,* 24/4 (Oct. 1962), 426, and 26/4 (Oct. 1964), 469. It was felt by some that we were "beating a dead horse" in dissecting formulas of theology textbooks which exegetes now recognize to be out-of-date. I hope this is true.

his misgivings about looking in the Hebrew revelation *at all* for information about such a Greek notion as the soul distinct from the body.[60]

Undoubtedly this is a great snare. On the other hand, it would seem that two human beings, even from eras and cultures much more divergent than Hebraic and Hellenic, can make assertions about some objective reality which they both have experienced. No matter how irreducible their viewpoint and their categories, they are nevertheless talking about the same *thing*. Hence it does not seem *always* or *a priori* excluded that the two assertions, or parts of them, can be somehow translated into a common idiom.

This has meanwhile turned out to be much better expressed by Martin Noth in these words:

> The possibility of transferring oneself into the outlook and thought world of another is the presupposition of any "understanding" among men at all, and this does not imply that the one who understands must thereby give up his own being. That possibility rests upon the fact that between man and man there is something ultimately in common, which lies deeper than the varying outlooks and modes of thought. But in each case there is need for effort to penetrate into another's world.[61]

For the up-to-date exegete, it is undoubtedly congenial just to tabulate objectively the occurrence of certain terms and then draw conclusions as to their meaning. This empirical objectivity accounts in large measure for the vogue of exegesis itself in our day, and for the vogue of Kittel's *Theological Dictionary*.[62] But the technique also proves to involve snares of its own, which have been articulately exposed by James Barr.[63]

Moreover the very same "existentialist versus essence mentality" which makes Scripture popular in the twentieth century, also would urge us to take up the biblical declarations as concrete units rather than dismember them. At any rate, my attempt to reorganize this chapter by

---

[60] Thus too Georges Pidoux, *L'homme dans l'Ancien Testament* (Cahiers Théologiques 32; Neuchâtel: 1953), 10, insists that the Israelite is "monist" in place of the dualism by which we oppose flesh and spirit. For us the soul is immaterial; for the Old Testament *nepeš* can be concrete (like blood, Dt 12:23), but it can also be vague ("you know the 'soul' of an alien," Ex 23:9); so also *rûaḥ*, life is breath (page 50). He concludes on page 72 that many of these Old Testament concepts about man are now out of date, and belong to "biblical archeology"; but not *all* of them.

[61] Martin Noth, "Gott, König, Volk im Alten Testament," *Zeitschrift für Theologie und Kirche*, 47/2 (1950), 159, relevant to H. Cadbury and G. Wright on "The Peril of Archaizing Ourselves," *Interpretation*, 3 (1949), 331, 450. Noth's essay is reprinted in *Gesammelte Studien* (Munich: 1957), 215.

[62] Gerhard Kittel, *Theological Dictionary of the New Testament* (Grand Rapids, Mich.: Eerdmans, 1964) = *Theologisches Wörterbuch* (Stuttgart: Kohlhammer, 1932–1966).

[63] James Barr, *Semantics of Biblical Language* (London: Oxford, 1961); *Biblical Words for Time* (Naperville: Allenson, 1962).

putting first what now comes last, showed that even more duplication and unproved presumptions would thus be involved. And some further friendly critics among my colleagues felt that the analysis of the major texts was indispensable and primary. Nevertheless, what now follows is the real meat of the answer to an unslanted question, "What if anything does Scripture tell us about the soul at all, about its nature, and directly or inferentially about its origin?"

1. *Nᵉšāmâ,* generally rendered "breath," is in Genesis 2:7 portrayed as vital and coming directly from God. Also in Job 32:8; 33:4; 34:14, *nᵉšāmâ* is God's breath in man. In Isaiah 57:16 it is a thing which God has made; and in Proverbs 20:27 it is "God's lamp" in man.

But strangely — and this has never been sufficiently noticed — the most frequent use of this "breath" is as a synonym of man himself. Thus *nᵉšāmâ* will be seen to be a genuine variant of *nepeš.* It means "the whole living being" in Deuteronomy 20:16; Joshua 10:40; 3 Kings 15:29. Even in Psalm 150:6, despite the parallel with other devices for producing music, we would render "let all *living being* praise Yah," rather than "let Yah be praised with the *breath* as well as with harps, flutes, and drums."

In some few cases this "breath" is attributed to God, and means his power, chiefly as it appears destructively: Isaiah 30:33; 2 Samuel 22:16; Job 4:9; 37:10. In Psalm 18H:16 the three anthropomorphisms *nᵉšāmâ, rûaḥ,* and *ap* (nostril, anger) are combined into one divine act, in which creation is significantly seen as a kind of rebuke (*ga⁽ᵃrâ*) to "something."

Finally, believe it or not, in no single case is *nᵉšāmâ* used to express biological or experiential features of what breath really means. If Isaiah 2:22 and Job 26:4 approximate this sense, it is only as a rhetorical negation.

Hence we must conclude that though doubtless derived from a root meaning "breathe," *nᵉšāmâ* itself as an actual existing word does not mean breath at all. Not metaphorically then, but in its literal and dictionary sense it should be defined as "the vital force present in man, due to God, and equatable with either."

2. *Nepeš* is one of the commonest nouns in the whole Hebrew bible, occurring some 750 times. In sixty-five percent of the cases, 487 times, it means simply "living being"; and *"as* living or acting" in 360 of these cases.[64] The other uses of *nepeš* focus some particular vital activity or its bodily organ; chiefly appetite or emotion, rarely a sense approaching

---

[64] A. Murtonen, *The Living Soul* (Helsinki: 1958), 10 f, 69; Johann Schwab, *Der Begriff der nefeš in den heiligen Schriften des Alten Testaments: ein Beitrag zur altjüdischen Religionsgeschichte* (Leipzig: Noske, 1913).

"breath" or perhaps better "scent": Proverbs 27:9; Job 41:13; Isaiah 3:20.[65]

In the Jewish apocalyptic writings, some of which are late-biblical and others not canonical at all, *nepeš* or its equivalent occurs 232 times. It has been found that only forty-six of these mean animate objects; 119 are said to mean "human consciousness" but in the context are seen to mean rather "the person" or self; eleven could be rendered "principle of life"; while no less than fifty-two are found to be synonymous with "shade" as an expression for the disembodied dead.[66]

On the other hand, in the earlier portions of the Hebrew bible, out of one hundred and twenty-four cases, forty refer to "what man is" and eighty to "something man *has*" (forty of these again being rendered in the King James version as "life"). But no less than forty-eight of these occurrences indicate that the human *nepeš* "dies." The conclusion is that before the Exile at least *nepeš* means simply "the living being that man is."[67]

A more ambitious effort to trace organic development from the earlier to the later usages of *nepeš* was made by Daniel Lys. He stipulates that a relative and approximate dating of the passages must suffice, not least because it is dangerous to apply the norms of source dissection too minutely. He takes as the earliest texts the books of Kings, in which he "acknowledges but does not distinguish" those same J and E sources as are found in the Pentateuch. In these earliest uses, *nepeš* means "life." But this is further declared "in the light of neighboring religions" to mean already "the soul-potentiality; or Being, 'Me'." During the Exile, there are a hundred occurrences of *nepeš,* and they mark a distinct turning point. The word now comes to mean "the whole living creature." In the postexilic priestly texts, this notion of individuality continues to dominate, but "the lost nuance of potentiality is recaptured." Finally in Qohelet the term is used "very materially, for the dynamic desire [? on the part] of the living being."[68]

---

[65] Richard B. Onians, *The Origin of European Thought about the Body, the Mind, the Soul, the World, Time, and Fate* (Cambridge: University, 1951), 93, remarks that Greek *psychē* is the "breath-soul." His claim to give evidence on Jewish beliefs is reduced to an appendix, pages 480–505, concerned rather with such organs as liver or knees as seat of emotions.

[66] D. S. Russell, *The Method and Message of Jewish Apocalyptic* (Philadelphia: Westminster, 1964), 145, 399. In the Qumran texts, the same meanings are found as in the Bible, with the addition of "take upon oneself," *hēqîm 'al nepeš,* according to H. A. Brongers, "Das Wort NPŠ in den Qumranschriften," *Revue de Qumran,* 4/3 (Oct. 1963), 407–415.

[67] E. W. Marter, "The Hebrew Concept of 'Soul' in Pre-Exilic Writings," *Andrews University Seminary Studies,* 2 (1964), 97–108.

[68] Daniel Lys, *Nèphèsh: histoire de l'âme dans la révélation d'Israël au sein des religions proche-orientales* (Études d'histoire et de philosophie religieuses de Stras-

From these various statistical and chronological studies, we may draw a provisional conclusion that *nepeš* means more universally than anything else "a being now living but capable of dying."

Sometimes in fact *nepeš* means "cadaver"! No other possible sense can be attached to it in the two cases in which it is joined with *mēt*, "dead": Numbers 6:6, "All the days of his Nazirate he shall not come upon a *nepeš* of a dead man"; Leviticus 21:7, "(The priest) shall not go upon all *napšôt mēt.*" We should expect in this second case a plural *metîm* to fit the plural of *nepeš;* but it can be readily agreed from this example that *nepeš mēt* had already become a single term, just as we say handfuls and not hands-full. In these two citations the *nepeš* cannot be considered something surviving apart from the dead body, but is something tangible belonging to the dead as dead. Perhaps from this arose the postbiblical usage of *nepeš* as "tombstone or monument."[69]

As for the eight further cases in which *nepeš* alone has been commonly rendered as "a corpse," I have reexamined these carefully and would say that taken by themselves they do not exclude some other sense such as divination (itself ultimately reducible to necromancy!) or possibly even "inner spiritual defilement."[70] In the light of the two existing cases where *mēt* is added, it seems reasonable to retain the rendering "corpse" but not to draw any lexical conclusions from it.[71]

Perhaps the sense of cadaver should be extended to Jeremiah 2:34, "on your hem are [!] found the blood of *napšot* of the unoffending poor." Recognition that *nepeš* is equated with blood in its materiality has always been widespread among exegetes.[72] Deuteronomy 12:23 f says explicitly "the blood is the *nepeš*," and even more concretely "you must not eat (this) *nepeš* along with the flesh (of living things), but pour it out upon the earth." This is also though less clearly the sense of Genesis 9:4,

---

bourg 50; Paris: Presses Universitaires, 1959), 114, 138, 175, 194. According to M.-Léon Ramlot, *Revue Thomiste*, 65/1 (Jan. 1965), 117, the most interesting conclusion of Lys is on page 165: *"Nepeš* is that by which man shares the sacred . . . the element in man which under certain conditions is worthy of encountering God."

[69] N. Avigad, *Ancient Monuments in the Kidron Valley* (Jerusalem: 1954); Duval, "Note sur le monument funéraire appelé nefeš," *Revue Sémantique* (1894), 259.

[70] "Those who are unclean for the *nepeš* of a man," Numbers 9:6–7; 5:2; 6:11; 9:10; Haggai 2:13; Leviticus 21:1; "tattooing for the *nepeš*," Leviticus 19:28; "the one touching anything unclean of *nepeš* shall not eat holy things," Leviticus 22:4.

[71] Miriam Seligson, *The Meaning of naefaeš met in the Old Testament* (Studia Societatis Orientalis Fennicae, 16/2; Helsinki: 1951), 86 holds the expression to mean "a death-demon"; see E. Kautzsch, "Der alttestamentliche Ausdruck nephesch met," Festschrift *Philothesia* (Berlin: 1907).

[72] J. Bainvel, "Âme dans la sainte Écriture," *Dictionnaire de Théologie Catholique* (Paris: Letouzey, 1909), 1, 969.

"You shall not eat flesh along with its *nepeš*, its blood." Again Leviticus 11:4, "the *nepeš* of flesh is in the blood."[73]

It has been claimed by Baab that not only is the blood equated with *nepeš*, but also the "bone" of man is equaled with *rûaḥ*, especially in Qohelet 11:5, "you know not what is the way of the *rûaḥ*, like bones in the teeming womb."[74] The example is not convincing. But it may be worth noticing that in modern Hebrew the grammatical function of reflexive pronoun is performed not by *nepeš* but by *'eṣem*, "bone." Even in biblical Hebrew, it is misleading to say that *nepeš* is used as a reflexive pronoun, "oneself." It has this rendering twenty times in the Authorized Version. But fifteen of these are among the forty-one cases in which the Septuagint seems to be based on a Hebrew text differing from the one which we now use.[75] The remaining cases can easily be explained from the fact that *nepeš* means "a person"; this does not make it a grammatical reflexive, any more than the occasional indignant or humorous English use of "spilled gravy on my sacred person." In Arabic, however, *nafs* means almost always "oneself"; only in counting, it means "(how many) people." Hebrew speakers laugh at hearing an Arabic-trained learner say "I washed my *nepeš*." Is not this because they have been misled by exegetes into thinking that their own Hebrew *nepeš* means "soul"? Anyway, isn't it even funnier to say "I washed my bone"?

From all that has been said, it will be seen that Gesenius-Briggs are fairly right in giving as the fundamental sense of *nepeš* "the breathing substance or being." But they are less warranted in equating this with *"psychē, anima*, soul, the inner being of man."[76] Moreover even their explicit emphasis on breathing, though legitimate enough insofar as coterminous with living, seems to presuppose an erroneous or unproved no-

---

[73] In Diogenes of Apollonia "the soul-breath which is breathed in, goes into the veins and is there mixed with the blood": Franz Rüsche, "Pneuma, Seele und Geist: ein Ausschnitt aus der antiken Pneumalehre," *Theologie und Glaube*, 23/5 (1931), 608, 606–625, see his *Blut, Leben und Seele* (Paderborn: 1930).

[74] Otto J. Baab, *The Theology of the Old Testament* (New York: Abingdon, 1949), 65. Baab rightly stresses that the Bible shows more kinship to the modern functional psychology than to the scholastic faculty-psychology. *Rûaḥ* "denotes deeper emotional drives, which move the soul to act or refrain from acting. In spite of this behavioristic emphasis, the biblical sources are in agreement that *rûaḥ* is a divine creation [but] although God-given, not mechanically implanted in the body. The biblical words which tell about the coming and the departure of the *rûaḥ* are necessarily figurative."

[75] The Septuagint also uses "body" to express person: Kendrick Grobel, *"Soma* as 'Self, Person' in the Septuagint," *Festschrift R. Bultmann* (Beiheft 21 to *ZNW*: Berlin: Töpelmann, 1954), 52–59. See now D. Lys, "The Israelite Soul According to the LXX," *Vetus Testamentum* 16/2 (April 1966), 181–228.

[76] (Gesenius-) Brown-Driver-Briggs, *Hebrew and English Lexicon of the Old Testament* (Oxford: 1954= 1906), 659; Charles A. Briggs, "The Use of *nepeš* in the Old Testament," *Journal of Biblical Literature*, 16/1 (1897), 17–30; Gesenius-Buhl, *Handwörterbuch*[17] (Berlin: Springer, 1954), 514.

tion of *how* this word came to mean "a living being." This presumption has since then been carried a step further by Dürr's claim that *nepeš* has basically the same meaning as in Accadian, namely "throat."[77] This sense has even penetrated into our Latin Bible with the Bea Psalter rendering of Psalm 69H:2, "the waters have risen up to my neck." Köhler's dictionary now gives this meaning to no fewer than thirty-eight biblical passages.[78] But competent Assyriologists assert that *napištu* does not have this concrete sense in even one single proved example.[79] Even in its commoner rendering, "breath," *napištu* means simply "life," oftenest in an expression equivalent to our "expire."

Radically, therefore, and not by any sort of metaphor or extension, we must conclude that biblical *nepeš* means "the individual, insofar as he is or at least was or can be alive." In *nepeš ḥayyâ* this transcendental relation or potency to life is emphasized as fully actuated, "a genuinely living individual."[80]

3. *Rûaḥ*. It has become almost axiomatic that just as *nepeš* acquired its meaning by progressive spiritualization of the concrete material "breath-producing) throat," so *rûaḥ* by spiritualization of the concrete almost-visible "storm-wind." What makes it hardest for us to evaluate just what man's *rûaḥ* means in the Bible is that the term is applied to God, while *nepeš* virtually never is; so that *rûaḥ* seems to be automatically nobler or more spiritual.[81] We ought to look first of all at the statistical

---

[77] Lorenz Dürr, "Hebr. *nepeš* = akk. *napištu* = Gurgel, Kehle," *Zeitschrift für die alttestamentliche Wissenschaft*, 43 (1925), 262–269. So now Werner Schmidt, "Anthropologische Begriffe im Alten Testament," *Evangelische Theologie*, 24/7 (July 1964), 374 (–388). He nevertheless concludes that biblical *nepeš* means "man as an individual, insofar as he is *out for* something." — V. Hamp, "Seele, biblisch," *Lexikon für Theologie und Kirche*[2] (Freiburg: Herder, 1964), 9, 569 holds the primitive sense of *nepeš* as "neck," though after exile it is identified with "spirit," and in the New Testament with "life."

[78] Ludwig Köhler, *Lexicon in Veteris Testamenti Libros* (Leiden: Brill, 1953), 626.

[79] See Karlheinz Deller cited by me in *American Ecclesiastical Review*, 152/6 (June 1965), 397.

[80] "The soul is not a part of man but the entire man as living; it does not inhabit a body but expresses itself by the body. Though Semites and Greeks both link soul with breath, this is spiritualized among the Greeks, whereas among the Semites it remains concrete and bodily. . . . Not the *nepeš* itself, but the *rûaḥ* of God, is the source of man's life": Xavier Léon-Dufour, "Âme," *Vocabulaire de Théologie biblique* (Paris: Cerf, 1962), 29, 31. Further Helmut Lamparter, *Das biblische Menschenbild* (Calwer Hefte 2; Stuttgart: 1956); G. E. Wright, *The Biblical Doctrine of Man in Society* (1954); C. Ryder Smith, *The Bible Doctrine of Man* (1953); M. Lichtenstein, *Das Wort Nephesch in der Bibel* (Berlin: 1920).

[81] Johannes H. Scheepers, *Die Gees van God en die Gees van die Mens in die Ou Testament* (Kampen: Kok, 1960), 307; English summary, 304–322; Paula

facts, and only then draw a conclusion which will fit all of them equally.

There are four hundred occurrences of *rûaḥ* evaluated by Briggs. Of these almost one hundred, or one-fourth, refer directly to the spirit of God. Even more, one hundred and seventeen, mean "wind." Man's "breath" (thirty-three) and "spirit or temperament" (seventy-six) together make up another quarter of the usages; and the remainder are synonymous with *nepeš* or *lēb* as "seat of life or attention."[82] These observations of Briggs do not emphasize sufficiently that even the secular uses of *rûaḥ* are often closely connected with God. Thus on the one hand "a *strong* wind" can be called "a wind of God," by a type of superlative abundantly attested in the Bible.[83] On the other hand, man's *rûaḥ* like his *nepeš* is often presented as a bit of the breath or wisdom of God stored up in him, in such passages as Job 27:3; Numbers 16:22; 27:16; Genesis 41:38; 4 Kings 2:15.[84] But "God's *rûaḥ*" in Micah 2:7 is simply an anthropomorphism for manlike *emotion* parallel to "nostrils" in the sense of anger.

It would seem that in not a single one of these cases (despite superficial resemblance of Numbers 16:22 to Hebrews 12:9) is *rûaḥ* a "spirit" in the sense of a preternatural disembodied being distinct from God. In striking contrast to this biblical embargo, we find no less than two hundred and thirty-three of the three hundred and eighty-three apocalyptic occurrences to refer to such a supernatural being; only thirty-nine designate God, and of the one hundred and eleven relating to man, in twenty-six it is his emotions and in thirteen his vital principle.[85]

We possess four studies that endeavor to trace *rûaḥ* through its chronological development.[86] Staples finds a growth "from *rûaḥ* as wind, to the

---

Seethaler, "Die Taube des Heiligen Geistes," *Bibel und Leben*, 4 (1963), 115–130; J. Köberle, "Gottesgeist und Menschengeist im Alten Testament," *Neue Kirchliche Zeitschrift*, 13 (1902), 321–347, 403–427; Alphonsus Benson, *The Spirit of God in the Didactic Books of the Old Testament* (Washington: 1949).

[82] Charles A. Briggs, "The Use of *rûaḥ* in the Old Testament," *Journal of Biblical Literature*, 19 (1900), 132–145; Gesenius-Briggs, *Hebrew and English Lexicon* (Oxford: 1954 = 1906), 925.

[83] J. M. Powis Smith, "The Use of Divine Names as Superlatives," *American Journal of Semetic Languages*, 45 (1929), 212 f; see above, footnote 31 on p. 94.

[84] See the portion of page 185 above, from which footnote 51 refers to here.

[85] D. S. Russell, *The Method and Message of Jewish Apocalyptic* (Philadelphia: Westminster, 1964), 150.

[86] Lys and Staples below; William R. Schoemaker, "The Use of *rûaḥ* in the Old Testament and of *pneûma* in the New Testament," *Journal of Biblical Literature*, 23 (1904), 13–67: Up to 700: wind or spirit, not breath; up to 550, same but never for the Spirit of God; up to 400, now also breath, and life itself by metonymy; till 160, wind, breath, prophetic spirit; but to express disembodied spirits, human or preternatural, not before Henoch, excepting Tobias 6:7.

E. Schweizer, "Gegenwart des Geistes und eschatologische Hoffnung bei Zarathustra, spätjüdischen Gruppen, Gnostikern und den Zeugen des Neuen Testaments," C. H. Dodd Festschrift, *The Background of the New Testament and its Eschatology*, edited by W. Davies and D. Daube (Cambridge: University, 1956), 482–508, as a sequel to Schweizer's *Pneuma* in *Theologisches Wörterbuch zum NT* (Stuttgart:

rûaḥ used by Yahweh for his work, to the *rûaḥ* Yahweh put into man to do his special work, to the *rûaḥ* Yahweh put into man to direct his life, to the *rûaḥ* Yahweh put in animals and man alike." It is acknowledged that the E-strand never shows man's *rûaḥ* coming from God as in the J-strand; though unlike the *nepeš* which can die, the *rûaḥ* categorically asserted to be *life* "belongs to Yahweh and will presumably return to him." But with Jeremiah 52:23, *rûaḥ* acquires a new meaning, "outdoors," which becomes in Ezekiel simply "side" in the sense of direction.[87]

Lys, in a sequel to his study on *nepeš,* concludes that *rûaḥ* at its earliest appearance in the Bible means "wind, somehow especially related to God." He suggests that this "divinization of natural forces" was not a *later* development but the *earliest* outlook; the revolutionary change in meaning came when the term was applied to man at all.[88] Though the transit from "wind" to "wind of God" is almost equally immediate in the earlier twentieth-century view crystallized by Staples, Lys has been praised as substituting a "dedivinization" process for the too naïve evolutionism from matter into spirit.[89] Cazelles reproaches Lys with being too much influenced by modern categories (entity; scientific; dynamic versus static); yet himself concludes that to the biblical authors *rûaḥ* is not so much wind or breath but "atmosphere."[90] This is surely a highly modern category, one of those words like "dimension" which French authors especially favor for recapturing biblical realities not easily conceptualized.

Kohlhammer, 1959), 6, (330–) 387–453, holds that Persian influence quietly transformed understanding of the Old Testament "spirit" from something of God's only transitorily in (some) men, into something always present within each man and determining his existence even before it actually occurred. On the relevance of this "spirit" to our alleged knowledge of angels, see Jean Daniélou, *The Theology of Jewish Christianity* (Chicago: Regnery, 1964), 117.

[87] W. E. Staples, "The 'Soul' in the Old Testament," *American Journal of Semitic Languages,* 44/3 (Apr. 1928), 168, 147 f. H. H. Wendt, *Die Begriffe Fleisch und Geist im biblischen Sprachgebrauch* (Gotha: Perthes, 1878), 34–41: *rûaḥ* evolved from "wind" to "a certain vital dynamism of varying degree, implying *invisible* and *immaterial* like the wind, but *divine* only in special connections."

[88] Daniel Lys, *"Ruach": le souffle dans l'Ancien Testament* (Études HPR Strasbourg 56; Paris: Presses Universitaires, 1962), 37, 348. Volume 49 of that series is *L'Esprit et le Messie dans le Bas-Judaïsme et le Nouveau Testament,* by Max-Alain Chevallier; see R. Koch, "Der Gottesgeist und der Messias," *Biblica,* 27 (1946), 241–268, and *Geist und Messias* (Beitrag zur Biblische Theologie des AT; Vienna: 1950).

[89] Paul Beauchamp, review of Lys, *Ruach,* in *Biblica,* 44/4 (Oct. 1963), 544. He is less pleased with a tendency of the author to confuse dogma with exegesis, and to draw excessive conclusions from the *silences* of Jeremiah and Ezekiel. — The view that "spirit" is a more primitive sense of *rûaḥ* than breath or air in König's Hebrew Dictionary furnishes the outset-point to Francis J. Crump's *Pneuma in the Gospels* (Washington: Catholic University, 1954), 1; see now J. Schmid, "Der Begriff der Seele im Neuen Testament," Festschrift G. Söhngen, *Einsicht und Glaube* (Freiburg: Herder, 1963), 112–132.

[90] Henri Cazelles, review of Lys, *Ruach,* in *Vetus Testamentum,* 14/3 (July 1964), 387 f.

A quite original insight of Haulotte shows that for the early Hebrews the *rûaḥ* was something of God in *some* men. It refers to the absolute power of God, and its possessor is called *ēl,* a variant form for the common-noun name of God, *elohîm.* In Isaiah 31:3 we read "The Egyptian is *ādām,* not *ēl;* his horses are *bāśār,* not *rûaḥ."*[91] It has not yet been explained why the largely shared vocabulary of Jeremiah and Deuteronomy avoid altogether the use of *rûaḥ* for God.

In all the recent lexical studies of *rûaḥ,* it would seem that insufficient account has been taken of Pedersen's "biblical panpsychism." Actually this amounts to imputing to the Bible a sort of teilhardian theory of pre-thought or pre-life inhering "on the inner side" of every particle of inorganic matter. But we are not trying here to draw any mutual support for these two scholars from each other's work. Rather we aim simply to emphasize how some recent scholarship would tend to find the biblical notion of "soul" in events and descriptions lying on a deeper level than mere similarity or consistency of term:

> We know that the Israelites do not acknowledge the distinction between the psychic and the corporeal. Earth and stones are alive, imbued with a soul, and therefore able to receive mental subject-matter and bear the impress of it. The relation between the earth and its owner is not that the earth, like a dead mass, makes part of his psychic whole. . . . [In Leviticus 25 and Exodus 23] the idea is that the earth is for a time to be free, so as not to be subjected to the will of man, but left to its own nature.[92]

4. *Rûaḥ and Nepeš Compared.* From careful counterpoising of the lexical usages of *nepeš* and *rûaḥ,* experts have drawn widely diverging conclusions which it would be well to take into account before adding our own. First of all we will note that surprisingly *rûaḥ* is more favored than *nepeš* to express certain less noble products of the human spirit such as anger, jealousy, impatience, vanity; and is more closely linked with the purely material "smell," especially via its cognate *rēaḥ.* Secondly the literal and unmistakable use of *rûaḥ* to express an ordinary physical phenomenon, "the wind," is more firmly attested than any alleged use of either *nepeš* or *nᵉšāmâ* even for "breath" and a fortiori for "throat."

Keeping these facts in mind will help us to guard due perspective while acknowledging another observation which must also correspond to what we notice in the uses of *rûaḥ:* "a certain tendency to establish a

---

[91] Edgar Haulotte, "L'esprit de Yahweh dans l'Ancien Testament," in *L'homme devant Dieu: mélanges H. de Lubac* (Paris: Aubier, 1963), 1, 34.

[92] Johannes Pedersen, *Israel, its Life and Culture* (London: Milford, 1926), 1, 479; examined along with V. Aptowitzer, "The Rewarding and Punishing of Animals and Inanimate Objects," *Hebrew Union College Annual,* 3 (1926), 117, in my *Sociology of the Biblical Jubilee* (Rome: Pontifical Biblical Institute, 1954), 113.

relation between the *nepeš* and man's earthly life, between the *rûaḥ* and his relations to God."[93]

Focusing now rather upon the mode of operation of the *rûaḥ* as against the *nepeš*, we find the almost-recent authors claiming that *nepeš* is used for purely animal functions, leaving thought the prerogative of *rûaḥ*. This is not only a correlative of unfounded presumptions about *napištu*, but seems to be an inference from the connection with God rather than an actual tabulation of the occurrences.

The claim that *nepeš* means "vegetative" life as distinct from the intellectual *rûaḥ* is further linked by Dussaud to a private communication from Adolphe Lods to the effect that some biblical texts show the *nepeš* as an individualized parcel of the *rûaḥ* "life-soul of the universe."[94]

More up-to-date is the view of van Imschoot, emphasizing that no *organs* of vegetative life are assigned to the *nepeš;* from this he goes on to deny that *nepeš* in the Bible ever designates the "person as such." Since it does designate the living individual, as we have seen, presumably what van Imschoot wishes to indicate is that long after the Hebrew bible was completed there arose a complex notion of *persona* combining data of Greek philosophy and of Christian revelation into a metaphor furnished by Roman drama.[95]

Apart from such sophisticated entanglements, we would agree with Podechard that "person" in its rough-and-ready sense of "human individual" is precisely the thing which is most designated by *nepeš*.[96] But we do not find faithful to the facts his further contention that *rûaḥ* more than *nepeš* means the more general breath of life which man shares with the animals. Animals too are *nepeš ḥayyâ,* and *nepeš* may be considered to fit them better than *rûaḥ* simply from the fact that God is not called a *nepeš*.

Ultimately therefore the conclusion may be suggested that *rûaḥ* expresses something like the "superior dynamism" of humans, as against the more static but precious "fact of being alive," *nepeš*. The "fact of being alive" is shown by experience to be something men share with animals and even with plants. The "superior dynamism," though it is indeed in its roots intellective, is grasped rather as something men have in common with the warrior God yHWH, or with the storm wind on which

---

[93] B. Hansoul, "Esquisse d'une théologie de l'homme," *Initiation théologique* (Paris: Cerf, 1962), 2, 355.

[94] René Dussaud, "La néphesh et la rouaḥ dans le 'livre de Job,'" *Revue de l'Histoire des Religions*, 129 (1945), 24, alleging Job 12:10; 32:8; 4:9; 33:4; page 29, Lods.

[95] P. van Imschoot, *Théologie de l'Ancien Testament 2. L'homme* (Paris: Desclée, 1956), 25; page 28 affirms that *rûaḥ* means wind or breath, also before the exile (Ps 19H:16; Ex 15:8; and notably at Ugarit).

[96] E. Podechard, *L'Ecclésiaste* (Paris: Gabalda, 1912), 311, 470; see above, footnote 15 to p. 171.

he rides (Psalm 18H:11), something which is expressed even in men's ignoble outbursts of passion or rage.[97]

As against both *rûaḥ* and *nepeš*, biblical *bāśār*, "flesh," also indicates the activities of the whole human composite, but now insofar as they are weak, pitiful, frustrated, and heteronomous.[98] Thus regarding our soul-creation problem, we will never be able to conclude from the Old Testament more than that God gave man his whole being as it is: the life which he shares with animals, the fleshly weakness coming into play even in his mental pursuits, and the manifestations of his animated body which are most powerful and godlike.

5. *Rûaḥ* and *Pneuma*. The word which the Greek translators chose normally for rendering *rûaḥ* is *pneûma* (two hundred and sixty-four times).[99] This means strictly "breath," and is thus *less* spiritual or noble than "soul," *psychē*, by which they render *nepeš*.

Since this Septuagint translation was made in Alexandria, it stood under the influence of a pagan Egyptian thought-world, as well as a Greek world, both differing from Hebrew tradition. One must wonder whether in the translators' formation of the idea of "soul," at the side of recognizable Greek influences there were also Egyptian strands of reflection. There is a thought-provoking originality in Preisigke's effort to approach our problem from the fact that in Egypt "fluid" was a synonym for soul, as well as for God.[100] The Arabs and we ourselves today think of God as "the ocean of being." But against Preisigke it has been claimed that the notion of "breath" was even more essential to the soul in Egypt than in Israel.[101]

The whole splendor of surviving pyramid and temple architecture is a monument to ancient Egyptian belief in the future life of the liberated soul. This soul is ambiguously referred to, sometimes as the *ba,* but

---

[97] Ceslas Spicq, *Dieu et l'homme selon le Nouveau Testament* (Lectio Divina 29; Paris: Cerf, 1961), 139.

[98] E. Schweizer, "The Church as the Missionary Body of Christ," *New Testament Studies,* 8 (1961), 4, apropos of the fact that there is no term for "body" in Hebrew; (p. 10) Christ as "body" is really "the world-soul permeating and ruling the whole cosmos."

[99] *Pneûma* is the Greek rendering of *nⁱšāmâ* only three times, and of *nepeš* only in Sirach 38:23: Friedrich Baumgärtel, "Pneûma im Alten Testament," in G. Kittel, *Theologisches Wörterbuch zum Neuen Testament* (Stuttgart: Kohlhammer, 1959), 6, 357–366; E. Hatch, H. Redpath, *Concordance to the Septuagint* (Oxford: 1897); J. Guillet, *Thèmes Bibliques* (Paris: Aubier, 1954), 218 = *Themes of the Bible,* translated by Albert J. La Mothe (Notre Dame: Fides, 1961), 235.

[100] Friedrich Preisigke, *Die Gotteskraft in der frühchristlichen Zeit* (Berlin: 1922); so already Paul Volz, *Der Geist Gottes und die verwandten Erscheinungen im Alten Testament und im anschliessenden Judentum* (Tübingen: Mohr, 1910), 23.

[101] Johannes Hehn, "Zum Problem des Geistes im Alten Orient und im Alten Testament," *Zeitschrift für die alttestamentliche Wissenschaft,* 43 (1925), 216.

sometimes as the *ka* or "double" of the deceased.[102] Rather than a surviving "part," the Egyptian soul seems to be a kind of shadow or diminished existence of the *whole* person.[103]

It has been pointed out that this "diminished shadow-like existence" has much in common with the early biblical descriptions of the mode of survival after death.[104] The future life is called in Hebrew Sheol, a mysterious and shadowy realm where bare survival seems to be equally the lot of the evil and the good.[105] These survivors are sometimes called Rephaim, from a word meaning weak or shadowy.[106] This meaning is not rendered dubious by the astonishing fact that the same term $r^e pa'im$ came to be applied also to "giants" of super-vitality, presumed to have inhabited Palestine before the Israelites.[107]

There seems to be no traceable influence whatever, even of the Rephaim and much less of the Egyptian *Ka,* in the Greek choice of *pneûma/psychē* to express *rûaḥ/nepeš*. The mutual influences of Greek and Semitic ideas in the development of the notion of *pneûma* have been studied by Verbeke. In word he denies it, but in his citations and trend of thought he rather leads the reader to think that the human *pneûma* is a properly Stoic invention. He takes up the Bible only at the point where it stands already under Stoic influence. Yet he concludes ". . . the Judeo-Christian religion is the principal factor of the evolution of ancient pneumatology in the direction of spiritualism, because it applied the term *pneûma* to the

---

[102] Maspéro's idea of the *Ka* as a "double" serving to house the *Ba* has been followed by some, but not most, of the recent inquirers, according to Ursula Schweitzer, *Das Wesen des Ka im Diesseits und Jenseits der alten Ägypter* (Altorientalische Forschungen 19; Glückstadt: Augustin, 1956), 13. On page 17 she holds that the *Ka* was originally the life principle of Horus-kingship; gradually it became a transmissible characteristic of the creator god, and in the Middle Kingdom more materialized.

[103] Junker called it "the needed supplement to fulfillment of the personality," but its abstract theological character always found expression in something visible and experienced, according to Liselotte Greven, *Der Ka in Theologie und Königskult der Ägypter des Alten Reiches* (Altorientalische Forschungen 17, 1952), 13, 11.

[104] Kurt Schubert, "Die Entwicklung der Auferstehungslehre von der nachexilischen bis zur frührabbinischen Zeit," *Biblische Zeitschrift,* 6 (1962), 177–214 [= *Theology Digest,* 12/3 (Autumn 1964), 203 f.]. Less convincing is the extent to which he finds these notions in early Babylon also.

[105] L. Hartman, *Encyclopedic Dictionary of the Bible* (New York: McGraw Hill, 1963), 2196, 508; T. H. Gaster, *Interpreter's Dictionary of the Bible* (New York: Abingdon, 1962), 1, 787.

[106] J. Gray, "The Rephaim," *Palestine Exploration Quarterly,* 81 (1949), 127–139; "DT'N and RP'UM in Ancient Ugarit," *PEQ,* 84 (1952), 39–41; C. Virolleaud, "Les Rephaïm," *Syria,* 22 (1941), 1–30; *Revue des Études Sémitiques,* 5 (1941), 77–83; Krister Stendahl, "Gamla Testamentets föreställningar om helandet [Refaim]," *Svensk Exegetisk Årsbok,* 15 (1950), 5–34.

[107] Paul Karge, *Rephaim, die vorgeschichtliche Kultur Palästinas und Phöniziens*[2] (Paderborn: 1925).

transcendent divinity and the immortal soul. Platonism helped secondarily to disengage the spiritualism latent in Judeo-Christian pneumatology."[108]

An earlier work claiming to analyze factors entering into the Greek terms for soul does no more than *juxtapose* some significant observations on the Semitic outlook. It sets forth the ordinary view that *rûaḥ* was originally wind, then came to mean God's power in the material universe, but was applied relatively late to religious or ethical effects in men; whereas *nepeš* was from the beginning used of men, and applied to God only rarely as a conscious anthropomorphism. But how this really entered into, or was illustrated by, the choice of *pneûma/psychē* is left unconsidered.[109]

A further complication in the choice of the Greek terms *psychē* and *pneûma* is the conviction widespread among the "Greek-thinking" Fathers of the Church, that man has *two* separate souls: a purely sensitive one called *psychē,* and an intellective one called *pneûma.* In our next chapter we will see what a long struggle was required for the Church to lay this "spirit" to rest.[110]

We will conclude that whatever notion of "survival after death" or "incorruptible substance" may be contained in *pneûma* or *psychē* is not at all found in the Hebrew *rûaḥ/nepeš* though it may have been read into them. This is not to say that the Hebrew bible has no notion of survival after death, or even of immortality.[111] It has; but these notions must be studied in connection with Sheol and Rephaim. So far as we can trace, there is no demonstrable interconnection or influence between these terms and *rûaḥ/nepeš.*

* * *

Whatever further conclusions anyone may wish to draw from the Old Testament about the immediate creation of the human soul as a divinely revealed doctrine must therefore proceed from these acquired results:

---

[108] Gérard Verbeke, *L'évolution de la doctrine du pneuma du stoïcisme à saint Augustin: étude philosophique* (Louvain: Desclée, 1945), 543. Verbeke finds in *pneuma* the sense of "an active bond of elements . . . vivifying, divine, intermediary," according to André Laurentin, "Le Pneuma dans la doctrine de Philon," *Ephemerides Theologicae Lovanienses* 27/3 (July 1951), 390; 435. On the soul in Augustine, see Philippe Delhaye, *La philosophie chrétienne au Moyen Âge* (Paris: Fayard, 1958), 49.

[109] Ernest D. Burton, *Spirit, soul, and flesh . . . in Greek writings and their equivalents in the Hebrew Old Testament* (Chicago: University, 1918), 71.

[110] See below, chapter 7, p. 224. A.-M. Dubarle, "La Bible a-t-elle une doctrine sur l'âme et le corps?" *Recherches et Débats du Centre Catholique d'Intellectuels Français,* 35 (Paris: Fayard, 1961), 183–200.

[111] E. F. Sutcliffe, *The Old Testament and the Future Life*² (Westminster: Newman, 1947).

(1) *Nepeš* means "the individual," insofar as he bears a relation to life as a state, normally suggesting "human" but somehow shared with animals. (2) *Rûah* means a certain dynamic quality shared by the human being with God, yet not always noble or spiritual in man or even in God. (3) These definitions cannot be proved to represent gradual metaphorical spiritualizations of an originally more concrete sense such as "breath, wind; throat." (4) No term for soul implies antithesis to body; "flesh" no less than *nepeš* means "the animated composite," but with emphasis on its weakness and frustrations; the contrast to soul is more likely to be called "man" than flesh. (5) Rare passages seeming to describe the origin of either *rûah* or *nepeš* require careful evaluation in their context.

SUMMARY OF THE SIXTH CHAPTER,
"SCRIPTURE PROOF-TEXTS"

In dependence upon the dogmas of Creation and Immortality, the soul is alleged to be produced by God with an immediacy essentially distinguishing it from the mode of origin of the vital principle in plants and animals. The link with immortality reduces to a purely speculative middle term: "a thing intrinsically independent of matter in its operations and destined to survive at least for a time in total severance from matter, cannot have arisen in dependence upon matter." However valid this reasoning may be, it is not *revealed*.

A sort of biblical proof of immediate creation of the soul was seen by the Fathers in Qohelet's "return of the spirit to its giver" (Ecclesiastes 12:7). But this means chiefly that *life* (in man as in animal) will *stop*. The life-principle of man and beast seems even to be *equated* in 3:19; but this means ultimately "we should not allow philosophizing about the unknown to impede our living according to our nature."

In Genesis 2:7 a living human being is the result of God's "molding mud" and "breathing." Both are metaphors, both express equal immediacy. Thus it was consistent when this verse was held to postulate God's immediate creation of both body and soul for man. But now scientific evidence and the pronouncement of Pius XII preclude seeing the first half as proof of nonevolutionary creation of the *body*. Since then, theologians have been unguarded in claiming to find *in this text* any greater creative immediacy for the soul than for the body. Both must be shown to be equally, truly, and immediately due to God's creative power, but without disregard for solidly assured scientific data.

Psalm 33:15, "God made the heart" (or "everything," Sirach 18:1); Hebrews 12:9, "father of spirits," strangely the only New Testament help; Second Maccabees 7:22, "creator of cosmos gives you spirit and life"; and Wisdom 15:11, "fashioner who breathed the soul and blew the spirit in": can only remotely and with difficulty be related to the divergence in mode of production between human and animal soul.

"Soul" in our English- or Latin-based bibles renders the Hebrew *nepeš*. This does not properly or primitively mean "breath" (much less "throat"), nor does *nešāmâ*. Both designate the concrete living individual. *Nešāmâ* focuses the life force which ceases when breathing ceases. *Nepeš* more directly signifies "the *individual*," connoting in varying degree his *state* of being "alive" (or *related* to life, in a sense applicable even to a dead body or a tombstone) and "human." "Spirit," *rûaḥ*, likewise did not mean primitively storm wind or anything so material, but the "superior dynamism" shared by humans with God, yet often violent and ignoble.

"Flesh," *bāsār*, is the nearest term in Hebrew for "body." No less than Soul and Spirit, Flesh too means "the *whole* man," but stressing his weaker and more frustrating aspects. Thus no Hebrew term of itself *means* "soul of man," as distinct from body, or from life of animal. From the terms themselves no argument can be drawn regarding the mode of *origin* of the human soul.

CHAPTER 7

SOUL-CREATION IN CHURCH TEACHING

Teilhard's hypothesis is that an "inner spiritual energy" compensates entropy in the tiniest units of inorganic matter, and combines into more complex consciousnesses culminating eventually in the human person.

This is obviously not what has been traditionally understood as the separate creation of the human soul out of nothing. Though Teilhard himself consented to acknowledge that such creation was compatible with his hypothesis, we have been more obstinate than he in persisting to inquire whether it is reasonable to postulate God intervening to produce what Nature was on the point of producing anyway.

We have seen that whatever be the speculative metaphysical arguments requiring this, they find no cogent basis in Scripture. But now we are prepared to submit fully to the decision of Christian tradition or the Magisterium of the Church if a loyal examination of the evidence shows that they authoritatively claim the immediate creation of the soul out of nothing to be a dogma or consequence or indispensable support of revelation.

Not that in formulating our exegesis of Scripture we have ignored the voice of Church tradition. Such exegesis of the single points as they arise must inevitably include advertence to the Fathers, and to pronouncements of the magisterium which bind a Catholic exegete. "Bind *and loose*," we should rather say, keeping intact Christ's metaphor of Matthew 16:19. The Keys of the Kingdom have been given to Peter undoubtedly for the partial purpose of *impeding* inquiry in a relatively few areas where revealed data would be ousted or jeopardized. But the power of teaching religious truth means also to *unloose* the growth and deepening of scientific theology by well refereed controversy.[1]

Hence we trust that even the Christian not committed to Papal authority, or the Jewish exegete or any scientist professing no religion, will view with sympathy our effort here to determine an area in which Catholic discussion is left more free than had been customarily imagined.

Even more securely we may confide that the Catholic will not allow any initial dismay to preclude his following objectively our inquiry into what the Church has really meant by identical formulas handed down in changing contexts since her earliest days.

It has been repugnant for us to state our conclusions in advance, because we have not ourselves formulated them in advance and then sought proofs for them, nor would we wish our reader to follow such a path. To some extent, and on the negative side, we have already indicated that our conclusions will end up rejecting the charge that Teilhard's notion of human spirituality is unorthodox.

At this point, however, we ought to make clear that on the positive side we will propose a coherent and constructive theory of the origin of the human soul which will safeguard and emphasize its immortality and also the immediacy of its creation by God.

But contrary to prevailing interpretations of these truths, we will also assert the interdependence of the human soul and of matter in the origin of the human being from God, and the essential identity of the operation by which God gives a vital principle to man, animal, and plant: *immediately,* yet not "out of nothing," but by a "creative concursus," as will be explained in the next chapter.

Proximately, then, what we are inquiring is whether this view is compatible with Church teaching. Our survey of Church documents has not been, and is not here, guided by the desire of finding proofs for the position just indicated. Nevertheless it may be of help to know in advance what we did and did not find those documents to warrant.

In our treatment of "creative concursus," it will be made clear that our view was worked out fully in detail without ever having got a hint that a similar view had meanwhile been published by Karl Rahner. However, once having seen and recognized the superior quality of his theological reasoning in defense of this position, it seemed more profitable to abandon any claim to originality and simply present his view, reformulated and explained to suit our present need. In this light, there is a certain paradox in the fact that most of our information in the present chapter is missing and is *missed* in Rahner's essay, but has been drawn

---

[1] R. North, "The Scope of Infallibility," *Continuum*, 2/4 (Winter 1965), 555–574.

by us almost wholly from Rahner's own edition of the binding documents of the Magisterium.[2]

Meanwhile a new edition of those documents has appeared, by a disciple of Rahner and along norms established by him.[3] Our references will be to the new numeration of this later work, DS, but accompanied by the DB-numeration which had been normative since the Bannwart edition in 1908: throughout the whole era in which most people living at the time this book was written learned their theology.

1. *Pius XII: "Faith Commands Retention"*

When Pope Paul VI in July 1966 summoned leading theologians concerned with human origins, before spurring them to renewed inquiry he reaffirmed some present formulations of Church teaching. These formulations seemed to echo intentionally what had rather recently been laid down by Pius XII.

In the Encyclical *Humani Generis* of 1950, Pope Pius XII declared that if the pros and cons of Evolution are duly set forth, the Catholic inquirer is at liberty to defend it "insofar as it deals with the origin of the human body out of preexistent living matter; the Catholic faith commands us to retain that souls are immediately created by God" (DS 3896 = DB 2327).

This declaration is parenthetical but emphatic. It uses the expression "commands," *iubet.* Since "Catholic faith" is the subject, this makes a rather conspicuous variant for the verb "teaches," which we would expect.

Again, the term "retain," *retinere,* is noticeably different from variants of the same verb meaning "hold" or "maintain" and more common in similar contexts. Whether either *iubet* or *retinere* was chosen for any other purpose than as a mere stylistic flourish, could scarcely be affirmed, and could scarcely be denied.

What seems clear is that the Pope here intends no dogmatic definition, nor indeed the conveying of any new information, but merely the *recall* of a doctrine in the form in which it is well known to Catholic theologians.

Yet despite this term "retain," a professor of the Gregorian University has written to acknowledge that *Humani Generis* is the *first* declaration ever made by the Magisterium on the immediacy of creation of the human soul.[4] The *formula* is earlier, and is "retained"; the doctrine also may be

---

[2] Henricus Denzinger, *Enchiridion Symbolorum,*[28] edidit Carolus Rahner (Freiburg: Herder, 1952).

[3] *Enchiridion symbolorum, definitionum et declarationum de rebus fidei et morum,*[32] quod primum edidit Henricus Denzinger, et quod funditus retractavit Adolfus Schönmetzer (Freiburg: Herder, 1963); page 1 on Rahner's role.

[4] See below, p. 229, n. 2 on Flick. — The allocution of Pope Paul VI was at first communicated to the secular press in a form different from that appearing in

earlier, but is not traceable in this formula.

Pius XII clearly qualifies the doctrine of soul-creation as "not optional." But its obligatory character is expressed in terms implying (so far as there can be a distinction — and there can!) *obedience* rather than certitude. The formulation itself does not go so far as to specify that the doctrine here imposed is simply a legitimate command of authority, to which the alternative would be *tuto doceri non potest*. Neither does it say that the prescribed doctrine is a part of revelation, to which the alternative would be heretical; or a necessary conclusion, to which the alternative would be erroneous — irreformably.

At any rate, to clarify the background of our Chapter 8, we are not here calling into question the *fact* that soul-creation is Church doctrine. We aim to focus on *what* precisely the Pope commands to be *retained*.

And as to this, the significant terms are "create" and "immediately." The qualification "out of nothing" is not explicitly appended after "create." *Animas* may be rendered either "souls" or "the souls," and from the context cannot be taken to refer to any other than human souls. But neither can any positive argument be drawn from the context as restricting them to human souls *alone,* or in any specific way as opposed or contrasted to the mode of origin of other vital principles to which the name *anima* is technically applied in theology.

In this part of the encyclical, incidentally, Teilhard de Chardin seems to be directly envisaged, though unnamed. This is apparent from an explanatory article published at that time by the now Cardinal Bea, utilizing terminology more explicitly drawn from Teilhard's writings.[5]

Our whole concern must now be to seek out that earlier ecclesiastical formulation of "immediate soul-creation" which Pius XII says we are "commanded" to "retain."

2. Nineteenth-Century Pronouncements

A precise statement concerning soul-creation had scarcely come up during the preceding thousand years of Magisterium utterances.

Leo XIII had indeed condemned as erroneous in 1887 the statement of Rosmini, "There is nothing inadmissible in the multiplication of the human soul by generation in such a way that it can be envisioned as proceeding from an imperfect or sensitive to a perfect or intellectual degree" (DS 3220 = DB 1910).

Osservatore Romano, July 16, 1966. It reiterates that polygenism "appears" irreconcilable with the dogma of original sin, and that evolution is "not worth considering where it does not clearly accord with the immediate creation of each and every soul by God." Flick and Rahner were both present at the meeting.

[5] Augustin Bea, "Die Enzyklika 'Humani Generis': ihre Grundgedanken und ihre Bedeutung," *Scholastik,* 26 (1951), 51.

This proposition must be assessed in the light of Rosmini's more general claim, which does in fact bear a resemblance to Teilhard's *"creari est uniri,* creation means being united."[6]

Says Rosmini, "Creation is the result of a synthesis effected by God between being in general and the possible beings which he has envisioned. In every creature there is a positive formal element which is *universal being,* and a material negative element or limitation which the creative spirit imposes upon the indeterminate."[7]

The proposition condemned in DS 3220 *mentions* the production of the soul by generation. But this is not condemned *in itself,* only in its alleged gradualness. Michel seems to put this wrongly.[8] Riva's lengthy inquiry into Christian traditions relevant to the condemnation formulates Rosmini's teaching as neither Traducianism nor Creationism but *trans-naturamento:*

> The sensitive soul is elevated and changes nature, by a divine intervention which manifests to the sentient principle a divine light, the ideal being. . . . [Even] traducianism does not deny divine causality in the question of the origin of the human soul.[9]

Our Denzinger handbook, in accord with its scope, contains no record of two energetic actions taken under Pius IX to preclude "The Defense of Generationism."[10] That was the title of a book of Frohschammer, put on the Index in 1857.

Around that time, a special command was transmitted to Ubaghs to

---

[6] See above, footnote 10, in chapter 4, p. 88.

[7] Antonio Rosmini-Serbati, *La Teosofia* (5 volumes, posthumous; Turin: 1859–1875), 1, 396; compare his *Antropologia in servigio della scienza morale*[2] (Novara: Miglio, 1847), 831: "In the generation of a human individual two causes concur, men by generation and God by illumination . . . God indeed creates the soul by illuminating it with his splendor and thus making it share in something of himself, Being as such." In his *Antropologia soprannaturale* of 1836 (Casale: Pana, 1884), Rosmini objects to soul-creation that it would postulate *two* miracles each time: God would not only create the soul, but would impede the parents' generative faculties from producing one, as in the case of other animals.

[8] A. Michel, "Rosmini," *Dictionnaire de Théologie Catholique* (Paris: Letouzey, 1937), 13, 2926 and 2939. Rosmini is further impugned by Albino Luciani, *L'origine dell' anima umana secondo Antonio Rosmini*[2] (Padua: Seminary, 1958; [1]1950).

[9] Clemente Riva, *Il problema dell' origine dell' anima intellettiva secondo Antonio Rosmini* (Domodossola: Sodalitas, 1956), 14: followed by a copious survey of patristic and scholastic views; see P. Barale, "L'origine dell' anima intellettiva secondo Rosmini," *Salesianum,* 20 (1958), 118–128; 119, creationism requires God's intervention only for what the parents cannot give, and Rosmini fits this.

[10] L. Frohschammer, *Über den Ursprung der menschlichen Seele: Rechtfertigung des Generatianismus* (Munich: 1854), is thus summarized by L. Janssens, *De hominis natura* (Rome: 1918), 597: "From the generative act of the parents, man is produced body and soul in virtue of a secondary creative power immanent in human nature from God's original donation." Frohschammer's more general views on the autonomy of reason were condemned in 1862: DS 2857 = DB 1673.

expunge from his *Anthropology* the phrase, "spiritual traducianism is more probable than creationism."[11]

In 1855 a decree of the Congregation of the Index had required A. Bonnetty to subscribe to the statement, "Reasoning can prove with certitude the existence of God, the spirituality of the soul, and the freedom of man." This is recorded in DS 2812 = DB 1650, but does not directly enunciate creation of the soul.

The First Vatican Council took over emphatically a statement of Fourth Lateran that God is creator of all reality, both material and spiritual, and "then, *deinde*" of man as a composite of both: DS 3003 = 800, DB 1783 = 428. This definition has been alleged to cover God's immediate creation of the human soul out of nothing. But upon closer examination its wording is seen not to require this interpretation any more than it requires his immediate creation of the human body out of nothing. The Lateran-Vatican statement is traceably a paraphrase of the Creeds' "father almighty, creator of heaven and earth, things visible and invisible."

3. Origins of the Soul-Creation Formula

Really the only relevant dogmatic pronouncement preceding Pius XII is the Armenian error condemned in 1341 by Benedict XII: "the human soul of the son is propagated by the soul of its father as body by body," DS 1007 = DB 533. The explicit point of this condemnation is a parallel alleged to exist between the mode of procedure in two operations. The only alternative to the one here condemned would seem to be "immediate creation by God."

And in fact the Armenian Bishops' Committee promptly rejoined that their church had always believed, "Souls are created *noviter* by God; and at the time of animation, the creation of the soul and its inserting in the body occur simultaneously."[12] The fairly Platonic soul-body relation underlying their statement, presumably formulated with an eye to assuring the Latin authorities of their orthodoxy, will not escape attention. But the condemnatory statement of Benedict XII had added no further precision as to how the origin of the human soul was to be positively understood. The subject was mentioned only casually in passing, as Sagüés rightly notes.[13]

---

[11] Gérard Ubaghs, *Anthropologia* (Louvain: 1848), 221, #428: to be corrected by the will of Pope Pius IX, according to an 1866 letter of Cardinal Patrizi to the Archbishop of Malines, *Acta Sanctae Sedis*, 3 (1867), 216. On Ubaghs' *Essai d'idéologie ontologique* (Louvain: 1869), see A. Fonck, "Ontologisme," *Dictionnaire de Théologie Catholique* (1931), 11, 1038.

[12] J.-D. Mansi, *Sacrorum conciliorum collectio amplissima* (Graz: 1924), 25, 1193.

[13] J. Sagüés, *De Deo creante* (Madrid: Biblioteca de autores cristianos, 1952), 2, 712.

The strongest formulation of soul-creation comes from a document of A.D. 1053. It is called "the Creed of Leo IX," but actually it seems to have been a widely used set of appropriate answers to the questions put to a new bishop in the ceremony of his consecration. Its statements include: "God's grace precedes and follows, without denial of human freedom. The soul is not a part of God, but created out of nothing; and apart from baptism it is subject to original sin"; DS 685 = DB 348.

We are already on the edge of a thought-world different from that of soul-body relationship, when "creation out of nothing" is set down as the alternative to being "a part of God." We will take this up presently.

In Leo's Creed the term *immediate* is not used, but in its place are two other useful clarifications. First of all there is an indication of the sort of origin which is disapproved as an alternative to creation. Secondly the creation itself is said to be *ex nihilo*. This means in its context first and foremost "not out of the divine substance itself," a seductive error which had frequently had to be combated.

Was this assertion under the authority of Leo IX intended also to exclude any simultaneous causality in the production of the human soul, on the part of the parents or the sperm-ovum union or any other existing material reality? Boyer admits quite candidly that it was not.[14] A proof of this answer would have to be sought in the use of similar formulas prior to Leo, and notably in the interpretation of Scripture which these involve.

Meanwhile one caution may be in place here. It is hard to avoid *imagining* the "nothingness" *out of* which the human soul was created as a sort of *stuff* or non-material potency. " 'To make something out of nothing' and 'pure spirit' seem to be simple and easy notions to one who receives them ready-made; our fathers in the faith [up through Tertullian and Origen] had a hard time to conceive them in their pure state."[15]

We have noted that the "chaos" of Genesis 1:2 may be the closest a primitive narrator could come to grasping the sophisticated notion of complete nothingness.[16] If we rid ourselves ruthlessly of the encumbrances of the imagination, ultimately it would seem that "God's creating out of nothing" means properly *"but for* God's immediate causal intervention, the human soul *would not be there."* It seems to deny that without God's immediate activity the human soul could simply *come out of* the sperm or the ovum or the fact of their union by natural processes.

"DB 348 condemns emanationism. In this perspective, the formula

---

[14] C. Boyer, *De Deo creante*[3] (Rome: Gregorian, 1940), 131.

[15] J. Bainvel, "Âme dans la sainte Écriture," *Dictionnaire de Théologie Catholique* (1930), 1, 1001.

[16] See above, footnote 29, in chapter 4, p. 94.

'out of nothing' does not necessarily include further also *immediate* creation," says Sagüés; nor does DB 170 exclude parental productiveness
affecting the soul.[17]

He goes on rather less convincingly to add that where the origin of
the soul is being treated and no *materia ex qua* is specifically indicated,
the theologian "can" conclude to creation, "especially since even at that
date theologians commonly condemned all traducianism." This vagueness
is surely not the language of the theologian determining the *binding force*
of an ecclesiastical pronouncement.

But now to take up Leo's insistence on soul-creation as an alternative
to its being "a part of God": that is, to emanationism. This formula is
taken over from a much earlier Creed, that of Toledo, DS 201 = DB 31:
"Man's soul is not the divine substance, or part of God, but a creature."[18]

The use of *creature* here instead of "created" is very significant for us.
Obviously the human soul is a creature, otherwise it would be God
himself! But that which is a creature is created. It is in this sense that
the human soul, in the primitive Christian belief expressed by this creed,
is created by God. In the sense in which the soul is a creature, the body
also, or even more so, is a creature. Yet from this it does not follow
that the body is created immediately by God out of nothing. The term
"immediately" is simply not relevant to this perspective, and is in fact
not inserted by Leo IX's creed in taking over the Toledo formula.

There is a further relevant phrase of the Toledo Creed, but in the
form in which it has been corruptly transmitted to us, it makes no usable
sense, and is simply omitted in DS. It is given by DB 20 as follows:
sed creaturam [animam dicimus] divina voluntate non prolapsam (?)
[*creatam*].

4. *The Declaration of Anastasius II*

Meanwhile, however, there was formulated in 498 against some unnamed heretics in Gaul a long statement of Pope Anastasius II. It will
be noted as highly relevant, but also highly rhetorical. The Latin is rather
special, and the qualified reader is urged to turn to it, since our rendition
can only hope to hint at the flavor or even the sense of the original;
but after the passage we will summarize what its theological teaching
seems to be:

---

[17] J. Sagüés, *De Deo creante* (Madrid: BAC, 1952), 2, 712.

[18] The same emphasis is found in this rejection of a Priscillianist error, in a
letter of A.D. 447 to the Spanish bishop Turribius, implausibly attributed to Pope
Leo I, now newly included in DS 285: "They claim that the soul of man is of the
divine substance, and that the nature of our condition does not differ from the
nature of the Creator. This impiety . . . the Catholic faith condemns: knowing
that nothing produced is so sublime and important that God is its nature."

DS 360 = DB 170 [Some heretics in Gaul think] that by a reasonable assertion they can arouse conviction for this: that, for the human race, parents, as from a material secretion they hand on bodies, so also contribute the spirit of the lifegiving soul. . . . How (therefore) against the divine pronouncement, by a too fleshly understanding, they think the soul made to the image of God is communicated and inserted by human intercourse; whereas on the part of him who from the beginning did this, the action itself even today does not cease. . . . They ought rather to understand what is written [Sirach 18:1], "He who lives forever, created everything simultaneously" [in the beginning potentially, but causally up till now, as explained by Augustine ML 34, 341]. Let them therefore assent to the sound doctrine, that *he* puts in the souls, who calls those things which are not, as if they were. . . . As for the possibility that they think they speak well and according to the faith, insofar as they claim that souls are rightly said to be given by the parents, because they are embroiled in sins . . . : by them nothing else can be given than what has been committed by their own evil presumptuousness, that is the guilt and punishment of sin, which the offspring following through the intervention of a tradux shows evidently.

There are some six theological assertions in this passage:

1. Parents do not give to human beings "the spirit of the lifegiving soul" in the same way in which they give bodies *ex materiali faece. Faex* means, in general, a residue left behind at the end of some process of change. According to Aristotle's *Animal generation* 1,18; 724b 22, the process of digestion in animals results in such "residues" as bile, phlegm, urine, faeces, and semen: some of which had a function in the body, while others were to be excreted. Whether or not the term *faex* was chosen here in tacit acceptance of the Aristotelian biology, it seems reasonable to suppose that in preferring this term to a more proper one like semen itself, the document affords at least a mild indication of the class of realities to which that substance is seen to belong.

2. It is against "the divine pronouncement," presumably Genesis 1:27, to imagine that "the soul made to the image of God," should be propagated and inserted by human intercourse. As we have seen above, it is unlikely that Scripture makes the image of God to consist in the soul any more than in the body; it is in the *whole man*.[19] But even assuming the image to be chiefly in the soul, it is not clear why this pronouncement of itself excludes the propagation of God's image from father to son, as seems suggested by the echoing of the wording of Genesis 1:27 in the fathering of Seth, 5:3.

3. The fact that God himself effects this human soul, each time now, just as in the beginning, is somehow put in relation to Sirach 18:1, which as we have seen says in Greek "He who lives forever, created all things in common."[20] Along with this verse is in fact cited also John 5:17,

---

[19] See above, footnote 38, to chapter 6, p. 182.
[20] See above, footnote 53, to chapter 6, p. 187.

"My father works up until now, and I work." This seems to be intended as an illustration, not of course a proof, of the continuing of some of the acts of creation.

4. The words of John, "(working) up till now," are echoed in the citation from Augustine, which seems to be interwoven into the wording of Anastasius as indicated by the italics: "If therefore, before Scripture disposed order and nature to each separate creature according to the separate species, *'potentially'* as cannot be denied, *'and causally in the work pertaining to the course of times he works up till now,'* therefore let them assent to the sound doctrine. . . ." Augustine's words seem to be taken to mean that God did *not* at the initial creation put into the reality then existing, the forces needed to work themselves out into later forms. However, this line of reasoning from Augustine's *Genesis Literally* seems rather to be saying that God is truly the cause *now* of those things which occur due to forces which he put into nature from the *beginning*. And in this sense it has often been seen as one of the strongest patristic justifications for admitting the doctrine of *bodily* evolution.

5. The true Catholic doctrine is that souls are inserted by the one who "calls those things which are not, as if they were."

6. The fact that souls are "(born) in sin" is not a reason for ascribing their origin to sinful parents. Anastasius excludes this error by an explanation whose force escapes us because it utilizes with apparent approval the term *tradux*. This term normally implies that the soul is produced by the parents. In the light of what precedes, it is plain that Anastasius does not approve what is called *"material* traducianism." Whether he is reluctantly leaving open some defense of the "spiritual traducianism" of Augustine is disputed by the experts.

The total force of the Anastasius passage is that the human soul owes its origin to God. Any effort to derive further qualifications regarding immediacy or *ex nihilo* would tend to show that the author's outlook is rather that "God is said to be the creator equally of the souls, and of the bodies whose creation is doubtless only mediate."[21]

The authority of Augustine, and the passage from Sirach which it is intended to clarify, would warrant concluding that God's creation of the new soul here and now is ultimately reducible to the forces which he put into nature from the beginning. The reference to man's creation in the image of God is as relevant to the body as to the soul.[22]

Before we take up specially the problems relevant to the term *tradux,* we may conclude and summarize here our survey of the whole two thousand years of Magisterium pronouncements. The basic assertion, "God

---

[21] J. Sagüés, *De Deo creante,* 2, 715. His assertion is framed to cover both the decree of Anastasius II and the letter to Turribius as in Migne's *Patrologia Latina,* 54, 684 and in J. A. de Aldama, *El Símbolo Toledano* I (Rome: 1934), 54.

[22] See above, footnote 38, in chapter 6, p. 187.

is the creator of the human soul," is inescapably Catholic doctrine. It means originally and chiefly that the soul is not the divine substance but a creature. The additions of immediacy and *ex nihilo* are nowhere found simultaneously. Where *ex nihilo* appears, it is proximately in explicit rejection of emanationism. The relation or antithesis between human and subhuman souls is nowhere a factor.

5. Pre-Aquinas Traducianism

The alternative to immediate creation of the soul by God, apart from pantheistic emanationism, is known in the history of dogma as traducianism. The term as coined was really an adversary's disparaging reference to the mode of transmission of original sin.[23] The *tradux* is spoken of as if it were some entity separate from the paternal sperm and ovum, but it seems to mean simply in the biology of that day "the parental contribution in conception."

Two possibilities are envisioned. If the purely material elements of sexual mating were considered to effect the spiritual soul, this was called material traducianism. It is regarded by modern theology manuals as more obviously untenable, and more directly condemned in the ecclesiastical pronouncements cited above. For it we may reserve the name traducianism without qualification.

Since however the parents *possess* a principle of life, which is the spiritual soul, it seemed possible to regard *this* as the tradux or entity responsible for the production of the soul of the fetus. This view is called "spiritual traducianism," and is regarded as *less* directly condemned by the Church. We will reserve for it here the name generationism, which in other contexts (and illogically spelled generatianism) may have the more generic sense of traducianism. The alternative to either kind of traducianism, as well as to emanationism, will be called creationism.

It will be noted that the manuals dispose rather handily of both "material" and "spiritual" traducianism, by this disjunction: "The new soul is produced either by matter or by a spirit. But neither makes sense." The point is, however, that the alleged producer is *neither* a pure spirit nor matter without spirit. And what is produced is, strictly speaking, an *individual living being* composed of body and soul: within which com-

---

[23] Explained by Augustine, *To Julian* 1, 6; *ML* 45, 1053. The form *traductianism(us)* is favored by Gabriel Huarte, *De Deo creante²* (Rome: Gregorian, 1935), 202. His *t* is defensible, but not the *a*. As a noun from *tradux*, "traducian" follows normal patterns, and would issue in "traducianism." By assimilation to this arose the *generatianism* and *creatianism* of our manuals (with *a*). There may be reason for preserving these hybrid forms to dramatize their inner relation to the traducianist controversy. But we may be pardoned for adopting the more etymological forms creationism, generationism.

posite, the soul is a *contributory principle* of being, rather than "a being" itself.

No dogma textbook has ever resolutely posed the problem: "What is the speculative disproof of the proposition, 'Animated beings produce an animated being'?" The closest we could indicate to this posing of the problem is Lacroix's rejection of this position of Poiret: "The creature has the power of producing or generating a thing like itself [matter from matter; spirit from spirit; and moreover] Active and fertile power is in the matter [of a human being] in the way that the mind itself is joined to the body."[24]

Principal among the names representing Catholic tradition in the traducianist controversy is Augustine. His position is given with fairness in the manuals. The question is not whether he *defended* traducianism. He did not, at least not clearly and consistently. He did, however, acknowledge vigorously that it was *better* than creationism and compatible with *some* requirements of Catholic dogma. In short, he was not conscious that *revelation itself* required creationism; nor was he sure that it did not.[25] Augustine's difficulty about God creating the soul at the moment of vivifying the body comes from his regarding the second chapter of Genesis as a *second* step after God had completed what is narrated in the first chapter.[26]

The DTC article on traducianism by Michel is conscientiously informative. But one may ask whether it does not prejudice the historical tracing of the question by its calling any early theologian's refusal to demand creationism "a hesitancy in face of the authority of Augustine," and any explicit proclamation of it "a clear condemnation of the error."[27] No less objective would be this counter-formulation: "Those who did not impose creationism were guided by a healthy respect for Catholic tradition, of which Augustine was a highly authoritative spokesman. Those who insisted upon creationism were presenting an original *extra chorum* speculation of their own."

Actually *neither* of the two ways of slanting the facts is commendable. The purpose of such a research should be simply to indicate *what* was being taught within the Church at each successive stage of its history.

---

[24] Pierre Poiret, *Cogitationum rationalium de Deo, animo et malo libri quattuor* (Amsterdam: Paulus, 1715), 148; Robert Lacroix, "L'origine de l'âme humaine," in a *Supplement* to the *Revue de l'Université d'Ottawa* 14-S (1944), 85, ascribing a similar view to Klee, and also to Domenico Gravina, O.S.B., *Sull' origine dell' anima umana e taluna verità che ne dipendono* (Palermo: 1870), 17.

[25] Augustine, *Letter* 166, 8, 25; *CSEL* 44, 580; *ML* 33, 471; Rouët de Journel 1441. The defense of creationism in his *De Anima* 2, 3, 6 (*ML* 44, 497; RJ 1879), expressly disclaims relevance to any soul except that of the first man.

[26] P. Galtier, "Saint Augustin et l'origine de l'homme," *Gregorianum*, 11 (1930), 7.

[27] A. Michel, "Traducianisme," *Dictionnaire de Théologie Catholique* (Paris: Letouzey, 1946), 15, 1355.

Michel admits that his approach is borrowed from Bellarmine, who "would have been better advised to take account of the development inherent in any argument from tradition, especially in areas where the faith is not directly involved."[28] Bellarmine's slantedness aroused the indignation of another Cardinal, Noris, whose work is commonly ranked among those denying that the creation of the soul is a doctrine of faith. But in reality his aim was merely to defend the uniqueness and legitimacy of Augustine's position as a witness to tradition.[29]

Despite his "loyal" slanting, Michel presents objectively a noteworthy number of evidences for a conviction within the early Church, that the origin of the soul was not a point on which our faith gives us any univocal guidance. The teaching of Gregory of Nyssa has been the subject of a protracted controversy.[30] Fulgentius states — and it is true! — "Nothing in Scripture condemns generationism."[31] The compilation called "Deflowering of the Holy Fathers" says that God creates the souls but we do not know "from what God makes them."[32] Rupert of Deutz is at pains to show that traducianism best satisfies the exigencies of *various* Catholic beliefs.[33]

From these citations of his own, we are at a loss to see in what sense Michel can conclude, "The condemnation of traducianism appears quite definitive, whatever may be the watered-down formulas suggested by respect for Augustine." More warrantably, though also with some exaggeration, Jerome concluded, "The majority of occidentals maintain with Tertullian and Apollinaris that soul is born of soul just as body is born of body."[34]

Hugh of St. Victor has a thesis, "The soul is not from a *tradux*." Here is what Michel says of it. "The reasons which he draws from Scripture are not very convincing. Neither is his example of the plants which communicate life without communicating a soul. But the only thing that matters is his conclusion [?!]: 'It turns out to be *more probable*

---

28 Robert Bellarmine, *Controversies* 4, 4, 11; Michel, *DTC* 15, 1358 f and 1364.

29 Henricus de Noris, *Historia pelagiana . . . additis Vindiciis augustianianis* (Padua: 1673), 4, 3; (Schelte ed., Louvain: 1702), 66 f. See D. Gutiérrez, *Augustinianum*, 1 (1961), 150 ff, reproaching *Lexikon für Theologie und Kirche*[2] (Freiburg: Herder, 1957), 1, 1092.

30 D. L. Rebecchi, "L'antropologia naturale di S. Gregorio Nisseno," *Divus Thomas Piacenza*, 20 (1943), 325–330.

31 Fulgentius, *Letter* 16, 16; *ML* 65, 1941.

32 Werner of St. Blaise, *Defloratio sanctorum Patrum*, *ML* 157, 1161.

33 Rupert of Deutz, *De Trinitate in Genesim*, 2, 21; *ML* 167, 267.

34 Jerome, *Letter* 126, 1; *ML* 22, 1085, cited as an "exaggeration" [of the true state of affairs] by B. Beraza, *De Deo creante* (Bilbao: Eléxpuru, 1921), 504, following Hurter, *Theologia dogmatica* 2, #280.

that souls are not from a tradux. The Catholic faith has chosen as *more worthy of belief* that souls daily come into being out of nothing in order to be joined to bodies and thereby be given life."[35]

6. Thirteenth Century: Traducianism Reappraised

A powerful new factor is brought into the discussion by the insistence of Saint Albert the Great that there is a soul in plants and in animals and in men. Moreover Albert is just as rigid in rejecting traducianism in the two lower cases as in the higher. "According to the Catholic Faith and according to the philosophers, no soul is transmitted, *nulla anima ex traduce,* neither in plants, nor in animals, nor in men."[36]

For Bonaventure the soul is a *hoc aliquid,* a Thing, which it was not for Albert.[37] He maintains soul-creation but expressly distinguishes the traducianists from heretics. Bonaventure defends both the substantiality of the soul and its union with the body, in virtue of a "plurality of forms," incompatible with the Aristotelian notion of the soul as the form of the body.[38]

The first to assign to traducianism the note "heretical" was thirteenth-century Moneta of Cremona, a Dominican.

He was quickly followed by another and most influential Dominican, Thomas Aquinas, whose genius in this area as in others is too apt to be uncritically equated with the consensus of tradition or with revelation itself.

Aquinas in his commentary on Romans 14:3 makes the singularly oblique statement, "In Augustine's time, the Church had not yet declared that the soul was not generated." The use of "declared" instead of "believed, became sure" or a similar expression, seems to indicate that Aquinas was aware of some published utterance of the Magisterium. Yet no proof has ever yet been discovered that the Church *did* make such a declaration in the meantime. In fact Thomas in the *De Potentia* 3,9, still dignifies the alternative view by the term "opinion." In the *Summa Theologiae* 1,118,12, he finally professes — in terms that are not merely "in appearance" hard to reconcile with those of his master Albert — that

---

[35] Hugh of St. Victor, *Sacraments* 1, 6, 30; *ML* 176, 300.

[36] Albert, *Second Sentences* 18, 8. According to Michel, Albert does not equate here the vegetable or animal soul with the spiritual soul. Yet no proof of the statement is cited, except the remotely-relevant *Summa* 2, 1, 4, 1, 2 ad 2.

[37] Eduard Lutz, *Die Psychologie Bonaventuras* (C. Bäumker *Beiträge*, 6/4; Münster: 1909), 9.

[38] Anton C. Pegis, *St. Thomas and the Problem of the Soul in the Thirteenth Century* (Toronto: St. Michael's, 1934), 52; 110.

the sensitive soul can be generated, but it is *heretical* to maintain that the spiritual soul is transmitted with the semen.[39]

It has been pointed out to me that both Aquinas and Albert accepted the Aristotelian teaching that the sensitive soul is not transmitted in the semen but is produced by a *virtus activa* in the semen. It would seem, however, that Aquinas differs from Albert at least in allowing that animal and plant souls are "educed from the potency of matter" and thus truly due to a *tradux* in a way which the human soul is not. The same colleague pointed out to me that there is no need to look for any "lost" condemnation of traducianism in order to account for the view of St. Thomas, since his reason for saying that traducianism is heretical is simply that it is incompatible with the doctrine of immortality of the soul, which was regarded as *de fide* in his day.[40] But I may be pardoned for continuing to think that Saint Thomas was too accurate a theologian

---

[39] Those who maintain that there is no contradiction here between the teaching of Albert and of Thomas point out: (a) both accepted the Aristotelian teaching that the sensitive soul is not transmitted in the semen but is produced by a *virtus activa* in the semen; (b) both state explicitly that this *virtus activa* is not itself a soul but merely a capacity to produce a soul in suitably disposed matter. For Albert, see *De Animalibus* 16, 1, 11; for Aquinas, *Summa Theologiae* 1, 118, 1 ad 3.

[40] George Vass, "The Immortality of the Soul and Life Everlasting," *Heythrop Journal,* 6/3 (July 1965), 270–288, deals with an indirect aspect of our present problem. Following A. Deneffe, *Scholastik,* 5 (1930), 383; 8 (1933), 359–379, he shows that neither Aquinas nor any scholastic ever tried to prove the immortality of the soul from its being the *forma substantialis* of the body. Vass says nothing about proving the *spirituality* of the soul from its immortality; but since he roundly asserts that its immortality is not positively knowable from reason, its spirituality could not be proved by reason from its immortality. Even after Lateran V, the immortality of the soul is a mystery of our faith, according to E. Verga, "L'immortalità dell' anima nel pensiero del Cardinal Gaetano," *Rivista di Filosofia Neoscolastica,* 27 (1935), 21–46; so F. Sciacca, *L'anima* (Brescia: 1954), 337 f, "morte ed immortalità personale." Vass's article, in reaction to C. Stange, "Die geradezu lächerliche Torheit der päpstlichen Theologie," *Zeitschrift für systematische Theologie,* 10 (1932), 306, shows that the Fifth Lateran Council in 1513 (DS 1440 = DB 738) in anonymously condemning P. Pomponazzi for his idea later published in *Tractatus de immortalitate animae* (1516: hylemorphism cannot be reconciled with the immortality of the soul; the soul's natural power to survive death is not clear, or is a mystery) does indeed give the impression that the soul's immortality is naturally knowable (whence even "the Christian hope of the Resurrection is made dependent on natural reasoning," Stange); Deneffe rightly shows that the decree does *not* require that immortality be held on other than *theological* grounds; but he should have gone on to conclude from the Lateran decree that the Church does in fact teach as a naturally knowable truth the *possibility* that the human soul is immortal; which after all is only a different way of stating the popular modern existentialist view that man is "a being unto death" (Rahner), an "orientation towards eternity," a being who "even in his has-been state is in God's hand" (K. Barth). — Vass, page 288, with Sciacca, page 337, concludes: "I confess that 'our dead exist, and I shall survive death.' But if I am asked, 'What is it exactly that remains of me after death?', I may answer, for the sake of convenience, 'My soul survives'; I may say 'I shall exist in the world that nurtured me, in men and women whom I loved and in God who has called me.' But I could just as well say (and perhaps with more justification) 'I do not know.' "

not to distinguish between "what the Church has *declared*" and "what reason shows to be incompatible with doctrines held by the Church as de fide."

Two questions invite the researcher to a serene but firm stand. First, was or was not Saint Thomas correct in saying that some "declaration" of the Church had intervened since Augustine? Not only if he was not correct, but even if he cannot be proved to have been correct in this very sidelong observation, his peculiarly authoritative position in theology does not suffice for admitting as infallible his witness to an otherwise unverifiable tradition.

Second, is it well to allow a speculative insight, however forceful and valid, to serve as the mouthpiece of tradition? Would it not be better to say that St. Thomas *solved* a problem which tradition *and revelation* had left unsolved? From this it would further follow that what St. Thomas solved by speculative insight on the basis of biological data known to him, can with his help be yet better solved by the use of increasingly accurate biological data.[41]

With fairness we may invoke here a forceful statement of Palmieri's relevant to another aspect of this very controversy. "So he made a mistake! What's surprising about that? Dismay of this kind betrays the mentality of those who surrender themselves completely to the leadership of a single man, a man after all, however learned he undoubtedly is; and look up to him as the sole, absolute, and almost infallible master, in comparison with whom others are disdained. Not for such a purpose did God raise up in the Church those whom we call Doctors."[42] He is speaking, not of Aquinas, but of Augustine as corrected by Aquinas. But what's sauce for the goose is sauce for the gander.

---

[41] Josef de Vries, "Zum thomistischen Beweis der Immaterialität der Geistseele," *Scholastik,* 40/1 (1965), 1–22, says on page 3: Though Aquinas really means by "matter" *materia prima* and *not* that "brain-stuff" which modern materialists mean, still this *materia prima* is ordered to extension (though Aquinas never managed to show exactly how), and thus his proofs of the soul's immortality still hold. His only really essential argument is that the intellectually knowing subject *becomes* all things (*De anima,* 25). Really this argument of his is based on some presuppositions, which are open to *big* objections: (a) only without individuating matter are things known intellectually (yet this is not true of God or angels); (b) "matter" as principle of individuation is meaningless to scientists, and is contested even by Catholic philosophers; (c) the immateriality of the soul's *act* is far from evident, and it would normally be known from the immateriality of the principle rather than vice versa. De Vries concludes that nevertheless the Thomistic argument is reductively true and valid: Any theory of knowledge would be impossible if all knowledge, even of spiritual things, were bound to material processes. [But it *is!* at least neither experience nor reason can conclusively reveal the contrary to our introspection. See pp. 21–22, chapter 1, above].

[42] Domenico Palmieri, *Tractatus de creatione et de praecipuis creaturis* (Paris: Giachetti, 1910), 298.

7. *Current Theological Qualifications*

What is the theological note assigned to the thesis defending creationism as against "spiritual traducianism"? Posed in exactly those terms, Sagüés answers the question very forthrightly, *de fide catholica ex magisterio ordinario.* However, he immediately adds the reservations, "This seems to have been made clear by the words of Pius XII. The above qualification holds certainly at least for the soul of the first parents."[43]

This is not a commendable theological procedure, to begin first by stating a resoundingly high note, and then take a look at the evidence which would suggest whittling it down a bit. The first thing to do is consider the evidences, all of them, and then draw from them the minimal sense which can and must be imposed as of obligation.

At any rate, the words of Pius XII here invoked do *not* seem to have had the intention of making the situation either firmer or clearer than it was already. He says *retinere iubet.*

This endeavor of theologians to be simultaneously loyal to the documentary evidence and to favored current formulas is already reflected as early as 1608, when Valencia held simultaneously the whole gamut of theological qualifications by calling spiritual traducianism "heretical or certainly erroneous and *rash.*" The minimum among these, rash, must be said to reduce to a high degree of probability combined with reverential respect for authority.

Before the pronouncement of Pius XII in 1950, I have found only Daffara assigning the note *de fide* without restriction.[44] Boyer ten years earlier thought that the thesis was already "not *de fide definita,* but now taught by the ordinary magisterium."[45]

Proxima fidei is the note assigned by Moran and Lercher, and equivalently by Beraza's *haeresi proximum* for the contrary.[46]

Theologice certa was preferred by Pignataro already in 1904, but with the addition "at least."[47] This was virtually Huarte's stand.[48] *Theologice*

---

[43] J. Sagüés, *De Deo creante* (Madrid: BAC, 1952), 2, 716.

[44] Marcolino Daffara, *De Deo creatore* (Turin: Marietti, 1947), 221.

[45] C. Boyer, *De Deo creante*³ (Rome: Gregorian, 1940), 146.

[46] John Moran, *Alpha et Omega: theses quaedam selectae de Deo uno et trino, creante et elevante, et de novissimis* (Worcester, Mass.: Harrigan, 1935), 109; Ludwig Lercher, *Institutiones theologiae dogmaticae 2. De Deo uno et trino, creante et elevante*⁴ (Barcelona: Herder, 1945, revised by anonymous Innsbruck professors; ³1940 was by F. Schlagenhaufen), 315; Blasio Beraza, *De Deo creante* (Bilbao: Eléxpuru, 1921), 509.

[47] Felice Pignataro, *De Deo Creatore commentarius in 1 P. Summae Theologicae S. Thomae* (Rome: S. Giuseppe, 1904), 245.

[48] G. Huarte, *De Deo creante*² (Rome: Gregorian, 1935), 202.

certa without such qualification is given since 1940 by Mors, Bozzola, and Pohle-Gummersbach.[49]

The much-admired volume of Gregorian University professors Flick-Alszeghy contained in its Italian edition the qualification "necessarily connected with faith: theologically certain."[50] But since its date of publication, Father Flick has published a resounding approbation of the position of Karl Rahner which we will set forth in the next chapter.[51] It seems that this must imply some reserves about the note to be assigned to the immediate creation of the human soul.

Doctrina catholica is the minimum required by Garrigou-Lagrange.[52] Hugon adds "doctrina *vere* Catholica," as if fearing theologians sometimes resorted to that term without being truly convinced.[53]

No particular note at all is assigned by van Noort.[54]

Here are two interesting samples of hesitancy or "thinking out loud." Pesch in 1895 wrote: "It must be admitted that until now there are no definitions of Church authority so clear as to make soul-creation *de fide,* but *no one can doubt which side ecclesiastical authority favors.*"[55] And van Hove in 1944: "It is certain Catholic doctrine, some even say *proxima fidei:* this is the view which the magisterium manifestly favors."[56]

These two formulations acknowledge to a certain extent that the *refusal* of nineteenth-century Popes to make a dogmatic pronouncement was in itself already a taking of dogmatic position. Their resolute policy was to effectuate the withdrawal or alteration of those formulations which they found repugnant. But they did *not* choose or feel prompted to make the declaration which would have warranted the note *de fide.*

At this point let us recall what we said of Sagüés: the notes here assigned are concerned not with "the immediate creation of the soul out of nothing" in general, but the rejection of that specific alternative called "spiritual traducianism." Actually this *presupposes* the disjunction which we already rejected: the soul if due to the parents must come from either

---

[49] José Mors, *Institutiones 2. De Deo creante* (Petropolis, Brazil: Vozes, 1940), 100; Carlo Bozzola, *De Deo uno et trino, creante et elevante* (Naples: d'Auria, 1948), 205; Josef Gummersbach, *Pohle: Lehrbuch der Dogmatik*[10] (Paderborn: Schöningh, 1952), 1, 560.

[50] M. Flick, Z. Alszeghy, *Il Creatore: l'inizio della salvezza*[2] (Florence: Fiorentina, 1961), 249.

[51] See below, footnote 2, to chapter 8, p. 229.

[52] Reginald Garrigou-Lagrange, *The Trinity and God the Creator* (Saint Louis: Herder, 1952), 613. In the English it is not really presented as a dogmatic note; a paragraph simply begins, "The Catholic doctrine is . . ."

[53] Édouard Hugon, *De Deo uno et trino, creatore et gubernatore* (Paris: Lethielleux, 1933), 769.

[54] G. van Noort, *Tractatus de Deo creatore*[3] (Bussum: Brand, 1920), 189.

[55] Christian Pesch, *Praelectiones dogmaticae 3. De Deo creante* (Freiburg: Herder, 1895), 66.

[56] Aloysius van Hove, *Tractatus de Deo creante et elevante* (Malines: Dessain, 1944), 219.

a material cause or a spiritual cause; but both are impossible. We repeat what we there said: no theologian has ever resolutely assigned a theological censure to the proposition "The soul as a thing separate from the body does not truly come into existence at all. Animated beings truly and properly cause the emergence of an animated being."

This declaration is, properly speaking, unaffected by the condemnation of "spiritual traducianism." In this sense it might be said that there is no inconsistency or alteration of view in Flick's defending Rahner's "creative concursus" while at the same time holding that the immediacy of the soul's creation is theologically certain. This immediacy is incompatible with making the soul a "being" produced either by the material part of the parents, or by the spiritual part of the parents. But the *immediacy* of God's creative intervention is not to be automatically equated with the contention that he is *more* the creator of the soul than of the body, or *more* the creator of the human soul than of the animal soul.

In the light of the relative reserve of ecclesiastical documents, up to and through the *Humani Generis* of Pius XII, we must really ask as a problem of historical theology: By what avenues and for what reasons was the creation of the soul promoted to its present (and not unanimous) high note?

This development seems linked with the reaction of the rank-and-file theology teachers to certain bold rethinkers around the year 1800. Whether these really taught that traducianism is not contrary to the Catholic faith is far from clear.

Berti's statement is: "Whether the soul was created out of nothing is a very difficult question; and there was reason for Augustine's hesitations in the matter. [But] it is an irrefutable Catholic teaching that the soul is not propagated by bodily semen."[57]

Klee, in his *History of Dogma* at least, calls generationism "opposed to Church doctrine"; and nowhere does he say formally that creationism is not certain, though his mildness in defending it accounts for the judgment passed on him by Mazzella.[58]

Berti and Klee, and others who speak like them, are not radicals. They accurately reflect the solid position of leading Fathers of the Church. Augustine rightly said, "It would be rash for human conjecture to presume that anything here has been defined."[59] And Gregory: "It has remained uncertain whether the soul descended from Adam, or was given afresh to each single man; the holy Fathers acknowledged that the ques-

---

[57] J. L. Berti, *De theologicis disciplinis* (1749; Bassano edition, 1792), 3, 12–15.

[58] C. Mazzella, *De Deo creante* (Woodstock, Maryland: 1877), 375 f; Heinrich Klee, *Manuel de l'Histoire des Dogmes chrétiens* (Paris: Lecoffre, 1848), 1, 405; *Katholische Dogmatik* (Mainz: 1835), 2, 234–308; *Specielle Dogmatik* (Munich: 1844), 1, 1, 3/7.

[59] Acknowledged by Boyer, *De Deo creante*[3] 129.

tion cannot be solved in this life."[60] Isidore states that *the* Catholic doctrine is, "the origin of the soul is uncertain."

In the First Vatican Council there was question of assigning the note *communis et certa* to the doctrine of the immediate creation of the soul. But the decision was contrary to cluttering up the decree with any such reference. Normally a council's refusal to assign a specified note could be taken as a hint that the least common denominator of their consensus would be somewhat lower. That conclusion is compatible, though not identical, with this one drawn by the historian of the Council:

> A formula indicating per transennam the immediate creation of souls, did not present this truth as a dogma of faith but as a common and certain doctrine, which would have sufficed to cut short the caprices of reviving views of traducianism and generationism. Finally it was decided to omit the phrase, and the conciliar definition left the question in that state and degree of certitude in which it then was.[61]

We too in turn are left with the same question which we have asked before. When Pius XII spoke of what the Catholic faith "commands us to retain," was he referring to the personal convictions of Aquinas, or to the official Catholic position as it objectively was in Aquinas' time?

8. *The Soul as Form of the Body*

Throughout all these twenty centuries, during which we have seen such reticence and vagueness in the pronouncements of the Magisterium on the mode of origin of the soul, we have in fact not been left without one extremely relevant declaration enjoying the very highest degree of the certitude of faith, *de fide definita.*

In those terms the council of Vienne in 1312 solemnly defined that the soul is the form of the body, rejecting the contrary opinion as heretical, DS 902 = DB 481.

The decree does not name the Franciscan Olivi, but there is no doubt that it is he whose teachings were being censured: only three theses, that is, out of a large number which had been denounced in the course of the inner-Franciscan "spirituals" controversy.

The precise issue being formally condemned was Olivi's contention of the duality of soul in man. This was shown rather convincingly by Palmieri.[62] It is true that Jansen thereupon made out a good case for his claim that the duality of soul was not a direct concern of the con-

---

[60] Gregory, *Letter* 53 to Secundinus; *ML* 77, 989.

[61] J.-D. Mansi, *Sacrorum conciliorum collectio* (Graz: 1924), 50, 109; schema, p. 70; see above, footnote 12 to p. 209.

[62] D. Palmieri, *De Deo creante* (Rome: 1878), 772.

ciliar fathers.[63] But this conclusion, echoed later still by Debièvre, leads him to an overall view more akin to Palmieri than he seems to recognize.[64]

Olivi truly held that the soul — by its sensitive "part" and not its intellective part — was the form of the body. He never uses the expression *anima intellectiva* but only *pars intellectiva animae rationalis,* whereas the Council of Vienne repeatedly uses the term *anima rationalis et intellectiva.* The basis for Olivi's view lay partly in the philosophic unsuitableness of a purely spiritual entity performing the material function of informing a body. [This scruple is highly relevant food for thought for metaphysicians attacking Teilhard today.] Secondly and more importantly, Olivi upheld, along with many Fathers interpreting the *psychē* distinct from *pneûma* in First Corinthians 15:44, the neo-Platonic or "Apollinarist" conviction of the sensitive soul as distinct from the intellective spirit in man.

Against Palmieri it has been claimed by Zigliara and Mandonnet that the intention of the council was not to condemn the duality of souls, but to affirm the nature of the *union* of the rational soul with its body.[65] In thus endeavoring to reverse the Council's intention from negative to positive terms, they inevitably fall into the snare of seeming to claim that a Thomistic theory on the *mode* of the union is here being imposed as a dogma of faith. This encroachment was promptly resented by modern experts.

Michel endeavors to agree that the Council by omitting the word "substantial" with *form,* refrained from imposing one philosophic system rather than another; and yet he tries to uphold Zigliara's claim that Olivi is condemned for denying the *immediacy* of the soul's informing of the body.[66] However, it must be noted that the Council also refrained from using the word *immediate.* Whether we are to consider as perfectly synonymous the words *per se et essentialiter* which the Council in fact does use, is a question upon which there will probably continue to be disagreement among the experts.

At any rate, when the Fifth Lateran council repeated this declaration, DS 1440 = DB 738, it continued to use the formula *per se et essentialiter* without *immediate.* But when Pope Pius IX echoed the wording

---

[63] Bernhard Jansen, "Die Definition des Konzils," *Zeitschrift für katholische Theologie,* 32 (1908), 289–307, 471–488; "Die Seelenlehre Olivis," *Franziskanische Studien,* 21 (1924), 297–314; also *Gregorianum,* 1 (1920), 83; and *Scholastik,* 10 (1935), 241.

[64] Michel Debièvre, "La définition du concile de Vienne sur l'âme," *Recherches de Science Religieuse,* 3 (1912), 335.

[65] T. Zigliara, *De mente concilii viennensis* (Rome: 1878), 96; P. Mandonnet, "Frères prêcheurs (La théologie dans l'Ordre des)," *Dictionnaire de Théologie Catholique,* 6, 896.

[66] A. Michel, "Forme du Corps humain," *Dictionnaire de Théologie Catholique* (Paris: Letouzey, 1947), 6, 547.

of Vienne but in retaining *per se* substituted for *essentialiter* the word *immediate,* he was rejecting the view of Günther that the human body possesses sensitive life apart from its union with the soul, DS 2828 = DB 1655.

Quite a tempest was caused when about the same time the redoubtable Pio Nono issued a letter in praise of the scholar heading a new Pontifical academy, "for following the principles of the Angelic Doctor on the union of the intellective soul with the human body, and on substantial form and prime matter."[67] These declarations were promptly and "gravely abused," as the Pope saw himself forced to clarify three years later, "in claiming that a certain philosophic system has been imposed. . . . Such Pontifical documents regard solely the substantial unity of human nature . . . [not] purely philosophical doctrines on which the Catholic schools legitimately follow varying views: because the supreme authority of the Church has never [!] rendered in favor of the one a verdict such as to exclude the other."[68]

The history of the dogma that the soul is the form of the body thus proves relevant in several ways.

First of all, it is at least superficially opposed to the doctrine that the soul is produced in a mode radically different from the body. All who formulated or used this terminology, right down through Pius IX, understood as its background that God created the body of the (first) human immediately out of mud. As for the explanations which have been offered for the paradox of subsequent bodies being produced with less immediacy than the corresponding souls, these explanations are not in themselves dogmas of faith.

Secondly, the dogmatic definition of Vienne enshrines an expression sacrosanct in what is somewhat tendentiously called "Christian philosophy," and that expression is one concerning which there is now a recognized consensus of the neo-Scholastic school. Yet the Church has recently insisted that in using such terms it did not intend to limit freedom of dispute in what was still strictly the realm of philosophy. Catholic philosophers, alas, persist in taking this freedom granted to them as if it meant that *they* enjoy a freedom which the custodians of revelation *deny* to *scientists*. But that is not the case. What is not revealed may be attacked and rejected just as laudably on the ground that it is incompatible with the known truths of science, as on the ground that it is incompatible with the known truths of philosophy.

"Form of the body" was a phrase chosen because in a general way it expressed the content of tradition and revelation regarding the utter

---

[67] Letter of Pius IX to Alfonso Travaglini, *Acta Sanctae Sedis,* 8 (1874), 496; background in *Civiltà Cattolica* (1874–4), 148–163.

[68] Pius IX, *Acta Sanctae Sedis,* 10 (1877), 258; see *Revue des Sciences Ecclésiastiques,* 2 (1877), 85.

unity of the human composite. How precisely the philosophical under-pinnings of this term were to be clarified was not the object of the definition. It warrants us and even encourages us to seek new avenues of explanation of the origin of the human soul, such that the importance and immediacy of God's creative part will be vindicated no less for the body than for the soul.

SUMMARY OF THE SEVENTH CHAPTER, ON THE MAGISTERIUM

Ecclesiastical declarations that the soul is created are far less peremptory than the declaration that it is the form of the body, with which they must be reconciled.

The most primitive formulation, which is traceably echoed in later pronouncements, aimed to safeguard the fact that the soul was a creature and not the divine substance itself.

Only *some* of the declarations on soul-creation add the term "immediately"; and *others* add "out of nothing."

The clarifications of revealed dogma do not truly take issue on the false disjunction, "Was the human soul produced by matter, or by a spirit, or by God?" Rather they assert that *but for* God's immediate intervention, in such a way that matter does not produce spirit, there would be no human composite.

Insofar as the soul is form of the body, God's creation of the soul must be regarded as an aspect of his creation of the body. This leaves room for discussing to what extent his creative immediacy is "out of nothing" as distinct from some connection with the living sperm and ovum of the spiritual-souled parents. No authentic clarification has been given of the mode in which the immediacy of God's intervention in the production of human souls differs from his concursus or his infusion of being in the production of animal souls.

Choice of Thomist formulas like "form" or "creation" to express the *sensus ecclesiae*, does not cloture debate about underlying explanations which Aquinas himself would have maintained to be purely philosophical or even scientific.

CHAPTER 8

RAHNER'S HYPOTHESIS OF HOMINIZATION

This chapter will outline the teaching of a leading dogmatic theologian on the mode of the creation of the human soul. He proposes it in a book whose title seems to have been borrowed from Teilhard: *Hominisation*. This word is so pivotal to Teilhard that some commentators think it is one of the many terms which he invented or at least brought into the theological purview from other contexts.[1] However, Rahner expressly avers that he is unacquainted with Teilhard's use of the term, or with the various teachings of Teilhard with which this book is concerned.

All the more intriguing, then, will be seen to be the relevance of what he has to say. And it seems only fair to indicate here emphatically that my own essential view of the creation of the human soul as a form of concursus was worked out in detail directly and solely in reflecting on the writings of Teilhard, and communicated in written and oral form before I had any chance to become acquainted with Rahner's contentions.

Moreover, the doctrine set forth in this chapter has been analyzed

---

[1] The English edition of *The Phenomenon of Man* (1959) has on page 164 this footnote: "French: *hominisation* — a word coined by the author." The volume called *Les processus de l'hominisation* (Colloques internationaux du Centre National de la Recherche Scientifique; Paris: 1958) has such titles as page 59 "L'hominisation de l'appareil masticateur" by G. von Koenigswald; page 149 "L'hominisation de la famille" by S. Zuckermann; page 179 "L'hominisation: selection, adaptation ou orthogenèse" by G. Héberer. A. Vandel's essay on page 193 is entitled "Le phénomène humain": "as a tribute to Teilhard."

and approved by an Italian expert in dogmatic theology.[2] And the same doctrine, put only indirectly in relation to Rahner, is found in these words of a Dutch theologian, "The genesis of the human soul is an (antithetical) aspect of the genesis of the whole person under God's transcendent creative causal activity."[3] Finding this view expressed in French, German, Italian, Dutch, and English should diminish any impression of singularity it might create. Though we must admit that all five writers concerned are Jesuits, there is no danger of assuming that the opposition to them is less strong among Jesuits than among other up-to-date inquirers.

1. *Concursus*

Though the view which we share seems daring, we will contend that it is rather the *objections* to it which are audacious. They involve rejection of two deeply-rooted Catholic traditions. One of these concerns God's cooperation with the acts of creatures in general. The other regards the precise instant at which the intellectual soul is united with the fertilized ovum. This will be treated in the next chapter, and also a rather technical and recent dispute about the very existence of concursus. For the present we will content ourselves with setting forth some notions traditional in Catholic philosophy and theology courses.

Concursus is a Latin word. It appears in two forms in English. "Concourse" is a place where people or cars *run along together*. "Concurrence" means simply occurring simultaneously, often with a nuance of agreement and cooperation, but sometimes nearer to its European sense of *competition*.

The semantic equivalent of concursus in English would be cooperation or collaboration. But both of these words in theology are unfortunately charged with pejorative moral implications. So we see ourselves forced to retain the Latin word concursus.

The book about *Hominisation* is coauthored by Rahner with Paul Overhage. The part signed by Rahner maintains expressly that the immediate creation of every human soul by God out of nothing is Catholic dogma.[4]

---

[2] Maurizio Flick, "Problemi teologici sull' ominazione," *Gregorianum*, 44/1 (Jan. 1963), 66, acknowledging that *Humani Generis* [despite its use of the term "retain"] is the first declaration ever made by the Magisterium on the immediacy of the creation of the human soul. Flick's article was summarized in *Theology Digest* 13/2 (Summer 1965), 122–128.

[3] P. Schoonenberg, "Evolutie," *Bijdragen*, 23/2 (1962), 138, 126. Also on page 138: Teilhard's "within of things" equals "subsistence or being-in-itself, which in animated beings develops as consciousness and spontaneity; in man as self-consciousness and liberty."

[4] Karl Rahner, Paul Overhage, *Das Problem der Hominisation* (Quaestiones Disputatae 12; Freiburg: Herder, 1961), 55 = *Hominisation: The Evolutionary Origin of Man as a Theological Problem,* translated by W. T. O'Hara (New York: Herder and Herder, 1966), 62.

But the equally Catholic dogma of the unity of body and soul in man, also the admissibleness of bodily evolution, also in general the new biological perspectives of our age, all require that we clarify more concretely what the "immediacy" and the "nothingness" as related to God's creative intervention mean.

Here is how Rahner's conclusion is formulated approvingly by Flick. God's creative "action" can be called with equal validity a creative "concursus." He gives origin to the soul, yet without producing by himself some new being which is not simultaneously the result of secondary causes.

In this perspective, there would be no essential distinction in the *mode* of operation by which God "creates immediately out of nothing" the human soul, and "concurs with the eduction from the potency of matter" of the sub-human vital principle. Rahner does not emphasize this comparison except to query whether we are really sure that there is an "individual" and therefore any vital principle at all in animals.[5]

When I first studied what Rahner has to say on this query, I took it to mean that he was thinking of the worm or some other animal which can survive in two or more parts. Some similar interesting experiments had been brought within the purview of philosophy as early as 1901.[6] To foster a methodic doubt that the dog or the horse possesses individual conscious reality may be fruitful. Such a methodology emphasizes that our *knowledge* of their individuality comes only by groping inferences from the human ego's own immediate experience of individuality.[7] But whatever may be the problems raised by some border-line cases, I found it unrealistic to deny that every dog is truly *one* living thing.

When I later had a chance to take up this problem directly with Rahner, to inquire whether I had rightly grasped what he was getting at, the matter seemed to be more complex. Naturally I do not pretend to give here an authentic interpretation of his meaning. But simply to guard against propagating to others my own rather naïve view expressed above, I will repeat what he briefly told me. Perhaps there is just *one* dog-soul which equally vivifies all dogs, in somewhat the same way as *my* vital principle extends itself to my *growth* of new material. Actually this is just an extension and rationalizing of what happens in the case of the bisected worm. On the other hand, *Sacramentum Mundi* denies that we must hold a vital principle in animals at all.[8]

---

[5] Rahner, *Hominisation*, 63, 81; English edition, pp. 71, 96.

[6] P.-M. de Munnynck, "L'individualité des animaux supérieurs," *Revue Thomiste*, 9 (1901), 639–651.

[7] See pp. 20 and 21 above.

[8] K. Rahner, *Sacramentum Mundi*, to appear in English: see *American Ecclesiastical Review*, 153/4 (Oct. 1965), 219.

It must be made emphatically clear that we are *not* here defending whatever Rahner holds about the individuality and vital principle of living things other than man. On the contrary, we find that the nature of God's creative concursus can be understood only by *forcing* an answer to the question of how it differs in the case of *human* and (if such there be) sub-human individuals.[9]

The eminent Teilhard commentator Pierre Smulders, though in general emphatic in demanding that God's immediate creation of the soul be admitted *both* as a part of Catholic teaching *and* as a thing perfectly compatible with the views of Teilhard, nevertheless explains "man's special creation" to mean "he is willed in and for himself."[10] He bases this view upon certain researches of the Catholic Richard.[11]

But really what they are saying is that there is no difference in the *process* by which a man-soul or a brute-soul owes its being to God's activity.[12] The difference is in the *term*. The human soul is essentially nobler, because it possesses some operations called "intrinsically independent of matter," both during its normal life and even mysteriously after death.

For this reason the human soul's mode of "coming into being," or rather of "dependence upon God's creative infusion of being," *ought* to be designated by a term different from what is used for animals. And on this, Rahner quite explicitly agrees.[13]

In a sense we have been unfaithful and unfair to his essay in thus leaping to his conclusions without following patiently the guarded reasonings by which he leads up to them. But since his book has been in print for some years now, we may assume that no one will pass any verdict on Rahner's stand from what we say here instead of going to verify his own assertions.

It may even be a service both to that author and to the public if the matter is here deliberately approached from a different angle. If it

---

[9] Aloys Müller, "Über den Unterschied der Menschen- und der Tierseele im Zusammenhang mit allgemeineren Fragen," *Theologie und Glaube,* 2 (1910), 387–395, concludes that we cannot admit the disjunction "different either essentially or nonessentially."

[10] Pierre Smulders, *La vision de Teilhard de Chardin* (Paris: Desclée, 1964), 88. In "Valeur et faiblesse théologiques de la synthèse teilhardienne," *Bijdragen,* 21/3 (1960), 277 f, Smulders admits that Teilhard's complexification-consciousness not only leaves place for creation of the soul, but implies it; however, (p. 279) sin and the cross are neglected.

[11] L. Richard, *Le mystère de la Rédemption* (Paris: Desclée, 1959), 229. *The Mystery of the Redemption,* translated by Joseph Horn (Baltimore: Helicon, 1966), also p. 229.

[12] The soul has *no* "nature," spiritual or otherwise! The *whole man* is a Spiritual Being, and is *created by God* in the sense of "unrepeatable," according to José F. Ocampo, "La visión de Teilhard de Chardin según Smulders," *Ecclesiástica Xaveriana,* 14 (1964), 133–137.

[13] Rahner, *Hominisation,* 83; English edition, p. 100.

turns out that we thereby end up imputing to Rahner something which he did not intend to say, it will still be of public interest to know why he would not wish that interpretation to be placed on his words. But a methodical and detailed check has been made with him and led to the conclusion that we are not far from what he meant to say.

2. *The Soul Is Not a Being Distinct From the Body*

In our last citation from Rahner above, we corrected and thereby rejected an expression about the soul's "coming into being." Many theologians today seem to have no hesitation in speaking about "the soul's coming into being" or "the soul's existence." This is unguarded. In a different age, the implications might have been unimportant. They are intolerable in a century so sensitive as ours to accuracy in formulations about biology and existential realities.

The soul as an individual entity does not exist and does not come into being. We doubtless find frightening or boring the metaphysical and dogmatic aspects of "the soul as form of the body."[14] Still, we cannot escape guarding in advance against the smuggling in of any expression which would imply for the soul a degree of individuality or a type of reality which it does not possess.

Like everything which shares Being in any way, the soul owes to God its share in Being. But to ask how God "brought this soul into existence" is to have fallen already victim to some wrong assumptions about what the soul actually is.

Here are a few clarifications on this subject from Rahner's *Hominisation*. In Thomism and the Council of Vienne the intellectual soul is by itself the form and act of indeterminate matter. Materiality is in this perspective not something objectively opposed to spirit, but is a factor (*Moment,* p. 52) of spirit and of its very fulness of being.

This does not mean that Rahner has arrived at, or would even tolerate, the teilhardian notion of spirit as an inner face or mere aspect of matter. Rahner explicitly declares that the spiritual soul in man is no mere aspect (*Erscheinungsform,* p. 23) of that which we call his materiality. Neither is matter just an aspect of spirit. "Each has an underivable possession of being, which can be conceived only as a whole, not as built up in combination out of other like elements." Man's ontological root and basis is "essentially" distinct from matter, and can arise only through a creative innovation.

On the one hand it is all wrong for the scientist to imagine that the only datum of experience is Matter, whereas Spirit is a thing that has to be painfully argued to. If the scientist has the conviction "only that

---

[14] Discussed at the end of chapter 7 above, pp. 223–226.

which *is* can be thought," then he is right; and he can call it Matter, but what he means by that is Being. "The really basically-encountered primitive reality is the relational unity between knowledge and the *a posteriori* self-revealing object." The first immediate datum of experience is my AWARENESS *of an object as external to my*SELF. It is thus from Spirit that we learn what Matter is.[15]

On the other hand, it is all wrong for the Christian to imagine that only that part of man which is not spirit owes its origin to matter in any way. The whole Christian tradition, alongside its insistence on the spirituality and createdness of the soul, also insists that *Man* is made from the earth, not that his "body" is made from the earth (p. 24).

Within the Church from 1850 to 1920 bodily evolution was rejected quite generally as an outright heresy. Yet between 1920 and 1950 the Church's awareness of her deposit had become so clarified that at the end of that period a papal document made it allowable to hold evolution as a theory. "The slow alteration of view took place therefore almost behind the façade of printed theology, a fact which cannot fail to provide food for thought."[16]

The Unity of Man precludes admitting evolution for his body as a price or bribe to bring scientists to concede that evolution will never be postulated for his soul. "Theology cannot hand over the body to science in order to save the soul for herself," says Rahner in at least three different books.[17] "We must therefore reserve for examination in a larger perspective the metaphysical and theological difficulty involved in the ecclesiastical declaration that there is no objection to holding an evolution of the human body, but that it is heretical to extend this to the 'soul.' "[18]

3. *God Really "Intervenes" Only for Salvation*

God has a salvation plan which he has actualized in human history. His interventions in working out this plan are called "miracles," and the information he conveys about himself by this activity is called "revelation." Apart from this *super*-natural salvation plan, wherever *else*

---

[15] Rahner, *Hominisation*, 48; English edition, 52; see above, footnote 71 to p. 32.

[16] Rahner, *Hominisation*, 30; English edition, 29; see above, footnote 8 to p. 37.

[17] *Ibid.*, 22; *Kleines theologisches Wörterbuch* (with H. Vorgrimler; Freiburg: Herder, 1961), 99. In his Editor's Introduction to Paul Overhage, *Um das Erscheinungsbild der ersten Menschen* (Quaestiones Disputatae, 7; Freiburg: Herder, 1959), 13, Rahner qualifies the soul's "immediacy" as "mediated" (*vermittelte Unmittelbarkeit*): "God's creative activity, and the soul in its own self-perfectioning (as *forma*) address themselves to something present in advance . . . the earthly *and* the divine origin must appear in both the soul and the body."

[18] *Hominisation*, 29; whether "heretical" seems applicable here, no matter what be the sense attached to "creation," seems doubtful from our Chapter 7, above.

in the world an effect can be observed, a cause *within* the world must be sought. God's causality is there *too* of course; but it is there as basic to *all* causality in the universe, and not as "a" cause at the side of others.[19]

The above paragraph reflects faithfully the content of page 80 of Rahner's *Hominisation,* as he agreed with me in a discussion some years after it was written. However, his honesty impelled him to add that the problem of miracle is perhaps not quite as easily soluble as it is there made out to be. He has meanwhile published along with Ratzinger an inquiry into "truth and the conquest of modernism."[20] And in Rahner's various essays from which Riesenhuber has gathered everything relating to the sense in which "Christianity is natural," we find candid acknowledgment of the measure of truth contained in efforts made by de Lubac and de Broglie to reformulate the textbook simplifications of the relation between faith, miracle, and nature.[21] Rahner would now like to leave open the possibility that miracle *need not* involve an "intervention" setting aside the laws of nature; and thus that *even* in the case of salvation history God's causality can be explained somewhat as in his cooperation with other secondary causalities.

Though we are anxious that the truth should appear, in whatever area and on whatever occasion, we must admit that this alteration or

---

[19] *Hominisation,* 80. Against J. Röösli's critique rather of Tresmontant than of Teilhard in "Die Idee der Evolution von P. Teilhard de Chardin," *Schweizerische Kirchenzeitung* (1961), 481 + 538, Ladislaus Boros, "Evolution und Metaphysik (eine Entgegnung)," *Orientierung,* 25/22 (Nov. 30, 1961), 239 replies, "God's intervention is one of the most problematical concepts of a metaphysical thought. . . . It must always be represented by a created cause. All reckonings go inerrantly without God, because he is not a reckonable cause," not a moment in world history. The creature *can* achieve more than it is.

[20] Rahner-Ratzinger, "New Testament Theology," *Offenbarung und Überlieferung* (Quaestiones Disputatae 25; Freiburg: Herder, 1965).

[21] Klaus Riesenhuber, "Der anonyme Christ nach Karl Rahner," *Zeitschrift für katholische Theologie* 86 (1964), 286–303 [= *Theology Digest,* 13/3 (1965), 163–171]. For the *Surnaturel,* see now H. Bouillard, "L'idée du surnaturel et le mystère chrétien," *Mélanges H. de Lubac,* 3, 153–166. As set forth by Charles Boyer, "Nature pure et surnaturel dans *Le Surnaturel* du P. de Lubac," *Gregorianum,* 28 (1947), 382, the ordinary view is that reason can prove only the non-repugnance of the beatific vision; for Garrigou-Lagrange, reason can provide a positive argument in its favor; for de Broglie, reason can positively prove its possibility; for de Lubac, reason can prove the *fact:* "the existence of the desire gives certitude that we have been elevated to the supernatural order"; Boyer in "De gratuitate ordinis supernaturalis ad quem homo elevatus est," *Gregorianum,* 29 (1948), 435–463 feels that de Broglie's *De fine ultimo humanae vitae* (Paris: Beauchesne, 1948), has overcome the de Lubac position; see also Philip Donnelly, "Discussion of the Supernatural Order," *Theological Studies,* 9/2 (Apr. 1948), 213–249 and 554–560; Hugo Rahner, "Wege zu einer 'neuen' Theologie?" *Orientierung,* 11 (1947), 213–217; also 14 (1950), 138–141–145, K. Rahner's answer to an anonymous contributor. On the relevance of the *Humani Generis* of Pius XII, see Cardinal Bea's article in *Scholastik,* 26 (1951), 48. See now Eulalio Baltazar, *Teilhard and the Supernatural* (Baltimore: Helicon, 1966); also p. 105 above.

rather diminishing of assurance in Rahner's view has made our present problem more difficult for us. Certainly we do not intend to defend here that miracle and revelation involve no more "intervention" of God than the creation of the human soul. Moreover by instinct and training I personally would like to cling much closer to the traditional interpretation of the First Vatican Council's *de fide* definitions to the effect that divine faith cannot be a reasonable act unless it is based on a logically-prior natural certitude that God in fact has demanded our assent to *this* revelation.[22] At any rate, we may hope to regard this vast and burning problem as *outside* the pale of what concerns us at present; or rather, we hope we may legitimately focus better the problem of the creation of the soul by contrasting it with God's assumed interventions in salvation history, exactly in the sense set forth in the paragraph of Rahner just cited.

God's causality in events *not* pertaining to salvation history is then in any event basic to *all* causality in the universe, and not "a" cause at the side of others. God is the transcendent cause of all reality, but he is not *one link* in any chain of created causality, as if he affected directly only the next-to-last link. "God is for every being equally immediately the condition of its possibility. Hence one and the same identical proof shows the existence of God and the immediate conservation and concursus exercised by God."[23]

---

[22] Teilhard de Chardin follows a similarly conservative line in his early essay, "Les miracles de Lourdes et les enquêtes canoniques," *Études* 118 (1909), 167 ff, taxing scientists with insincerity for not facing the fact of miracles. But in his 1934 "Comment je crois," he says, *"In the old apologetics, the choice of a religion was guided chiefly by the consideration of miracle (a power 'surpassing the forces of nature' guaranteed divine origin). I personally have no difficulty about accepting miracle, provided that it be not (as is required also by Church teaching) contrary to the rules which we are discovering to be ever more numerous and precise in the natural evolution of the world. (This constant upward movement toward the limit of our possibilities defines at the same time miracle and the meaning of Evolution itself; hence I have given up seeing a sundered character equivalent to a rending by God of the seamless veil of phenomena). Miracle rightly understood remains in my eyes a criterion of truth, but subordinate and secondary."* See the observations on this passage by Georges Crespy, *Revue de Philosophie et de Théologie*, 9 (1959), 298. For a most recent Catholic approach, Guy de Broglie, "Les signes de crédibilité et la Révélation chrétienne" (Recherches et débats CCIF; Paris: Fayard, 1964) = *Revelation and Reason*, tr. M. Pontifex (New York: Hawthorn, 1965).

[23] Rahner, *Hominisation*, 58. Says Teilhard, *"God doesn't so much do things as make them do themselves"* (in "Comment se pose aujourd'hui la question du transformisme," 1921, page 39 of *La vision du passé*): on which Émile Rideau, *La pensée du Père Teilhard de Chardin* (Paris: Seuil, 1964), 336 f observes, "The concursus of God and of his creation: . . . God gives at once to exist, to be structured, and to act. . . . This gift implies a permanent concursus." On pages 404, n. 103, and 421, n. 144, Rideau gives parts of a letter of Maréchal to Teilhard on July 3, 1934, criticizing his *Christologie et évolution* from a rather rigidly Aristotelian viewpoint and for not making the cosmic role of Christ inferior to that of sanctifier.

God's part is indispensable everywhere, but (leaving out of account the problem of salvation-plan miracles) is not to be postulated as an explanation of natural events. If we are asked the question "Why is there lightning?" it is against sound metaphysics no less than sound science to answer "Because God made lightning."

"So also," says Rahner's page 59, "must we not say 'Of course God is also cause of the "Soul," because he is by definition cause of everything: cause however in the way that befits him alone, not in such a way that this causing of the soul is to be ascribed to him differently from everything else that at a given moment and place comes into being within the world'?"[24]

4. *Does the Less Then Produce the Greater?*

When we say, therefore, "God creates men's souls immediately," this is not a denial that the parents produce the whole man. Rather it is a clarification that theirs is one of the numerous created causalities in which the agent by his contact with the divine causality really surpasses the limits of his own being (p. 82).

The Scholastic thinker had unhesitating assurance that the life-forms which he held to exist in sub-human "individuals" were "educed from the potency of matter." But thereby he supposed as true that *a creature can produce a new reality,* something more than a mere "regrouping" (p. 63). His alternative to "a new reality" was called "local motion," but that term really covers what today would be called "a re-combining of atoms or molecules."

The "plus" which the Scholastics thus serenely saw introduced by means of the creature's causality could have happened only in virtue of the participation of unlimited being (p. 66). *Similarly the human parents are the cause of the one and whole man, including the soul.* The operation of a creature must be grasped — no differently in this case from those others — as "self-surpassing." The effect cannot be totally traced to the Being of this acting creature, and yet must be reckoned as effected by it (p. 82).

What Rahner here says is in accord with Saint Thomas *Gentes* 3,22, "the ultimate step of all generation is the human soul, and toward this as an ultimate form matter tends."

---

[24] *Hominisation*, English edition, p. 67. Among Rahner's applications of this doctrine to the ethical and sacramental life, see Donald L. Gelpi, *Life and Light: a Guide to the Theology of Karl Rahner* (New York: Sheed and Ward, 1966). Note further Olivier A. Rabut, *Valeur spirituelle du profane: les énergies du monde et l'exigence religieuse* (Paris: Cerf, 1963), 33: to a reader of Teilhard who has reproached Rabut with making too great a distinction between nature and grace, he replies, "Grace *will* be provided on *occasion* of the upward climb of evolution."

"If [1] all becoming is really self-transcendence, even in some cases over to a new being; if [2] this occurs only in virtue of the dynamism of absolute Being, but without destroying the fact that a real *self-*transcendence is involved; and if [3] matter and spirit are not disparate, but matter is to some extent congealed spirit, and only makes sense by rendering Spirit an existing reality: — *then* the evolution of matter into spirit is not an unmanageable concept."[25]

This phenomenon of a finite thing "outdoing itself" is basically identical with the simple experience of transit from potency to act, from less to more. It is precisely *this* which can only be accounted for by the part which divine causality plays within the very structure of the finite causality.

The real function of a doctrine on concursus is thus to explain the datum of *becoming as such* (p. 66). This is true even though Rahner acknowledges that there is in scholastic philosophy a dispute about the exact concept of physical and immediate concursus, as we will take up in the next chapter.

But we may indicate here at once a recent Thomist reaction to this line of thought, specifically put in relation with Teilhard. Corvez holds, "Whether there be question of the totality of the world, of being as such, of the human soul and divine grace, we have seen that the notions of creation, or of 'continued creation,' are applied either not in the same sense or not at all: the basic principle of the distinctions being that the divine motion and production of being are not identical with veritable creation."[26] It is indeed astonishing to learn that creation is not identical with the divine production of being. We are further told that even conservation is *not* an aspect of the creative function, *nor* as immediate. Moreover, every *movement* supposes a subject there to receive it; and it is *qua* created rather than *qua* being that created being cannot be conceived except in the relation of dependence on God.

It is far beyond our competence to evaluate these highly metaphysical thrusts. But it is not beyond our competence to recognize that they *are* metaphysical. Even if it should turn out that Corvez is right and Rahner wrong, it will be on a purely metaphysical terrain, not in the name of revelation. This means that if the support which Rahner gives to Teilhard

---

[25] Rahner, *Hominisation*, 78/92. A recent Protestant effort to defend evolution against a fundamentalism legislated as recently as 1949, S. du Toit, *Progressive Creation* (Potchefstroom, South Africa: Pro-Rege, 1962), 47, protests against reducing God's creative activity to something which happened only once for all at the beginning, and in this perspective sees no need to postulate an "intervention" for creating the soul.

[26] Maurice Corvez, "Création et évolution du monde," *Revue Thomiste*, 64/4 (Oct. 1964), 568, 550 ff; see now his *De la science à la foi: Teilhard de Chardin* (Tours: Mame, 1964).

regarding the creation of the soul is to be rejected, it will be as a matter open to free philosophic discussion outside the realm of dogma.

If we have done justice to Rahner's speculation, and if it is in fact compatible with Scripture and tradition as our preceding chapters have led us to conclude, then Teilhard was not deserving of rebuke for failing to see and state that "the presence of a being capable of reflection" requires "immediate creation of the soul out of nothing" as part of the observed phenomenon. No intervention of Almighty God at the emergence of the soul is needed, *different* from his continuous cooperation with all stages of the evolution inaugurated by him.

If then Teilhard is deserving of any reprehension at all, it is for having yielded to the pressure of censors and inserted those footnotes claiming that the traditional notion of the creation of the soul fits well enough with his analysis of the phenomenon. He was far closer to the truth than they.[27]

---

[27] Efforts have been made to clarify whether it was the Paris archdiocese or his own Jesuit confreres that were more instrumental in preventing the publication of Teilhard's works in his lifetime. Any information on this subject, even if too little and too late, would seem to be of service to the science of theology and the theology of science. And by "information" is not meant such pure inventions as that of G. Bosio, "Il fenomeno umano nell' ipotesi dell' evoluzione integrale," *Civiltà cattolica,* 106–IV (Dec. 10, 1955), 623: the *Phenomenon* was written by Teilhard but "never intended for publication," *mai voluto dare alle stampe;* page 631: "His friends have done a poor service to his memory in publishing this book [without which] there would have been no loss to his prestige, to science, or to the faith." What Teilhard most needed was to be subject to the battering of open public criticism; as E. F. O'Doherty's review of *The Phenomenon* in *Philosophical Studies,* 9 (Dec. 1959), 162–165 says, "Quite honestly, it is not easy to see what all the fuss is about. . . . One wonders how much of the enthusiasm is due to the fact that Teilhard was not allowed to publish his philosophical thought in his own lifetime." And J. Franklin Ewing, "The Human Phenomenon," *Theological Studies,* 22/1 (March 1961), 87: "Whatever the reasons were, [the prevention of publication] had several bad effects. One was that Teilhard was not subjected to the give-and-take of reviewers and critics. . . . Dogmatic theologians and metaphysicians with a cooperative spirit could have corrected certain points and rounded out others." Ewing also claims that Teilhard's passing of his manuscripts to friends outside the Jesuit order for publication after his death is not as compatible with the Jesuit commitment as some confreres had assured Teilhard; there is a further inconclusive exchange on this topic between Robert Francoeur and P. D. Fehlner in *Homiletic and Pastoral Review,* 61/1 (Oct. 1960), 36, 46. Anticlerical R. Teldy Naïm, *Faut-il brûler Teilhard?* (Paris: Calmann-Levy, 1959), 21, praises the Society of Jesus for the loyalty it shows toward its members who are under fire. One effect of the clandestine circulation of Teilhard's often-unsigned writings was to imperil proper attribution of their contents. Max Begouën narrowly averted the publication, among Saint-Exupéry's posthumous works, of a Teilhard manuscript he had lent him, says A. Devaux, *Teilhard et Saint-Exupéry* (Carnets Teilhard, 3; Paris: 1962), 4.

SUMMARY OF THE EIGHTH CHAPTER, "RAHNER'S CREATIVE CONCURSUS"

Hominization is a word used independently by both Teilhard and Rahner to express the theological problem involved in the fact that a *material* being can perform spiritual acts and thus be the subject of *eternal* destiny and supernatural life. Revelation and tradition insist that the matter and spirit of man make a *single* reality owing its *whole* being to God. Theological reasoning has further worked out that the "soul" (or "form of the body") is due to God's immediate creation.

Essentially our problem is to explain how one single immutable eternal act within God can have *differing* effects outside of God. In this light we are on firm ground in saying that the *procedure* by which God produces the human soul differs in no way from the procedure by which he produces the animal soul. Only because the *end result* of his action is so different in the case of "a Personal Being willed in and for himself," there is good reason to reserve for this special event a special name, "immediate creation of the soul out of nothing."

Yet there is also good reason for *not* tolerating the implication that God's creative activity plays no role in the production of each single human "body." (This is especially true for those who hold that all those perceptible qualities which we associate with the term "body" are actually the contribution of the "form," our soul, its "matter" being nothing other than pure indeterminacy.) Also infelicitous is the implication that the *parents* contribute *less* to the total living reality in human than in animal generation; or that the animal soul's "eduction from the potency of matter" is a production of new being in which God is not directly involved.

Rahner's solution is that God's creative power does not appear in nature as *one* cause ranged in its place alongside various others, but God's causality is equally operative in *all* emergence of new beings. This is a revitalized doctrine of concursus. *Every* production of a new being means that the cause outdid itself, "the less produced the greater." This is accounted for by the fact that God as *co-producer* furnishes the Being, the *new* Being, the *plus*.

Human parents do not really produce a human soul, but no one else does either. The soul is not a separate reality, a bird to be put into a cage as Plato thought. There is no soul unless there is a *being*. The parents produce a human *being*. And God produces the human being. Each exerts the causality of its own order. The human parents "outdo themselves" in producing a being with a soul, in the same general way that animal or inorganic agents "outdo themselves" in producing any new being. God is truly and immediately the creator of the human "soul" or life-principle of the living being. Essentially his activity here is the same as in his production of new animal or inorganic being; but the special term "creation" is applied because of the dignity of its end product.

CHAPTER 9

THOMISM ON CONCURSUS
AND THE MOMENT OF INFUSION

The doctrine of concursus, as Rahner was seen to hint, is very shabbily handled in our textbooks. If there is such a thing at all, it is of primary importance throughout the whole of metaphysics. Against it, scarcely a single serious voice is raised. A violent and rather unrefuted attack on concursus by Stufler, echoing Durandus but claiming to give the pure doctrine of St. Thomas, is the sole warrant for recent textbooks' skirting the doctrine as "controverted." It is unclear whether another significant trend inaugurated by Lonergan is relevant here.

Before addressing ourselves to these two very independent Jesuits, it may be opportune to tabulate first the degree of adherence to the doctrine of concursus in the approved authors of the treatise on God as Creator.

1. Survey of Manuals and Monographs

Proximate to Faith in Beraza is the highest note assigned to concursus by any dogmatic theologian. "It is not an express dogma of the faith, but certain, and rash to deny; and the contrary is considered by some to be heretical."[1] In 1895 Pesch seemed to be hinting at some such high note when he said the doctrine is "not *de fide*"; but when he continues

---

[1] Blasio Beraza, *De Deo creante* (Bilbao: Eléxpuru, 1921), 735.

"otherwise held by all except Durandus," he must be interpreted as mean-ing merely "more common," which in the peculiar jargon of theologians means *"less* than common; *not* certain."[2]

Theologically certain is the note assigned by Muldoon and Bozzola.[3]

Universal and irreformable (communis et certa) was claimed by Pohle-Gummersbach in 1952, with full awareness of the opposition of both Durandus and Stufler.[4] Mors also holds concursus to be *communis,* though mentioning it only in a scholion on creation.[5] Hugon fits less explicitly in this perspective by his assertion that it is *error* to deny concursus in natural operations.[6] So also van Noort.[7]

Merely *quite widely held* (communior) is maintained by van Hove to be the proper conclusion from the fact that there are several adversaries of good standing within the Catholic fold.[8] This is virtually the verdict of Daffara, "everyone but Durandus," as we saw in Pesch above.[9]

No note seems to be assigned by Garrigou-Lagrange, Lercher-Schlagen-haufen, or Pignataro.[10] It is surprising that the only mention of concursus in Boyer's 1948 edition is apropos of conservation, referring to an article of his which in fact does not deal with concursus at all.[11]

"Very important" (not a theological note) is the only qualification as-signed by Flick-Alszeghy, along with the observation that concursus would have been treated by Vatican I but unfortunately the schema was not sufficiently well prepared in advance.[12] Though the Flick-Alszeghy thesis is enunciated, "The world depends wholly on God in its being *and opera-tion,"* still in the analysis of Scripture which precedes, there is no attention to the *operation.*

---

[2] Christian Pesch, *Praelectiones dogmaticae 3. De Deo creante* (Freiburg: Herder, 1895), 29.

[3] T. Muldoon, *De Deo creante* (Rome: Catholic Book Agency, 1959), 233; Carlo Bozzola, *De Deo uno et trino, creante et elevante* (Naples: d'Auria, 1948), 182.

[4] Josef Gummersbach, *Pohle: Lehrbuch der Dogmatik*[10] (Paderborn: Schöningh, 1952), 1, 511.

[5] José Mors, *Institutiones 2. De Deo creante* (Petropolis: Vozes, 1940), 70.

[6] Édouard Hugon, *De Deo uno et trino, creatore et gubernatore* (Paris: Lethiel-leux, 1933), 537.

[7] G. van Noort, *Tractatus de Deo creatore*[3] (Bussum: Brand, 1920), 34.

[8] Aloysius van Hove, *Tractatus de Deo creante et elevante* (Malines: Dessain, 1944), 105.

[9] Marcolino Daffara, *De Deo Creatore* (Turin: Marietti, 1947), 78; "at least morally certain," J. Sagüés, *BAC Summa 2,* 568.

[10] Reginald Garrigou-Lagrange, *The Trinity and God the Creator* (Saint Louis: Herder, 1952); L. Lercher, [3]F. Schlagenhaufen, *De Deo uno et trino, creante et elevante* (Innsbruck: 1940); F. Pignataro, *De Deo creatore* (Rome: 1904).

[11] Charles Boyer, *De Deo creante*[4] (Rome: Gregorian, 1948), 118; "Providence et liberté dans un texte de saint Thomas," *Gregorianum* 19/2 (June 1938), 194–209. Boyer's textbook refers also to his *De gratia*[2] (1946), 271.

[12] Maurizio Flick, Zoltan Alszeghy, *Il Creatore: l'inizio della salvezza*[2] (Florence: Fiorentina, 1961), 33; *Collationes Lacenses,* 7, 99.

The only theologian's effort to supply this exegetical documentation is that of Teixidor.[13]

He gives in first place John 5:17, "my Father works even until now, and I work," as referred by Augustine to "not only static but dynamic conservation."[14] Neither Teixidor nor Maldonado as cited by him adverts to the fact that God's working "now" (even on the Sabbath) may be taken equally as asserting the *eternity* of God's *First* creation.

Other texts not more convincingly set forth by Teixidor are Psalms 103; 144:14; 145 f; Matthew 6:30 and 10:29; Job 10:8 ff.

Acts 17:28 is given the interpretation favored by Bellarmine: "It would have been enough to say, 'In him we live and have our being,' if God only gave and conserved our nature and powers of acting, but did not work together with us. But the word 'move' was there inserted to make clear that we can no more move without the present help of God, than we can be or live without his conservation."[15]

With very little help from traceable sources of revelation, therefore, our problem turns out to be whether the opinion of Durandus and Stufler enjoys sufficient probability, either internally or as acknowledged by "several" contemporary authorities, to diminish our assurance that concursus is a certain tenet of natural reason and/or a traditional doctrine of the Catholic faith.

The fact that just in this particular moment, concursus lends itself to being "exploited" toward radical reappraisal of another Catholic doctrine, on soul-creation, does not really excuse us from assessing the ecclesiastical status of concursus in itself with complete objectivity.

2.   What CAN Act, Really Can ACT

Stufler's negation of concursus revolves about a point which is worthy of our most sympathetic consideration. If we say a thing *can* act, then go on to say that an outside thing *must* help along when it *does* act, this means it was only double-talk in the first place to say the thing really *can* act.

In more technical terms, we say that in virtue of its creation and conservation by God, the self-moving creature possesses the *possibility* and genuine *capacity* of immanent action. And yet something essential is lacking, right up to the moment of completing the action, if God's actual cooperation is required.

To say "able *now*" does not mean "able *if and when* an element is supplied which is not *present*."

---

[13] Luis Teixidor, "Del concurso inmediato de Dios en todas las acciones y efectos de sus criaturas," *Estudios Eclesiásticos*, 7/1 (Jan. 1928), 5–23; 7/2 (Apr. 1928), 146–160; 8/3 (July 1929), 332–362; 9/3 (July 1930), 321–350; 11/2 (Apr. 1932), 190–227; 11/3 (July 1932), 289–322.

[14] Augustine, *ML* 34, 335.   [15] Robert Bellarmine, *Grace and Freedom*, 4, 4.

What answer can be given to Stufler? Here is one attempt: "Nothing can enrich its own reality. But to-actually-act is something over and above to-be-able-to-act." This formulation is cited by Manya only to be rejected.[16] And doubtless this way of looking at things has something of the absurdity of Zeno's claim that man can never walk because before he can cover a full step he will have to cover a half-step, and before that a quarter-step and so on infinitely.

To-actually-act is indeed something over and above to-be-able-to-act; but it is *not* a something for which an additional enrichment of reality is required. Hence Manya ends up *rejecting* the need of immediate concursus, at least in the form in which it was taught by nineteenth-century theologians Liberatore, Zigliara, and Lercher.

"Being active is an aspect of being created itself" is the title of an approach to this problem by De Coninck. *Every* being is active, and its activity is not a thing separate from its being. Thus any talk at all of creaturely causality as "secondary" is misleading. Three different possibilities of "a push from God" are enumerated; but they all come down to this, that the creature is already active insofar as it is being — but of course in dependence upon God.[17]

Superficially at an opposite extreme, but at root identical, is De Raeymaeker's denial that there is any proper causality in second causes at all.[18] Thus "the divine cooperation in the action of second causes is simply the conservation of the created agent in faithfulness to its law."[19]

The Stufler position, which these reflect, was originally expressed in a doctorate thesis entitled, "The Teaching of Saint Thomas Aquinas on God operating in every operation of nature especially where free will is involved."[20] As the title shows, it was a plunge into the turbid waters of sixteenth-century Jesuit versus Dominican passion over how God's universal governance and foreknowledge is to be reconciled with the freedom of man's will.

A storm of comment can be seen in the various theological periodicals of the years following Stufler's publication of his thesis in 1923.[21] He

---

[16] Juan Manya, *De Deo Cooperante* (Theologumena 1; Dertosa, Alguero, 1946).

[17] A. de Coninck, "Creari et moveri convertuntur," *Collectanea Mechlinensia,* 17 (1928), 641–656. But see A. Gazzana, "Come le cause create producono l"esse simpliciter' dei loro effetti," *Divus Thomas Piacenza,* 18 (1941), 417 f.

[18] L. De Raeymaeker, *Philosophie de l'Être²* (Louvain: Institut Supérieur de Philosophie, 1947), 329.

[19] Joseph de Finance, *Être et agir dans la philosophie de S. Thomas* (Paris: Beauchesne, 1945), 230.

[20] Johann Stufler, *Divi Thomae Aquinatis doctrina de Deo operante in omni operatione naturae creatae praesertim liberi arbitrii* (Innsbruck: Tyrolia, 1923).

[21] Beside Martin and Lange cited below: B. Geyer in *Philosophisches Jahrbuch,* 37 (1924), 339–359; G. Huarte in *Gregorianum,* 6 (1925), 82–114; Reginald Schultes in *Divus Thomas Fribourg,* 3 (1925), 361; 1 (1923), 123–145; F. Žigon, *Divus Thomas arbiter controversiae de concursu divino* (Gorizia: 1925).

gathered up some of these criticisms in an article four years later.[22] Then in 1936 he published a restatement of his position under the title "God the First Mover of All Things."[23]

Since he here assigns chief weight precisely to those contentions which the intervening years had shown to be most vulnerable, we may limit our observations to this volume.

3.   A Key Text and Some Objections

Stufler's initial argumentation had been wholly taken up with showing that Saint Thomas denied the necessity of immediate concursus. If a thing *can* act, then it can *act!*

You may say if you wish that every action of a non-living being, perhaps even every action of a non-free being, is rather a passivity, and comes from the agent which generated the being rather than from the being itself.[24] But Stufler rightly acknowledges that God must not be inserted as first in a chain of natural causes.

The key text from Aquinas is *On Truth* 24:14: "God is the cause of natural operation insofar as he is the giver and conserver of that which within the thing is the principle of natural operation." At several points Stufler declares that our insistence on God's creation and especially *conservation* is sufficient guarantee that the *Being* in any operation is caused only by the First Cause.

In this position, from the standpoint of commonsense logic rather than the grounding in theological metaphysics as a specialty which would be required for speaking authoritatively here, I wish to note what seem to be three weaknesses:

a. Stufler's own paraphrase of Saint Thomas is carried away by rhetoric into denying (just after he has affirmed) the conservation itself as well as the concursus. "God called the cosmos of natural agents out of nothing into being; he upholds them continuously and keeps them in being . . . but the becoming and happening in this cosmos takes place exactly in the manner in which it would take place if — to take the impossible case as possible — there were no creator at the side of the creatures."[25]

---

[22] J. Stufler, "Ergebnisse der Kontroverse über die thomistische Konkurslehre," *Zeitschrift für katholische Theologie*, 51 (1927), 329–369; cf. 47 (1923), 533–564; 49 (1925), 62–86, 186–218.

[23] J. Stufler, *Gott der erste Beweger aller Dinge* (Philosophie und Grenzwissenschaften, 6/3; Innsbruck: Rauch, 1936). This is *not* the little booklet of Stufler translated by E. Sutcliffe, *Why God Created the World, or the purpose of the creator and of creatures, a study in the teaching of St. Thomas Aquinas* (Stanbrook Abbey: 1937). Nothing of the concursus controversy seems to have been hitherto available in English. Stufler's view that the creature can produce being of itself is favored by E. Iglesias, *De Deo in operatione naturae vel voluntatis operante* (Mexico: 1946) = *Ciencia y Fe*, 7 (1945), 84–106; cf. 9 (1947), 34–57; 11 (1949), 44–46.

[24] Aquinas: *Gentes*, 2, 47; *De Veritate*, 5, 9, 4; *2 Physics*, 10.

[25] Stufler, *Gott der erste Beweger* (1936), 21.

b. Saint Thomas himself in that passage of the treatise on Truth goes on to add an example which relates only to local motion and not even to the production of new being. "God is the cause of natural operation insofar as he is the giver and conserver of that which within the thing is the principle of natural operation, from which principle necessarily follows a determinate act, as when he conserves gravity on earth, which is the principle of movement downwards."

Stufler says, "This passage is so clear and unambiguous that even de Lemos, O.P., admits that according to Aquinas all nonfree secondary causes are 'moved' by God through the mere giving and conserving of their powers."[26]

Today we would say that in falling a body merely continues in that state of moving which had been impeded by an obstacle outside itself. Doubtless the two-way attraction which we call gravity has something in common with the same molecular activity which produces new beings. But it is difficult to see how on the sub-vital level these new beings are more than mere reassembling of components by local motion. For Rahner indeed this is possibly true even on the level of sub-human life; and for most biochemists today, even on the level of human life.

c. The Being which Stufler admits to be due to God's causality without concursus is explained as a thing so utterly indeterminate that it is rather in the line of potency than of act, like prime matter.[27] Anyway, the being which God produces via secondary causes is not *per se* but *per accidens,* since there was already being *there.* When a man makes a green thing red, red is caused *per se;* but color is caused only *per accidens,* since the thing already had a color. This distinction seems to be less convincing than most of those in Saint Thomas, since it implies that "color" *remains,* while green "goes" and red "comes"; but what actually happens is that "red color" comes, while "green color" either goes or is simply covered up. Since St. Thomas was not thinking of wave-or-particle-motion from the colored surface, it is useless to salvage his example by saying that "motion" remains, but only its speed or cycle is varied.

Stufler apparently does not welcome being classed with Durandus on the concursus issue. He claims that Durandus has *two* adversaries in view when speaking of concursus.[28] Aquinas is *not* there attacked for holding immediate concursus, but rather for evading the issue. The adversary

---

[26] *Ibid.,* 19; Thomas de Lemos, *Panoplia Gratiae* (Leodio: Landas, 1676), 3, 1, 1.

[27] *Ibid.,* 70. On page 75 this objection is in fact faced, citing *Summa Theologiae,* 1, 65, 3 and *Separated Substances,* 10; on the colors, *Gentes,* 21.

[28] Durand de Saint-Pourçain, *Commentarius in libros Sententiarum* (1310), Book 2, 1, 5. Ninety-one propositions of this work were condemned as anti-Thomist by a Dominican board in 1314; see J. Koch, *Durandus de S. Porciano* (Münster: 1927).

whom Durandus opposes for holding immediate concursus is Giles of Rome.[29]

A reviewer objected that the Durandus-Stufler position of purely mediate concursus is basically that adopted by those who before Peter Lombard's time denied that God could concur with sinful acts.[30] To this Stufler answers that the error of these people lay rather in denying to God *any* authorship of the act, even mediate. And this is tantamount to saying that they denied that God even *created* man, as Olivi in fact retorted to these pre-Lombardites.

Stufler rests his case of rightly interpreting Saint Thomas chiefly on the above mentioned passage *On Truth* 24,14. Two other passages which seem to support Stufler's view, really are saying that the fact of God's concursus does not remove or do violence to true secondary causality.[31]

The classic statement of Saint Thomas invoked *in favor* of concursus is in the *De Potentia* 3,7.[32] It is there said that God is in *four* ways cause of all creaturely activity: (a) he *gives* the power of acting; (b) he *conserves* it; (c) he *applies* it as principal cause; (d) he uses secondary causes as his instruments.

This fourth "way" has a sinister ring, and doubtless disposes Stufler's partisans to agree that Thomas does not here mean exactly what he seems to mean.

But Lange, a Jesuit confrère whose review is claimed by Dörholt to praise Stufler far too much, cites against him the further passage in the *De Potentia* 7,2 ad 9: "Being (*esse*) is the actuality of all acts, and is therefore the perfection of all perfections. This is not to be understood in the sense that to that which I call *esse* something more formal is added, determining it as act determines potency. *Esse* is not determined by another thing as potency is determined by act, but rather as act is determined by potency."[33]

The Thomist Martin cites numerous texts in which God is said to be cause not only of being *in communi* but also of that whereby the common

[29] Giles of Rome, *Essence and Being*, 4; Stufler, *Gott der erste Beweger* (1936), 111; Louis Rasolo, *Le dilemme du concours divin: primat de l'essence ou primat de l'existence* (Analecta Gregoriana 30; Rome: 1956) 30; L. Becker, *À propos de l'influence de Dieu dans l'opération des créatures* (Annales de Philosophie, 3; Louvain: 1914).

[30] L. Teixidor, *Estudios Eclesiásticos*, 8 (1929), 352; Stufler, *Gott der erste Beweger* (1936), 109.

[31] Aquinas, *Fourth Sentences*, 49, 1, 3, 1; *De Caritate*, 1.

[32] V. Frins, "Concours divin," *Dictionnaire de Théologie Catholique* (Paris: Letouzey, 1923), 3, 782. The long inquiry of Bishop T. Muldoon, *De Deo Creante* (Rome: Catholic Book Agency, 1959), 216–234, concludes that for St. Thomas concursus is "a certain created force like a quality, by which God as principal cause moves the creature as instrumental cause for the performance of its proper action."

[33] H. Lange, *Theologische Revue*, 23 (1924), 346 ff; so also *Summa Theologiae*, 1, 3, 4; 1, 4, 1 ad 3; B. Dorhölt, *Divus Thomas Fribourg*, 6 (1928), 236.

nature is determined.[34] Stufler thinks this objection is answered by recognizing in it the confusion between two things that are in fact distinct: "God's Activity" and "God's *proper* activity."

A kindred objection is formulated thus: "If the character of the First Cause demands that its causality extend to everything that in any way is found among created perfections, then its proper working is not merely being *in communi* but the determinate being; and if this is the case, then there is nothing more for second causes to add." To this Stufler replies, "The objection confuses two concepts. For God to be First Cause of all being requires that every *proper* operation of the *second* cause be also God's *operation* and reducible to his causality — but not that this be in God a *proper* operation."

In summary, it cannot be denied that there is a strong dose of common sense in Stufler's basic position that "to be able to act" means *to possess already what is required for the action* and not to be still in need of a further help from outside. On the other hand the very nature of Being is such, and the nature of God's communication of Being is such, that wherever there is in any way a new production of Being, God's creative influx must be immediately involved. Despite Stufler's own claim to the contrary, he would seem to be envisioning God's activity as one in a continuing series of causalities, rather than as a power in a different order, parallel and immediately present to all created causality.

4.   *Lonergan's Work on God's Cooperation*

The influential book of Bernard Lonergan seems to be backing up Stufler — and falling into the same tender trap — when it says that God's concursus consists simply in the fact that he is the first agent of all occurrences.

But Lonergan rightly insists, and sees the problem solved in this fact, that God is first agent of all these occurrences *now,* not at some time in the past distinct from the moment of the act whose concursus is in question.

> Only the cause of the order of the universe can be the sufficient ground for the occurrence of any event; further, since every development and every emergence depends upon a complex of events, only the cause of the order of the universe can be the sufficient ground for any development or emergence. It follows, further, that God applies every contingent agent to its operation. For the agent operates in accord with the pattern of world order when the conditions of operation are fulfilled; but the condi-

---

[34] Stufler, *Gott der erste Beweger,* 95, 75; Raymond Martin, *Pour saint Thomas et les Thomistes contre le R. P. Jean Stufler, S.J., dans le débat touchant l'influx de Dieu sur les causes sécondaires* (Saint-Maximin: École de Théologie, 1926) = *Revue Thomiste,* 29 (1924), 579–595; 30 (1925), 167–186, 567–578; 31 (1926), 73–85.

tions are fulfilled when other events occur; and God is the first agent of each of those occurrences. Moreover, it follows that every created agent is an instrument in executing the divine plan; for its operation is the fulfillment of a condition for other events; and so it is used by a higher agent for an ulterior end. Finally, it follows that God by his intelligence moves all things to their proper ends; for God causes every event and applies every agent and uses every operation inasmuch as he is the cause of the order of the universe. [Bañez and Molina both] ascribe divine control of all events to the fact that God by a peculiar activity controls each. But on the above analysis God controls each event because he controls all, and he controls all because he alone can be the cause of the order of the universe on which every event depends.[35]

Lonergan at that point refers the reader to his 1942 articles on God's cooperating grace. But it is not easy to see how his clarifications there are applicable in the "purely natural" order and apart from free will.[36]

And this is not only true of Lonergan. We might deplore that almost all the numerous treatments of concursus are actuated by a concern for solving a problem — or defending a position antecedently imposed by non-academic intramural authorities, as in the case of the Jesuits — on the *De auxiliis* controversy relating free will to the divine governance.

Praemotio is a term which has not entered into my above explanations. Friends have remonstrated that only this term can lay down an adequate antecedent framework of God's action always "logically and ontologically, though not temporally, *prior*" to any act of creatures. *Praemotio* would thus eliminate "the assumption that God acts contemporaneously with his creatures. If we use the term *praemotio,* as Thomists do, then it must be understood without time. And if we understand it this way, then the term *concursus* becomes unnecessary. The only distinction between *praemotio* and concursus is one which we *imagine in God,* according as we imagine him before time and during time." To my failure to see the genuinely *metaphysical* implications of *praemotio* are ascribed ambiguities in understanding "secondary" causality, "continued creation," and the precise increase of reality which *"actually* acting" involves over "being *able* to act."

This aid is welcomed in loyally putting before the reader every really relevant evidence, even evidence that this chapter is ill-founded. My acceptance of the peculiar type of divine priority called premotion

---

[35] Bernard J. F. Lonergan, *Insight, a Study in Human Understanding* (New York: The Philosophical Library, 1957), 664. Privately Lonergan has assured me that his only objection to concursus lies in regarding it as an answer to Durandus wrongly interrogating Aquinas, "Besides existing and creating, what *more* did God have to do for this specific act?" But he sees no difficulty in holding that the concursus which we here require, and which we feel suffices to explain the origin of the human soul, is simply God's present eternal creative act.

[36] B. Lonergan, "St. Thomas' Thought on *Gratia Operans,*" *Theological Studies,* 2/3 (Sept. 1941), 289–324; 3/1 (Feb. 1942), 69–88; 3/4 (Dec. 1942), 533–578.

is impeded chiefly by the normal English or Latin usage of both *prae* and *prior* implying time and negating contemporaneous. God's action is admittedly not "contemporaneous" as if to imply that God is *within* time as creatures are. Yet God is equally *present* to every moment of the action of creatures who are within time. What is called *"pre*-motion" is really explained as "a non-temporal *superior* moving, a *transcendent* moving, or a *hyper*-motion" of creatures to their goals. And if this is precisely what is meant by concursus, then a *con*-compound seems in some ways preferable to a *pre*-compound for expressing it.

5. *Some Questionable Formulas*

If we have to choose, rather than a clear forceful inaccuracy we would of course prefer a vague indecisiveness. Such an elusive formula has at least the merit of leaving a way open toward the truth, or embodying the truth in concealed form. Such must perhaps be our judgment on this thoughtful but evasive paragraph:

> Whatever may be the manner in which we study scientifically the genesis of the human being, it is a waste of effort to try to decipher empirically a fact such as the appearance of the spiritual soul. For precisely the fact of the appearance of the spiritual soul is recognizable only from within, so to speak, when, already present, it manifests itself with evidence either through the act of consciousness of the subject, or through the modes of behavior which translate it unmistakably to the outside. Thus the soul of each human being experiences and allows itself to recognize its own spirituality only subsequently to its awakening within the individual. Neither its appearance in being nor the initial instant of its activity can be the object of an experimental inventory. It is the same, and for a still greater reason, when we go back to the original source of humanity. From the descriptive point of view, the naturalist attains only retrospectively a fact which seems to be produced quite "naturally" with precision at an indeterminable moment in time. The scholastic theologians were well acquainted with the discussions on the animation of the fetus and their insolubility from the point of view of physiological science. That does not prevent them in any way from acknowledging the intervention of divine causality creative of the human soul on account of its immateriality, an immateriality recognized quite otherwise than by a genetic method of differentiation. . . . The theology of St. Thomas states in principle that the generative act of the parents has to do only with the sensitive soul, the particular creative action of God calling forth from the midst of the human being the dimensions of a spiritual consciousness.[37]

Anything we would *like* to believe, but cannot prove, we can always say is not a fact but a *dimension* of our thought. Who can disprove it?

Here is another formula which we find "encouragingly frustrating." It

---

[37] Dominique Dubarle, "Theology of the cosmos," in A.-M. Henry, *God and his Creation* (Dubuque Priory, 1958), 303.

expressly espouses both the "occasionalism" which we found sinister above, and the creative concursus of Rahner:

> We do not see why the human organism itself may not also enter into the scheme of evolution understood in this way, and constitute its highest point. Doubtless, here the generative activity of the immediate ancestor of man would have as its function merely the disposing of the material cause of the human organism for the reception of the form which is to give it its internal unity, and this action would attain its term only by a special Divine concursus, like that required by the production of every natural species. . . . This special Divine concursus, activating in certain beings some virtualities which the latter could not exercise unaided, would manifestly be distinct from the ordinary Divine concursus cooperating with the natural activities of secondary causes, but, even so, it should not be regarded as a sort of intrusion or interference with nature, making the production of new species a sort of miracle or new creation: on the contrary, it would be exercised in accordance with the natural exigencies of the production of species by way of evolution, and in that sense we could describe it as "natural" though not as "ordinary."[38]

The above analysis adopts the formula *"special* concursus" for one which is *natural* and takes place in the emergence of any new species. It would seem both likely and undesirable that this ground for distinguishing "special" from "ordinary" concursus will be confused with a somewhat different use of those terms preempted at least ten years earlier. The DTC article by Frins, whether or not compatible with the Brisbois line of thought, has the doubtful merit of making up a new term to describe the problem and then acting as if that solved the problem.

Frins so defines universal and special concursus that there is no difference between them except what he calls a "supposition." The supposition is that in the case under consideration (the human soul), an immediate divine intervention is indispensable. To give his case its due, we may presume that by "supposition" he means here a thing which has been *proved.* However, he falls into the snare of saying or at least seeming to say that the production of the human soul is a *miracle:* a thing which no theologian would tolerate.

"The question of concursus in general treats only of created causes producing their fully connatural effects. If by hypothesis the creation in its order was lacking in any of the elements making it fully capable of producing its act, there would be need of a particular intervention of the divine omnipotence, that special action which produces miracle."[39]

---

[38] Edmond Brisbois, "Transformisme et philosophie," *Nouvelle Revue Théologique,* 59/7 (July 1932), 591 f, 577–595; given in English in E. Messenger's *Theology and Evolution* (London: Sands, 1949).

[39] V. Frins, "Concours divin," *Dictionnaire de Théologie Catholique* (1923), 3, 782.

To say that concursus is a continued creation may be a bit sloganized. We have seen Corvez objecting to it, and also to the claim that creation is to be equated with infusion of being.[40] But all experts will recognize that the slogan of "continuing creation" has become deeply intrenched within Christian theologizing.

God's proper causality applies to the transit from non-being to being, not only as regards initial existence, but also as regards each subsequent action or modification of the existent. But, warns my colleague Francis Wade of Marquette University, "this second causality of God is not to us the same as the first. The second causality presupposes the existing effect of the first. It seems unjustified to identify creation (as in the effect) with concursus (as in the effect). And that is all that such terms can mean. In God his causality has no distinguishable features, nor is his causality distinct from himself, as ours is. But this mystery in God is no help to us when we are trying to explain different effects in nature," such as the immediacy of God's production of the human or animal soul.

It would be rash to oppose the judgment of modern experts like Stufler and Lonergan, at least to the extent of claiming that concursus as a metaphysical problem has been definitely solved.

But the shoe pinches both ways. As long as second causality in general remains somewhat mysterious, there seems to be no cogent reason for not investigating serenely and independently other problems such as the origin of the soul. If solutions commended by twentieth-century chemistry and theology force concursus into a better light than metaphysics alone sheds upon it, then metaphysics will be the grateful gainer.

We have admittedly an ulteriorly motivated, but not therefore unfounded, basis for maintaining the Catholic theologian's obligation of defending concursus. It is every bit as solidly intrenched in the tradition of the Church as is the immediate creation of the soul. But concursus is at the same time more congenial to the perspectives of an evolution-centered science.

Hence, subtly or unconsciously perhaps, the anti-evolutionary theologian may find himself benignly disposed to ignore or eventually renounce concursus, while fighting for the creation of the soul on the ground that it is Catholic tradition. Is he not perhaps thereby fighting a dogged last-ditch battle to resist evolution on every front where success can be hoped for — and when it can no longer be rationally hoped, then as Rahner says "handing over the body to science if theology can keep the soul" for its good old static creationism?

Not that it was the opponents of evolution who in fact excogitated the twentieth-century attack on concursus. Stufler and his supporters set out

---

[40] M. Corvez, "Création et évolution du monde," *Revue Thomiste*, 64 (1964), 550–568, cited in footnote 26 to chapter 8 above, p. 237.

from an entirely different point of departure, and were actuated by motives of the most progressive order.

The danger is that their innovation may be evaluated, not with that serene objectivity which it deserves, but uncritically as a *deus ex machina*. It could be used to discredit what must otherwise seem an altogether Catholic explanation of the immediacy and creativeness of God's intervention in the emergence of the human vital principle.

6. *Moment of Infusion of the Soul*

The extended citation from Dubarle above pointed to a historical connection between the problem of defining or defending concursus, and a quite different type of objection against our view of soul-creation. It would seem that this view of ours is too wedded to the nineteenth-century assurance that the intellectual soul is present in the human organism from the very instant of conception.

Actually I think that assurance is justified. But I also think that Rahner's essential proposals would be unaffected if it could be proved that the intellectual soul "emerges" only at an advanced stage in the development of the embryo.

At any rate, we must set in perspective here the genuine or equal "theological probability" that the living individual becomes animated by an intellectual soul only in the fifth or tenth week of its existence.

Dr. Ernest Messenger, the intrepid promoter of Catholic evolutionism, was fiercely in favor of this view. Moreover it was the view of Saint Thomas; though, concerning the biological information and assumptions on which he was basing himself, "the less said the better."

Messenger rightly sees that Aquinas lays down in this regard some norms of conciliability with theological tradition, and that their validity is not bound up with that of the biological information. Moreover, even as rational philosophers, we are greatly intrigued by an incidental question which for the anti-vitalist biology of our day is of no concern whatever: namely *whether* and *whose* "Life" is present in the sperm and ovum before, during, and after the instant of their union.

Messenger gives unqualified support to the view that the spermatozoon as well as the ovum before union has a life of its own distinct from that of the parent.[41]

This is maintained also in an article of Chollet, which unhesitatingly draws this conclusion: Therefore *each* of these unassociated gametes has a principle of life, a soul.[42]

---

[41] Ernest Messenger, *Theology and Evolution* (London: Sands, 1949), 230. This book is in large part a compilation from other authorities favorable to his earlier *Evolution and Theology* (London: Burns Oates, 1931).

[42] A. Chollet, "Animation," *Dictionnaire de Théologie Catholique* (Paris: Letouzey, 1923), 1, 1317.

This is qualified by Messenger: but not a *rational* soul; they are not two separate human beings. And the name rational is denied them not merely because only through *union* can they become human, since it is at least theoretically possible that by some artificially-induced parthenogenesis, either one separately could divide and grow into a man, if only it were located in a suitable milieu.

An eminent moral theologian maintains, "When the sexual gametes are united, there does not seem to be so great or so radical a change that the composite ought to be said to live already by a rational soul. Each element when separated lived with its own principle of life, which was not a rational soul. A similar life-principle seems to account for their life when united."[43]

Rahner too maintains that the gamete is "not simply and from every viewpoint merely a piece of the parent-organism."[44] He is also favorably impressed by the relevant contribution of Sauser to the Festschrift in his honor.[45] Biologists distinguish ontogenesis, or evolution of the individual, from phylogenesis, or evolution of the species. They maintain that the ontogenesis of the individual *repeats* the phylogenesis of the tribe. Thus the self-transcendence in *any* new production can occur by *steps,* as in the old scholastic view.

Another and quite differently oriented dogmatic theologian maintains as "beyond doubt that not only the fecundated ovum but also the seed and the ovum before union are animated by the same kind of true life."[46]

Messenger makes his own this teaching of Saint Thomas: The animal soul is caused to supersede the vegetative soul by the efficiency of the same "form-making power, *virtus formativa"* out of the parent-soul, by which the vegetative soul itself was formed.[47] The soul is not created, according to St. Thomas, until the body has the disposition and organization necessary to make it a specifically *human* body. It is the *form* of *this* body.

---

[43] Benedikt Merkelbach, *Quaestiones de embryologia et de administratione baptismatis* (Liège: Pensée Catholique, 1937); Hyacinthus-M. Hering, "De tempore animationis foetus humani," *Angelicum,* 28/1 (Jan. 1951), 18–29.

[44] Karl Rahner, *Das Problem der Hominisation* (Quaestiones Disputatae, 12; Freiburg: Herder, 1961), 79.

[45] G. Sauser, "Mediko-Theologisches," in Festgabe K. Rahner, *Gott in Welt* (Freiburg: Herder, 1961), 2, 850.

[46] B. Beraza, *De Deo creante* (Bilbao: 1921), 537.

[47] E. Messenger, *Theology and Evolution* (1949), 251, citing Aquinas, *Second Sentences,* 18, 2, 1, 3; *Gentes,* 2, 88; *Potentia,* 3, 9–12; *Summa Theologiae,* 1, 118, 1–3. — Note the further statement of Saint Thomas in *Gentes,* 3, 22, "The ultimate end of the whole process of generation is the human soul, and to it matter tends as toward its final form." It is interesting that Aquinas says here "the human *soul"* rather than the human *being.* C. Vollert, "Evolution of the Human Body," *Proceedings of the Catholic Theological Society,* 6 (1951), 132 = *Catholic Mind,* 50 (1952), 144: "St. Thomas perceived no difficulty in admitting the succession of forms in the human embryo."

With Dorlodot, Messenger denounces as a picayune scholastic apriorism the trick of "showing somebody an ovule and asking if it is a human body."[48] But it is a question we cannot help feeling a yearning to know the answer to.

A misplaced Scripture proof. Alphonsus Liguori declared it to be both morally and scripturally wrong to hold that the fetus is animated in the first moment of conception.[49]

As for the moral part, we may note that an opinion of Busenbaum following Saint Thomas, that male conception is completed the fortieth day and female the eightieth, was adopted by the Vatican congregation concerned with administering the sacrament of penance, as basis of their decision in certain cases regarding canonical irregularity under Gregory XV.[50]

A directly contrary "moral" conclusion, however, was drawn by Pius XII in an address to the Family Front in 1951. He expressly alluded to those penal consequences of former Vatican juridicists; but went on to show that it is forbidden for the obstetrician to act on any assumption that the human being is not fully present from the first moment of conception.[51]

We are still bound by Canon 747, which restricts the baptism of certain fetuses by adding the condition "si certo vivant." However, this can plausibly be taken as meaning, "if this unusual growth is really a human being, possessed of rational life."

As for the Scriptural proof invoked by Saint Alphonsus: The Septuagint renders Exodus 21:22, "If two men while fighting strike a pregnant woman, and her child comes out 'without having received its form,' a fine shall be imposed; (23) but if it 'had received its form,' *he* shall give soul for soul; (24) an eye for an eye, a tooth for a tooth."

In the Hebrew text, instead of "her child comes out," we have "her children come out." And the expression which the Greek translators rendered *mē ex-eikon-isménon,* "without having received its form," really means "without damage." The word for damage is in Hebrew *asōn,* for which the Greek translators could hardly have misread *sělěm, mar'eh, dimyōn,* or other word for the Greek *eikōn* "image, form."

Thus only in the hypothesis that the Septuagint was independently inspired could there be foundation in Scripture for a dogmatic or biological assertion regarding the moment of infusion of the "soul as form."

---

[48] E. Messenger, *Theology and Evolution,* 297.

[49] Alphonsus Liguori, *Theologia Moralis,* Book 3, 4, 1 #394 (ed. L. Gaudé, Rome: Vatican, 1905), p. 648, citing also Busenbaum; St. Thomas, *Third Sentences,* 3, 5, 2.

[50] William Reany, *The Creation of the Human Soul* (London: Ouseley, 1929), 195.

[51] Francis Hürth, *De re matrimoniali: allocutiones Pii XII* (Rome: Gregorian, 1955).

We may reasonably ask common sense and science, "When is there really a *human body* there in the womb?" And their answer may well be, "After eighty days." But in asking "When does the *soul* inform the *body?*", we are using body in a *hylemorphic* sense that has nothing to do with biological structure. We are asking, "When does the substantial form of this individual inform (prime) matter?" And to this question the biologist will exhibit a sublime indifference.

7. Can the Being Make Its Own Structure?

Bishop MacDonald holds, as does Messenger, that the intellectual soul can only animate matter which has already a structure proportioned to operations that are distinctively human. It would seem that a thoroughly adequate answer to this was given by Austin O'Malley. "If the *anima intellectiva* is not present in the primordial cell solely because its formal facultative action is not needed, that soul is not in the new-born babe for the same reason."[52] Putting it another way, it is the function of the vital principle not only to effect *operations* maximally suited to the being's capacity, but also to effect (out of a very tiny and undifferentiated outset point) precisely that *structure* which will be capable of such operations.

This was pointed out by Hürth in editing Pius XII's Family Front allocution. In this he counters the 1940 position of A. Lanza, who since became an archbishop: "The substantial form cannot be the efficient cause of the organism with which it concurs to form one substance" and "is terminus, not beginning, of the generative process."[53]

We should say rather that from the instant of union of the gametes, there is present a single unified *being and operation* toward the goal of complete "personhood" which is never really finished until death. There is no biological or metaphysical reason for postulating *different* forms to preside over successive phases of that unified operation.

It could *not* be said that the adequate human soul *must* have been present in the separated gametes. Although from one point of view the "nature" or goal or function of every gamete is to develop into a human being, from a more realistic and existential point of view it must be recognized that the *normal* fate of a gamete *as such* is *not* to develop into one. Most gametes are "destined to disappear," *in* nature's plan and not as a frustration of it. One spermatozoon out of some two million in each male ejaculation can *possibly* develop into a human being, and this

---

[52] Austin O'Malley, M.D., "When Does the Intellectual Soul Enter the Body?", *American Ecclesiastical Review,* 49 (1913), 568–587, also 50 (1914), 182–196, 456–461, rejoinders to objections from Bishop Alexander MacDonald, pp. 13–19, 453–456.

[53] Antonio Lanza, *La questione del momento in cui l'anima razionale è infusa nel corpo* (Rome: Lateran, 1939; 303 pages).

proportion is considerably lessened by factors present in the female contribution: even if we leave out of account the loss of seed apart from
intercourse, which is in a high proportion of the cases neither culpable
nor "unnatural."

What must be admitted, however, is that a tremendous *mystery* remains as to the "type of life" possessed by the gamete before fertiliza-
tion. But basically this frustrating mystery is no different from that posed
by artificial preservation of an animal heart or other organ in uninterrupted functioning long after the death of the organism from which it
was taken.

As long as only the heart of a chicken or monkey is involved, no
great problem will be created, at least for those who are unsure whether
animals possess genuine individuality. But the human heart seems equally
capable of such indefinite test-tube survival. No scientist or philosopher
could then deny that *"it* lives." But neither could any say *"what* lives."
Is it the individual from whom the heart was taken, who is thus technically still alive and deprived of whatever retribution theology sees awaiting beyond the threshold of death? Or can that detached heart somehow
be said to have received a temporary and perhaps sub-human vital principle of its own, either by some altogether incidental local motion, or by
the cessation of vitality in the organism where it originated?

A second biological dilemma must further be noticed, to which both
Hürth and Schmaus attach paramount importance.[54] A single fertilized
ovum, after several days of life and growth within the womb, has been
known to divide and grow into twins. Indeed, this seems to be the case
with all "identical twins," so that the occurrence cannot be called monstrous or unnatural.

We must perhaps ultimately admit that one or both of the twins receives its substantial form long after the union of sperm and ovum from
which it grew. Even if that is the *only* solution which can be envisioned,
it does not automatically constitute a reason for generalizing this to *more
normal* human situations which are quite different.

No one can give satisfactory answers to these questions about the
late-starting twin, or the test-tube heart. And no one can satisfactorily
answer the same questions about the normal gamete. *"It* lives," certainly.
"What lives? *Who* lives?" Unanswerable.

The gamete, when once it has been produced and channeled into a
store chamber of the parent body, is really no more living by the life
of that body than when it has been ejected into the point of union and
new life. Moreover a spermatozoon can be preserved indefinitely outside
any human body and eventually used for artificial insemination of an
ovum.

---

[54] Michael Schmaus, *Gott der Schöpfer* (Munich: 1954), 324.

During the interval, is it "a living being"? And if so, is it a plant, an animal, or a man? I would say simply, and against Rahner, that it is a piece of the parent organism, preserved in existence by a procedure which for the species is "natural," but for the organism itself is "transitory," and if protracted becomes "violent" or unnatural. The fact that *this* answer to the question may be faulty is no argument against the fact that after the instant of union a single *human* being continues uninterruptedly in existence.

8. *The Parent Produces the Whole Child*

Sertillanges, Rahner, and almost all theologians who have recently tackled the problem, deplore the evil of a terminology which makes it appear that the parents produce one part of the child and God produces a different part.

"It has never been easy to fit the doctrine of the creation of the soul by God into the experimental datum of procreation. God creates the *body, in* giving the soul as substantial form for the body."[55]

"God's creative activity, and the soul in its own self-perfecting (as *forma*) address themselves to something present in advance. . . . The earthly *and* the divine origin must appear in *both* the soul and the body."[56] The "peculiar creation of the soul" cannot be interpreted otherwise than as an aspect of the peculiar creation *of the body* or rather *of the individual.*

In this perspective, some favorite older expressions of Catholics must be repudiated. "According to the tenets of Creationism, generation, as such, does not produce the human compound, namely man, but only his body," wrote Reany confidently.[57] He might well be confident, because his first patristic proof was the letter of Diognetus, "The flesh hates the soul and wars against it. . . . The soul loves the flesh. The soul has been shut up in the body, and itself restrains the body."[58]

Another exposition, enlightened and progressive for its day, nevertheless contains these words: "The act of generation conspires to the origin of the soul . . . [but] it is not a causal relation: . . . the act of generation is an occasion."[59]

Every "natural" or *generating* agent produces a being like himself. This is the sense of the scholastic axiom *omne agens agit sibi simile,*

---

[55] Pierre Smulders, *La vision de Teilhard de Chardin* (Paris: Desclée, 1964), 8.
[56] Karl Rahner, introduction to Paul Overhage, *Um das Erscheinungsbild der ersten Menschen* (Quaestiones disputatae 7; Freiburg: Herder, 1959), 13, 11, 18.
[57] William Reany, *Creation of the Human Soul* (1929), 44, 61.
[58] Diognetus letter, *MG* 2, 1176.
[59] John T. Driscoll, *Christian Philosophy: a Treatise on the Human Soul* (New York: Benziger, 1898), 212.

invoked as recently as 1952 by Boyer precisely to prove that evolution is wrong, because the body of an animal cannot give rise to the body of a man. He then goes on to state, "Only beings *animated* by a spiritual soul will engender bodies *capable of being animated* by a spiritual soul."[60] The variation which he admits between the two terms we have italicized is unfaithful to the principle he claims to be following. He would have to say either "Only animated beings can produce an animated being," or "only beings capable of being animated can produce a being capable of being animated." What he actually says is, in effect, "Animated living beings *cannot* produce animated living beings, but can only produce that which is *neither* life *nor* animation within the living being."

Either the axiom is simply not applicable here at all; or else it says, "The parents produce neither the body alone, nor the soul alone, but the animated being, body and soul." And this is in fact the case — whether or not the axiom has any validity at all, here or anywhere else.

Every time parents' coitus bears fruit, there is present a human soul animating a human body. Either we must say the parents really *produce* the animated body, or we must say that their act in a certain true sense forces or causes God to produce whatever in the animated body the parents do not produce.

The notion of "forcing" God to act is not quite as repugnant as it sounds. Within the order willed by God, the free agent in performing any act, brings it about that God *must* cooperate and presently produce the very being of the act, even a sinful act.

Nevertheless, theologians have shown little sympathy for the claim of Cardinal Mercier that the parents' coitus is the "determining cause" of God's creative act. "The formation of a man consists in the *uniting* of a rational soul to what the parents furnish: matter," he says. It is not in fact correct that the matter furnished by the parents is not *living,* but he does not exactly say that. "This uniting is without doubt the work of God, because God is the author of the creation of the soul; but it is also the work of the parents, because their generative act is the determining cause of the creative act."[61]

It seems profoundly ill-advised to adopt any terminology which implies a causality exerted upon God by creatures. Even *prayer,* which

---

[60] Charles Boyer, "De l'évolutionnisme anthropologique," *Laval Théologique et Philosophique,* 8/2 (1952), 205, 203–207.

[61] D. Mercier, *Cours de Philosophie: Psychologie*[8] (Paris: Alcan, 1923), 2, 335. — R. Lavocat, "La pensée de saint Thomas sur la génération humaine et la vision évolutive du monde," *Revue des Questions Scientifiques,* 133 (1962), 81–87, on *Potency* 3, 9–12, favoring E. MacMullin against R. Gleason in *Darwin's Vision* (p. 64, n. 4 above), holds *overall* evolutionary organization of matter to culminate in true *exigency* of spiritual soul.

"moves" God to help, is more properly an occasion; and it leaves God a sovereign freedom, of which he frequently avails himself.

It would be much more theistic to say that God gives to parents the power to produce a human being, than to say that parents have the power to cause God to produce something.

It is a datum of common sense and experience that human parents produce a human child just as truly as animals produce their respective offspring. To reconcile this commonsense view with the claim that God's intervention is *divergently* indispensable in the two cases, Sagüés brings forward a classic argument: "It is not an essential of generation that the generator produce the total effect. If you kill a *man,* it does not follow that you killed his *soul.*"[62]

He gives no word to show that what holds of destruction holds also of production. This is not obvious. And in fact it is not true.

A work of art embodies not only determinate quantities of matter but also an idea. The work of art can be smashed. The vandal has not destroyed the idea. But from this it cannot be concluded that the idea was not furnished by the producer who put together the materials.

Human parents, with God's creative concursus, produce a human being, body and soul.

---

[62] J. Sagüés, *De Deo creante* (Madrid: BAC, 1952), 727. — We must note here the emphasis on post-conception emergence of the soul, in Joseph Donceel, "Teilhard de Chardin and the Body-Soul Relation," *Thought,* 40/158 (Autumn 1965), 376. This essay enriches our view of "creative concursus hominization" by a warning against the "angelism" of Denis the Fake (p. 374), and by stimulating perspectives on *Death* (p. 378 ff) as possibly the moment of resurrection itself [Roger Trois-fontaines, *I Do Not Die* (New York: Desclée, 1963), 138, qualified 292]; or of "pancosmic openness to matter" [Karl Rahner, *On the Theology of Death* (New York: Herder and Herder, 1961), 31].

SUMMARY OF THE NINTH CHAPTER,
"DIFFICULTIES ABOUT CONCURSUS AND INFUSION"

Concursus is normally maintained by Catholic textbooks, though not in a very assured connection with revelation. In this there is something awry. Concursus is the kind of doctrine which either ought to be thrown out as not true at all, or ought to be made the very pivot of all our speculation about God.

Some theologians, even quite recently, have had the courage and consistency to throw it out. This is even claimed to be faithful to Aquinas, on the ground that any rational person ought to mean what he says: "What CAN act, really can ACT." On the other hand, it is true both for Aquinas and in fact that God's creative inpouring of Being is not something that took place once for all, long long ago, but is a constant dependence of every form of being — every new form of being here and now — on God's creativity as first cause.

Some alleged adversaries or objectors to concursus really are adverse only to ignoring how God's creative act is *single* and equally *present* to every created effect throughout all time. It is misleading to pose the question of concursus in the terms, "Besides existing and creating, what *more* did God have to do for the occurrence of a specific created act?" The concursus which we require, and which we feel suffices to explain the origin of the human soul, is simply God's present eternal creative act.

At any rate, concursus has sufficient right to be defended as a solidly tenable Catholic doctrine. And if by invoking this doctrine, an evolutionist view of the origin of the human soul can be proposed, then this cannot be called heretical or "less Christian" because of the reliance it places upon concursus.

Our line of reasoning has tacitly presupposed that a new human life begins at the instant of conception. This is not necessarily true. Moderns competent in both biology and theology show a strong trend to revive the Thomistic teaching that the definitive intellectual soul is present only several weeks after conception. Actually their problem is really the more complex one of *"Whose* life is present in the sperm and ovum before union? or in the identical twin?" We cannot give an answer to these questions, and we cannot exclude the commonsense and moral-theology view that the new individual human life begins at the moment of conception.

But the inquiry is beneficial, chiefly as reinforcing our assurance that the human parents truly *produce* the human being, body and soul, just as God in his own order truly produces each new human being, body and soul.

CHAPTER 10

THE SOUL OF THE ONE BODY

God created the soul. But his work is not stopped or finished. In a dynamic universe, "creation is cosmogenesis" applies to the soul too. The future of man is involved.

God created the human soul, each human soul, and immediately. But not separate from matter. This is no part of Christian revelation reasonably reappraised. What we understand as the soul arose inextricably fused with matter. God created our body just as inexorably as our soul, just as inexorably as he created the animal soul. Or rather, the only proper terminus of the creative act was the Individual Being, the single person, body and soul.

God's creative concern for man is not diminished by our seeing the formation of the human *body* as terminus of a billion-year-long gradual rearrangement of forces put into inorganic matter from the beginning. Just as little is his power and wisdom lessened by our seeing the emergence of the human *soul* too as a natural step in the ever increasing complexification of forces present from the beginning.

It may be *philosophically* very difficult, or even eventually impossible, to maintain that the intellectual powers of man are not due to an intervention of God "intrinsically independent of matter." But this philosophical tenet is not a part of Christian revelation. You may think a man is wrong for denying it, but you cannot think him heretical as long as he maintains that the human soul owes its being to God and is immortal.[1]

Much of what we have so far said about Teilhard emphasizes that he is concerned with the future far more than with the past. He thinks of Creation chiefly as the correlative of man's eventual reabsorption in God as his final goal.

1. *Planetization, Megalopolis, and the Bomb*

A new direction, centripetal instead of centrifugal, was given to the whole process of evolution by the creation of the human soul, that is by the occurrence of "Hominization."

The same forces within nature itself which — always dependent upon God's guiding infusion of Being — worked out this stupendous "critical threshold," have not ceased operating. In fact during our twentieth century they seem to have brought us to the verge of another threshold scarcely less critical.

"Planetization" is a favorite Teilhard term for this. As a term, it is slightly illogical. It should mean the formation of new planets, or of a planet. But it really means the unification of mankind into a single reality embracing our whole planet. Planetization is expressly set forth to be merely a synonym of hominization itself looking ahead toward the future, as "orthogenesis" also is a synonym looking ahead *from* the past.

Perhaps, logic quite apart, it is unfortunate that he chose a term exclusivizing our one planet, just during the generation in which man is seriously and practically concerned with occupying other planets. Nevertheless, for those who have sympathetically followed what Teilhard is really getting at, there is in his dream of planetization a wonderful challenge and inspiration, whose essential lines hold good or are even reinforced in a perspective of many planets fused into a still higher unity by the presence on them of one-and-only Man.

"The envelope woven by humanity about the terrestrial globe is not formed of elements grossly juxtaposed or irregularly distributed, but it tends to form a network in which a common vitality circulates. . . . Our view of life is obscured and inhibited by the absolute barrier which we persistently set between Natural and Artificial. Because of having laid down as a principle that nothing artificial is natural (and this means failing to recognize that the artificial is the humanized natural), we overlook vital analogies as clear as between bird and airplane, fish and submarine.

---

[1] This was the formulation proposed and accepted by Carmelite Father Philippe de la Trinité in a very sympathetic interview on the theme of this volume; though in his writings *Teilhard et Teilhardisme* (Rome: Lateran, 1962) on De Lubac and Crespy, and *Rome et Teilhard de Chardin* (Paris: Fayard, 1964) on Leys, he severely concludes (page 191 of this latter work), "Teilhard is objectively dangerous." See on Jean Rambaud [his bibliographical name] in Chapter 4, pp. 87 and 107 above.

Under the influence of this same abominable principle, we have been for years uncomprehendingly watching, as it forms itself before our eyes, the astonishing system of land-sea-air routes, mails, wires, cables, airwaves, daily more and more closing in the face of the earth. . . . This represents the creation of a veritable nervous system of humanity: the development of a common consciousness. On a higher level, and with other means, we are thereby continuing the uninterrupted work of biological evolution."[2]

Perhaps there is today no more challenging and crystallized sample of man making his future by uniting himself in quasi-biological higher units than The City. Lewis Mumford's work finds relevant to this a sentence which he claims comes from Emerson: "Our civilization and these ideas are reducing the earth to a brain. See how by telegraph and steam the earth is anthropolized."[3]

At the 1964 Fordham University Teilhard gathering, it seemed altogether natural to accord a special focus of prominence to the rethinking of urbanization. Instead of just sprawling out in ever vaster fringes on the outskirts of slum-or-industrial blight, man should take in hand the rational remaking of his cities, as an indispensable first step in remaking his planet.[4]

Megalopolis, this phenomenon of the sprawling, teeming, blighted, but alluring urban cosmos, gains a special poignancy by its relevance to atomic destruction. In cold fact, the threat of megaton bombs would be a less powerful instrument of international policy if population were not most concentrated precisely where the precariousness of its structures makes it most vulnerable. There rests on every thinking human a terribly serious responsibility for searching out every avenue of controlling and preventing the use of The Bomb. This obligation is rightly seen as correlative of the extent to which intense concentration of cultural and productive resources within the megalopolis has made possible for mankind unique progress which we would like to see continued and increased.

Nevertheless some of the attitudes taken in face of The City and

---

[2] Teilhard, "L'hominisation" (1924), in Œuvres 3, *La vision du passé* (Paris: Seuil, 1957), 87 f. On Art itself as an aspect of this "Artificial" which is the "humanly natural," see Monique Périgord, *L'esthétique de Teilhard* (Paris: Éditions Universitaires, 1965), 129.

[3] Cited without reference by Lewis Mumford, *The City in History* (New York: Harcourt, 1961), 567; on page 589 he notes that "world unification as the next step in human development" is foreseen also by Carleton S. Coon, *The Story of Man: From the First Human to Primitive Culture and Beyond* (New York: Knopf, 1954), 406.

[4] On cities formed by panic-streaming, see Jean Baboulène, "Le phénomène urbain aujourd'hui," in *Recherches et Débats du Centre Catholique d'Intellectuels Français*, 38, *"Vers une nouvelle civilisation urbaine"* (Paris: Fayard, March 1962), 27(–39). Now the epoch-making New Look: Harvey Cox, *The Secular City* (New York: Macmillan, 1965), 38.

The Bomb seem to be a point-blank denial of the very values which Teilhard has most successfully asserted. And first of all, whatever may be done to "control" or "renounce" atomic bombing, The Bomb itself cannot be unmade. Nuclear fission is here to stay. Of this weapon is uniquely true what Teilhard wrote has been true since the invention of the sling and the arrow:

"The weapons which each people forges desperately to defend and separate itself become immediately the property of all the others, and are transformed into bonds augmenting human solidarity."[5] Americans and Russians have seen themselves simply forced to keep avenues of communication open, not because either sees the slightest positive value in what the other has to offer (alas!), but simply to keep abreast of nuclear developments in physics and diplomacy.

The Bomb cannot be unmade, but Megalopolis can. Of course we love big cities, and have no desire to see humanity fractioned into little agglomerations spread evenly over the midwestern prairies with no libraries or symphonies. But rationally it would seem that our best defense against bombing is decentralization. If a really significant step could be taken in that direction, the threat of the bomb would automatically lose much of its significance.

Frankly, it is not easy to see this happening. We love our urban delights too much. Equally frankly, without this it is not easy to foresee a world in which the hydrogen bomb will not be used, with the biggest cities as its targets. Though this will be a great crime for which all humanity will share the guilt, still if it happens it can achieve what rational planning has been unable to achieve: destroy the cesspool-adjuncts of big-city culture which are now constituting the manifold maximum barrier to humanity's progress.

Teilhard was an optimist. And his optimism was never more radiant than in face of the threat of failure. That is the very meaning of optimism. There is no particular mentality involved in being cheerful about success. The only real optimist is the one who possesses reasons for seeing that *in and through* the present failure a plan is being methodically worked out. For overall success, any number of foreseen failures play their indispensable role.

Whatever we are to say about Megalopolis and The Bomb, it must not betray an attitude of cringing or doubt. Man makes his own future: constructively if he has courage and realism enough to do so; but even if by his own failures and consequent agonies, man is headed toward a glorious future of which he himself is the producer.

---

[5] Teilhard, "Les unités humaines naturelles," cited on p. 101, note 51 to Chapter 4 above. See too "Some Reflections on the Spiritual Repercussions of the Atom Bomb" (*Études*, 1946) in *The Future of Man* (= Œuvres 5; New York: Harper, 1964), 140–148.

Urbanism, at any rate, is by its very nature only a midway station in man's goal of unifying his kind. To decide at what point mankind now is on its curve of species life, we must notice that other species have had a moment of maximum socialization, in John XXIII's sense, to be qualified below. This socialization in animal species has been successful in varying degree. In our own day, it would seem, the *human* species is reaching just such a "boiling point" of increased unification. This is apparent on the one hand from technology, and on the other hand from the politico-economic ferment interwoven with it.

"Man originally lived in little units. Then links were established, first between tribes. . . . From neolithic times onward, has not the parcel of land remained the symbol and shelter of freedom under its original form? But now under the eyes of our century, a transformation has been taking place. In the 'totalitarian' political systems, whose excesses will certainly be corrected by the future but only in order to accentuate their basic tendencies or intuitions, the citizen sees his center of gravity transferred little by little, or at least pivoted upon that of the national or ethnic group to which he belongs. . . . An organizing trend, based on the findings of science, geometrizes the masses and tends to impose a specialized function on each individual" — just as each organ of skeletal structure had had to become more completely specialized before the animal was at the threshold of being transformed into the human.[6]

In these facts unfold the three steps of a "great option" now confronting mankind. First is the choice of optimism instead of pessimism. Second is the choice of an optimism of evolution instead of an optimism of escape. Third is the choice of a unified instead of a pluralized evolution.

"I am overmastered by these complex impressions that the earth is too small and that this straitness is nevertheless the condition of our centeredness and of our human compenetration, then too perhaps of our 'escape' or ecstasy. . . . While this [whole human layer] *is formed and welded together by the very impossibility of spreading out any farther, we experience that our domain is ridiculously restricted, and we feel arising an anxiety about finding the way out. Nothing but the earth — it's too little! Anyway, I'd like to express the psychology (the mingled sentiments of*

---

[6] Teilhard, "La grande option" (1935), *Cahiers du monde nouveau*, 1/3 (1945): in Œuvres 5, *L'avenir de l'homme* (Paris: Seuil, 1959), 59. His "Super-Person" toward which nature is tending has evidently nothing in common with the Nietzsche Superman, cut off from and above the mass of humanity surrounding it. But there is a more than coincidental likeness to this analysis of the biblical people by W. Robertson Smith, *Religion of the Semites*[2] (New York: Meridian, 1956 = 1889), 273 f: "Kin formed a physical unity with a common life . . . considered themselves a single living whole, a single mass animated with blood, flesh, bones."

See now J. Chaix-Ruy, *Le surhomme de Nietzsche à Teilhard de Chardin* (Paris: Centurion, 1965), 249–344. Teilhard's views are traced by Philippe Périer to "L'abbé [Henri] de Tourville [*Pensées de piété confiante:* Gabalda, 1916], inspirateur du P. Teilhard," *Revue Teilhard de Chardin* 11 (June 1962), 5–8.

pride, hope, disappointment, expectation) of the man who regards him-self no longer as French or Chinese but as Earthan. The farther I go, the more I feel determined to live above all political and national con-cerns whatever, and say openly what I think without caring for what others have said."[7]

"*The moment has come to rip the old cloth. Fascism, communism, democracy mean nothing any more. I dream of . . . Universalism, Futur-ism, Personalism.*"[8] This noble and somewhat alarming anti-chauvinism gains piquancy from Teilhard's paradoxical lack of interest in learning the language of the people among whom his mature life was set.[9] We will see presently his conviction that neither all men nor all races were created equal.[10] But what calls now most of all for a special inquiry is his much-discussed and much-hushed insistence on some elements of rightness within communism.

2. Communizing and Communication

It has been said, in the brash ardor of twentieth-century ecumenism, that the worst harm done to the Catholic Church by Luther lay not in any errors he taught but in the number of solid truths he claimed for his own and thereby induced Catholics to renounce interest in them. Similarly it will doubtless be seen one day that communism more than by any of its errors has done harm to the theistic community by laying claim to certain genuine truths which its enemies were thereupon content to yield to it. For the moment, we must simply take philosophically in stride the fact that any effort to evaluate or defend such truths, especially on the part of a member of the academic community, will be written off with a rich vocabulary of slurs like dupe or pinko.

Where could we better begin than by noticing the howl of protest that went up when John XXIII's social justice encyclical employed favor-ingly the term "socialization."[11] For the solid bourgeois backbone of parish life, Leo XIII had said all that would ever have to be said, in lumping together anything socialistic along with Marx and communism and Hegel

---

[7] Teilhard, Letter of Sept. 1, 1926 from Tsientsin; *Lettres de voyage* (edited by his cousin Marguérite Teillard-Chambon [*sic*] under the pseudonym Claude Aragonnès; Paris: Grasset, 1956), 1, 97. Alternative translation in *Letters from a Traveller* (London: Collins, 1962), 132 ff.

[8] Letter of April, 1936; *Lettres de voyage,* 1, 206; *Letters from a Traveller,* 224.

[9] George B. Barbour, "At Work in the Field," in Robert T. Francoeur, ed., *The World of Teilhard* (Baltimore: Helicon, 1961), 31; and *In the Field with Teilhard de Chardin* (New York: Herder and Herder, 1965) 23: Teilhard never learned to write more than the middle character of his Chinese name Teh Jih Chin 德日進 ["virtue day-by-day increases"; in Korean *Tog-Il-Jin*].

[10] N. Corte (= Léon Cristiani), *Teilhard* (New York: Macmillan, 1957), 55.

[11] Donald R. Campion, "The Pope and 'Socialization,' " *America,* 105 (March 10, 1962), 749 (–752): "For that matter, some . . . Catholics would still be reciting their rosary daily for the 'conversion' of Leo XIII from socialism if he had not died in 1903."

and all the other ideologies that constituted a menace to the European feudal structure. Such things as public school education and public health services, which we regard as the very bone of the American way of life, were in fact boldly socialistic in the context of their origin, and even in the United States met opposition on this ground almost until this century.

But the charge of philo-communist leveled against Teilhard is not based on any concern he showed for social justice by alteration of the feudal structure. He admired a chateau as *"proud affirmation of the need of an 'elite,' which I find to be one of my most decisive and definitive convictions acquired during these past years. Those proud towers founded on the rock above the torrent could never have been conceived and constructed except by a powerful race aware of having surpassed the others. The whole difficulty (and the secret) of real democracy consists in favoring the renewal and recruitment and admission of as wide a circle as possible into the elite. But IN ITSELF the plebs is profoundly inferior and hateful."*[12] "Snobbish," "far-fetched," sums up Teilhard for Albright.

"Reading an article on alcoholism, I was struck by the need which there is for many people to be upheld or corrected BY FORCE in the conditions and paths of health or well-being. Obviously in the case of religion, where an interior assent is required, and where the assurances are not of the experiential order, the use of constraint is infinitely delicate. . . .Anyway I am more convinced than ever that humanity is not now (if it ever will be!) ripe for being led by reason. The masses will still have to be led by a leash for a long time to come."[13]

These immature and regrettable outbursts, this naïve assurance that all will go well if ecclesiastical restraint is delicately applied to prevent mere reason and humanity from doing harm, were doubtless greatly tempered over the years by Teilhard's experience of the benefits of such superior guidance as applied precisely to himself! But harsh as were his youthful judgments on the vulgar mob of his own occidental world, they are surpassed by his out-of-character pessimism about the rest of the human race.

"Teilhard cavalierly dismisses the history of Chinese civilization as too 'neolithic,' and that of India as 'too passive and detached' to contribute much to the noösphere."[14] His memorandum to UNESCO on his views of democracy in 1949 was a dud.[15]

---

[12] Teilhard, Letter of September 8, 1918, cited with courageous fulness by Rideau, *Pensée*, 35. — W. F. Albright, *History, Archaeology, and Christian Humanism* (New York: McGraw, 1964), 79, n. 36 — The incorrigibleness of Modern Youth, its "promiscuous desire to be free of parental domination . . . and of school and home lessons" *refutes* Teilhard's optimism, thinks Francis Neilson, *American Journal of Economics* 20 (Oct. 1960), 102.

[13] Teilhard, Letter of July 10, 1916; Rideau, 35.

[14] *Time* (December 14, 1959), 60; *Phenomenon of Man*, 209.

[15] Teilhard, in Œuvres 5, *L'avenir de l'homme* (Paris: Seuil, 1959), 245–249.

"India . . . seems as incapable of governing itself as China or Malaysia. The more ground I cover abroad, the more I fear that my basically-admired Geneva, many liberal Catholics, and most of all my 'missiologist' confreres made a bad mistake in holding against all biology the equality of the races. Universalism is not democracy (egalitarianism)."[16]

Perhaps by a sort of compensation, at the end of his life he exhibited an almost feverish interest in Africa as the ultimate origin of all human culture.[17]

Painful though these sentiments are to us who have so much benefited by the values of democracy, we must turn away our eyes in order not to see the many areas in which the strange Teilhard pessimism finds its applicability today. Crime and juvenile delinquency and addiction are not kept within endurable limits by reasoning with the sufferers, however much we may sympathize with their backgrounds and esteem their human dignity even as superior to our own. The Rules Committee and other gentlemen's-agreement procedures are needed for the United States Congress or other government bureaus to attain some measure of ponderous efficiency. At base this implies that *just* letting everybody have an equal say sounds better in Fourth of July speeches than it actually works out in practice. The communists too in many of their public policies adopt formulas which mask their true operational procedures; the reason why we find this reprehensible is ultimately that not their procedures but their goals and ideology are unacceptable. But it will give food for thought to communists and Christians alike to see how brutal a recognition of the limits of human reason and reliability lay at the base of Teilhard's socializing optimism.

As we saw in Chapter 4, the totalitarian systems, fascist as well as communist, earned Teilhard's awed respect not because of their ideologies (which were opposed), but because they succeeded in galvanizing or "geometrizing" toward a worthy goal the masses of mankind who do rather tend to scurry off all in contrary directions. Democracies attempt to impose similarly a worthy goal with less efficiency and more dignity, by grade school lessons and pledges, and later by parades and speeches, especially as background to the outpouring of the blood of the nation's uniformed youth. Hence it is a little superficial, though understandable, when Teilhard's respect for marshaling mankind toward its goal is called a dangerous threat to men's freedom.[18]

---

[16] Teilhard, Letter of Jan. 21, 1936 between Java and Hong-Kong; *Lettres*, 1, 197.

[17] Teilhard, in Œuvres 2, *L'apparition de l'homme* (Paris: Seuil, 1956), 235–374. See L. S. Senghor, *Pierre Teilhard de Chardin et la politique africaine* (Cahiers Teilhard, 3; Paris: Seuil, 1962).

[18] James M. Connolly, *The Voices of France: A Survey of Contemporary Theology* (New York: Macmillan, 1961), 126; similarly Roger Aubert, *La théologie catholique au milieu du XXe siècle* (Paris: Casterman, 1954), 49, 65.

"Democracy has emancipated instead of liberating. With emancipation each cell has thought itself free to set up a center of its own. Hence the proliferation of false intellectual and social liberalisms . . . the disastrous equalitarianism which constitutes a threat to any serious construction of a new Earth. . . . By fragmenting and leveling the human mass, democracy . . . has seen Communism break away from it to the left, and all the forms of Fascism rise against it on the right. In Communism, at any rate in its origins, faith in a universal human organism reached a magnificent state of exaltation. The temptation of Russian neo-Marxism for the elite consists far less in its humanitarian gospel than in its vision of a totalitarian civilization strongly linked with the cosmic powers of matter. The true name of communism would be earthism."[19]

Among legitimate needs of modern man advocated both by Marx and by Teilhard have been social unification, progress of technology, advance of thought.[20] But really, any or all of these three slogans might equally be claimed as an attainment and ideal of the anti-communist secular world.[21] It would be hard to sift out how much of our modern rapture for these goals owes anything to what Marx added to what he got from the directions in which capitalist industrialism itself was heading. As things stand now, especially since the first sputnik and the climb of Leontov from his capsule out into space, it cannot reasonably be denied that communism does value and promote those three goals. But it is hard to see that approval of aims like these should have occasioned for Teilhard, upon his arrival at one Jesuit house, a greeting by his new superior such as this: "We know enough about your kind; you're an evolutionist and a communist."[22]

Courageously and convincingly, Bruns wrote that for Teilhard the only God whom we can worship today "in spirit and truth" is a synthesis of the Christian "God up above" and the Marxist "God up ahead." "We are dying" of the old metaphysics; it must yield to an ultraphysics "where

[19] Teilhard, *Building the Earth* (Paris: Seuil, 1958), 51. The French text is there given, enabling us to make adaptations in the English.

[20] Madeleine Barthélemy-Madaule, "Teilhard de Chardin, Neo-Marxism, Existentialism: a Confrontation," *International Philosophical Quarterly*, 1/4 (Dec. 1961), 654, 648–667.

[21] More relevantly Hélène Bourgoin-Moudrova, "L'homme comme création de l'homme selon Friedrich Engels et selon Pierre Teilhard de Chardin," *Actes du IX⁰ Congrès des Sociétés de Philosophie de langue française, "L'homme et ses oeuvres"* (Paris: Presses Universitaires, 1957), 467 (–470) attributes to Teilhard as "Hegelian themes" (1) the ultimate invention of matter is man; (b) the proper invention of man is man. See also by Rudolf Karisch (author of a book on "The Christian and Dialectical Materialism"), *Teilhard de Chardin: Anliegen und Aussagen seiner Entwicklungslehre* (Essen: 1962).

[22] C. Cuénot, *Teilhard de Chardin* (Paris: Club des Éditeurs, 1958), 289. See also Cuénot's "La morale et l'homme selon Pierre Teilhard de Chardin" in *Morale chrétienne et morale marxiste* (Paris: Palatine, 1960), 117–147.

matter and spirit will be encompassed in one single coherent and homogeneous explanation of the world." As Cuénot puts it, evolution is the only theological interpretation of the universe which could get through to a thinking Marxist.[23]

To this I would add that nothing in Teilhard is more Marxist, but in a legitimate and defensible way, than his insistence on finding out the direction in which history is heading so that he can put himself in the same direction. *"For hundreds of millions of years, Consciousness has been ceaselessly mounting on earth's surface. Could we think that the direction of that tide will be reversed at the very moment we were beginning to perceive its flow? . . . Truly our reasons, even natural, for believing in a final success of man are of a higher order than anything that could happen."*[24]

Thus too Rideau opens his key chapter with the observation, "The phenomenology of Teilhard is, like that of Hegel and of Marx, historical. . . . Essentially unfinished, the reality of the universe is *temporal:* in tension toward a goal. . . . History is not turbulence, not just metamorphosis, but directed growth of human beings toward a maximum of being. . . . Teilhard acknowledged the importance of the social datum, he links up with Marx in his acceptance of modern technology, though perhaps he did not allow quite the place due to the economico-political factor. . . . Even without turning to Marx, a more attentive reading of the Old Testament could have awakened Teilhard to the capital role of the 'poor' in history."[25]

Bivort, perhaps having Teilhard in mind only subconsciously or not at all, in his preface to an otherwise fairly advanced anthology sets down among principles basic to communism "a virtually godless universe, integral evolution (including that of 'spirit' from 'matter' as a substitute for religion). . . . The immediate danger is not Marxist-Leninism as a systematic scheme of thought, but that superficial 'scientianism' which is the fundamental weakness of the West's resistance to communism."[26]

Indeed such an "integral evolution, including that of spirit from matter" is common to occidental scientists and to Marxism, and bears a

---

[23] J. Edgar Bruns, "God Up Above — or Up Ahead?" *Catholic World*, 191/1 (April 1960), 23–30.

[24] Teilhard, "L'heure de choisir" (Christmas 1939), citing from "La crise présente" in *Études*, 233/2 (Oct. 20, 1937), 145–165 = Cahier 3: *Sauvons l'humanité;* in Œuvres 7, *L'activation de l'énergie* (Paris: Seuil, 1963), 20.

[25] Émile Rideau, *La pensée du Père Teilhard de Chardin* (Paris: Seuil, 1964), 106; 127. This neglect of economics is here regarded as an even worse lacuna than Teilhard's inadequacy in safeguarding God's transcendence and human freedom. — One must perhaps question whether Rideau's proposal involves a too facile equating of the Old Testament "poor" with economic standards rather than "pious confidence in God": see my " 'Humilis Corde' in luce Psalmorum," *Verbum Domini*, 28/3 (May 1950), 153–161; and A. Gelin, *Les Pauvres de Yahvé* (Paris: Cerf, 1953).

[26] J. Bivort de la Saudée, *God, Man, and the Universe* (1953), vi.

very close resemblance to the very thing which this book was written to clarify and defend. Whether it is fair to call "superficial scientianism" "a substitute for religion" this or any other effort to rethink tried theological tags in the light of assured modern science, we must leave to the decision of the reader who has followed our tracing of the relevant pronouncements of revelation.

The esteem of technology is undoubtedly teilhardian. *"What charac-terizes man is hands and brain."* But the *hand* has been prolonged into the machine: a tool invented and passed to the group. And the separate brains all fall into their place in a sort of dome or network of com-munications.[27] Surely this valuation of technology is today no less pro-foundly American and Western-European than communist!

Another "accusation" against Teilhard which will be perhaps more welcomed than deplored by his defenders, is that he "situates himself in the Marxist perspective of hopes for humanity [!] . . . The adventure of Teilhard is exactly that of the priest-workers. He buried himself in the mass of matter as they in the mass of humanity. From both these ad-ventures it is Marxism that comes out victorious."[28] In Teilhard's think-ing it is doubtless true that "the priest-worker movement proves Marxism stronger than an ideology."[29] This comment is cited in a book whose author observes that Teilhard is on the side of both Marx and Aquinas, as against "the American way of life," whose ultimate answer to *Why* any particular activity is "To have more comfort."

An open-minded and self-critical people like the Americans will surely not become prejudiced against Teilhard by hearing a few more hard things he has to say about them in their relation to communism. After all, Karl Barth received a hero's welcome in Chicago after having written that for the true Christian there is very little choice offered between the American and the communist way of life, since both are at base equally godless and destructive of irreplaceable human values.[30]

As for Teilhard, it is bad enough to find him writing from New York in 1948 that the American attitude toward communism is hysterical.[31]

---

[27] Teilhard, "La place de la technique dans une biologie générale de l'humanité" (Jan. 16, 1947), in Œuvres 7, *L'activation de l'énergie* (Paris: Seuil, 1963), 165. On page 232, from "Pour y voir clair" (1950): Oriental mysticism aims to identify with the outer periphery, the multiple. Marxism tries to unify about the center. And this is what we need. We need a mysticism of the West, in place of the juridical-ism which our religion has been offering us. [Teilhard's views.]

[28] Louis Salleron, "La pensée du Père Teilhard de Chardin constitue-t-elle un dépassement de la pensée de masse?" Conférence du C.E.R.E.C. (1958), 18.

[29] François-Albert Viallet, *L'univers personnel de Teilhard de Chardin* (Paris: Amiot-Dumont, 1955), 230, 142. See further attacks on Teilhard's Marxism by Jean Joublin, "L'évolutionnisme soi-disant 'chrétien'" and "Examen de l'alibi 'scientifique' du teilhardisme," *La Pensée Catholique* 78 (1962) 96; 86–138; and 81 (1962) 59–97.

[30] Karl Barth, *How to Serve God in a Marxist Land* (New York: 1959), 52.

[31] Teilhard, Letter of March 20, 1948; cited in C. Cuénot, *Teilhard de Chardin* (Paris: Plon, 1958), 332. (= Baltimore: Helicon, 1965), 281.

More unendurable still would be his Barthian snippet that no two peoples
are so suited to understanding each other as the Americans and the Russians, save for its naïveté and the surprise compliment it ends with.
He begins by saying that he met Malik of Russia at a United Nations
gathering, and liked him. Then, *"I couldn't refrain from telling him that
as an impartial observer, I didn't understand how the tension could keep
up so long between two peoples so suited to understand each other as the
Americans and the Russians. But for that it would be required that Russia
renounce its 'morality of lying,' and that's the whole question."*[32]

On the other hand, much has been made of Teilhard's lifelong sympathetic friendship for scholars of English tongue,[33] and the significance
of New York as the only refuge of his harassed old age. Not only is this
altogether true, but we are doubtless going to discover from continuing
published memoirs many more samples of his touching devotedness to
our people. But there are also strange blanks in the narrative, and research will probably ferret out some less flattering islands within them.

In his vast correspondence, amid comments about the American scene,
occurs almost no single sympathetic word about any Jesuit university
either singly or as part of a system or larger Catholic or secular whole.
His admiration for their sunny open spaces and fresh unspoiled recruits
is almost belittling. His relations to any and all American Jesuits ought
to be even now at long last examined and written up in minutest unfettered detail to satisfy public demand: instead of being shrouded in
a silence which confronts even the most well-intentioned inquiry with an
evasive answer.

The fact that in his last years Teilhard's home was in a hotel outside
the Jesuit house is fully explainable as due to a temporary need which
hit also other members of the Park Avenue community. But this leaves
altogether unexplained why the intellectual centers of his adopted province
and country did not move heaven and earth to secure for at least temporary or private sessions a confrere who within the decade would turn
out to be one of the world's most influential academic figures. No matter
how much the truth about these matters may hurt, it is ultimately going
to hurt *less* than any effort made to conceal it. Americans make a great
deal of freedom of all kinds, freedom of expression and freedom of the
press; yet the frankness and honesty of French Jesuit publications about
Teilhard through Leroy, de Lubac, and Rideau find no echo in America.

The upshot of it all is that we must neither ignore nor misinterpret
the fact that Teilhard, like John XXIII, has been acclaimed by the communists among their patrons. The most articulate exponent of this view
is Garaudy, who was even invited to a Catholic dialogue organized to

[32] Teilhard, Letter of May 29, 1952.
[33] See above, footnote 19 to chapter 1, p. 6.

keep open intellectual lines of communication with communists. Nevertheless in his book Garaudy says that Teilhard was not "in any sense" a Marxist, and had "little and poor" information on the subject. Only independently he came to some of the conclusions which the "Comrades" do in fact emphasize.[34]

One may wonder whether the effort to defend Teilhard against the charge of favoring communist ideas is not an unhealthy concession to the mentality that Truth comes in blocks of black and white. It is inevitable that any widespread and fascinating intellectualism will contain within itself genuine truths, many of them borrowed from the very rivals whom it combats, others inevitably marking an *advance* upon the rivals. When such things happen, the only sensible thing to do is what Thomas Aquinas did in enriching the Catholic theological framework by any number of insights and principles borrowed from Muslim or Jewish interpreters of Aristotle.

For this the works of Aquinas were in his own time regarded with mistrust, and were burned at a public ceremony by the Paris theology faculty. This too is natural, because the maxim "if you can't beat 'em, join 'em," is in all times taken to imply that if you admit any doctrine of the adversaries as superior to your own or tenable at all, you are thereby subscribing to and even promoting an overall goal which is intolerable. Unfortunately the opposite is true: in failing to appraise the true strength (and what is stronger than truth?) of the enemy weapons, we are condemning ourselves to a defeat from which no building up of defensive barriers can save us.

Still, due consideration may be given also to the reserves made by Catholic defenders concerning Teilhard's rapprochements with the communist outlook.[35] Following Fessard and Calvez, Rideau writes, "By his affirmation of a definitive end to history, Teilhard sharply separates himself from Marxism, which by a deep-rooted contradiction holds simultaneously that history must complete itself and must continue."[36] And Russo

---

[34] Roger Garaudy, *Perspectives de l'homme: existentialisme, pensée catholique, marxisme* (Paris: Presses Universitaires, 1959), 196–347. Garaudy's striving to understand Teilhard is commended by Georges Morel, "Karl Marx et le père Teilhard de Chardin," *Études*, 304/1 (Jan. 1960), 86; on page 82 he objects that Garaudy's page 182 does not sufficiently insist upon the "critical thresholds"; but this seems relevant rather to a letter of page 204 citing Cuénot to the effect that Teilhard is "of course a monist." See above, pp. 112 ff, 189.

[35] Étienne Borne, " 'Matière et esprit' dans la philosophie de Teilhard de Chardin," *Recherches et Débats du Centre Catholique d'Intellectuels Français*, 40, *"Essais sur Teilhard"* (Paris: Fayard, Oct. 1962), 51: "Teilhard's philosophy is realist and non-dialectic"; page 47: the real reveals itself; Teilhard has confidence in the human mind, as did Hegel and Bergson.

[36] Émile Rideau, *La Pensée du Père Teilhard* (1964), 144; G. Fessard, *Le dialogue catholique-communiste est-il possible?* (Paris: Grasset, 1937); P. Calvez, *Le pensée de Karl Marx* (Paris: Seuil, 1956).

says of Teilhard's "ultra-personalism": "We have here a conception that is completely opposed to the totalitarianism of the Marxist when he discusses the 'end' of humanity, a destiny wherein we discover in only a very feeble degree anything like a care for the individual human person and his dignity."[37]

"Some few Christians, in France, Italy, Poland, are under the impression that of its nature communism is a progressive movement taking its place in the line of history. They are confirmed in this idea by the fact that Teilhard too finds humanity's only hope of escape from threatening anarchy in the 'socialization' of human coexistence. But whoever identifies this 'socialization' with communism shows that he has a very poor understanding of teilhardian teaching."[38]

3. *Teilhard's Anti-Existentialism*

A more constructive evaluation of Teilhard's divergence from communism might take rise from the fact that he showed to it a favor which he refused to existentialism. In one way, his conscious severance from the existentialists may have masked a congeniality more profound than he was ever able to notice. In fact most of the authors whom we saw inquiring into his communist leanings call attention to his existentialist features too.

But from another point of view, existentialist anguish is for Teilhard at an opposite pole from communist confidence of victory. Since he read relatively little, especially of anything uncongenial to his academic tastes and qualifications, it is not surprising that Teilhard reduced existentialism to the single word "pessimism." It is obvious then how instinctively abhorrent it would have been to his radiant optimism.

What is less obvious is this. How could a so passionately twentieth-century mentality have rested content with a so superficial characterization of the philosophy which has had more influence than any other upon our century? His simplification of it, by a paradoxical irony, is scarcely

---

[37] François Russo, "The Phenomenon of Man," *America*, 103/5 (April 30, 1960), 186. Russo continues, "Like all great creative minds, Teilhard was not slowed down by methodological discussions. Such exercises in the minutiae of scholarship never seem to have greatly interested him." Though one must question whether the given example, "Is science here really invading the domain of philosophy?" is a "mere exercise in minutiae" (see in chap. 1, p. 29 above), still the conclusion of page 188 earns approval: "One might wish that Teilhard's synthesis were more open, more unfinished." See also Norbertus M. Luyten's "Réflexions sur la Méthode de Teilhard de Chardin" in the *Festschrift* for Sovietologist Joseph M. Bocheński (Fribourg: 1965), 290–314.

[38] Ignace Lepp, *Teilhard et la foi des hommes* (Paris: Éditions Universitaires, 1963), 158.

less than that with which existentialism is globally rejected at the side of teilhardism itself in the *Humani Generis* of Pius XII.[39]

Some head-on clashes of Teilhard with existentialists are noted in Cuénot's biography.[40] In June 1946 he took part in a panel discussion with Berdyaev on "Marxists and existentialists." On January 21, 1947, his views on planetization were strongly opposed by Gabriel Marcel in a dialogue chaired by Dubarle.

Tresmontant justly observes that Teilhard's "philosophy of birth, being-for-life" is the antipodes of Heidegger's "being for death."[41] Yet one may notice how harmonious in Karl Rahner is the fusion of teilhardian themes with those elements of Heidegger's philosophy which he defends.[42]

"Against existentialist anguish, Teilhard feels perfectly secure that man's situation in the universe, scientifically located, grasped and understood in the movement from which it proceeds, suggests grandeur and solidity; man and the universe afford each other a consistency which is at once double and unique."[43]

While cheerfully adept at detaching from Marxism or pantheism some usable elements, or even seeing in the position of atheists some valid truths they were groping for, Teilhard judged both existentialism and Husserl-style phenomenology to move in a pre-Copernican universe.[44]

---

[39] Pius XII, "Humani Generis," *Acta Apostolicae Sedis* 42 (1950), 563 = DS 3877 f = DB 2305 f: "An immoderate monistic-pantheistic evolutionism, exploited by communism for furtherance of its dialectical materialism . . . has paved the way for a new erroneous philosophy . . . called 'existentialism' because it does not concern itself with the unchanging essences of things, but only with the existence of single individuals; to which 'historicism' is allied. . . ."

[40] Cuénot, *Teilhard de Chardin* (1958), 302, 438.

[41] Tresmontant, *Teilhard de Chardin: His Thought* (Baltimore: Helicon, 1959), 44.

[42] The exegete will be specially attracted by an effort to confront Teilhard with the existentialist-Heidegger current which finds its expression in Bultmann: Georges Crespy, *Le pensée théologique de Teilhard de Chardin* (Paris: Éditions Universitaires, 1963), 159–186, Chapter 6, "Teilhard, Bultmann, existence, and history"; page 178 "For Teilhard, history is a continuous process; for Bultmann a succession of instants . . . points; for Teilhard the movement of history comports a theologically discernible finality; for Bultmann history accomplishes nothing." Unfortunately this confrontation did not attract the Catholic Bultmann-expert L. Malevez, "La méthode du père Teilhard de Chardin et la phénoménologie," *Nouvelle Revue Théologique*, 79/6 (June 1957), 579–599, where he is preoccupied with the fact that Teilhard did not make room for the creation of the soul (p. 597); as also J. Galot in *NRT*, 78/2 (Feb. 1956), 178, "[he is] reasoning as if biological energy were transformed into spirit."

[43] Christian d'Armagnac, "Philosophie de la nature et méthode chez le Père Teilhard de Chardin," *Archives de Philosophie*, 20/1 (Jan. 1957), 9; see 21/2 (Apr. 1958), 298–312, "De Blondel à Teilhard: nature et intériorité;" 23/1 (Jan. 1960), 151–163, "Épistémologie et philosophie de l'Évolution."

[44] Paul-Bernard Grenet, *Teilhard* (Savants du Monde; Paris: Seghers, 1961), 45. On page 29 it is observed, "Teilhard did not feel he was understood by Claudel, who was to write of him later cruelly and often unjustly." See now Mme. Claude Rivière, *Teilhard, Claudel et Mauriac* (Carnets Teilhard 7; Paris: Éditions Universitaires, 1963).

Yet despite the differences in their worlds, on some basic points Teilhard was more akin to the existentialists than divergent from them. Even the validity of *Angst* is acknowledged in his portrayal of our hurtling toward the crisis of an existential anguish born with consciousness itself — the terror of our powers and our destiny: *"By our intellect and will we thought to have a unique simplicity and self-mastery. In place of that we discover with horror all kinds of fibres holding us together even to those most sacred depths by their monstrous knot: fibres that come from all over and far away, each with its own history and its own life, ever threatening to escape our control and come untied."*[45]

His kinship with existentialism is discerned most validly perhaps in his insistence on concrete individual reality itself, as distinct from abstracted essences. Undoubtedly Teilhard was fond of generalizing, and he really loses sight of individuals in the vast cosmic surge of his synthesis of reality. But at the same time he constantly gives vent to his distaste for a world of metaphysical essences, a metaphysics of geometry.

Rideau's chapter on the "Anthropology" (rather, in English, rational psychology) of Teilhard begins with the remark that a "scientific perspective spontaneously opens out on an existentialist outlook" and ends, "Teilhard's anthropology deserves to be called *existential* because it brings in the problem of destiny and does not overlook the function of personal fulfilment, or the drama of choice deciding a being's value. . . . But his thought surmounts the narrowness of existentialism by inserting man at the heart of the cosmic surge and the history of the universe, calling upon him to consummate the unification of the world in the one-souledness of persons."

Again, Rideau's chapter on the spirituality of Teilhard starts out, "His global project is of the *existential* order"; from the 1933 *Christology and Evolution* he quotes that the universe *"has ceased to be the garden all planted where a fantasy of the creator exiles us for a while; it has become the great work in course of realization, which we are to save in saving ourselves."* The elements of an existential philosophy seen by Rideau as incorporated in Teilhard's "radical rationalism" are: interiority, human disquiet, conflicts and crises of the self, freedom. "All Teilhard's research has an existential character. It focuses on the problem of man's perfecting in solidarity with the universe, and defines the conditions of this perfecting."[46]

Regrettably many intellectuals who today forcefully commend an "existentialist" attitude seem to mean by that no more than a vague protest

---

[45] Teilhard, "Un phénomène de contre-évolution en biologie ou la peur de l'existence," (Paris, 1949), in Œuvres 7, *L'activation de l'énergie* (Paris: Seuil, 1963), 194; cf. 189.

[46] Émile Rideau, *La pensée de Teilhard de Chardin* (Paris: Seuil, 1964), 263, 438, 443, 510, 51.

against the extent to which the peddling of scholasticism has lost touch with the vital concrete interests of the learners. Admittedly it is this loss of contact which provoked first Descartes and then Kierkegaard to their work of rethinking; and this is a function of existentialism which is highly popular with extensive areas of cultivated and well-disposed inquirers. But it would be a pity to lose sight of the extent to which even Thomas Aquinas based himself on concrete experienced realities, on the best science of his time, on the existent reality which *esse* meant to him. In this perspective, a recent book rightly classes the better recent interpreters of Thomism among existentialists.[47]

To take up now a more specific, or rather peripheral, feature: one branch of the existentialist movement is Emmanuel Mounier's "personalism." Toward this, Teilhard felt unconcealed sympathy. In fact the basis of the present chapter as culmination of Teilhard's notion of the soul is a renewed discovery of the absoluteness of the Person. Mounier like Teilhard speaks of "Holy Matter," and links his thought with Teilhard's as a "movement of personalization which strictly speaking begins only with man, though one may discern a preparation for it throughout the history of the universe."[48]

Walter Ong shows how Teilhard adds to personalism something of which its existentialist roots had left it bereft: "One trouble with personalism is an inadequate awareness . . . of the fact that the human person appears in the universe only after an incredibly long period of impersonal evolution. . . . Teilhard's thought does not lack this awareness, despite its personalist center."[49]

Before pursuing the somewhat vexed problem of how Teilhard's absolutizing of the person is compatible with his even more cherished absorption of individuals into a higher unity, we must notice one of his recurrent motifs which fits here perhaps more aptly than in any other connection.

4.   *The Phenomenon of Woman*

Celibate commentators feel rather as if the carpet has been pulled out from under them when they find Teilhard ascribing to femininity a dimension no less universal than to evolution itself.

---

[47] F. Temple Kingston, *French Existentialism* (Toronto: 1961).

[48] Emmanuel Mounier, *Personalism* [= *Le personnalisme* (Paris: Presses Universitaires, 1950), 24], translated by P. Mairet (London: Routledge, 1952), 7. See further Jean-Marie Domenach, "Le personnalisme de Teilhard de Chardin," *Esprit* (March 1963), 340 ff. See page 107, note 62 above.

[49] Walter J. Ong, "Personalism and the Wilderness," review of Henry G. Bugbee, *The Inward Morning* (State College, Louisiana: 1959), in *Kenyon Review*, 21/2 (Spring 1959), 303; see also his review of H. McLuhan's *Mechanical Bride* in *Social Order*, 5/2 (Feb. 1952), 84; and now McLuhan's *Understanding Media: the Extensions of Man* (New York: McGraw-Hill, 1964), 23, linking Kierkegaard's angst with the telegraph or satellite as outering of man's nervous system.

"It seems to me unquestionable, as a law and not merely as a fact, that no man however devoted he be to a Cause or a God, can have access to spiritual maturity and fulness apart from some 'sentimental' influence coming to link his intelligence more closely with sense operation, and effect an at least initial excitation of his powers of loving. No more than he can do without light or oxygen or vitamines can a man — ANY *man — (and the evidence is daily more clamorous) do without the Feminine."*[50]

"By means of woman, and only by her, can man escape the isolation in which his very perfection tends to fetter him."[51]

More personally still, his *Heart of the Matter* pays *"general almost worshipful homage to those women whose warmth and charm have passed drop by drop into the blood of* [his own] *dearest ideas. . . . Nothing has developed in me other than under some woman's look and influence."*[52]

These words almost prompt a blush of embarrassment equal to that felt in intruding upon someone in an indiscretion. But actually it is our rash judgment for which we should blush instead: Teilhard's words are quite applicable to his sisters and cousins who from his correspondence are known to have exerted a lifelong fostering influence upon him.[53] In fact one might well get the impression that a good percentage of the

---

[50] Teilhard, "Le coeur de la matière" (1950), announced for the volume of the same title as Œuvres 10. See also A. A. Devaux, *Teilhard et la vocation de la femme,* (Carnets Teilhard, 12; Paris: Éditions Universitaires, 1964).

[51] Teilhard, "Esquisse d'un univers personnel" (1938) in Œuvres 6, *L'énergie humaine* (Paris: Seuil, 1962), 93.

[52] Teilhard, "Le coeur de la matière" (1950), cited in Rideau, *Pensée de Teilhard,* 40; cf. 247. Among collections of his letters to women, note the American sculptress Lucile Swan's "Memories and Letters," in *Teilhard de Chardin: Pilgrim of the Future,* edited by Neville Braybrooke (New York: Seabury, 1964), 40–49; and Teilhard, *Lettres à Léontine Zanta* (Paris: Desclée de Brouwer, 1965).

[53] The Dante-Beatrice theme is here evoked by Giancarlo Vigorelli, *Il Gesuita proibito: vita e opere di P. Teilhard de Chardin* (La cultura 58; Milan: Saggiatore, 1963), 19; and by Xavier Tilliette, "La femme et la fémininité" in *Recherches et Débats du Centre Catholique des Intellectuels Français,* 45, "La Femme: nature et vocation" (Paris: Fayard, Dec. 1963), 110. On pages 120–138 of that issue, André-A. Devaux, "Le féminin selon Teilhard de Chardin," begins with his love for his mother (p. 134) and culminates in his love of the Mother of Christ, on the lines of Ottilie Mosshamer, *Prêtre et Femme* (Paris: Alsatia, 1961), 69. Devaux on page 136 reproduces (perhaps more serenely and understandably than Crespy, *Pensée Théologique de Teilhard,* p. 93), this paragraph from a letter of Teilhard to Mme. M. Choisy, published by her in *Psyché,* 99, page 8: *"My conviction is that the remarkable rise of Mariology in comparison with Christology [le Marial à côté du Christique] is chiefly the work of men (especially those vowed to celibacy). The basis (and the interest) of the Marian question (the 'Marian fact') is to my mind that it betrays an irresistible Christian need of 'feminizing' (if only by an external atmosphere or envelope) a God (Yahweh) horribly masculinized. That is only one of the present faces of the superdiscovery of God: God at once 'cosmized' and 'feminized' in reaction against a certain 'neolithic paternalism' too often presented as the definitive essence of the Gospel."*

little reading Teilhard ever did was in proximate compliance with the urgings of his cousin Marguerite.

Not that his emphatic words restrict his debt to those women who happen to be relatives. With equal detachment we may think of the natural qualities which make women almost indispensable as secretaries, housekeepers, nurses, and in any number of other innocent functions rather needed by men even if they are celibates, and not always best performed by their wives if they are not.

Still, it would be unrealistic to overlook that those same feminine qualities which come by nature's ordination into play for certain types of work are also an echo and answer to some deep-seated longing rooted in the fundamental complementarity of man toward woman. Womanly effectiveness is never altogether dissociated from girlish charm. And so it is always seductive; or even (if one prefers to call things by their gloomiest names) it is always a temptation — to the happily married no less than to the bachelor. And this is perhaps the most characteristic facet of the grandeur and misery of our human situation.

We learn from a book by a Jesuit author, whose printing was authorized by a Jesuit provincial, that "there is no reason to conceal" the fact that Teilhard discovered sex tardily, at the age of 32, by a "sentimental" experience.[54] We are given to understand that four pages of details can be found in an even less inhibited volume.[55] Also, a visit in Paris at the age of 47 saw a "renewal" of the (presumably same) attachment, but in a degree which was easy to conquer.

The authors who have communicated these details are undoubtedly aware that by far the largest part of the information they convey is by what they leave unsaid. This has obvious disadvantages, even unfairnesses. What the circumspect and sympathetic authors austerely call "temptation" will fit rather as "dalliance" in the vocabulary of the average male reader. And the fact that these two cases can be so concretely pinpointed in date and place invites even the most objective evaluator to suppose that only by chance, in a matter so subject to secrecy, were these samples recorded. Moreover, there are wholly unrealistic undertones in the assertion that with this trial sex was "discovered" or "awakened" in this un-

---

[54] Émile Rideau, *Pensée du père Teilhard de Chardin* (1964), 14.

[55] J. Madaule, *Initiation à Teilhard de Chardin* (Paris: Cerf, 1963), 23–26. The Dutch equivalent, *Teilhard de Chardin: een eerste kennismaking met zijn leven en denken* (Turnhout: Brepols, 1964), on page 16 tells only that Teilhard was seized with a fascination for leftist thinking by meeting Ida Treat, the first wife of Paul Vaillant-Couturier; and on page 18 is cited Teilhard's generalized observation about some need of sentiment in a man's life; page 49 gives no indication of the alleged experience in 1927. Unless Rideau has some further basis for this "late discovery of sex," the phrase is misleading. The "discovery" is related to his cousin Marguerite, and with Pierre Leroy rather discounted, in Claude Cuénot, "Pierre Teilhard de Chardin: ébauche d'un portrait," *Livres de France* 17/4 (Apr. 1966), 7.

usual man. What must undoubtedly be meant is that the urge and power of sex impulses were then for the first time related to an available feminine companion. But if we were in a position to read and evaluate one by one all the thoughtful and prayerful reactions of the younger Teilhard to a whole gamut of gradually unfolding awarenesses of adolescent sex, these would almost certainly constitute a banally edifying record into which the crises of 1913 and 1927 and others which might similarly have occurred would slip unnoticed.

On the other hand, the honesty and naturalness which dictated the recording of these particular events can only inspire confidence and appeasement of thirst for truth in the mature reader. Teilhard's whole life-striving was toward taking concrete facts as our point of departure, and gazing with unflinching steadiness at the observable phenomenon. Whatever use we intend to make of his original and helpful generalizations about the role of Eve can only gain in inspirational convincingness from being based on concrete actualities.

This said, we will go on to marvel that Teilhard's writings show constantly an unswerving defense of and satisfaction in the vocation of celibacy. This in an age when clerical mores are being seriously re-examined by the highest ecclesiastical authorities under the crossfire of psychiatry, sociology, and scandals. Even the scientific insights of Teilhard would seem to have converged on a restoring of biology and bodily matter to a share in the life of the spirit, not only for "second-rate" citizens in the Kingdom of God but in those who are called to be its leaders and examples. Yet he never for an instant saw it this way. Why?

Most of all, it would seem, because his very love of biology and of nature recoiled from the wastefulness and inefficiency and degradation so prominent in the use of sex around us. In a "Discourse on Marriage" in 1938 he said, *"On some days the world resembles an immense chaos."* And on another occasion he penned these poignant and poetic words:

"It is really the universe which, through Woman, is advancing towards Man. If Man fails to recognize the true nature and the true object of his love, the disorder which follows is profound and irremediable. Desperately striving to appease upon something too small a passion which is addressed to [the] All, he inevitably tries to cure a fundamental disequilibrium by constantly increasing the number of his experiences, or making them more material in character. . . . Look quite coldly, as a biologist or engineer, at the reddening sky over a great city at night. There, and indeed everywhere else, the Earth is constantly dissipating, in pure loss, its most miraculous power. . . . How much energy do you think is lost to the Spirit of Earth in one night? . . . Man must, instead, perceive the universal Reality which shines spiritually through the flesh. . . . Woman is put before him as the attraction and symbol of the World. He can only unite

with her by enlarging himself in turn to the scale of the World . . . can only reach Woman through the consummation of the universal Union."[56]

"I was a bit peeved with Péguy for having taken the theme of EVE, *the 'natural' mother, whose so mysterious features merge with the remote past in a veil of symbols and legends: what an admirable personification of the needed and utterly vital bonds inseparably attaching our human bundle to the laborious and patient procedures of nature."*[57]

If Teilhard thus deplores even a single night's deviation of the powers of sexual energy which were intended to bring the human race in ever greater amplitude toward its goal, how could he tolerate the frustration and loss due to centuries of celibacy? It is because he envisions the true constructive energy of sex as a creative release more extensive and on the whole of a nobler order than *only* the procreation of children.

Life *"does not propagate just to propagate, but only to accumulate the elements needful for its personalizing. As Earth approaches the maturing of its Personality, Men must recognize that their concern is not just to regulate births, but especially to find a full blossoming for the quantum of love exempted from the duty of reproduction. Under the pressure of this new need, the essentially personalizing function of love will detach itself more or less completely from that which has had to be for a time the organ of propagation, 'the flesh.' Without ceasing to be physical, indeed in order to remain physical, love will become more spiritual. For man the sexual will find its fulfillment in the pure Feminine. Is not this the reality Chastity dreams of?"*[58]

Teilhard conceives *sexuality*, disciplined by reason, in the perspective of this activation of spiritual energy in the service of the world, as if the principal function of the senses were to release or disengage an ever greater "quantum of love." The future of human kind depends largely on a utilization of sexual energy sublimated by chastity: "Not flight (by refusal), but conquest (by sublimation) of the unsearchable spiritual forces still dormant beneath the mutual attraction of the sexes. . . ." Teilhard discerns "a gradual increase of the spiritual availability of the sexes, with a gradual reduction of the 'reproductive' side and the acts leading to it; as mankind is gradually transformed in nearing its maturity, the multiplication of the species will simply be limited to the optimum demanded by eugenics."[59]

Frankly we find in all this an element of the mystic dreamer to which neither the biologist nor the theologian is apt to subscribe. But

---

[56] Teilhard, *Construire la terre* (Paris: Seuil, 1958), 58.

[57] Teilhard, Letter of Jan. 1, 1917; see Jean Onimus, *Pierre Teilhard de Chardin ou la foi au monde* (Paris: Plon, 1963), 26.

[58] Teilhard, "Esquisse d'un univers personnel" (1936), in Œuvres 6, *L'énergie humaine* (Paris: Seuil, 1962), 96.

[59] Émile Rideau, *La pensée du Père Teilhard de Chardin* (Paris: Seuil, 1964), 250. The citations are from "Coeur de la matière" (1950), and an unpublished letter of November 11, 1934.

there is also a hardheaded commonsense substrate of realism, which comes out more clearly in Teilhard's application of these norms directly to the evaluation of religious celibacy. *"By its spontaneity and universality, the call to chastity is too close to the infallible instincts of Life to be a dated value."*[60]

Nevertheless, he goes on to acknowledge, *"the fully satisfactory formula has not yet been found either in practice or in theory."* Our practice is based on the dated formula that except for procreation all relation between the sexes is to be kept down to a minimum. By its animal raptures and swooning of the personality, sex is fringed in human instinct with a *horror* combined of animality, shame, excitement, fear, and mystery: all summed up in the slogan found ready-made in Apocalypse 14:4, "unpolluted by contact with women."

And yet the very energy which nourishes and weaves our interior life is originally of a passionate nature. The gradual liberation of social usages regarding women is a consequence of having some leisure left over for the spirit instead of being wholly taken up as primitives are with food and procreation. The Feminine always seems to be more dangerous than some other attractions thought to be less material, like ideas or stars. And yet the more dangerous a thing is, the more its conquest is commanded by Life. Dangers attract the sportive soul.

He continues: Are we to keep our heart for God, undivided? Surely; but our heart is not a glass of water, which has less for each if two drink from it. God as a lover is not in the same category of love as ourselves.

Teilhard even advocates the principle which most of those who follow it in practice would shrink from formulating so bluntly: *"We should seek above all greater richness even though we may be muddied in attaining it; rather than make our supreme goal to commit no fault, even though we may be less rich for it."* Virginity excludes for a man and woman "union for this child"; but not "union for this idea," "union for this work." Yet somehow it doesn't seem to work out that way. Why? Perhaps because we hope that by *saving ourselves up,* the moment of the total gift to another would coincide with the divine encounter.

Is it impractical? *"Someday we will capture for God the energies of love. Then for the second time in his history man will have made the Promethean discovery of fire."*

To any who may be tempted to protest that this is no defense of celibacy but a veiled attack on it, insofar as the "muddying" is not necessary but only a consequence of living a freely and questionably chosen state, there is an obvious answer. History and literature alike

---

[60] Teilhard, "L'évolution de la chasteté," conference given at Peking in 1934 made available to me in manuscript form by Richard Zehnle, S.M.; to appear in Œuvres 11, *Christianisme et évolution.*

are full of how often not the celibate but the married, from prolonged
and intimate association on the plane of work or ideas, have been drawn
to sexual releases of a kind not foreseen nor indeed wanted. This is a
problem which passes far beyond the specific risks involved for celibates
living in a way calculated to allow legitimate exploitation of their spiritual energies by such catalysts as are in principle compatible with their
state. Even so, one must admit, as Teilhard began his essay by admitting,
that these are only gropings toward the solution of some genuine unsolved
problems latent in the real values of celibacy.

But as the title and structure of this chapter suggest, we are not at
all concerned here with what Teilhard thought about sex in its biological
and moral aspects. We aim to focus solely on that *complementarity* which
a human being finds in *some* of his fellow-beings drawing him toward
a more intimate union of souls. This urge is proximately *exclusive,* and
therefore in a certain sense "narrowing."

But on the other hand, there is simply no way to unite ourselves with
the whole world except through individuals one by one. "Communion with
the world-soul," if it is not a mere metaphor or the symbol of a mysticism
to which we do not subscribe, can be attained only by union with individual souls. Some recent experts maintain that just as God does
not exert his indispensable causality around us except by means of
recognizable secondary causes, so also even God cannot be loved by
us except in our loving of created things.[61]

Teilhard drew a sketch to show a friend how the multiple is integrated in the one without that loss of individuality which is postulated
in the Vedanta; but even our more personal occidental avenues of union
with the whole world are in some way recognized by the Upanishad
declaration: "The wife loves her husband not for love of her husband but
for the *Atman.*"[62]

---

[61] This was the theme of an ordinary class by Karl Rahner at the University of
Munich, which by chance it was my privilege to hear in February, 1965.

[62] Maryse Choisy, *Teilhard et l'Inde* (Carnets Teilhard 11; Paris: Éditions Universitaires, 1964), 13, 47. See R. C. Zaehner, *Matter and Spirit: Their Convergence
in Eastern Religions: Marx and Teilhard de Chardin* (New York: Harper and Row,
1963; apparently entitled only "The Convergent Spirit" in the London edition).
Zaehner's excellent *Introduction to the Catholic Church and World Religions*
(Faith and Fact 140; London: Burns Oates, 1964), 35, equates *atman* with "the
true transcendent self" of Thomas Merton, which he calls also the image of God
in the human soul; *perhaps* identified in the Bhagavad-Gita with Krishna as the
god Vishnu incarnate; (p. 38) the ultimate in Indian religion (Hinduism influenced by Buddhism) is thus "love of the incarnate God"! Zaehner gives on page 19
this citation from Merton's *New Seeds of Contemplation,* page 44: "The 'I' that
works in the world, thinks about itself, observes its own reactions and talks about
itself, is not the true 'I' that has been united to God in Christ. . . . It is our 'individuality' and our 'empirical self' but it is not truly the hidden and mysterious
person in whom we subsist before the eyes of God . . . that unknown 'self' whom
most of us will never discover until we are dead."

Whatever built-in trends of our nature may help to open out our soul toward union with "the not-I" are *of themselves* a step in the right direction, despite incidental barriers which they may put in our way. As has been done from time immemorial, our nature itself invites us to consider *which* elements of a man's love for his woman can be successfully isolated from the strictly biologically reproductive sequence in which they occur, and then applied with due proportion elsewhere. Thus we can hope to attain harmonious personal union with less attractive relatives, neighbors, co-workers, and people of like competences and tastes in the search for truth and beauty.

All this is a rather risky business, of course. "Platonic love" has been defined as "the gun we didn't know was loaded." Yet the principle that *love* as such is basically *one* must be called legitimate. Teilhard is likely enough to some extent mistaken and ill-advised, either in his analysis of religious celibacy, or in his recommendations and practice regarding idolization of "the pure feminine." But we can still draw from his reflections a help toward a consistent theory of how the universe tends toward union of human beings with each other in Christ.

In a somewhat different direction, another important conclusion regarding the use or rather transformation of sex is drawn by Teilhard in the commendation of *eugenics*. *"So far we have certainly allowed our race to develop at random, and we have given too little thought to the question of what medical and moral factors* MUST REPLACE THE CRUDE FORCES OF NATURAL SELECTION *should we suppress them. In the course of the coming centuries it is indispensable that a nobly human form of eugenics, on a standard worthy of our personalities, should be discovered and developed.*

"Eugenics applied to individuals leads to eugenics applied to society. It would be more convenient, and we would incline to think it safe, to leave the contours of that great body made of all our bodies to take shape on their own, influenced only by the automatic play of individual urges and whims. 'Better not interfere with the forces of the world!' Once more we are up against the mirage of instinct, the so-called infallibility of nature. But is it not precisely the world itself which, culminating in thought, expects us to think out again the instinctive impulses of nature so as to perfect them? Reflective substance requires reflective treatment. If there is a future for mankind, it can only be imagined in terms of a harmonious conciliation of what is free with what is levelled up and totalized. Points involved are: the distribution of the resources of the globe; 'promotion of movement' towards unpopulated areas; the optimum use of the powers set free by mechanization; the physiology of nations and races; geo-economy, geo-politics, geo-demography; the organization of research developing into a reasoned organization of the earth. Whether

we like it or not, all the signs and all our needs converge in the same direction. We need and are irresistibly being led to create, by means of and beyond all physics, all biology and all psychology, A SCIENCE OF HUMAN ENERGETICS."[63]

5. *"Let's Talk About What's Real"*

In spite of a mystic and poetic aura clinging to much of what Teilhard has to say, especially about the subjects treated in this chapter, we must not forget that he claims to be simply "observing the phenomenon."

And in fact the satisfaction he gives to our latter twentieth century is largely bound up with the extent to which he takes as his point of departure the established and urgent facts of modern physics and psychology. We might and indeed ought to deplore the superficiality with which many of his admirers derive from him chiefly a negative or contemptuous attitude toward the out-of-touch aspects of scholasticism against which he revolted.

As noted above, Aquinas and the constructive original Christian Aristotelians very insistently started from *the concrete facts furnished by science* in order to build upon them their "theoretical" or *working-hypothesis* synthesis of all knowable reality.

This is exactly what Teilhard has done, even though the "science" on which he bases himself has so far outstripped its medieval predecessors that many people sincerely believe science did not exist two centuries ago.

Even giving due weight to these warnings, we must agree that "where there's smoke there's fire." There must be *something* out of kilter in the teaching of Catholic philosophy and theology in some places, to have provoked such an enthusiasm for Teilhard. And that something may be summed up in the phrase: Look first at the facts.

Yet precisely his failure to do this in a given case furnishes one of the commonest criticisms from orthodox theologians against the Teilhard synthesis. He leaves almost wholly out of account one of the most perceptible and pervasive of all phenomena in the world today: Sin.[64]

Censors consider it to be somehow morally reprehensible in a priest not to keep hammering away at what is the great problem and concern of organized religion everywhere.

Even theoretically, a system must be worthless which is built on a

---

[63] Teilhard, *The Phenomenon of Man* (New York: Harper, 1959), 282 f. In pursuit of this suggestion, there has been founded at Fordham University a Human Energetics Institute. See also Théodor Monod, "L'énergie humaine," *Christianisme social,* 71 (1963), 307–340.

[64] Teilhard, *The Phenomenon of Man,* appendix, page 309. On page 311 he still insists that what he does is to leave room for *theology* to tell what observation does not tell.

sampling of the data excluding systematically all the evidences and effects of human failure and wickedness.

This criticism becomes paramount as we approach the goal and climax of his whole work, union of mankind in God. Every one of the facets of this union revolves around areas charged with value concepts and human guilt: not only the favorite whipping-boys, communism-existentialism-sex; but even such words as God and collaboration and love evoke men's millionfold failures all around us in relation to what should be their guideposts. How can Teilhard plan for the future of man without taking into account more realistically what man actually is?

This complaint has been answered voluminously by de Lubac, Smulders, Rideau, and even Teilhard himself. *Too* voluminously, in my opinion. The mere fact that from his writings and views can be drawn extensive proofs that he *does* in fact thus keep sin close to the forefront of his attention is a kind of admission that no other policy is legitimate. And this is false, a betrayal not only of teilhardism, not only of Christianity, but of human reason.

The only possible goal of the human spirit is "what *is.*" Sin is by definition "what is *not.*"

This is one of those truly powerful and enduring achievements of the Thomist world-view which somehow we are ready to let slip away from the focus of awareness when something really important comes up. Evil is by definition the absence of good; good is by definition "whatever *is.*" Pain is evil, because by pain we mean the absence of a good that ought to be there. Sin is one specific form of evil, which means it is one specific way of not being anything at all.

What then of our human *experience* of pain, evil, sin? If a thing is not there at all, how can we have experienced it? Or, if we are to admit that evil is nothingness, then must we not end up with Sartre finding in this "nothingness" an even more dynamic reality than our colorless "being" itself? "Nothingness is curled up like a worm at the very heart of being," he says. And in what he says, there is in fact a *voice of experience* which we would gain a great deal by striving to evaluate sympathetically. We could draw from it useful lessons to enrich our Christian philosophy, instead of first demonstrating by a sort of geometry that he simply can't be right and so to hell with his experiences, which is what they deserve anyway because they are so immoral.

On the positive side, however, there is much to be said for the traditional Thomist view that evil is the absence of good. By this definition, since everything whatsoever lacks something of what its being might have and ideally ought to have, nothing is left good in the universe except God. And this is what Jesus also thought (Luke 18:19). But *normally* we speak of evil as "privation": i.e., the absence of that reality which the thing concretely and indispensably *needs* to have, either in the physical order (mutilation, pain, sorrow, failure), or in the moral order (a human act not tending toward the goal of the one who performed it; sin).

In all these cases, we can recognize the difference between the "evil as such" and "the evil *thing*," and further removed still is what we call "an evil *person*." The evil kiss or the suffering kidney is evidently a *reality* in itself, and good not only by this very fact, but also because of some especially attractive values within it, brought out by the very fact of its "evil" being perceived. Its evil therefore is just one particular way of looking at a thing which is good in itself.

We cannot even say that evil is an "abstraction." It is even *less* than an abstraction. We "abstract" an element or aspect which is really there, and focus it by detaching it from what it is embodied in. But in evil that which is really there is *nothing,* simply the *absence* of what ought to be there. Hence in speaking about "the evils" or "the sins" of which our world is full, we are talking about *realities,* and realities in which there is a preponderant amount of *good* along with "something missing." But in talking about "Evil" or "Sin" we are talking about nothing at all.

In this altogether Christian perspective we can see, if we really *want* to see, why Teilhard gives the impression that he has nothing to say about sin or suffering or the danger of failure overhanging the whole cosmic enterprise.

He prefers to accentuate the positive; to focus on what *is*. The popular song says: "Let's talk about living; let's talk about love." The scientist and thinker says: "Let's talk about facts; let's talk about what's real." And even in talking about what's real, we can choose to stress either its deficiencies or its *realities*.

Oddly, the same dissatisfaction which meets Teilhard's alleged soft-pedaling of sin is felt by many Protestants for the smugness they see in our Church's definition of itself as "without stain or wrinkle." "The main emphasis behind many of the [Vatican II] observers' comments was a feeling that *De Ecclesia* does not yet come to grips with the reality of sin in the church. The church it describes is not the church as it actually is, but only the church as it ought to be. [But . . .] Catholicism is moving beyond 'triumphalism' and uncritical self-adulation."[65]

Must we not agree that the very group within the Church which is most pained by Teilhard's refusal to talk of the real world all sinful as it is, is also the most pained by Protestants' insistence on talking about the real Church all sinful as it is?

The majesty of human achievement stands out most recognizably in the background of danger and failure against which it is set. Great

---

[65] Robert McAfee Brown, *Observer in Rome* (Garden City, N. Y.: Doubleday, 1964), 73.

dramatists and journalists as well as theologians have known well how to exploit this poignancy of the human situation. A portrayal of reality in which no due allotment is made for the background effect of evil would be hollow and unconvincing.

But surely not *every* interpreter of the human situation has to focus on the bleak side. Surely "a man with a new idea" can take for granted *many* of the banal realities with which the life of us all is surrounded. Is it so bad, after all, to talk resolutely about the "Things" rather than the "Un-Things"?

Teilhard is assured of the success of the human enterprise. Though not everything in 1950 was better than in 1940, though Beethoven or Plato may never be surpassed, still *"It is better to be than not to be; it is better to be more than to be less; it is better to be conscious than not to be conscious; it is better to be more conscious rather than less."*[66] And since all this has been perceptibly the direction of the universe, we can say legitimately and without qualification that it is getting better and better.

The purpose of his 1920 *Note sur le progrès* is *"not to show that there is a* NECESSARY AND INFALLIBLE *progress; I wish only to establish that for* MANKIND AS A WHOLE *there is a progress* OFFERED AND AWAITED, *akin to that which individuals cannot reject without fault and condemnation."*[67]

Cosmic energy, *"in its effects, is prey to uncertainties in cross-play: from below there is chance, from above there is freedom. In the case of very big groupings, such as the human mass represents, the process tends to 'infallibilize' itself, the chances of success diminishing on the side of freedoms, with the multiplicity of elements involved."*[68] *"By a sort of 'infallibility of big numbers,' Humanity as the current front of evolution's wave, cannot in its groping fail to come out on the right road and on some outlet up ahead. By a sort of interplay, the more freedoms are multiplied, the more they redirect and correct themselves in the direction toward which they are interiorly polarized: instead of neutralizing themselves by mob-effects. It is not as a gamble but as a reasoned calculation that I*

[66] Teilhard, "Mon univers" (1924), cited by M. Barthélemy-Madaule, *Bergson et Teilhard* (Paris: Seuil, 1963), 606; compare the letter of May 11, 1923, *Lettres de voyage* 1, 31: *"If one admits that being is better than its contrary, it is hard to stop short of God. If one does not admit it, no discussion is possible."* See Josef Vital Kopp, *Entstehung und Zukunft des Menschen: Pierre Teilhard de Chardin und sein Weltbild* (Munich: Rex, 1961), 67.

[67] Teilhard, in Œuvres 5, *L'avenir de l'homme* (Paris: Seuil, 1959), 31; variant translation of Michael Denny in *The Future of Man* (New York: Harper, 1964), 19 n. 1. In "Esquisse d'un univers personnel" (1936), Œuvres 6, *L'énergie humaine* (Paris: Seuil, 1962), Teilhard emphasizes how "personalizing costs suffering," as shown by Madeleine Barthélemy-Madaule, "La personne dans la perspective teilhardienne," *Recherches et Débats du Centre Catholique des Intellectuels Français*, 40, *"Essais sur Teilhard"* (Paris: Fayard, Oct. 1962), 77, 66–78.

[68] Teilhard, *The Phenomenon of Man* [= p. 307], my translation.

unhesitatingly bet for the ultimate triumph of Hominization over all the evil chances threatening the progress of its evolution."[69] *"When freedoms are expressed statistically in a crowd, their likelihood of error and misdirection are diminished. They head in the right direction. Nothing impedes the advance of humanity toward its goal. But it is a determinism above freedom, not beneath freedom."*[70]

Who can deny that there is a validity in the statistical observation of big numbers of free human acts, or even of complex acts influenced by interplay of a large number of free and non-free components? The number of fatal auto accidents over a holiday weekend can be foretold with appalling precision. The whole science of sociology is based on the recognition that in a sum total of which every single act is free, the proportions are nevertheless predictable and thus in a certain sense necessary. To this extent Teilhard's observations are *not truly* demolished by Smulders' aphorism, "The personal Yes or No can never be calculated in advance."[71]

Still it would seem that Teilhard's hopes for humanity are not truly of the statistical order. The "law of big numbers" is merely invoked as a suggestion or sample of *one* way in which freedom is compatible with inevitableness.

His real assurance comes rather from discerning some kind of scientific law that "an ultimate implausibility once realized must be irreversible."[72] That the forces within nature should have ever combined into the highly successful synthesis which is man was so utterly unlikely, that when once this has happened, it can no longer be imagined that any

---

[69] Teilhard, "Les directions et les conditions de l'avenir" (1948), Œuvres 5, *L'avenir de l'homme* (Paris: Seuil, 1959), 304; *The Future of Man,* 236.

[70] Teilhard, "Le néo-humanisme moderne et ses réactions sur le christianisme," a conference of 1948 cited in Rideau, *Pensée de Teilhard* (1964), 416, together with a letter of Teilhard to Rideau restating his position; to appear in Œuvres 11.

[71] Pierre Smulders, *La vision du Père Teilhard de Chardin* (Paris: Desclée, 1964), 159. Similarly Joseph Meurers, *Die Sehnsucht nach dem verlorenen Weltbild: Verlockung und Gefahr der Thesen Teilhard de Chardin's* (Munich: A. Pustet, 1963), 96: "The real way to put the question is 'Am "I," are "You" then only the product of an evolution? Am I and are you "only" the result of our progenitors?' Is not the truth rather that every I and every you is once-for-all?" But Karl Rahner, "Über die Frage einer formalen Existentialethik," *Schriften zur Theologie* (Cologne: Benziger, 1962), 2, 237, against the objection that man's *act* is not just one case of a general principle, distinguishes: Insofar as he is concretely bound up with matter, yes it is; but "insofar as the same man subsists in his spirituality and individuality, *no;* each one is called by his name." And in *The Church and the Sacraments* (1961, translated by W. J. O'Hara; New York: Herder and Herder, 1963), 38, Rahner says, "The body is the manifestation [and 'intrinsic symbol'] of the soul, through which and in which the soul realizes its own essence. The sign is therefore a cause of what it signifies by being the way in which what is signified effects itself."

[72] See above, footnote 24, p. 270; and also n. 45, p. 100.

cataclysm or failure will impede the universe from carrying forward this enterprise to its goal of definitive final success.

As a scientific law, this may be quite unconvincing, "whistling in the dark." It is quite understandably rejected by the many scientists to whom finality and orthogenesis are anathema. But it would be strange that the Christian to whom that "implausibility" is really God's guiding hand should fail to share Teilhard's optimism and assurance.

Our generation's economic prosperity, it has been said, is just a glorious fireworks display due to a destructive exploitation of earth's resources which cannot keep up much longer. Once the capital of accumulated coal and oil is burned up, no waterfalls or solar radiations or uranium deposits will permit continuance of the twentieth-century pace; restrictions and famine will once again reduce the population.[73] Teilhard flatly denies these forebodings, but the repeated play he gives to them suggests that his optimism about the success of the human enterprise would not be threatened even by such setbacks as a mammoth diminution in comforts or even in population statistics.[74]

Even if a hydrogen conflict were to blast the universe into uninhabited chaos tomorrow, the Christian could not think for one moment that nature's goal had not been fully achieved, because this would mean that God's goal had not been achieved.

The many humans who are assumed to end up in hell, the many failures in the performance of every human individual, are no more a negation of the radiant success of the human project than are all the millions of seeds that rot in the forest for every one that grows into a tree.

On the contrary, that *exuberance* of nature is the most impressive and glorious part of her efficiency: she attains her end not by precluding failures, but by reckoning with them. And yet it remains true that a book or a Disney movie about all the seeds that never grew into anything would be pretty dull. "Let's talk about life."

6.   *Super-Personalism of the Third Millennium*

As we edge forward to the brink of our third thousand years of the era inaugurated by Christ, the world and humanity are undergoing a critical change. Like puberty, this emergence of a new sense or direction is at first vague and is not well understood by the one undergoing it.[75]

A sort of spiritual temperature around us has been gradually rising

---

[73] Charles Galton-Darwin, *The Next Million Years* (1953), 389 n. 1.

[74] Teilhard, "L'énergie d'évolution" (New York, 1953); "L'activation de l'énergie humaine" (1953), in Œuvres 7, *L'activation de l'énergie* (Paris: Seuil, 1963), 391, 491.

[75] Teilhard, "Les conditions psychologiques de l'unification humaine," *Psyché* (Dec. 1948), Œuvres 7, *L'activation de l'énergie,* 182.

so that it is now at the verge of the boiling point. A new orthogenesis is taking place; the human phylum is turned in upon itself to "super-personalize" by sublimating the sexual sense and exploiting the awareness of the humanity which we have as a common bond.

The network of communications folding the whole earth in on itself is more and more recognizable as "a nervous system of a higher order," betokening the unification of mankind into a Super-Person, which like the human composite will act in the common interest of the whole rather than in the conflicting interests of the parts.[76]

On the crowded earth, *we already form only one sole body. In this body itself, thanks to the gradual setting up of a uniform and universal system of industry and science, the thought of separate individuals tends more and more to function as the cells of a single brain. What does this mean other than that this transformation will follow its natural line, and we can foresee the moment when men will know what it is to desire, hope, and love all together the same thing at the same time as by a single heart.*[77]

Since this biological goal of mankind is so noble in itself, and fits so well into what revelation tells us of the creation of the whole material universe in and for Christ, it follows that the religious and supernatural forces of revealed religion should support and foster Nature's plan rather than mistrust and oppose it.[78]

In *The Divine Milieu* is outlined the need of a new kind of "state of evangelical perfection," passing as far again as the classical religious institutes have been passed by Opus Dei or de Foucauld or priest-worker ideals all variously claiming to vitalize what the Gospel has to offer specifically for the needs of our times.[79] Teilhard says what we need

---

[76] Teilhard, "Le sens de l'espèce chez l'homme" (Saint-Germain en Laye, 1949), Œuvres 7, *L'activation de l'énergie*, 209.

[77] Teilhard, "Réflexions sur le bonheur" (1933), cited from *Cahiers Teilhard 2*, p. 63 by Rideau, *Pensée*, 417; on page 429 he adds from "La Crise présente" [footnote 24, above] *"Only the Christian dogma of the Mystical Body, the belief in a spiritual organism whose principle of unity exists prior to the aggregation of its members, assigns a real term to our march toward 'catholicity.'"*

[78] S. Geerts (-A. Hulsbosch), "De Kosmogenese van Teilhard de Chardin: I. van natuurwetenschappelijk standpunt," *Annalen van het Thijmgenootschap*, 47 (1959), 312(-323): the world is not one in which we are by accident, or which is hidden from us; but is *our* world in which we must work out *our* part. — The chief contribution of a critique cleverly entitled "Teilhardogenèse?" by Msgr. André Combes, *Ephemerides Carmeliticae*, 14/1 (1963), 155–194; 15/1 (1964), 200–223, replying to de Lubac, 190–199, is to bring out on page 192 that 2995 pages of Teilhard's writings are in circulation, of which de Lubac's *Pensée religieuse* cites nearly half!

[79] Justus G. Lawler, "Chardin and Human Knowledge," *Commonweal*, 68/2 (April 11, 1958), 48, considers the *Milieu* vulnerable for its failure to include illustrations from classical theological authorities; see further Mary T. Clark, R.S.C.J., "The *Divine Milieu* in Philosophical Perspective," *Downside Review*, 80/258 (Jan. 1962), 12–25.

most of all is a group of men consecrated to doing Earth's *natural* tasks with that holiness which is proper to them.[80]

His proposal, though in itself constructive and positive, must be admitted to reflect some of his criticisms and dissatisfactions at the present orientations of Christianity:[81] *"We must acknowledge that in consequence of a certain anthropomorphism or primitive nationalism, the current of Judeo-Christian mysticism has had trouble disengaging itself from a perspective in which 'Oneness' or absolute unity was sought too narrowly in* SINGULARITY *rather than in the* UNITIVE POWER OF GOD. *This is the unfortunate implication of loving God 'above' all things, rather than in and* THROUGH *all things. From this has resulted a certain 'meagerness' in the mysticism of the prophets and many saints: a mysticism too 'Jewish' or too 'human' in a limitative sense, that is to say, not sufficiently universalist and cosmic. Of course there have been exceptions: Eckhart, Francis of Assisi, John of the Cross. One example of a perverse quest of Oneness is in destruction and death, on the ground that death suppresses the Multiple and leaves only God subsisting. One may doubt whether such a morbid interpretation has ever nourished a true current of mysticism. But as a sample of awkwardness and perversion it is worth keeping in view, as a danger that is always possible, since it amounts to mistaking the* SUFFERING OF ANNIHILATION *for the suffering of* TRANSFORMATION. *Is it really*

---

[80] Teilhard, *The Divine Milieu* (Fontana edition, 1964), 67; "Le phénomène spirituel" (1937) in *Œuvres* 6, *L'énergie humaine* (Paris: Seuil, 1962), 136: *"The time has passed when God could simply impose himself upon us from the outside, like a master and an owner. The world will never again kneel except before the organic center of its evolution. What more or less all of us need at this moment is a new formulation of sanctity."* Further Jean-Marie LeBlond, "Consacrer l'effort humain," *Études*, 296/3 (Jan. 1958), 60. *"The Church must rejuvenate herself by humanization,"* says Teilhard in "Le Christ évoluteur" (Peking, Oct. 8, 1942), *Cahiers Pierre Teilhard de Chardin*, 5 (Paris: Seuil, 1965), 26; see 86–112, "La planétisation à partir des communautés humaines," by André Tunc; and now Philip Hefner, "Teilhard de Chardin: the Cosmic Dimensions of Catholicity," *Una Sancta* 23/2 (1966), 61–70.

[81] Teilhard, "Le sens humain" (1929): *"The truth is that if Christianity has today ceased to give satisfaction, this is not at all because (as its defenders claim) it is too difficult and too lofty, but on the contrary because its ideal does not seem either sufficiently pure or sufficiently elevated. Under its actual current presentation, the Christian religion seems narrow to our spirit and chokes our heart":* cited by N. Wildiers, *Teilhard* (Paris: Presses Universitaires, 1960), 82, along with Teilhard's further observation (p. 87), *"Isn't it strange that Christology, in contrast to Mariology, has made no progress for centuries?"* And in a Letter of March 16, 1921 (Rideau, *Pensée*, p. 74): *"What continues to dominate my perspective is the ever-sharper view of a crushing disproportion between the grandeur of the realities engaged in the march of the world (physical, biological, intellectual, social), and the tininess, the narrowness, or the provisional character of the philosophico-dogmatic solutions by which we claim to have stowed the Universe away for ever. We are trying to put the ocean into a nutshell."*

so sure that some commentaries on the meaning of the Cross do not betray traces of that 'illusion'?"[82]

Rideau summarizes with remarkable lucidity the "Three Steps of Personalizing" which crown the Teilhard edifice.[83]

"Where can we today seek a *scientific* and positive solution for the problem of happiness otherwise than in nature itself and in the facts themselves, as set forth by physics and biology?

"What these show is that in conflict with the material trend toward disintegration of energies, Life has chosen to mount upward toward a *consciousness* ever more interiorized and personal. This climb of the Universe toward consciousness has found its summit in man. To conform oneself with the direction of the facts themselves, it is impossible to escape from this movement, which has no other exit except onward and upward. *'To turn back for the sake of being a bit less; to pause awhile to play'* are stupid moves, *'reverse eddies in the universal flow.'* The only solution for the problem of man and the problem of happiness is spiritual growth, a cooperative yielding to the surge pushing history toward its goal. *This* is the human vocation. In it three steps can be discerned: centering, decentralization, supercentering.

"*Centering upon one's true self:* In countering a scattery agitation, source of enslavement and of maladjustment, every individual must first of all possess his own *being* to a maximum degree: grow and increase in it, emancipate and possess it. This is a struggle of total and organized *culture,* which will result in giving to the personality more order, unity, and worth.

"*Decentralization upon others:* The cult of the person would risk becoming a masked selfishness unless it found expression in love, and put

---

[82] Teilhard, "Quelques remarques pour y voir clair sur l'essence du sentiment mystique" (1951) cited in Rideau, *Pensée de Teilhard* (1964), 507, along with protests on behalf of the "Jewish prophets." Really neither the divine revelation nor the Jewish people need apology for having progressed from a "holy war — chosen people" exclusivism before the Exile, to the universalist perspectives which guided them since then: even though truly "cosmic" elements could be exploited only after a sufficient progress of humanity in scientific knowledge. On Teilhard's appreciation of the Cross, see what the *Divine Milieu* says of "diminishments of passivity"; and Dr. Paul Chauchard, *Teilhard et l'optimisme de la Croix* (Carnets Teilhard 20; Paris: Éditions universitaires, 1964); also his *La création évolutive* (Paris: Spes, 1957).

[83] Émile Rideau, *La pensée du père Teilhard de Chardin* (Paris: Seuil, 1964), 454 f, preceded by an analysis of the three options with which life confronts man: (1) choice of weariness or pessimism ("life's not worth living") as in Hinduism, Schopenhauer, or even sometimes Christianity regarded as an escape; (2) choice of epicureanism, Gide-style enjoyment of the most intensified natural pleasures; (3) "The choice of those who in spite of all its pain and sorrow put their bet on life, plunge forward toward the future, assent to all the appeals of the world and of man. Without seeking happiness directly, they get it as a bonus in the joy of creation and of outdoing themselves, of sacrifice and generosity, in the inexhaustible fulness of being"; see *The Divine Milieu* (Fontana edition), 97, 102.

itself at the service of others.[84] Here again we must yield to nature, where everything is linking, interdependence, and solidarity of elements pushing toward the unification of individuals. Love means coexistence and collaboration, welcoming and giving, sacrifice and renunciation. The only kind of love which gives happiness is the kind which expresses itself by a forward step of the spirit worked out in common.

"*Supercentering on the absolute:* Once the above movement of decentralization has begun, it outstrips itself, beyond all closed circles or groups, toward the effecting of an entire humanity perfectly unified in a sort of single soul [*unanime*]. Again, this effort is in harmony with the evident fact of the present-day increase of human unity. '*We can foresee the moment when men will know what it means to desire and love together the same thing at the same time as it were with a single heart.*' This is the trend also of a recent phenomenon of the spirit, which has drawn the human elite toward the conquest of some value beyond themselves: the epic of explorers, technologists, and scholars.

"That value which they are seeking has not yet a name, but it is already an absolute. The secret of happiness thus turns out to be, to become lost in what is 'bigger than oneself': to do the smallest things in a grand style, '*add a single dot, however tiny it be, to the gorgeous embroidery of life, then find in that dot the immensity which is in course of producing itself*'; '*sink one's own interests and hopes in those of the world and particularly of Humanity, by putting oneself at the service of Progress.*'"

Whether what Teilhard dreams of as the "Super-Person" of the twenty-first century is anything more than a metaphor would not seem to be of vital importance to decide, as long as we cannot really decide whether the Mystical Body of Christ drawn from St. Paul is metaphorical or has some physical reality.[85] If such a "Super-Person" will someday exist, it will be doubtless only for an instant at the consummation of all things in the divine being for which they were made.

"*In a convergent universe, each element finds its completion not directly in its own consummation, but in its incorporation within a higher pole*

84 Rideau here (note p. 510) cites Teilhard's own avowal in "Le coeur de la matière" (1950) that his *Divine Milieu* and "La Messe sur le monde" were still too egocentric! — Source of the other citations not indicated, presumably Teilhard where italicized. See now Rideau, "Teilhards Botschaft der Hoffnung — ihre Möglichkeit und Grenzen," *Dokumente* 22/3 (June 1966), 187–200.

85 In *Gli errori di Teilhard de Chardin* edited by G. Frénaud (Turin: Albero, 1963), 39, the Dominican R. T. Calmel finds it unacceptable that a dogma and mystery of faith like the Mystical Body should be "subordinated" to what is only a scientific opinion, since Teilhard holds that a fixist universe cannot give a solid base for the Mystical Body. Similar objections to "Teilhard's Eschatology" in comparison with Nietzsche and Sri Aurobindo are developed by Ernst Benz, *Schöpfungsglaube und Endzeiterwartung: Antwort auf Teilhard de Chardins Theologie der Evolution* (Munich: Nymphenburger, 1965), 252.

of consciousness where alone it can enter into contact with all the others. By a sort of turning in on The Other, its growth culminates in giving and in decentralizing. . . . To pass into the beyond, the World and its elements must first attain what might be called 'their point of anni- hilation.' "[86]

Even in his headiest vision, Teilhard never speaks of "the one soul of the Super-Person." The closest he comes to this is when he speaks of all loving the same thing "as it were with a single heart."

Nevertheless we may properly conclude that only here we find the keystone to the story of the creation of the human soul. To understand this final chapter it is important to have recognized at its true nobility the procedure by which God wished his immediate and creative role in the emergence of the human soul to be intimately linked with the material and vital universe.

---

[86] Teilhard, "La grande option" (1939), in Œuvres 5, *L'avenir de l'homme* (Paris: Seuil, 1959), 77 = *The Future of Man* (New York: Harper, 1964), 55 f. To the ever-increasing favor of Christians for this world-uniting view, add now Richard Towers, *Teilhard de Chardin* (Richmond: Knox, 1966); Philip E. Hughes, *Creative Minds in Contemporary Theology* (Grand Rapids: Eerdmans, 1966), 407–450; Perry LeFevre, *Understandings of Man* (Philadelphia: Westminster, 1966).

SUMMARY OF THE TENTH CHAPTER,
ON "SUPER-PERSONALIZING"

God created man body and soul; but his work is not finished as long as men are not united into that higher "Body" toward which they are tending. It is hard to delimit exactly the extent to which this higher "Body" is some unified physical reality as distinct from a mere metaphor. But in that same possibly metaphorical sense there will be a corresponding "Soul" with which our inquiry may worthily conclude.

The human spirit has succeeded in producing high-speed communication channels which amount to a mammoth nervous system uniting all humanity over the surface of our planet. Thus mankind has been brought to a new "critical threshold," typified by the sprawling Big City in its wonder and its horror, especially as counterpoised to the menace of nuclear destruction. Teilhard sees man's duty to lie in organizing and uniting his forces in the direction in which history is going.

He does not deny a certain kinship in this outlook to that of communism. Unduly mistrustful of "the masses" and "the retarded races," he was nevertheless optimistic in his hope that the right technique could be found for galvanizing them toward a worthy goal. The measure of success which communism has had, even in "duping" the masses, is due ultimately less to its ideological errors than to its elements of truth. Yet in his ultra-personalism Teilhard is most irreducibly hostile to Marxist ideology.

Teilhard's optimism in planning for the future, in proportion as it gravitated toward the unifying forces evoked by communism, gravitated away from the deadening *angst* of Existentialism. But at heart Teilhard was existentialist to the extent that he was twentieth-century. An even more concrete kinship is discerned in his rebellion against formulas confining revelation within a static and fixist world outlook.

Lyric praise of woman's role in the evolution of the nobler cosmos doubtless betrays in Teilhard a certain amount of fantasy or illusion, possibly not without danger. But he heartily advocated religious celibacy, and even saw the future of mankind as a whole to consist in the transformation of inter-sex intimacies from the reproductive to the more spiritually creative plane. More fundamental to his mystique of femininity is that it gives a lead or clue toward that higher union in which separate individual personalities can be fused.

The super-personalizing forward goal of the human planet is called irresistible and irreversible. Teilhard does not ignore the immense negative areas of failure, sin, suffering. But he has a right to focus on the "reality" in which they appear, and which grows *out of* them rather than in spite of them. The "religious order of the future," and even the Christian religion itself, must be oriented toward realizing the unifying trend nobly contained within our biological nature itself. First men must be brought to "be themselves," to will and seek their personal fulfilment more intensely. In a second step they lose themselves in someone else, many someones in circles spreading ever wider outward. Only thus can man attain his third step, of super-centering on an absolute goal: the "return of the soul to God who gave it."

Index (A) of Scripture References

Genesis
1: 91
1-3: 92[27]
1:1: 122, 133
1:2: 94[30], 210
1:21: 177[25]
1:24: 177
1:26: 54, 122, 128, 160[150], 181[34]
1:27: 165, 180, 212
1:28: 124
2-3: 54, 96[38]
2:7: 35, 37, 48, 136[57], 165, 175, 185, 187, 190
2:19: 177 f
2:21 f: 48
2:23: 186
3:17: 124 f
3:20: 54
5:1: 182[37]
5:3: 212
7:22: 178
8:21: 125[18]
9:4: 192
9:11: 125[18]
41:38: 195
49:3: 134

Exodus
3:2: 4
15:8: 198[95]
21:22 ff: 254
23: 197[92]
23:9: 189[60]

Leviticus
11:4: 193
19:28: 192[70]
21:1: 192[70]
21:7: 192
22:4: 192[70]
25: 197[92]

Numbers
5:2: 192[70]
6:6: 192
6:11: 192[70]
9:6 f: 192[70]
9:10: 192[70]
16:22: 186, 195
27:16: 186, 195

Deuteronomy
20:16: 190
12:23: 189[60]
12:23 f: 192

Joshua
10:40: 190

Second Samuel
22:16: 190

Third Kings
8:27: 135
15:29: 190

Fourth Kings
2:15: 195

Tobias
6:7: 195[86]

Second Maccabees
7:22 f: 187
7:28: 94, 187

Isaiah
2:22: 190
3:20: 191
10:18: 179
30:33: 190
31:3: 197[91]
44:24-27: 96[36]
51:9-15: 96[36]
57:16: 190
65:17: 125
66:22: 125

Jeremiah
2:34: 192

Ezekiel
18:23: 154

Micah
2:7: 195

Haggai
2:13: 192[70]

Psalms (Hebrew Numbering)
18:11: 199
18:16: 190
19:16: 198[95]
33:6: 185
33:9: 185
33:15: 185
63:2: 179
68:17: 135
69:2: 194
82:6: 89[17]
89:28: 132[40]
104: 242
104:23-30: 175
104:29: 172, 175, 178
139:2: 185
139:14: 185
144:14: 242
145 f: 242
150:6: 190

Job
4:9: 190, 198[94]
10:8 ff: 242
12:10: 198[94]
14:22: 179
26:4: 190
27:3: 195
32:8: 190, 198[94]
33:4: 190, 198[94]
34:14: 172, 178, 190
37:10: 190
41:13: 191

Proverbs
3:19: 122
8:22: 122, 130[33], 132, 158
9:16: 158
20:27: 190
27:9: 191

Qohelet (Ecclesiastes)
1:9: 174
1:18: 174
2:14: 174
2:24: 174
3:2 ff: 174
3:10 ff: 174
3:17: 171
3:19: 170 ff[15]
3:20 ff: 170
3:21: 171, 175
4:1: 170
9:4 f: 170
9:10: 170, 174
11:5: 193
11:9: 174
12:1: 172
12:1-7: 168[9]
12:7: 167-175
12:12: 173

Wisdom of Solomon
7:26: 133[47]
8:19 f: 188
15:11: 187

Sirach (Ecclesiasticus)
18:1: 187, 212
24: 1-31: 158
24:9: 122
38:23: 199[99]
51: 23-30: 131[38]

Matthew
6:30: 242
10:29: 242
10:39: 131[38]
11:25: 131
16:19: 204

Luke
2:7: 130 f
18:19: 286
19:10: 121, 143

John
1:1: 130[32]
1:3: 134
1:14: 130[32]
3:18: 130[32]
5:17: 212 f, 242
8:25: 134
9:4: 174

Acts
3:21: 125
14:16: 125[18]
17:28: 242

Romans
1:20: 109, 122 f
5:10: 139
5:12: 54, 57, 122
8:18-23: 122
8:19: 123
8:19-22: 126
8:21: 4
8:22: 134
8:23: 129, 133
8:29: 129, 131, 134
8:28 f: 123
8:29: 111
14:3: 217
16: 136[57]

First Corinthians
3:22: 161[150]
7:11: 138
8:6: 132, 134
9:9: 123[9]
11:7: 160
12:27: 137
15:20: 129
15:23: 148[111]
15:28: 4, 103[55], 112, 120[4]
15:44: 136[57], 224

Second Corinthians
4:4: 128[27 f], 134, 160
5:18: 139

Index (B) of Subjects and Authors Cited

Index (C) of All Teilhard Writings, Here Cited or Not

An indispensable tool of research has been Claude Cuénot's updated bibliography in *Livres de France* 17/4 (April 1966) 27–30, which we had the good fortune to receive by gracious gift of the author after long frustration in tracking down references. We venture to call the special attention of our readers to the usefulness of the subjoined list, especially since we have been able to add to Cuénot's data some few items unearthed elsewhere, as well as English equivalents and page-references to our own citation in the present work. See too Ladislas Polgar, *Internationale Teilhard-Bibliographie* (Freiburg: Alber, 1965). The symbols to the left are explained in the box on page 309 opposite.

9 Action et activation (1945).

7 L'activation de l'énergie humaine (1953), 290[74].

2 L'Afrique et les origines humaines (1954–5), 268[17].

5 Agitation ou genèse? [+ Y a-t-il dans l'univers un axe principal d'évolution? (un effort pour voir clair) (1947) = Position de l'homme et signification de la socialisation humaine dans la nature (1948)].

04 L'âme du monde (1918).

7 L'analyse de la vie (1945).

3 Apparent Discontinuity Inevitable in Any Evolutionary Series (1926).

SYMBOLS indicating PUBLISHED COMPILATIONS of Teilhard's (shorter) writings
"ŒUVRES" series (Paris: Éditions du Seuil);
in English, London: Collins = New York: Harper.

1 = *Le phénomène humain,* 1955; = *The Phenomenon of Man,* translated by Bernard Wall, 1959.
2 = *L'apparition de l'homme,* 1956; = *The Appearance of Man,* translated by J. M. Cohen with notes by Desmond Collins and preface by Robert T. Francoeur, 1965.
3 = *La vision du passé,* 1957.
4 = *Le milieu divin,* 1957; = *The Divine Milieu,* translated by Bernard Wall, 1960.
5 = *L'avenir de l'homme,* 1959; = *The Future of Man,* translated by Norman Denny, 1964.
6 = *L'énergie humaine,* 1962.
7 = *L'activation de l'énergie,* 1963.
8 = *La place de l'homme dans la nature* (= *Le groupe zoölogique humain;* Paris: Albin Michel, 1956); = *Man's Place in Nature,* translated by René Hague, 1966.
9 = *Science et Christ,* 1965.
10 = *Le coeur de la matière* (to appear proximately).
11 = *Christianisme et évolution* (to appear proximately).

PUBLISHED LETTERS

01 = *Lettres d'Égypte* (1905–1908), with preface by Henri de Lubac (Paris: Aubier, 1963); = *Letters from Egypt,* translated by Mary Ilford (New York: Herder and Herder, 1965).
02 = *Lettres d'Hastings et de Paris 1908–1914,* edited by Auguste Demoment and H. de Lubac (Paris: Aubier, 1965).
03 = *Genèse d'une pensée: Lettres (1914–1919)* (Paris: Grasset, 1961); = *The Making of a Mind: Letters from a Soldier-Priest, 1914–1919,* translated by René Hague (New York: Harper, 1965).
04 = *Écrits du temps de la guerre* (1916–1919) (Paris: Grasset, 1965).
05 = *Lettres de voyage, [I.] 1923–1939,* edited by Claude Aragonnès, pseudonym of Marguérite Teillard-Chambon (Paris: Grasset, 1956): translation, see 06.
06 = *Nouvelles Lettres de voyage, II. 1939–1955* (1957): translated together with 05 as *Letters from a Traveller* by René Hague and others (New York: Harper, 1962).
07 = *Blondel et Teilhard de Chardin: correspondance commentée,* by Henri de Lubac (Paris: Beauchesne, 1965).
08 = Other collections: *Lettres à Léontine Zanta* (Paris: Desclée de Brouwer, 1965); "Memories and Letters" [to] Lucile Swan, in *Teilhard de Chardin, Pilgrim of the Future,* edited by Neville Braybrooke (New York: Seabury, 1964) 40–49; George B. Barbour, *In the Field with Teilhard de Chardin* (New York: Herder and Herder, 1965).
09 = Letters CITED in other published works, especially Claude Cuénot, *Teilhard de Chardin* (Baltimore: Helicon, 1965).

CAHIERS and similar (Seuil) collections

001 = *Construire la terre,* 1958.
002 = *Réflexions sur le bonheur,* 1960.
003 = *Pierre Teilhard de Chardin et la politique africaine,* 1962.
004 = *La parole attendue,* 1963.
005 = *Le Christ évoluteur; Socialisation et religion; Carrière scientifique,* 1965.
006 = *Choses mongoles; Activités en Chine* (to appear proximately).
(There is no 007.)
008 = *Hymne de l'univers,* 1961; *Je m'explique,* 1966; *Images et paroles,* 1966; *Élevations et prières* (1967).
009 = *La messe sur le monde* (Paris: Desclée de Brouwer, 1962).

The Idea of Fossil Man [in A. Krober, *Anthropology Today* (Chicago: University, 1953) 93–101], 91[21].

2 Une importante découverte en paléontologie humaine: le Sinathropus Pekinensis (1930).

9 L'incroyance moderne: cause profonde et remède (1933).

9 Ingredients of the Human Body (1919).

5 Une interprétation biologique plausible de l'histoire humaine: la formation de la "noösphère" (1947).

11 Introduction à la vie chrétienne (1944).

3 The Law of Irreversibleness and Evolution (1923).

01 Letters from Egypt (1905–1908), 1[1].

02 Lettres d'Hastings et de Paris (1908–1914), 1[1].

06 Letters from a Traveller (1923–1955), 3[6], 4[9], 25[52], 266[7] [f], 268[16], 288[66].

08 Lettres à Léontine Zanta, 278[52].

09 Lettre à Emmanuel Mounier, 1947).

08 Letters to Lucile Swan, 278[52].

09 Letters cited in published works, 6[17,19], 44[32], 49[43], 60[70], 103[55], 112[77], 271 f[31], 267[12] [f], 278[53], 281[59], 289[70], 292[81].

Lexique, 107[62].

5 Life and the Planets (1945 f).

5 [Life on Other Planets:] Plurality of Inhabited Worlds as a Sequel to the Problem of Human Origins (1953), 262.

3 Life's Movements (1928).

3 La loi d'irréversibilité et évolution (1923).

7 Looking at a Cyclotron: Human Energy Folded Back in upon itself (1953).

04 La lutte contre la multitude: interprétation possible de la figure du monde (1917).

04 La maîtrise du monde et le règne de Dieu (1916).

10 Ma position intellectuelle (1948).

8 Man's Place in Nature (1949), 9 f[25] [f], 42[22].

3 Man's Place in the Universe: reflections on complexity (1942), 26[53].

009 [Mass over the World] La messe sur le monde (1923), 294[84].

F. Meyer, recension (1955), 16[42].

4 Le milieu divin (1926), 63[2], 110[74], 112 ff[76, 81, 83], 291 ff[79 f, 83].

04 Le milieu mystique (1917).

Les miracles de Lourdes et les enquêtes canoniques [*Études* 118 (1909) 167]. 235[22].

11 Modern Scientific Neo–Humanism and its Effects on Working Men's Christianity (1948), 289[70].

7 The Moment of Decision: a Way to make Sense out of the War (1939).

04 Mon univers (1918): not =

9 Mon univers (1924), 55[65], 288[66].

04 Monism (The Big Monad) (1918).

11 Monogénisme et monophylétisme (1950), 41[20].

7 La montée de l'autre (1942).

11 La morale peut-elle se passer de soubassements métaphysiques avoués ou inavoués? (1945).

3 Les mouvements de la vie (1928).

10 My Credo (1934).

10 My Intellectual Position (1948).

6 La mystique de la science (1939).

04 Names for Matter (1919).

3 Natural Human Units: Race in Biology and Morality (1939), 101[51], 264[5].

The number-symbols to the left refer to published compilations as classified on page 309, above.